Transforming Community Policing

Mobilization, Engagement, and Collaboration

Hugh C. Russell

Contributors

Stephanie Ashton, Kwantlen University
Henri Berube, Humber College
Arun Dhanota, Humber College
Stephen Duggan, Humber College
Sarah Gilliss, New Brunswick Community College
Cindy McDonald, Niagara College
Mark Simchison, Niagara College

emond ▪ Toronto, Canada ▪ 2017

Emond Montgomery Publications Limited
60 Shaftesbury Avenue
Toronto ON M4T 1A3
http://www.emond.ca/highered

Printed in Canada.

We acknowledge the financial support of the Government of Canada. Canadä

Vice-president, publishing: Anthony Rezek
Publisher: Lindsay Sutherland
Managing editor, development: Kelly Dickson
Developmental editor: Heather Gough
Senior editor, production: Jim Lyons
Production supervisor: Laura Bast
Copy editor: David Handelsman
Proofreader: Francine Geraci
Permissions editor: Marnie Lamb
Indexer: David Gargaro
Typesetter: Christopher Hudson
Cover designer: Nicole Gaasenbeek
Cover image: Photography by Jeremy Ashley/Belleville Police Service

Library and Archives Canada Cataloguing in Publication

Russell, Hugh C., 1943-, author
    Transforming community policing : mobilization, engagement, and collaboration / Hugh C. Russell.

Includes bibliographical references and index.

    1. Community policing.   I. Title.

HV7936.C83R88 2017   363.2'3   C2016-905819-0

To all those police officers, and people who are considering becoming police officers, who realize that their primary job is to help bring out the best in all those whom they serve.

BRIEF CONTENTS

DETAILED CONTENTS

PART I   COMMUNITIES AND COMMUNITY POLICING

1 Communities, Crime, and Social Disorder

2 Evolution of Community Policing

PART II   POLICE ROLES AND CAPABILITIES

3 What Police Do Well, and What Police Do Poorly

4 Police Roles in Community Safety and Well-Being

PART III   MOBILIZATION AND ENGAGEMENT

5 Problem-Solving and Problem-Oriented Policing

6 Transformative Community-Building Practices

7 Collaborating with Other Agencies and Organizations

8 Collaboration, Information, Knowledge, and Risks

PART IV   KNOWING WHAT TO DO, AND SEEING IF YOU DID IT

9 Community Safety Planning

10 Applying Risk Analysis to Violent Extremism

11 Evaluating Community Policing Initiatives

EPILOGUE (It Is All About Relationships)

FOREWORD

I have often said that effective contemporary community policing can address issues ranging from vandalism to terrorism. That statement raises eyebrows and the doubt of critics of community policing, who remain undeterred from their view that community policing is soft on crime, a mere philosophy, and surely not evidence of core police functions or tactical operations. In this book, Hugh Russell skillfully shares insightful views on the transformation of community policing to challenge such myths and perspectives and inform a wide range of readers.

Crime control and law enforcement is approximately 20 percent of an officer's average work load; roughly 80 percent is focused on providing assistance, intervening, diffusing, guiding, supporting, and problem-solving. As crime rates decline, some decision-makers have narrowed their view of what is needed to build and maintain safe and secure communities. Surely, if crime rates are declining, the thinking goes, there is even less need for police officers. But if community safety and well-being are the targets, and we know that 80 percent of an officer's time is spent on non-criminal matters, we need to take a closer look at the function and priorities of the police and that which belongs more appropriately within a community web of support.

As traditional police organizations have transformed over the past 40 years, we have come to understand it is essential to clearly define what is meant by "community" and "contemporary policing." The world's constant flux continually changes the types of request for policing services, and the police and their partners must remain nimble in order to adapt to changing issues and threats, whether man-made or natural. To do so effectively, police, government leaders, and communities must be prepared to strategically adapt to our ever-changing landscape. Policing in the 21st century involves a host of complex issues—some new and some that have existed for a millennium or more. The following 11 chapters trace the evolution of policing from its earliest roots through the traditional, professional, and research eras to provide a full picture of contemporary community policing. As Dr. Russell so aptly writes, "It's time to put the community back into community policing."

As our world changes, police legitimacy is increasingly challenged by societies that demand transparency and accountability. Public trust and confidence is further shaken when high profile events are exacerbated by social and traditional media. Most certainly, a citizenry that is distrustful of its police will shy away from building a partnership that involves them in a meaningful way. The police alone cannot "build social capital" with troubled people and in troubled neighbourhoods. The inroads into a healthy community must begin with trust and collaboration. However, the reality is that the round-the-clock shift worker who is pegged into response-based policing has difficulty effectively understanding and applying some of the most basic tenets of contemporary community policing—that is, the time to invest in building rapport, trust, and relationships in their policing location.

Community safety and well-being isn't about the police "doing" policing to the community. It is, rather, about the police and community merging their common interests to create and maintain peaceful and safe neighbourhoods together. Policing is about people and our ability to build meaningful relationships and bring together a web of resources to help identify, prioritize, and address a variety of complex criminal and social issues that often, by default, require the attention of police. The bulk of policing in Canadian society is focused on the "human condition," and that condition has many tentacles. Policing is about people, and to a lesser extent their "things." The complexities of effective modern policing require a community web of support that does not lie, and cannot lie, at the feet of any one organization. As Dr. Russell notes in the epilogue to this book, "It's all about relationships," which is the fundamental truth of the matter.

Relationship-building, problem-solving, and crime prevention are cost-effective in the long run; they are more productive than rapid response and rapid arrest. However, the returns on investment of time and resources may take an entire generation to bear fruit. There will always be a need for reactive policing, but this need must be balanced with proactive, preventative, and interventionist strategies. Citizen engagement is a critical component for effective policing; trying to pull tactical policing from community policing is akin to trying to drive a car on only its rims—you likely won't get very far, and it will be a noisy and uncomfortable ride. As Dr. Russell writes, we do a disservice to ourselves when we think that community policing belongs in one unit and tactical policing in another. Contemporary community policing belongs to everyone.

Dr. Russell encourages the reader to apply critical thinking skills and to test assumptions through a series of scenarios; for this reason, among others, this book is a "must read" for police officers, police leaders, strategic community partners, and political decision-makers who ultimately have a say in policing mandates and function in their respective communities.

Leanne J. Fitch
December 2016

Transforming Community Policing illuminates a significant change in our understanding and expectations of community policing. Up to this point in history, community policing has been about things police can or should do differently in order to achieve the goals of community safety. But, in the past few years, community policing has shifted its focus to what the rest of the community can do to achieve these goals—that is, *community* policing. The key to this text, however, is that that transformation cannot and will not happen without significant efforts on the part of police agencies and individual officers to engage, mobilize, and collaborate with all their community members. This is the first text which clearly depicts these transformations.

Transforming Community Policing draws on the latest qualified research on the subject from around the world. The assertions and generalizations made here and shared with the readers are well supported by data and evidence presented by experts. But the text also benefits from the author's career and experience in community-building and policing, which spans the globe and covers almost 50 years of practice.

This text will be of equal value to practicing police officers and police agencies, as well as to persons considering whether they would like to become police officers. The transformations discussed here will help practicing officers improve their impact on community safety and well-being. They will also inform the aspirant about the kinds of duties and relationships they must be willing to have with all community members should they choose a career in policing.

Chapter 1 provides a foundation for the entire book by focusing on "community." Here we uncover the social-psychological characteristics of true community and observe that those characteristics are lacking where police are responding most often. Hence community policing has to strive to rebuild those foundations so that true community may emerge from the chaos and dysfunction that leads to crime and social disorder.

Chapter 2 provides a historical perspective on community policing—starting from the 7th century and up to the present day. One of the most important aspects of that history is the transformation of policing models from traditional policing to community policing.

Chapter 3 draws on contemporary research, which shows what police are particularly well qualified to accomplish and what they are not. For example, this research clearly shows that police are not particularly adept at crime prevention—beyond enforcement and a visible presence—and, further, that many other people and organizations in community are much better at crime prevention and should be mobilized and engaged to provide it.

Chapter 4 draws on the observations of Canada's 2014 Expert Panel on the Future of Canadian Policing Models. The Expert Panel discovered from worldwide research that everyone in community has to be actively involved in achieving the goals of safety, security, and well-being and that police should not hold sovereignty over community safety.

Chapter 5 introduces standard problem-solving models and reflects on the challenges police face when trying to implement them. The approach to these challenges lies in engaging other community members to make significant contributions to community problem-solving, and engaging them is a police job.

Chapter 6 is a hands-on chapter where we learn specific tactics and techniques police may use to rekindle community where it least exists. The chapter discusses some of the tools police may use to mobilize people who are not contributing to community-building because of their distractions with poverty, addictions, mental health, single parenting, and other personal and social pressures.

Chapter 7 moves the discussion into the realm of police relationships with other agencies and organizations in community. It introduces the concept of interagency collaboration and discusses the challenges that all agencies face when trying to collaborate with one another.

Chapter 8 is about communication and information-sharing. The key to this chapter is the notion of reciprocity. Police need to insist that all agencies, organizations, and individuals in community communicate clearly and often with police. By the same token, police have to become more transparent and communicative with those community members with whom they seek to collaborate in the enterprise of community safety and well-being.

Chapter 9 presents a framework for planning to increase community safety and well-being. The framework is generic; it can be applied to any specific community problem or risk factor. An example is provided in applying the planning framework to the problem of addictions and mental health.

Chapter 10 provides another example of planning for community safety. This one focuses on the risk of violent extremism. One of the purposes of this chapter is to demonstrate that community policing should be applied to even the most severe, violent, and harmful risks that Canadian and other police agencies around the world are currently facing.

Chapter 11 focuses on trends in police agencies toward becoming more data-driven and evidence-based. The chapter deals with evaluation of community policing initiatives. The chapter's focus is on how to get qualified research and evaluation done; it is not about making qualified researchers and evaluators out of police officers, whose talents lie elsewhere.

The last chapter, "Epilogue," is more of an essay. Although it summarizes key lessons in all the previous chapters, its focus is on one social-psychological factor that can make or break a community policing initiative—police legitimacy.

The bottom line for community policing is "relationships"—relationships among the people who strive to resolve community problems; relationships between these people and other community agencies and organizations; and, above all, relationships between police and all the people and organizations in the communities they serve. Community policing will not transform community members into behaving more responsibly if community members do not hold their police services and all individual officers in the highest esteem. And police are the only ones who can effect that transformation.

Hugh C. Russell
January 2017

ACKNOWLEDGMENTS

While one name may appear as the "author" of a text like this, a whole raft of people actually live, breathe, and move throughout all the ideas and concepts that appear here. They deserve special acknowledgment because this text would not exist without their significant contributions to the subject that brings all of us between these book covers.

Thank you, Chief Leanne Fitch (Fredericton Police Service), not only for agreeing to write the foreword to *Transforming Community Policing* but also for providing conceptual and practical inspiration and leadership to all Canadian police leaders who believe that community policing holds some answers to the challenges of community safety and well-being.

Seven scholars, lecturers, and retired and active police and corrections officers have contributed poignant anecdotes from their professional experience, which are peppered throughout *Transforming Community Policing*. All of them believe in community policing and built time into their full schedules to contribute meaningful and practical experiences to the concepts and lessons offered in this text. The publisher joins me in thanking them for their experiences in policing, their commitment to learning, and their stories and words that we have captured here. They are:

- Sarah Gilliss, New Brunswick Community College;
- Mark Simchison, Niagara College;
- Cindy McDonald, Niagara College;
- Stephanie Ashton, Kwantlen University;
- Stephen Duggan, Humber College;
- Arun Dhanota, Humber College; and
- Henri Berube, Humber College.

My personal inspiration for this text and all the ideas within it comes from over 45 years of experience around the world. In that sense, this book has been a privilege to write because it affords me the opportunity to see if the ideas gathered over that time hang together in a cohesive, logical, and meaningful way. Most of those ideas and concepts emerged through the hard work and inspiration of a lot of people with whom I have had the privilege to problem-solve in community. I owe a profound debt of gratitude to far too many to list here. But some of those most directly connected to the major ideas in this text over the past 15 years, include:

- Senior Constable (Ret.) Rob Davis, Waterloo Regional Police Service;
- Deputy Minister Matthew Torigian, Ontario Ministry of Community Safety and Correctional Services;

- Director Stephen Waldie, Ontario Ministry of Community Safety and Correctional Services;
- Inspector (Ret.) Mark Allen, Ontario Provincial Police;
- Inspector Robyn MacEachern, Ontario Provincial Police;
- Chief (Ret.) Dennis Poole, Chatham-Kent Police Service;
- Chief Paul Pederson, Greater Sudbury Police Service;
- Director (Ret.) Bill Stephens, Ontario Police College;
- Chief Robert Keetch, Sault Ste. Marie Police Service;
- Staff Superintendent Peter Lennox, Toronto Police Service;
- Staff Sergeant Steve Pipe, Toronto Police Service;
- Deputy Chief Andrew Fletcher, South Simcoe Police; and
- Executive Director Ron Bain, Ontario Association of Chiefs of Police.

Throughout my professional career I have written hundreds of reports (many of them book-length), manuals, training courses, texts, guidelines, analyses, speeches, and the like. It was always a relatively solitary exercise, benefiting from the assistance of the occasional professional colleague only. Before *Transforming Community Policing*, never have I written for a professional publishing house. Hence I am delighted to report what a great pleasure it has been to write for Emond Publishing. They are professional and competent, know their market and how to meet it with a new product, and above all provide excellent technical support to their authors. A whole team of skilled people backed me up, including (but not limited to):

- Lindsay Sutherland, publisher;
- Heather Gough, developmental editor;
- David Handelsman, copy editor;
- Marnie Lamb, permissions editor; and
- Laura Bast, production supervisor.

Thank you, Emond Publishing, for the privilege of working with you.

Finally, thank you to the reviewers who provided feedback both during the initial planning stages and on draft chapters:

- Heather Hodgson Schleich, formerly of Niagara College and triOS College;
- Doug King, Mount Royal University;
- Sarah Gilliss, New Brunswick Community College;
- Marcy Birgeneau, Centennial College;
- Tanya Philp, Sheridan College;
- Dave Sinclair, Mohawk College; and
- Laura Norman, St. Lawrence College.

ABOUT THE AUTHOR

Hugh C. Russell, PhD, is a thought leader with more than 45 years of globe-spanning applied community research that focuses on mobilizing and supporting all community members to address their social and criminal justice issues. His work is predicated on the principle that safety, security, and justice will not be realized unless and until communities are fully engaged in resolving their own issues of conflict and social disorder. This requires that police and other justice and social services assume special roles in assisting communities to take more responsibility for these issues.

Dr. Russell is principal architect of three major policies: (1) community mobilization, in which police help people in high-demand neighbourhoods take more responsibility for crime reduction, crime prevention, and increased safety and security; (2) safety promotion within a framework for collaborative, risk-driven planning for community safety and well-being; and (3) promotion, development, training, evaluation, and support for community risk mitigation strategies.

Dr. Russell is the author of a manual for risk mitigation through "situation tables" that is freely available through an e-learning program offered by Wilfrid Laurier University. It can be accessed at <https://www.wlu.ca/academics/faculties/faculty-of-human-and-social-sciences/centre-for-public-safety-and-well-being/situation-table.html>.

Dr. Russell is a proponent and trainer of the community justice strategy known as "community conferencing." He has trained police officers, lawyers, professional mediators, and community members in applications of conferencing to resolve conflicts in schools, the community, and workplaces.

Awarded a life membership in the Ontario Association of Chiefs of Police, and recipient of the Ontario Provincial Police Commissioner's Commendation for his work with Ontario police services, Dr. Russell has also advised other provincial governments, as well as the armed forces, state governments, and police in the United States. He is a speaker and public educator on community justice practices.

PART I

Communities and Community Policing

CHAPTER 1

Communities, Crime, and Social Disorder

Police from the Toronto Police Service 55 Division attend a community event for Police Week, 2016. Police Week, held nationally in Canada since 1970, celebrates the connection between police services and the communities that they serve.

LEARNING OUTCOMES

Upon completion of this chapter, you should be able to:

- Explain the meaning of the word "community" as it appears in the phrase "community policing"
- Define "community" as it relates to crime and social disorder
- Explain how the concept of "social control" relates to policing in low-demand and high-demand neighbourhoods
- Explain the role of community policing in reshaping community life in neighbourhoods where police respond most often
- Identify the main parties that must be mobilized and engaged in reshaping community life

Introduction

This first chapter is all about "community," because in truth, community policing is all about community. Community refers to people who share common values and to people who work together to resolve their own neighbourhood problems. Fostering community well-being is both the primary goal of community policing and the outcome of successful community policing.

A review of the community policing literature over the past decade reveals that few authors or practitioners who have written knowledgably about the subject have clearly defined the meaning of the word "community" in "community policing."[1] But all who use the phrase "community policing" to differentiate it from other forms of policing are investing heavily in the meaning of that word. Otherwise, these would simply be books about "policing."

The concept and practices of community policing have been changing, adapting, and transforming over time—as they should! (In Chapter 2 we briefly review the history of community policing.) These transformations are forced by increasing awareness on the part of municipal governments and police agencies that police alone cannot create and sustain safety for all. Police are essential: we rely on them to respond 24/7/365 to any crisis that threatens harm or victimization, and there is no other group of professionals better trained to do what they do. But it is not enough. Communities that experience the greatest threats to safety and well-being need far more than the most effective police agency to reduce those threats and thus reduce the harm and victimization that result from them.

That is what brings us back to the notion of community, and its relationship to policing. What does a community need to keep it safe, if policing is not enough? How can a basically unsafe community (where police are in high demand) get what it needs to make it safer, and in so doing, reduce the demand for police and other emergency services? Ultimately, what is the role of police in helping the community become safer and healthier for all? We explore the answers to these questions in the remainder of this chapter.

ON PATROL

Low-Demand Neighbourhood with High Social Control

It is a beautiful Saturday afternoon. You turn your cruiser into a neighbourhood you have never visited before. Up ahead you see the elementary school where the playground was recently renovated by the community. The new, bright, and shiny equipment is crawling with youngsters; you can hear their laughter through your open window. Off to the side are chatting parents, drinking coffee. Heading down the street you see a Neighbourhood Watch sign, which always reassures you that the neighbours are looking out for each other. The streets are lined with similarly styled homes, well-manicured front lawns, and at least two vehicles per driveway. A man from the neighbourhood is washing one of those vehicles, so you stop for a few minutes in front of his house to have a friendly chat. You notice for the first time that the majority of these houses have floodlights above their garages and home security stickers on their front doors, and you're impressed with how organized and proactive this neighbourhood seems. It is no wonder that you never get a service call to this neighbourhood. As you are just about to drive out of the neighbourhood, you see a community garden to your left, full of volunteers, who turn, smile, and wave. This is definitely one of those neighbourhoods in which there are high levels of social control that keep everybody safe and secure—thereby not requiring police attention as often as some other neighbourhoods.

While this neighbourhood could be anywhere in Canada, it is very similar to the one in the city of Richmond in British Columbia. Richmond is actively working to create an inviting and safe community by coming together to beautify all aspects of the city. To see the work they have been doing, see <http://www.richmond.ca/parks/about/beautification/about.htm>.

Consider the following questions:

1. You do not know who lives in this neighbourhood, how much money they make, or what their politics are. But you can tell a lot about this neighbourhood just by the observations you made through your cruiser's windshield. What do your observations tell you about the relationships among these neighbours?

2. On the basis of what you can tell about the relationships among these neighbours, how much crime and social disorder would you guess these people experience in this neighbourhood?

Community's Influence on Policing

Think about the word "community." When you use that word, what does it mean to you? When you think of your own community, how would you describe it? Is it about the people with whom you share a belief system—like those who attend your church, synagogue, mosque, or other place of worship? Is it about geographic location—like the neighbours on the street where you live? Or maybe it is about the people who share the stages and activities in your life—like your fellow students who are studying this text. Community could be about culture and ethnicity—like Somali Canadians who gather at a community centre for traditional holidays and celebrations. Community could be about all of these things: consider a Portuguese Canadian whose community members attend the same Catholic church and live in the same neighbourhood, supporting each other in raising their children and in employment.

Why is your community important to you? What does it do for you? What do you do for it? What makes a community important for anyone? How does a community serve its members? What are the underlying qualities of community that make it an important aspect of our broader social and political systems? Think about your answers to that last question as we explore the meaning of "community policing" in this chapter and the ones that follow.

James et al. define "**community**" as "a social unit of any size that shares common values ... a group of people who are connected by durable relations."[2]

Now review the On Patrol scenario at the beginning of this chapter. That is a description of what one officer sees when driving through a particular neighbourhood. If you were that officer, would you guess that the most important qualities of community that you have identified in your life exist in this neighbourhood? In looking at this neighbourhood, would you guess that the people share "common values" and seem to have "**durable relations**"? How can you tell? What are the visual cues you can use to assess the quality of community in this neighbourhood?

Below is another On Patrol scenario. Read it and answer the same question: would you guess that the most important qualities of community that you have identified in your life exist in this neighbourhood? Do the folks in this neighbourhood share common values and have durable relations with each other? How can you tell? What are the visual cues you can use to assess the quality of community in this neighbourhood?

ON PATROL

High-Demand Neighbourhood with Low Social Control

It is a chilly Saturday night as you patrol through the high-crime zone of the downtown core. You are fresh out of the academy, and have already experienced more than you thought you would in a lifetime of policing in this small sector of the city. As you drive by an old and beaten-up playground, you see children playing on a broken swing set, unattended, even though it is dark out. As you continue down the street, it's hard not to feel a sense of pity for the neighbourhood. The alleyways are littered with trash and makeshift shelters. There is garbage blowing across the street and so many of the streetlights have been broken, making the street dark and shadowy. As you approach one of the corners, you see a group of girls, not properly dressed for the elements, who turn to walk in the other direction. Not far up ahead you see a group of young men sitting on the stoop of an apartment building. Strewn across the front lawn are broken toys, a derelict barbeque, and broken glass.

---

community a social unit of any size that shares common values; a group of people who are connected by durable relations

durable relations relationships that are strong, lasting, and endure through the pressures and changes that life, family, and neighbourhood can bring

As you drive by, some of the men look away as if to avoid attention, while others stare at you with contempt. You joined the force to help others, but on nights like tonight, as all the citizens under your care turn away from you, you question your choice.

Although this neighbourhood could be anywhere in Canada, the lower east side of Vancouver, known as East Hastings or the Downtown Eastside, epitomizes it. The lower east side has been battling these types of issues and epidemic levels of drug use. One group of police officers, nicknamed "The Odd Squad," sought to chronicle these issues in a film about the lower east side entitled *Through a Blue Lens* (see <https://www.nfb.ca/film/through_a_blue_lens>).

Consider the following questions:

1. What does your cruise through this neighbourhood tell you about the relationships among all these "neighbours"?
2. What does all the trash in the neighbourhood tell you about the social standards for street and yard maintenance and upkeep?
3. What can you tell about the relationship between police and these neighbours? Why is the relationship that way?

The late Jane Jacobs, one of the world's finest contemporary urban planning experts, reflected on neighbourhoods like those in our two scenarios when she said: "A successful city neighborhood is a place that keeps sufficiently abreast of its problems so it is not destroyed by them. An unsuccessful neighborhood is a place that is overwhelmed by its defects and problems and is progressively more helpless before them."[3] Is the low-demand neighbourhood in the first On Patrol scenario one that is keeping "sufficiently abreast of its problems"? How can you tell? What about the second neighbourhood scenario: is this a neighbourhood that is "overwhelmed by its defects and problems and ... progressively more helpless before them"? How can you tell?

Now the big question! Which of our two scenario neighbourhoods is responsible for the largest number of public calls for police assistance and other emergency services like fire, ambulance, and children's aid? Of course, it is the high-demand neighbourhood that generates the most calls for police assistance. Throughout this text we will refer to neighbourhoods that require the most police assistance as "high-demand neighbourhoods" and those that generate fewer calls for police assistance as "low-demand neighbourhoods."

Our first take-away from this analysis is that these neighbourhoods show significant differences. In a high-demand neighbourhood, members share fewer common values and have less durable relations with each other. In contrast, in a low-demand neighbourhood, members share far more common values and have far more durable relations with each other. We might say that there is far less true community in high-demand neighbourhoods than in low-demand neighbourhoods.

Both of these scenarios depict neighbourhoods, but only one of these neighbourhoods could be called a "community." In the high-demand neighbourhood there is no evidence that people are friendly and help each other to solve common problems. The officer patrolling through our high-demand neighbourhood observed that children were playing unsupervised, and that broken glass and other debris represented a safety risk for them. Yet high-demand neighbourhoods are where police respond most often—where there is the least "community." So what does community policing look like in high-demand neighbourhoods? To stretch the analogy for the sake of learning, how does a police service implement community policing where there is not any (or not much) community? In contrast, what is the role of community policing in a low-demand neighbourhood? Is it the same in both of these neighbourhoods, or does community policing play different roles, in different ways, in each? We explore these questions below in our discussion of the mobilization and engagement model of community policing and in the sections that follow.

The Mobilization and Engagement Model of Community Policing

Police leaders in Ontario struggled with these questions when they produced that province's "Mobilization & Engagement Model of Community Policing" in 2010 (see Figure 1.1).

Without paying attention to the bull's-eye, look at the headings in the four corners of this graphic and how those police leaders answered the question about whether community policing is one thing done the same way in all kinds of neighbourhoods. They divided neighbourhoods into four "zones": red, amber, blue, and green. In this representation they are saying that at any given time, police officers may find themselves responding in a range of neighbourhoods, from those that have very little semblance of real community (red zone, highest demand) to those that benefit from all of the qualities of community (green zone, lowest demand). Of course, many neighbourhoods fall in between those two extremes. Amber zone neighbourhoods are those that request many calls for service and have many repeat calls but where there are some people and organizations that share common values and work hard to promote safety and security. Blue zone neighbourhoods are those in which there are far more people and organizations that share common values and work together to deal with common threats to safety and well-being, and request fewer calls for police assistance.

FIGURE 1.1 Ontario's Mobilization & Engagement Model of Community Policing

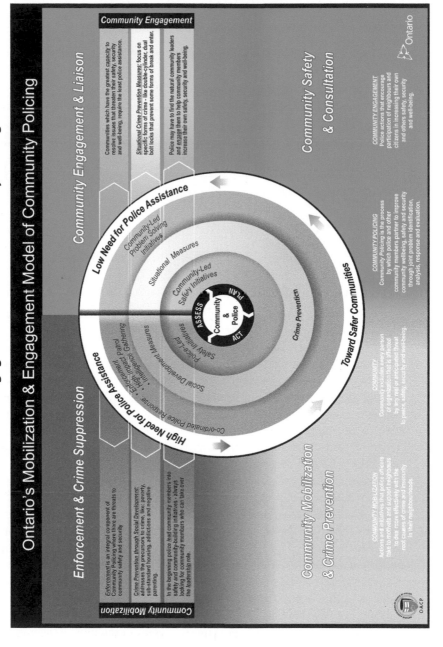

CHECK YOUR UNDERSTANDING

1. What does the word "community" mean, in the context of community policing?
2. What do we mean when we say that there is less community in high-demand neighbourhoods than there is in low-demand neighbourhoods?
3. Will an effective community policing program be applied in the same way in all neighbourhoods? Why or why not?

Community Policing in High- and Low-Demand Neighbourhoods

What is the role of community policing in each kind of neighbourhood?

Higher-Demand Neighbourhoods

In the high-demand neighbourhoods, where there are the largest number of repeat calls for service and greatest levels of **victimization** as a result of crime and social disorder (red zone), the highest priority for effective community policing is crime suppression and enforcement. This means ensuring that people in these neighbourhoods are living and relating lawfully. That becomes the highest-priority community policing goal, not only because it is the job of police to reduce harm and victimization but also because it is nearly impossible to do anything else to make the community stronger if criminal behaviour and social disorder are so extreme that people cannot reach out to each other and find constructive ways to resolve community problems. It is simply not safe to try to create community in a neighbourhood that is plagued by crime and social disorder.

Targeted enforcement bolstered by good intelligence and reliable data is a good strategy to achieve this community policing goal. If we accept the notion that enforcement and crime suppression are the highest-priority community policing goals in a red-zone neighbourhood, we can effectively mitigate the oft-heard criticism that community policing is "soft" on crime. If a neighbourhood situation warrants rigorous enforcement, then the best community policing strategy is to make enforcement the highest priority. In fact, some of the most effective community policing strategies in the most dangerous and

---

victimization ill-treatment like bullying, oppression, discrimination, abuse, and harassment at the hands of another person or people

crime-ridden neighbourhoods start with rigorous enforcement. For an excellent example of this strategy, see the *60 Minutes* video "Counterinsurgency Cops: Military Tactics Fight Street Crime."[4]

If, on the other hand, police analysis of the target neighbourhood shows that crime is not the biggest problem, and that the greatest threat to common values and durable relations among the neighbours is too much social disorder (amber-zone neighbourhood), then enforcement is not the first priority of effective community policing. Rather, officers can begin to identify key individuals (for example, community leaders), groups (for example, members of a church or mosque), and organizations (for example, Big Brothers or Big Sisters) in the neighbourhood and motivate and support them to be more effective in pulling neighbours together to solve their social disorder problems.

Of course, the fewer the crime and social disorder problems, the easier it is for community policing officers to identify effective local groups and individuals to deal with viable threats to safety and well-being in the neighbourhood. For example, in a blue-zone neighbourhood, little police-initiated "mobilization" is needed because members of the community are already mobilized. Here, the primary task of community policing is to identify neighbourhood members who are working together and provide them with support and outreach to others who can help them keep their neighbourhood as safe as possible for everyone.

Lower-Demand Neighbourhoods

In the lowest-demand neighbourhoods there are the fewest illegal activities and the least social disorder (green zone). In fact, our drive through the On Patrol neighbourhood at the start of this chapter showed that we can expect very few reasons for police to be in this neighbourhood at all. That is because the people here share common values for a safe and secure neighbourhood and they have sufficiently durable relations to keep it that way. Therefore, effective community policing in green-zone neighbourhoods remains largely a matter of keeping abreast of whatever is happening there and ensuring that the neighbours and community organizations working there feel effectively connected to the police so that should they ever need technical advice or assistance that is appropriate for police to provide, they can obtain it easily and efficiently.

The nature of community influences the tactical choices of community policing. Therefore, in designing a community policing strategy for any neighbourhood it is important to

- consult with crime and other data analysts to get the clearest and most reliable estimates of crime and social disorder in the neighbourhood;
- define community policing goals accordingly;

- determine whether targeted enforcement should be used initially (for example, in a higher-demand neighbourhood); and
- determine whether it is sufficient for police to simply liaise with community partners (for example, in a lower-demand neighbourhood).

Building Community

The qualities of community that we value so much in our own lives and neighbourhoods—mutual trust and durable relationships—exist in insufficient measure to build and sustain community safety in those neighbourhoods where police respond most often. So we need police (among others) to take steps to help people there create those qualities. We have already identified that police most often have to get this ball rolling by using enforcement and crime suppression so that it is safe for neighbours to begin to learn about each other and experiment in working together to make their neighbourhood stronger. But after that, so much more needs to be done to build up the neighbourhood's natural resistance to crime and social disorder.

Recall the description of the On Patrol high-demand neighbourhood. What were the visual and verbal cues that told you this is most likely a high-demand neighbourhood? Remember that through your cruiser windshield you observed: a decrepit playground; unsupervised children playing; trash and litter; young men loitering; and a lawn littered with broken glass and other debris. These characteristics are known in criminological circles as **criminogenic factors**: these are community or personal characteristics that can signal the probability of crime or social disorder (like trash and litter, broken windows, and derelict vehicles); create opportunities for them (like leaving bikes, toys, and other personal possessions outside); or actually cause them (like domestic violence and poor parenting).[5] It is important to acknowledge that the mere presence of criminogenic factors does not perfectly predict criminal behaviour or social disorder. But taken together, a lot of them suggest that crime and social disorder are more likely in the high-demand neighbourhood than in the low-demand neighbourhood. They signal that the high-demand neighbourhood has less social control than a low-demand neighbourhood. Social control, together with community capacity-building and police–community relations, is essential for building community. We explore these topics in the following sections.

---

criminogenic factors community or personal characteristics that can signal the probability of crime or social disorder (like broken windows), create opportunities for them (like leaving valuables unattended), or actually cause them (like domestic violence and poor parenting)

Social Control

Social control refers to the ways in which people influence each other's thoughts, values, feelings, and behaviour in their neighbourhood. That influence actually shapes community values and encourages all members of the community to adhere to those values.[6]

The criminogenic factors you can see in the high-demand neighbourhood suggest that very little social control exists there. The three strongest sources of social control in any neighbourhood are, in order of influence, family, friends, and neighbours.[7] Without those sources of social control, a neighbourhood has to rely on rules, laws, and external influences like police and other social agencies to maintain order and keep everybody safe. But if most of the families in the high-demand neighbourhood are single-parent families, and those parents are plagued by a combination of parenting pressures, poverty, unemployment, underemployment, and health issues, it is less likely that family exerts much social control on the behaviour of their own children—much less those of their neighbours. Furthermore, if the youth of distracted parents are experiencing rejection in their broader social networks (like racism outside the neighbourhood, or being shunned or bullied in school) and they turn to friends whose influence is at all anti-social, then that source of social control disappears. If the neighbours are similarly plagued, and further, there has been no experience of working together on common problems sufficient to foster respect and trust between them, then likely that source of social control is obstructed as well.

The bottom line in this analysis is that in neighbourhoods where police have to respond most often, the neighbours are not exerting sufficient levels of social control on each other. As a result, police are needed to exert social control from outside the neighbourhood. Unfortunately, by the time police are called, deficiencies in social control have too often already led to harm and victimization. Therefore, an important goal of community policing is to get ahead of this cycle—to exert some external social controls (through police and other agencies) before anyone is victimized, or ideally, to kindle internal sources of social control in the neighbourhood.

Police officers who know the people and personalities of the neighbourhood are in an excellent position to know which neighbours are anti-social and likely not capable of being encouraged or supported to behave in pro-social ways. Similarly, they know who in this neighbourhood has the right attitudes, values, energy, and credibility to begin the process of developing some internal social control, whether they can be identified, whether it is safe for them to do so, and whether they are supported in doing so—all three of which are jobs for community policing.

---

social control the ways in which people influence each other's thoughts, values, feelings, and behaviour in their neighbourhood

Community Capacity-Building

In the following In the Community feature, consider how police use the people and resources of a neighbourhood to build community.

IN THE COMMUNITY

Community Capacity-Building in Cloverdale

In Cloverdale, a high-demand neighbourhood in southwestern Ontario composed of 250 single-family townhouses, police were called to respond every day, all year long. Family and Children's Services recruited five parents to discuss what could be done to tackle the problems. Also in attendance were three social workers, one police officer, and a social psychologist. Before the discussion got very far, one parent asked the lead social worker to find someone in the neighbourhood to provide child care so that the parents could meet without having to be distracted by childcare demands. The lead social worker replied: "No one in the neighbourhood is qualified to provide these services or we would not be out here on child protection issues as often as we are!" The other parents in the meeting agreed with the social worker. The social worker then suggested that her agency could hire an early childhood educator from a nearby community college to come into the neighbourhood and provide child care. However, the police officer, thinking that a neighbourhood of 250 families had to have at least one neighbour who could provide these services, said that he would go out and find a volunteer to do it.

Within 20 minutes, he found the perfect neighbour. He did it by asking several neighbourhood children, "If someone had to watch over you for an hour or two once in awhile, who would you like it to be?" Upon hearing the answer "Mrs. Robertson!" three or four times, he asked an 11-year-old boy to show him where Mrs. Robertson lived. Being a uniformed police officer, the constable had no difficulty getting Mrs. Robertson to open her door to him when he knocked. He explained what he needed, and Mrs. Robertson said that she would be delighted to help her neighbourhood by providing some occasional childcare services. He asked her to give him her qualifications so that he could take her back to the group that was meeting and tell them why she should do this work. She said, "I work part time in a daycare centre across town, but my strongest qualification is that I've raised ten children in this neighbourhood by myself. Further, half of them are in university or community college, and the other half intend on going." Mrs. Robertson did that work and went on to do many other things that strengthened this community. But it took a police officer to find her. That is community policing at its best.

Despite this recent success, patrol officers who have to respond to this neighbourhood repeatedly often begin to feel frustrated, and eventually, that frustration turns into cynicism. The cynicism turns into serious doubts, not only about the capacity of people in this neighbourhood to solve their own problems but also about the ability of police and enforcement to help them do so.

In contrast, think about what the police officer who found Mrs. Robertson actually achieved. What did he do? The obvious answer is: he found someone to provide child care so that parents could have their meetings. Of course that is true—and commendable! But where community policing is concerned, he did so much more!

This officer sensed that it was important to find an internal source for the child care. The social worker actually offered to spend money out of her agency's budget to hire an early childhood educator from a nearby community college to come into this neighbourhood and provide these services. But the officer, having watched the municipality and a host of external agencies throw resources and programming into this neighbourhood for 20 years without noticeable improvements in either crime or social disorder, knew that sourcing external childcare workers and bringing them into this neighbourhood to solve an internal problem was not a sustainable solution. So he found an internal source of quality child care.

The second thing he did, by asking children who they would like to have provide these services, was tap into the social capital of this neighbourhood. He probed the children and discovered that they had a trusting relationship with Mrs. Robertson. Social capital is like money in the bank: it can be used to get things done in the community. This officer found the one person these children most liked, trusted, and respected. Hence, he knew that she would be able to exert the social control over the children that would be necessary for adequate child care.

Finally, by bringing Mrs. Robertson back to the parents and introducing her—thus giving her a chance to demonstrate that she was an asset to the whole neighbourhood—the officer was strengthening trust and durable relationships among these neighbours. He was providing social control over the children and increasing social capital among the adults. That is community building; that is community policing. It strengthens the community's ability to control the behaviour of at least some of its own members. The more successful police are at increasing a community's capacity to control itself, the less police have to invest in policing there, and the safer the neighbourhood will be.

That is called "**community capacity-building**": the identification, strengthening, and linking of a neighbourhood's tangible resources, like people,

---

community capacity-building the identification, strengthening, and linking of the neighbourhood's tangible resources like people, organizations, businesses, housing and natural environment, and intangible resources like relationships among residents, spirit of community, pride in the neighbourhood, and willingness to work together for the common good

organizations, businesses, housing, and natural environment, and intangible resources, like relationships among residents, spirit of community, pride in the neighbourhood, and willingness to work together for the common good. Community capacity-building has almost limitless possibilities. It is instrumental in

- improving housing values;
- creating playgrounds and recreational facilities for neighbours;
- organizing community gardens and teaching neighbours how to grow, harvest, and cook fresh vegetables;
- bringing social and human service agencies into one nearby facility to provide one-stop shopping for the neighbours;
- providing onsite daycare so that parents have an opportunity to do other things;
- creating after-school programs for children, run by neighbours on a cooperative basis; and
- providing peer mentoring for high school students to help them stay in school and succeed.

All of those are examples of helping the people in this neighbourhood do things that strengthen them as individuals, and through them, the whole neighbourhood as a collective of people who are making their neighbourhood stronger. All of those things strengthen community capacity to grow and thrive—and over time, they move a neighbourhood from the red zone into the amber zone, and eventually even into the blue zone or green zone.

One way to interpret the Mrs. Robertson story is that the police officer recognized the neighbourhood problem of child care and solved it by finding a qualified person to provide this service. But to fully comprehend what problems are faced by high-demand neighbourhoods, and what needs to be accomplished through effective community policing, we have to recognize that a lack of child care is only a symptom of a much more profound problem. Police and others who wish to find sustainable solutions to local problems have to analyze these problems on a deeper level.

Most high-demand neighbourhoods have insufficient levels of **social capital**: positive relationships between people that enable them to work together for the common good. The building blocks of social capital are mutual trust and respect, caring about each other, sharing information, and cooperating (see Figure 1.2).

One of the fundamental jobs of community policing officers is to create social capital in high-demand neighbourhoods. It is not just about providing

---

social capital positive relationships between people that enable them to work together for the common good

FIGURE 1.2   **The Building Blocks of Social Capital**

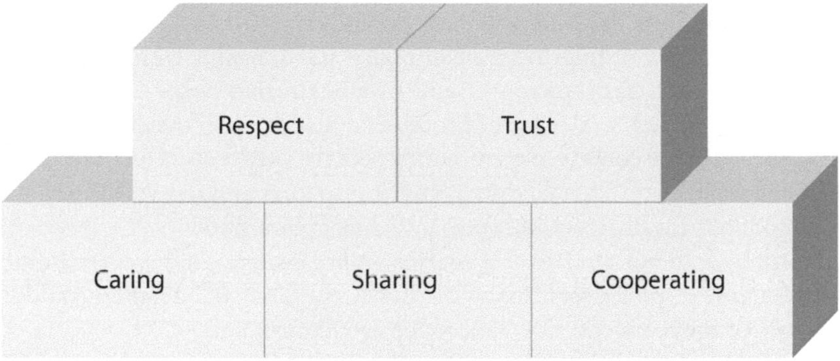

Social capital's building blocks create the foundation for community building.

child care; rather, the need for child care provides the officers with an opportunity to increase social capital. Similarly, it is not just about improving
police–community relations. Although police will not be able to increase
social capital if their own relations with the community are not positive, police
legitimacy is only a foundation on which police can work to build social capital in high-demand neighbourhoods.

Social Capital and Police–Community Relations

The introduction to this chapter mentioned that community policing continues to adapt and transform in response to changing times and demands. The
concept of social capital is one of the most recent transformations in our
understanding of community policing. Police are realizing that part of their
role is to help neighbours in the most broken neighbourhoods reconnect
with each other; learn that they do share common values; and relate to each
other in ways that will give them a chance to learn to trust each other. In
effect, police have a significant role to play in reweaving the social fabric that
constitutes true community, and which is so lacking in the highest-demand
neighbourhoods.

That is a relatively new idea for many police agencies, which are more
accustomed to struggling with the challenge of getting people in these neighbourhoods to work with and trust the police. Of course, that has to be accomplished as well. It is known as **police legitimacy**. Police legitimacy means that
neighbours value what the police do in their neighbourhood, and they value

---

police legitimacy neighbours value what the police do in their neighbourhood and
they value how the police do it

how police do it. Police legitimacy has been shown to be one of the strongest police-based crime- and **recidivism**-prevention measures.[8] Where police legitimacy is low in high-demand neighbourhoods, very little that police do there will have the effect of improving neighbours' relationships with each other. Qualified research has shown over and over again that police legitimacy is derived from neighbours' sense of procedural justice when they have to deal with police.[9] In the context of community policing, **procedural justice** means neighbours' feelings that police are being transparent and fair when they are called to intervene or resolve disputes in the neighbourhood.

Think back to our On Patrol scenarios. What evidence did you see in the first scenario of police legitimacy in that Richmond, BC neighbourhood? What about the lower east side Vancouver neighbourhood?

That raises the question: what is the role of police in community capacity-building, especially in high-demand neighbourhoods? The short answer is community policing. Even before we further unpack what that phrase means, notice that now the word "community" takes on new meaning because we have acknowledged that where police have to respond most often, the qualities of community are in least evidence. There are not people there who likely welcome police—much less want to "partner" with them. There are other human and social service agencies there, but they show very little inclination to do more than their responsibility for providing emergency assistance requires, and they too rarely reach out to police to foster any kind of partnership on behalf of community building. Hence, policing there has to include measures that help the people and agencies reconnect with each other and work together to solve shared problems. Many of those other agencies and organizations have roles to play in community capacity-building. In some respects, which we will explain later, police are very limited and very specialized in what they can contribute to community capacity-building. Police officers have a great responsibility to build and sustain police legitimacy not only with neighbours in high-demand neighbourhoods, but also with all of the other agencies and organizations that care about what is happening in that neighbourhood. Police legitimacy has to come first, but when it is established, police can have a significant, positive impact on improving what we could call "neighbour legitimacy"—that is, neighbours valuing each other and how they behave in the neighbourhood. That opens the door to consideration of all kinds of police strategies and tactics for increasing neighbour legitimacy. We will touch on some of them in Chapter 6.

---

recidivism   reoffending that occurs after the completion of treatment or sanctions for previous criminal behaviour

procedural justice   fairness or perceived fairness in procedures

In 1974 an English social psychologist put his finger on the differences between our two scenario neighbourhoods. He recognized that where community is obviously thriving, people have a sense of belonging and they take responsibility for themselves and other community members. But where community does not exist, although there is a neighbourhood and there are people there, they do not relate particularly well and they do not share responsibility for themselves and each other.[10] Research in 1986 identified four elements required for a "sense of belonging" in a community: a feeling of membership; the ability to influence others and be influenced by them; fulfillment of personal needs; and a shared emotional connection with other members.[11] That sense of belonging and mutually supportive relationships are the keys to community capacity-building.

Now think about your own community. Can you see evidence of social capital operating there? What about in our second scenario neighbourhood? It naturally follows that where police respond most often, community policing has to include efforts to get people to trust and respect each other, share information, and cooperate in solving community problems. Police have very specialized and important roles in generating social capital in these neighbourhoods.

CHECK YOUR UNDERSTANDING

1. What do we mean by the phrase "social control" and how does it apply to community policing?
2. What are the sources of social control in both high-demand and low-demand neighbourhoods?
3. What is the role of social capital in building community?
4. What can police do to help build and strengthen social capital in a high-demand neighbourhood?
5. Provide three examples of activities that police officers could support in order to strengthen social capital in a high-demand neighbourhood.

Social Disorder

Statistics Canada says that police-reported crime rates in Canada continue on a 40-year decline to the present day.[12] However, most Canadian police services are recording increasing calls for police assistance, which contributes to public outcries about the escalating costs of policing.[13] What accounts for this disparity? If crime is down, and police are our specialized crime fighters, then one would think that calls for police assistance would be down too.

This disparity is accounted for by a statistic compiled by the Canadian Association of Chiefs of Police, which reported that in 2013, 70 to 80 percent of all calls for police assistance involved something other than chargeable offences (crimes). These include occurrences like reports of suspicious persons, family disputes, disputes between neighbours, and safety issues associated with addictions and mental health. We use the label "social disorder" to characterize these occurrences—and they are trending upward.

The Ontario Association of Chiefs of Police (OACP) defines **social disorder** as a "condition in which the behaviour and activities of people at a specific location lack sufficient control or order, deviating significantly from what would be considered by most to be comfortable, reasonable or safe."[14] Social disorder is the first thing we notice when we drive through a high-demand neighbourhood like the one in our second On Patrol scenario, and it affects everybody. Far from engendering a sense of safety, trust, respect, and a willingness to cooperate in solving community problems, social disorder drives people apart; makes them suspicious and fearful of each other; and breaks down **community cohesion**. There goes the social capital!

That raises the question: what is driving social disorder up? As any police officer who has frequented a high-demand neighbourhood will tell you, "It's mental health, addictions, poverty, negative parenting, and a host of other social ills." These are known, in the health sector, as the **social determinants of health**. The OACP defines "social determinants of health" as

> protective factors such as access to income, education, employment and job security, safe and healthy working conditions, early childhood development, food security, quality housing, social inclusion, cohesive social safety network, health services, which ensure equal access to all of the qualities, conditions, and benefits of life without regard to any socio-demographic differences.[15]

---

social disorder a condition in which the behaviour and activities of people at a specific location lack sufficient control or order, deviating significantly from what would be considered by most to be comfortable, reasonable, or safe

community cohesion strong and positive relationships between people who may have different backgrounds, tackling community problems together and developing a positive climate for community building

social determinants of health "protective factors such as access to income, education, employment and job security, safe and healthy working conditions, early childhood development, food security, quality housing, social inclusion, cohesive social safety network, health services, which ensure equal access to all of the qualities, conditions, and benefits of life without regard to any socio-demographic differences"; in the policing sector, they are often called the "social determinants of safety"

In the policing sector, we call these the "social determinants of safety." Both terms mean the same thing.

This observation is a game changer for community policing. Most front-line police activities deal not with crime, but with social disorder. Most community policing focuses on promoting the social determinants of health—what the health community calls "health promotion," but what we, in policing, can call "safety promotion."

Before we move on to our next topic of discussion, community well-being, it is helpful to summarize what we have learned in the chapter so far:

- "Community" is not about place, ethnicity, activity, or ideology as much as it is about community cohesion: a feeling of belonging, being a member, and wanting to work with others to solve community problems.
- Community exists less in neighbourhoods where police are called more often.
- Social disorder predominates in neighbourhoods that demand the most police assistance.
- If our goal is to reduce police calls for service and make people safer, we will have to invest in community capacity-building.
- Police will have to acknowledge and exert their very specialized capacities to foster social capital in high-demand neighbourhoods.

Community Well-Being

"Well-being" is the word we use to describe a person, a family, a group, or even a location for which the social determinants of health are all positive—that is, people's economic, social, health, psychological, spiritual, and relationship factors are all positive. Obviously, well-being encompasses more than just safety. Police can rush into a situation and make it safe for everybody, but if the social determinants of health are not there, it will rapidly become unsafe again and police will have to rush back.

So, well-being becomes our target state, especially in high-demand neighbourhoods. That has led a number of municipalities across Canada and elsewhere to develop indexes of well-being. One, called a "sense of community index," has been widely applied in schools, workplaces, and a variety of communities.[16] It and others document both the characteristics of community well-being, like average income levels, employment rates, and family conditions, and how people feel about their community, such as whether they feel safe and trust their neighbours.

The City of Calgary, Alberta has developed an index that provides scores on three main dimensions: economic well-being, social well-being, and physical well-being.[17] Canada has its own index known as the Canadian Index of

Wellbeing.[18] It provides measures in eight categories: community vitality, democratic engagement, education, environment, healthy populations, leisure and culture, living standards, and time use. A score for each of those categories is generated from eight different measures per category. Three of those measures per category are shown in Table 1.1 in order to provide some idea of how well-being scores are generated.

A number of Canadian municipalities have developed their own well-being indexes because they are one of the best predictors of crime, social disorder, and needs for social and economic development. All of these indexes are evidence based and statistically founded. For example, statisticians and researchers measure neighbourhood characteristics and neighbours' feelings of safety and then statistically measure whether those factors correlate with crime and social disorder. Wherever they find a strong correlation, they add that factor to their index of safety and well-being.

Because well-being is so highly correlated with crime and social disorder, incidents of crime and social disorder become good indicators of the well-being status of neighbourhoods. Police can map occurrences, and in so doing, identify those neighbourhoods that are in particular need of more investment in community capacity-building (see Figure 4.8 in Chapter 4 for an example of such a map). It also helps to overlay on those occurrence maps data from the Canadian census about income levels, single-parent families, levels of education, and other social determinants of health. Most often, those maps will coincide—thus isolating for police, and their community partners, neighbourhoods where everyone has to work on building community. If they do not invest in community capacity-building, then neighbours there will experience increasing levels of harm and victimization, thereby escalating the demand for and costs of emergency response—and the cycle goes on and on.

Because they collect data about crime and social disorder occurrences, police can serve the rest of us in other human and social service agencies, and in municipal governments, in learning where the priority neighbourhoods are for community capacity-building. Most human and social service agencies and organizations operate within the resource and mandate constraints provided in their area of specialization. For example, a health care provider limits its efforts in community to health resources, technologies, and advice; it does not apply itself to other issues like housing quality, employment, or landlord–tenant relationships. By the same token, a housing agency does not consider issues of health, nutrition, and exercise. Basically, our human and social service agencies are mandated and organized by specialization. Yet we have recently learned that most crime and social disorder results from the confluence of multiple risk factors, like poverty, substandard housing, addictions, single parenting, and mental illness. There is no single agency that is mandated and has the resources to look at all those factors. So when crime and social disorder escalate in these neighbourhoods,

TABLE 1.1 **Canadian Index of Wellbeing: Categories and Selected Measures**

Domain	Selected Measures
Community Vitality	Property crime
	Violent crime
	Participation in organized activities
Democratic Engagement	Voter turnout
	Satisfaction with democracy in Canada
	Women in Parliament
Education	University degrees
	Youth completing high school
	Socio-emotional competence of young teens
Environment	Greenhouse gas emissions
	Ground-level ozone
	Energy production
Healthy Populations	Life expectancy at birth
	Self-reported excellent health
	Probable depression
Leisure and Culture	Time spent on social leisure activities
	Volunteer hours
	Expenditures on culture
Living Standards	Median income
	Population in low income
	Employment rates
Time Use	Workday commute times
	Labour force working 50+ hours/week
	3-5 year olds read to daily by parent

we call police. Police are the ones who can see and recognize the results of deficiencies in the social determinants of safety. They do not get called into neighbourhoods where these determinants are satisfactory. As a result, police can be the first ones to blow the whistle for all the rest of us in establishing priorities for improving the social determinants of health and well-being. That is one of the unique capacities of police agencies. They have the data; they know where the problems are. They can make that clear to all of the rest of us.

Reshaping Community Life

On crime prevention, criminologist Lawrence Sherman has said:

> Communities are the central institution for crime prevention, the stage on which all other institutions perform. Families, schools, labor markets, retail establishments, police and corrections must all confront the consequences of community life. Much of the success or failure of these other institutions is affected by the community context in which they operate. Our ... ability to prevent serious violent crime may depend heavily on our ability to help reshape community life, at least in our most troubled communities.[19]

His reference to "our most troubled communities" represents what we have called high-demand neighbourhoods. In using the phrase "reshape community life," he appears to go even further than community capacity-building. This statement raises questions about just what is required to reshape community life and whether there are any limits to what community mobilization and community policing can achieve.

Community policing is not a magic bullet. It can help reshape community life, but it alone is not sufficient, not least because police have neither the full range of skills, nor the resources needed, to reshape community life. In this context, we are saying that community policing is a useful tool for police to bring to the task. It has special qualities and contributions to make. But a host of other people, agencies, organizations, political will, and resources must be part of this equation too.

Police are not community development experts. But they most often end up being the responder of last resort where social disorder is at its worst. This is because the highest-demand communities have degenerated to the point where people at severe risk of harm and victimization. In those conditions, few others than police have what it takes for emergency intervention. That approach to dealing with high-demand neighbourhoods will work so long as society is willing to tolerate the harms and victimization that occur there, and also willing to pay the escalating costs of policing.

IN THE COMMUNITY

Reshaping Community Life in Bancroft, Ontario

Faced with a $50,000 surcharge from provincial police at the end of its fiscal year, Bancroft, Ontario, which had insufficient funds to do public works maintenance, passed a resolution in council that rejected the surcharge and refused to pay the bill. After a "cooling-off" period afforded by the Christmas and New Year's break, council rescinded that resolution, paid the bill, and went into negotiations with police about the sources of the surcharge. They learned that it was directly related to the types and frequency of calls for police assistance within the municipality. That is when it occurred to the municipality that if they could do something to get the calls for service down, they might also experience smaller bills from their police service. They asked police for a breakdown of the types and frequency of calls for service, and that information led them to focus on those community-building strategies that would have the greatest impact in reducing the most prevalent occurrences, thereby increasing people's safety and reducing the costs of policing.

This is a good example of police advising and engaging municipal governments on issues of community safety and well-being. By simply passing the costs of policing on to the municipality, they got the municipality to reconsider what it could do to make its citizens safer—and thereby reduce policing costs. Then, by sharing occurrence data and helping municipal governments and partnering community agencies figure out what to do to reduce the incidence of these calls, people became safer, calls for service dropped, and the costs of policing stabilized. That is effective community policing because it shows how police actions get community to begin to figure out how to do things differently, and better, so that their people become safer.

Web of Organizations Reshaping Community Life

Let's review the logic and science that underpins community policing. It starts with the observation that police have to go most often to those neighbourhoods where people are experiencing the most harm and victimization from crime and social disorder. Crime and social disorder happen most often in neighbourhoods where neighbours have the least social cohesion. They do not stick together, and they do not know each other (much less trust and respect each other) sufficiently to join together in fighting the very conditions that put them at risk in the first place. Often these neighbours are preoccupied with their own personal challenges, which can range from poverty to addictions, to parenting pressures, to mental health issues, to physical disability, to substandard housing, to social injustices and other negatives on the social determinants of health continuum. Police are society's last line of defence in these neighbourhoods; hence, they know where these conditions prevail. They can inform those of us who wish to collaborate in "reshaping community life" about what the risk factors are and where this work is most needed.

But—and this is a big "but"—police cannot reshape community life alone. Police must use community policing as a tool to mobilize and engage others in reshaping community life. Most fundamentally, community policing means police doing things that kick-start efforts to reshape community life in neighbourhoods where the characteristics of community do not exist. Community policing is about creating community in order to reduce harms and victimization. We know that if community exists, people are safer and more secure because they trust and respect each other sufficiently to enjoy common values for safety and well-being, and to band together to deal with community problems as they arise. That is why we make the very important distinction that community policing, in neighbourhoods where community does not exist, is about creating community. If community building is done well, people are safer and there is less demand for police or other emergency responses.

Our Mrs. Robertson scenario showed what can happen when a creative police officer mobilizes a neighbourhood asset who adds tremendous value to the process of reshaping community from the inside out. Most high-demand neighbourhoods are home to community assets like Mrs. Robertson. The challenges in mobilizing them are:

- first and foremost, figuring out which neighbours are assets and which are not (a job for which street-wise and experienced police officers are uniquely qualified);
- making it safe for these assets to reach out to their neighbours and begin to apply themselves to reshaping community life (again, police are uniquely qualified to do this); and
- providing these assets with the supports they need to succeed at reshaping community life.

IN THE COMMUNITY

Using Community Assets to Reshape Community Life

For years the local Optimist Club, whose motto is "Friends of youth," donated $10,000 to the local police service to channel into summer activities and programs for youth from high-demand neighbourhoods. A community asset whom police had identified in one such neighbourhood asked an officer who happened to be a member of the Optimist Club if he would try to steer some of those funds directly into the neighbourhood.

Recognizing that this was an opportunity to develop the advocacy skills of a key figure in the community, the officer answered: "No, but you can! Write a letter to the club president requesting a chance to ask members for this support, and I'll be sure that letter gets to him." With panic on her face, the community asset said, "I can't do that! I wouldn't know what to say." The officer gently replied, "You agree to write the letter and I'll help you." Encouraged, the woman wrote the letter. The club president invited her to attend a regular club meeting and make her pitch to members. The officer attended, in uniform, and sat beside her during the club dinner, then stood up and introduced her. She made her pitch and got thousands of dollars to provide a range of summer craft and recreation services for neighbourhood youth and children whose families could not afford to send them to summer camp. The Optimists benefited too: they felt better connected to the youth they were supporting in the first place.

The Optimist Club scenario exemplifies what is meant by the third condition of community mobilization: providing community assets with the supports they need to succeed at reshaping community life. In this case it was a simple matter of coaching the community asset on how to write a letter, and attending with her when she made her pitch to this fraternal organization. The best part of this approach is that this particular neighbourhood asset learned something about how to write a business letter, approach a local community-based organization, and raise some much-needed funds for her own neighbourhood youth. Through that simple exchange she became even more of an asset for reshaping community life in her high-demand neighbourhood—all because of the astute handling of the situation by a police officer who refused to do it for her, but supported her in learning how to do it for herself and for her neighbourhood.

Mobilizing assets in the neighbourhood—while necessary—is insufficient to reshape community life to the point where harms and victimization are significantly reduced and where police and other acute care providers are required to respond less often. As Professor Sherman has commented:

Ironically, a central tenet of community prevention programs has been the empowerment of local community leaders to design and implement their own ... prevention strategies. This philosophy may amount to throwing people overboard and then letting them design their own life preserver. The scientific literature shows that the policies and market forces causing criminogenic [factors] are beyond the control of neighborhood residents, and that "empowerment" does not include the power to change those policies ... . It is one thing, for example, for tenants to manage the security guards in a public housing project. It is another thing entirely to let tenants design a new public housing policy and determine where, in a metropolitan area, households with public housing support will live.[20]

So if police and local neighbourhood assets are insufficient for the task, who else can we engage in helping reshape community life in high-demand neighbourhoods? The answer lies in a whole web of other agencies and organizations that have a stake in what is happening in these neighbourhoods. The example above of the Optimist Club shows one **community-based organization** (an organization of community members that is usually dedicated to community service of some kind, frequently but not always incorporated, and most often a not-for-profit organization that raises funds to support its activities) that rallied to the cause of reshaping community life, at least for youth, in this small neighbourhood. But there are so many more community-based organizations that can be usefully engaged in rebuilding community where it is most lacking. These include service clubs, faith groups, and activity groups (like parenting, childcare, sports, and educational groups), among others. An effective community policing initiative will identify who and where those community-based organizations are; liaise with their leadership; and engage them in community-building initiatives where their particular strengths will serve best.

Another important category of organizations that are essential for reshaping community life is the publicly funded human and social service agencies that serve these neighbourhoods. Many of them, like those that deal with child security, income maintenance, social housing, assistance to persons with disabilities, public transit, and health care, serve the widest variety of needs and are mandated and funded by various levels of government.

Each of these publicly funded agencies operates under rigorous legislated standards and operational policies and procedures. As a result, many of these mandates, policies, and procedures can inhibit these agencies from effectively collaborating with each other in reshaping community life in a high-demand neighbourhood. An agency may, for example, operate an acute care service in a neighbourhood on behalf of its own mandate and resource base, but find it challenging to work together with other agencies and realize the value of collaboration. This is another critical issue where police have the capacity to engage other human and social service agency partners in more collaborative ventures on behalf of the same neighbourhoods and neighbours where all agencies are already responding too often.

---

community-based organization organization of community members that is usually dedicated to community service of some kind; frequently but not always incorporated; and most often a not-for-profit organization that raises funds to support its activities

A third category of organizations that are needed to effectively reshape community life is municipal offices and agencies. It forms an important part of the web of organizations and includes a variety of offices and agencies. In a large urban centre, for example, a municipal government may operate an office that focuses on community development—and what a natural partner it is for reshaping community life in a high-demand neighbourhood. In a small, rural municipality, however, no such office may exist. More likely a small municipality operates specialized offices in only a few areas, such as public works (water, electricity, sewerage, etc.), roads, fire and other emergency services, garbage and recycling, and bylaws. Usually, decisions about something as substantial as reshaping community life are made by an elected council and sometimes supported by an administration that does background work like social surveys, economic development, and municipal planning.

Because rural municipalities are small, their tax base does not afford the wide range of government offices and functions that are available in larger municipalities. So the small municipality relies on regional and county offices to provide the services that they cannot afford to run locally. That means that any effort to engage public agencies in a local effort to reshape community in a high-demand neighbourhood will require reaching out to agencies and organizations at higher levels of government (regional, county, and even provincial). This is not possible if the team doing this work does not know who or where the agencies are, and does not know the roles, resources, mandates, and leadership of those agencies. Hence, any effort to reshape community life has to be grounded in good research, outreach, and knowledge about the wide

FIGURE 1.3 Three Types of Agencies That Populate the Web of Organizations

Municipal agencies		
Public works	Police	Others

Publicly funded agencies			
Children's aid	Health	School boards	Others

Community-based organizations			
Women's support groups	Service clubs	Business associations	Others

range of agencies, services, resources, and advocates that can be engaged to join in this work.

All of which brings us back to the meaning of "community" in community policing. We have already established that community means that people know and trust each other sufficiently to join in creating and sustaining a safe and healthy neighbourhood. Further, we have asserted that where police have to respond most often, community does not exist sufficiently to sustain safety and well-being for all. Hence, at least in part, community policing means reshaping community life in these neighbourhoods. But another interpretation of "community" in community policing is that it requires community-based organizations, human and social service agencies, and municipal and county governance to reshape community life in high-demand neighbourhoods. In short, it takes the whole community to build community where community is lacking to the degree that people's safety and well-being are in serious jeopardy. That is the "community" side of this equation. In Chapter 3 we will begin to unpack the "policing" side of community policing.

CHECK YOUR UNDERSTANDING

1. Are officers in an effective community policing service able to reshape community life sufficiently so that a high-demand neighbourhood becomes a low-demand neighbourhood? Why or why not?

2. With reference to a high-demand neighbourhood where officers respond most often, what do we mean by a "community asset"?

3. What other agencies and organizations need to be engaged by community policing in reshaping community life in high-demand neighbourhoods?

CHAPTER SUMMARY

When applied to community policing, the word "community" has very special meanings. First and foremost, it means that community is not the same in every neighbourhood; therefore, community policing cannot and should not be the same in every neighbourhood. Before police launch any community policing initiative in any neighbourhood, they have to examine the neighbourhood and find out the extent to which true community operates there—meaning the extent to which the people in that neighbourhood share common values for safety and well-being and have the collaborative capacity necessary to resolve neighbourhood problems.

Second, we know that where neighbours do share common values for safety and well-being, and have durable personal relationships that allow them to work together to resolve neighbourhood problems, police are rarely called to provide assistance. In contrast, where neighbours do not share common values and durable personal relationships, police are called to respond most often. Therefore, the primary goal of community policing is to create in these neighbourhoods common values for safety and well-being and the durable personal relationships that are necessary to achieve these goals.

Third, "community" in the context of community policing means everyone. Police cannot expect to solve profound neighbourhood problems by themselves. What is required is the participation of all possible neighbourhood assets, working together and in partnership with diverse agencies, organizations, and government offices from outside the neighbourhood. Together, they have a good chance at improving the conditions of safety and well-being in even the most marginalized neighbourhoods. The main job for community policing, therefore, is to mobilize neighbourhood assets, engage community partners, and ensure that it is safe for them to collaborate constructively in reshaping community life.

REVIEW AND DISCUSSION QUESTIONS

1. What does "community" mean?
2. Can we assume that all neighbourhoods under the jurisdiction of a single police service have the same degree of community? Why or why not?
3. When police are planning a community policing strategy for a target neighbourhood, what kinds of analysis and research do you think they should do first?
4. On what bases do police decide the main goals or objectives of a targeted community policing initiative?

5. What is the meaning of "social control," and what are its implications for community policing in high-demand neighbourhoods and in low-demand neighbourhoods?

6. What do we mean by "social capital" in the context of community policing? How can social capital be used in community policing?

7. What does "police legitimacy" mean, and how does it relate to community policing?

8. What are the "social determinants of health," and what do they have to do with community policing?

9. In the highest-demand neighbourhoods where police respond most often, who can police turn to in order to reshape community life by targeting the social determinants of health?

10. If police cannot, and should not, be the sole community builders in high-demand neighbourhoods, what is their role in community policing?

KEY TERMS

community, 6
community capacity-building, 15
community cohesion, 20
community-based organization, 28
criminogenic factors, 12
durable relations, 6
police legitimacy, 17
procedural justice, 18
recidivism, 18
social capital, 16
social control, 13
social determinants of health, 20
social disorder, 20
victimization, 10

NOTES

1   The most notable exception is Victor E Kappeler & Larry K Gaines, *Community Policing: A Contemporary Perspective*, 6th ed (Waltham, Mass: Anderson, 2011) 97-132, which devotes 135 pages to an academic literature review of the meaning of "community" in relation to the concept of community policing.

2   Paul James et al, *Sustainable Communities, Sustainable Development: Other Paths for Papua New Guinea* (Honolulu: University of Hawaii Press, 2012) at 14.

3   Jane Jacobs, *The Death and Life of Great American Cities* (New York: Vintage Books, 1992) at 112.

4   CBS News, "Counterinsurgency Cops: Military Tactics Fight Street Crime," *60 Minutes* (4 August 2013), online: <https://www.youtube.com/watch?v=KhFKmZDC_ho>.

5   Jeanette Kinard & Jessica Johnson, "Criminogenic Risk Assessments: What Are They and What Do They Mean for Your Client?" *Voice for the Defense Online* (2 October 2014), online: <http://www.voiceforthedefenseonline.com/story/criminogenic-risk-assessments-what-are-they-and-what-do-they-mean-your-client>; and Edward J Latessa & Christopher Lowenkamp, "What Are Criminogenic Needs and Why Are They Important?" *For the Record* (2005), online: <https://www.uc.edu/content/dam/uc/ccjr/docs/articles/What_Are_Criminogenic_Needs.pdf>.

6   David Garland, *The Culture of Control: Crime and Social Order in Contemporary Society* (Oxford: Oxford University Press, 2001).

7   Morris Janowitz, "Sociological Theory and Social Control" (1975) 81:1 Am J Sociol 82.

8   Lawrence W Sherman, "Policing for Crime Prevention" in Lawrence W Sherman et al, *Preventing Crime: What Works, What Doesn't, What's Promising: A Report to the United States Congress* (Washington, DC: National Institute of Justice, 1997) ch 8.

9   Lynn Hinds & Kristina Murphy, "Public Satisfaction with Police: Using Procedural Justice to Improve Police Legitimacy" (2007) 40:1 Aust NZ J Criminol 27.

10   Seymour B Sarason, *The Psychological Sense of Community: Prospects for a Community Psychology* (Oxford: Jossey-Bass, 1974).

11   DW McMillan & DM Chavis, "Sense of Community: A Definition and Theory" (1986) 14 J Community Psychol 16.

12   Statistics Canada, "Police-Reported Crime Statistics in Canada, 2014," by Jillian Boyce, in *Juristat* 35:1, Catalogue No 85-002-X (Ottawa: Statistics Canada, 2015).

13   Hugh C Russell, "II: A Focus Beyond Crime" in Hugh C Russell & Norman E Taylor, *New Directions in Community Safety: Consolidating Lessons Learned about Risk and Collaboration* (Toronto: Ontario Working Group on Collaborative, Risk-driven Community Safety and Well-being, Ontario Association of Chiefs of Police, April 2014) at 5, online: <http://www.oacp.on.ca/Userfiles/StandingCommittees/CommunityPolicing/ResourceDocs/OWG%20New%20Directions%20in%20Community%20Safety.pdf>.

14   Community Safety and Crime Prevention Committee, "Definitions of Words and Concepts That Are Important in Promoting Community Safety and Well-Being" (Toronto: Ontario Association of Chiefs of Police, 2016).

15   *Ibid*.

16   DD Perkins et al, "Participation and the Social and Physical Environment of Residential Blocks: Crime and Community Context" (1990) 18:1 Am J Commun Psychol 83.

17   City of Calgary, *Indices of Community Well-Being, 2006 for Calgary Neighbourhoods* (Calgary: Community and Neighbourhood Services, Social Policy and Planning, 2010), online: <http://www.calgary.ca/CSPS/CNS/Documents/indices_of_well_being.pdf> at 2-3.

18   Canadian Index of Wellbeing, *How Are Canadians Really Doing? The 2012 CIW Report* (Waterloo, Ont: Canadian Index of Wellbeing and University of Waterloo, 2012).

19   Lawrence W Sherman, "Communities and Crime Prevention" in Lawrence W Sherman et al, *Preventing Crime, supra* note 8, ch 3.

20   Sherman, *ibid.*

CHAPTER 2

Evolution of Community Policing

The Halifax Police Court and City Hall, originally built in 1810 to house the county courthouse, sat in the centre of town next to the city market. This photograph, taken in July 1886, shows the police court and market on a busy Saturday morning.

LEARNING OUTCOMES

Upon completion of this chapter, you should be able to:

- List the principal characteristics of "traditional policing"
- Explain why traditional policing began to fail and what new approaches were added
- Describe how the following three characteristics influenced the nature of policing: community partnerships, problem-solving, and crime prevention
- Distinguish between police efforts to form partnerships with the community and police undertaking community mobilization and engagement
- Explain what the roots of crime and social disorder are, and what the main roles and responsibilities of police are in resolving them

Introduction

All communities regularly face threats to safety and well-being. They may originate from natural hazards like storms and wildfires or they may come from the criminal actions of individuals striving to adapt to the challenges of life and making choices that threaten the capacities of others to live well and safely. Consequently, communities rely on police to mobilize quickly and apply special skills and abilities that minimize harm and victimization from such threats and risks.

The modern police service is based on a model that dates back approximately 1,500 years—to a time when Indigenous tribes and communities of what are now the British Isles struggled with the remnants of Roman colonialism and Frankish and Germanic invasions from northern Europe. Typical of colonial movements throughout history, these early invaders sought ways to control the peoples they conquered while at the same time benefiting from their hard work and productivity. Prior to the rule of King Ethelbert of Kent, Celtic communities relied on their own abilities and resources to deal with threats to community safety—whether natural hazards, such as storms, or human conflicts. Archaeological and historical evidence[1] suggests that Ethelbert was the first settler authority to write down and articulate the role of the king—what today we would call the "state"—in securing safety and well-being for all in a community. Not unlike today's *Criminal Code*[2] of Canada, Ethelbert's document lists offences and sanctions that would be adjudicated by the king and his court.[3] In exchange for that service, the king would extract tithes (taxes). In effect, Ethelbert took away from community the people's responsibility for their own safety, security, and well-being and placed it in the hands of the state—in exchange for the wealth of the people.

Ever since, Western law enforcement has been a function of public authority—an arm of the state in which the public invests significant resources with increasing expectations for a safe and secure community. Over time, and to varying degrees, police services have delivered on that promise. But also over time, the public has exerted significant influence on the ways in which police services organize and how they do their work. This chapter is the story of those influences and how the institution of policing has evolved in adapting to them.

The evolution of community policing is less a chronology of community policing events and ideas than it is a description of a natural evolution in policing itself. It is about how policing has changed over time in response to changes in the environment in which it worked, world events (like the mobilization of large armies), and evolving mandates from the people police serve. Ironically, the advent of "community policing" in the last 40 years has brought us full circle—back to the days before King Ethelbert of Kent. Experience and circumstances have created pressure for those currently involved in policing (public policy-makers, police agencies and associations, police leaders and officers, municipal leaders, and local organizations and individuals) to seriously reconsider the role of community in ensuring everyone's safety and well-being. The opportunity has arisen to relearn what Celtic communities may have known over 1,500 years ago—that only community can achieve safety and well-being for all. That achievement has to originate with the efforts of those most directly affected by any threats to safety and well-being—community members, not the state, welfare agencies, police, or other external providers.

Much of the last half of the 20th century saw community policing applied as an overarching concept or philosophy that influenced policing style. In the spirit of community policing, officers were encouraged to relate more openly and congenially with the public they encountered in the course of their duties. The emphasis was on how police officers carried themselves. However, in the first decade of the 21st century the term took on new meaning with an emphasis on the role of non-police—community members—in increasing their own and their neighbours' safety and well-being. The term now signals an effort to put "community" back into the community policing equation.

ON PATROL

Street Crime Unit

Club "Z" was a favourite place for youth to hang out on weekends, listening to music and dancing. One night, witnesses reported a stabbing between two young men who had been on the dance floor. According to these witnesses, the incident began after the victim glared disrespectfully at the perpetrator. The perpetrator then produced a knife and stabbed the victim twice, killing him. The motive for murder seemed unrealistic but investigations revealed that youth were swarming and beating up other youths for no apparent reason. Swarming erupted in schools, and in one case two young men burst into a busy classroom and beat up a student. These youths did not fear traditional school sanctions, and police enforcement tactics were ineffectual.

Police, a clinical psychologist specializing in youth violence, and school officials formed a partnership to address the swarming behaviour. They created a Street Crime Unit composed of social workers and young, plainclothes officers who could relate to school-aged youth. On call 24 hours a day, members of the unit were embedded in particular schools so that youth could get to know them. The unit's mandate was to increase reporting of victimization and collaborate with school and justice officials in finding sustainable solutions, which included, whenever possible, extrajudicial measures (measures that do not require court proceedings).

Through this initiative, the partnership discovered that community policing is most effective when police and others listen to the community and victims and attempt to understand the problems they face. They found that the Street Crime Unit provided effective support to the victims, and collaboratively it identified meaningful sanctions for the offenders that would help ensure that this unacceptable behaviour would never occur again. As a male student told police during an interview, "If you get to know someone better, you feel more comfortable. If you get to feel more comfortable around police, seeing them around more, you react a lot differently."

Consider the following questions:

1. Why didn't school discipline or police enforcement work in this situation?
2. What could be gained by police collaborating with the school board and a psychologist specializing in youth violence?
3. What did the Street Crime Unit achieve that traditional enforcement was not able to achieve?

The Chronology of Community Policing

The Western European Experience

From 1100 to 1700, control of people's behaviours in community (later to become known as "law enforcement" and even later than that, "policing") in western Europe was organized around the feudal system. Feudal masters appointed local sheriffs to rally villagers when someone needed to be caught or held accountable for some breach, and to collect taxes to compensate the feudal lord for this service. As villages and population centres grew, layers of enforcement authorities were added to this system. A judicial layer was added in England through passage of the *Justices of the Peace Act* in 1361.[4] Appointed by the king, justices of the peace had supreme authority over all enforcement as well as prosecutions and sanctions—thereby setting the stage for collusion between justice officials and lower levels of enforcement. By the 1500s large urban centres like London made such systems impracticable. As the Industrial Revolution (18th century) stimulated private sector growth, companies began to hire their own police to protect their properties and those of their workers and village officials. That system broke down when production efficiencies led to layoffs of large numbers of people and increased poverty led to more crime and disorder. Private constabularies could not keep up, in part because they were directing too many resources into competing with each other and bribing local officials. Meanwhile, the local populace demanded improved security and policing.

Similar pressures emerged in France and by the end of the 18th century, that nation organized a highly militarized and secretive national police force. The English people did not like what they saw happening in France. That led England's home secretary, Sir Robert Peel (in 1822), to try to design a more transparent and publicly accessible police service. The model on which most contemporary Western policing is based emerged from Sir Robert's efforts, which culminated in the *Metropolitan Police Act* of 1829.[5] It established London's Metropolitan Police Service, known today as "the Met."

The Met was publicized by its first two commissioners and Sir Robert as "policing by consent" of the people, as opposed to policing by authority of the monarch. Officers were depicted as citizens in uniform, acting with the consent of fellow citizens, and committed to the principles of transparency, integrity, and accountability to the public they served. Those values may be seen in the nine principles of policing, which are popularly known as "Peelian principles":[6]

1. To prevent crime and disorder, as an alternative to their repression by military force and severity of legal punishment.
2. To recognize always that the power of the police to fulfil their functions and duties is dependent on public approval of their existence, actions and behaviour, and on their ability to secure and maintain public respect.
3. To recognize always that to secure and maintain the respect and approval of the public means also the securing of the willing co-operation of the public in the task of securing observance of laws.
4. To recognize always that the extent to which the co-operation of the public can be secured diminishes proportionately the necessity of the use of physical force and compulsion for achieving police objectives.
5. To seek and preserve public favour, not by pandering to public opinion, but by constantly demonstrating absolutely impartial service to law, in complete independence of policy, and without regard to the justice or injustice of the substance of individual laws, by ready offering of individual service and friendship to all members of the public without regard to their wealth or social standing, by ready exercise of courtesy and friendly good humour, and by ready offering of individual sacrifice in protecting and preserving life.
6. To use physical force only when the exercise of persuasion, advice and warning is found to be insufficient to obtain public co-operation to an extent necessary to secure observance of law or to restore order, and to use only the minimum degree of physical force which is necessary on any particular occasion for achieving a police objective.
7. To maintain at all times a relationship with the public that gives reality to the historic tradition that the police are the public and that the public are the police, the police being only members of the public who are paid to give full-time attention to duties which are incumbent on every citizen in the interests of community welfare and existence.
8. To recognize always the need for strict adherence to police-executive functions, and to refrain from even seeming to usurp the

powers of the judiciary of avenging individuals or the State, and of authoritatively judging guilt and punishing the guilty.

9. To recognize always that the test of police efficiency is the absence of crime and disorder, and not the visible evidence of police action in dealing with them.

CHECK YOUR UNDERSTANDING

1. Review the Peelian principles of policing and explain which principles reinforce the goal of "policing by consent."
2. Which principles address the idea of police legitimacy?
3. Which principles reinforce the separation of powers between police and the judiciary?
4. Which principles paint a picture of police as citizens in uniform?

Traditional Policing

Notwithstanding its founding principles, by the late 19th century, policing in the United Kingdom and the United States began to suffer significant levels of public criticism because it was too deeply embedded with politics and municipal bodies. In effect, police were seen as agents of political leaders, who used police to manipulate the people for the sake of personal gain or a preferred public policy. One way of interpreting this stage in the evolution of modern policing is that the Peelian principles failed to bring about the accountable and transparent service they strived for. On the other hand, the Peelian principles were quite successful in empowering the people to demand and expect a transparent and publicly accountable service. (That is an expectation that prevails today: look at the Black Lives Matter movement in Canada and in the United States.) By the end of that century, public pressures produced another transformation in policing—one that would inject more substantial boundaries between policing and political influence.

What has become known as "professional policing" or "traditional policing" emerged at the turn of the 20th century.[7] This was a more militarized model that emphasized command and control, logistical efficiencies, uniform standards and practices, and a rigid hierarchy of authorities. The military form of organization accommodated large numbers of members, ensured effective decision-making, and created efficiencies in service, especially in times of emergency. Further, the military model emphasized social control, and the new perception of the role of police similarly emphasized social control. At that time the military model enjoyed popular legitimacy; its uniforms spoke of order, ethics, and direct authority, as opposed to authority rendered by a patron government or politician.[8]

In the **traditional policing** model, the focus was on reactive policing, which entailed:

- responding as quickly as possible upon report of a crime;
- investigating the incident, victims, and perpetrators;
- documenting every stage of the investigation;
- catching criminals and making arrests;
- supporting prosecutions of those arrested; and
- conducting random patrols to deter other potential perpetrators.

The traditional model prevailed through almost three-quarters of the 20th century. But it began to change owing to the advent of technologies like telephones in homes and businesses, radio dispatch, air-conditioned police cruisers, and computers—all of which contributed to fewer face-to-face interactions between police and the communities they served. Furthermore, the traditional model failed to address the roots of crime and social disorder. Hence, police found themselves responding repeatedly to the same incidents, at the same locations, in response to the same perpetrators.

By the 1970s qualified research and evaluation of police practices also challenged the traditional model of policing. For example, two of its precepts fell under the scrutiny of behavioural scientists. George Kelling et al. proved that rapid response rarely led to speedy arrests or higher-quality investigations (although it did minimize harms and speed victim access to treatment and supports).[9] Boydstun and Sherry disproved the assumption that random patrol was a strong deterrent to crime and social disorder. They concluded that more constructive relationships between officers and the public they served were more important and more effective deterrents, and that they also speeded investigations and arrests.[10] In the wake of these findings, police leaders and researchers began to embrace the idea that investigations would be more timely and successful, and intelligence would be higher quality, if police had a more open and consultative relationship with neighbours in the community. Moreover, the desire to increase policing efficiencies and reduce costs led them to notice the high incidence of repeat calls for service and consider whether engaging in problem-solving might be more effective and economical than speedy response and quick arrests.

---

traditional policing reactive policing based on the military model of rapid response and efficient follow-up to harmful incidents

CHECK YOUR UNDERSTANDING

1. Even today, we hear police officers refer to "traditional policing." What are its characteristics?
2. When did this model arise and what factors led to its creation?
3. How long has traditional policing been around, and do you think it will continue to be relevant?
4. What are the strengths of traditional policing? What are its weaknesses?

The Adoption of Community Policing into the Traditional Policing Model

In the mid-1970s the words "community policing" began to circulate in policing circles and beyond (in municipal agencies, among human and social service providers, and in communities). No doubt this phrase was coined to distinguish evolving changes in the style of police service delivery from the traditional model that had prevailed for three-quarters of a century. But the bottom line was not the addition of a new service to traditional policing, but changes in the delivery of policing services across the board. To this day, police services employ many of the methods of traditional policing—speedy incident response when warranted, thorough, well-documented investigations, arrests, and prosecutions, and assistance to victims—because the law requires them to and because community requires them to. However, after acknowledging that most police time and effort is not related to chargeable offences, but rather social disorder and problem-solving, police services began to try to figure out how to integrate some of the principles of "community policing" into their service-delivery models. Before we continue our discussion, it is useful to note the distinctions between the tactics of traditional policing and those of community policing (see Table 2.1):

TABLE 2.1 **Features of Traditional Policing and Community Policing**

Traditional Policing	Community Policing
Police solely responsible	Collaborative
Incident-driven	Risk-driven
Reactive	Proactive
Speedy response	Timeliness of intervention
Investigative	Supportive
Minimizing harms	Preventing harms
Arrests and prosecutions	Problem-solving

The distinctions shown in the table, above, are important to understand. But neither approach is better than the other; nor are they mutually exclusive. Both are needed by the modern police service and the communities they serve. Which tactics are applied by a police service, or individual officer, at any moment in time relates exclusively to the nature of the situation that police are addressing. Police need the full repertoire of service-delivery tactics to do their job well.

Some services accommodated these distinctions by organizing, virtually, two sides of their house: traditional policing on one side, and community policing on the other. They set up "community policing units" to which they assigned "community policing officers." In effect, they reinforced the apparent distinctions between traditional policing and emerging community policing tactics. However, they failed to acknowledge the issues that forced the advent of community policing tactics in the first place—that improved relationships with the public and other community agencies and organizations would not only help prevent crime and social disorder, but also improve the quality of intelligence and the speed and quality of investigations, arrests, and prosecutions.

Worse yet, distinguishing between traditional and community policing set up a dynamic in the squad room that was totally dysfunctional—the distinction between "real policing" and "soft policing." That forced many criminologists, researchers, and police leaders to spend inordinate amounts of time explaining to their own members as well as the broader public what community policing was not—for example, soft on crime, a silver bullet, a specialized unit, or a mere program, activity, or person.

In some ways, use of the words "community policing" suggested something different from "policing" when in truth, the inclusion of "community" in that phrase was simply intended to make "policing" more effective and more efficient. Whitelaw and Parent said it best:

> Community policing is best viewed as the most recent phase in the evolution of police work that, ironically, has resulted in police services returning to the original roots of policing as set forth by Sir Robert Peel early in the 19th century.[11]

The notion of community policing as a "philosophy" emerged from sincere efforts to integrate traditional and community policing tactics. Police leaders were trying to figure out how to integrate proactive policing, problem-solving, crime prevention, collaboration, and other ideas into the traditional, enforcement model. They strived to instill in their front-line officers the value that the people whom police serve deserve to have input into policing decisions and processes. This idea of community policing as a broad philosophy that should influence all police decisions and processes predominated in the 1990s but began slowly fading away in the early 2000s. This is principally because police agencies have learned that community policing involves much more than abstract belief systems about the value of public input to police decisions. It also requires practical actions and specialized police tactics. Most significantly, current practices have shown that even traditional police tactics will not succeed and their effects will not be sustainable without citizen involvement and collaboration. Citizen involvement is a prerequisite to successful policing. It is not a question of philosophy or belief; it is a reality. Today, policing is seen as traditional tactics merged with community problem-solving based upon equitable partnerships between the police agency and other agencies, organizations, businesses, and citizens in community.

CHECK YOUR UNDERSTANDING

1. What are some of the characteristics of community policing?
2. How are the characteristics of community policing different from the characteristics of traditional policing?
3. Carefully consider and then defend your answer to the following question: which is better, traditional policing or community policing?
4. Why is the notion of community policing as a broad philosophy that should influence all police decisions and processes inadequate?
5. What are some of the practical police tactics that community policing has brought into the traditional policing model?

The Tactics of Community Policing

A description of the evolution of traditional policing would be incomplete without a look at the particular tactics of community involvement in problem-solving and crime prevention, and how they came about.

Public Consultation

A customer-focused approach emerged in the 1950s and 1960s in response to popular complaints about poor police–community relations. Initially, it took the form of public relations, in which police agencies channelled messages through local media in order to present police decisions and actions in the most positive light. Community relations units were established and select officers were charged with spinning pro-policing messages in hopes that they would at least reduce the number and substance of community complaints about police actions. But when public relations seemed not to totally satisfy the public, police turned to **consultation**: seeking, from the broader public, information, advice, input, and reactions to policing priorities, investigations, and actions.

Sometimes consultation meant police informing citizens of safety or other concerns—for example, a "notification of community crime" program in

---

consultation seeking, from the broader public, information, advice, input, and reactions to policing priorities, investigations, and actions

which officers canvassed neighbourhoods in order to inform neighbours of recent incidents in the neighbourhood and the need for increased vigilance and safety precautions. More often, consultation took the form of police soliciting intelligence, information, and surveillance from citizens in order to inform ongoing investigations. The On Patrol scenario in the Introduction to this chapter told the story of Toronto police consulting a psychologist and the school boards in order to try to figure out what to do about youth swarming other youth. Eventually, such consultation tactics worked well enough that police sought community inputs on targeted safety initiatives like Citizens on Patrol. To this day, consultation continues in most police services as citizens serve on boards and committees that help determine policing priorities and facilitate police operations. Through consultation tactics, police have learned that they are not solely responsible for policing decisions, and that their success will in large part depend on their capacity to maintain a reciprocal and open relationship with the public they serve.[12]

Location Policing

The consultation tactic alone had a huge impact in altering the traditional model of policing. But another influential tactic was the rediscovery of **location policing**: assigning select officers to specific neighbourhoods so that they could get to know the neighbourhood and neighbours could get to know them. This idea harks back to the days of the beat officer. But the advent of patrol cars and radio dispatch increased police efficiencies by providing dispatch with the choice to mobilize officers away from their assigned beats when circumstances merited it. So location policing had to be rediscovered in the 1970s and 1980s.

This tactic influenced another significant aspect of the traditional model of policing—the rigid hierarchy of decision-making. Location policing yielded front-line officers who better understood the needs and dynamics of their neighbourhoods than did supervising officers. That meant that in order to benefit from this tactic, the hierarchy of decision-making had to be stood on its head by empowering front-line officers to make some decisions that had previously been the exclusive domain of their bosses. The impacts of this more team-oriented approach to policing were largely positive. The public approved, neighbourhood conditions improved, and crime and disorder rates declined in these neighbourhoods.[13]

Location policing had trouble competing with dispatch efficiencies, however, in a budget environment that was minimizing the number of police officers available to respond to incidents. Nevertheless, some police services found location policing so helpful in not only reducing crime and social disorder but also improving police–community relationships that they adapted the model to fit current budget constraints. For example, the Toronto Police Service, as

---

location policing having select officers dedicated to specific neighbourhoods so that they can get to know the neighbourhood and neighbours can get to know them

of this writing, is completing an evaluation of their Neighbourhood Officer Program in which they are doing location policing in 17 select, high-demand neighbourhoods, and comparing the results with outcomes in 17 "control" neighbourhoods where police are dispatched in the traditional fashion. Preliminary results are looking very positive. This lends credence to the idea that even if location policing cannot be used in all neighbourhoods, at least it may be worth applying in those neighbourhoods where crime and social disorder generate the most calls for police assistance.

Reassurance Policing

Location policing correlates nicely with an approach that British police have named **reassurance policing**: maintaining relationships with the public that actually reduce their fears of crime and social disorder. Reducing fear of crime became a priority in the 1970s and 1980s when police noted that it was difficult to enlist the help of community members, even in rectifying disorder, if neighbours feared retribution from some of their own. Police noticed that fear of crime frequently exceeded what police knew to be actual levels of crime; hence, they realized that reducing fear of crime meant something different from simply fighting crime.

Both of these factors led police to attempt to reduce fear of crime by mounting visible patrols and by policing various kinds of disorder. In Britain, the Met combined location policing and reassurance policing by mobilizing thousands of uniformed civilians known as "police community support officers" (PCSOs). The PCSOs were selected from the very communities to which they were assigned to patrol and engage citizens in problem-solving. Evaluations showed that this approach was very effective in reducing fears of crime and instilling confidence in the police service—even though the PCSOs were not sworn officers. Results included reduced crime and anti-social behaviour; increased feelings of safety; increased trust and confidence in policing; and increased public engagement with police in community problem-solving.[14]

Reassurance policing took a slightly different form in North America. In the early 1980s James Wilson and George Kelling proposed a "broken windows theory."[15] Their theory was that disorder bred more disorder, thereby creating more opportunities for crime and greater fear of crime. They further hypothesized that if neighbours could be mobilized to rectify disorder (fix the broken window) as soon as it was noticed, not only would they reduce the chances of more disorder, but they would begin to exert the social control in the neighbourhood that was lacking. In so doing, they would also overcome their fear of crime. That part of the broken windows theory stood up fairly well under evaluative scrutiny. Neighbours worked better with police and feared crime less, thereby

---

reassurance policing maintaining relationships with the public that actually reduce their fears of crime and social disorder

empowering themselves to exert more social control on everything that happened in their neighbourhoods. But another component of the theory that did not bear up so well was the notion that social disorder was a precursor to crime and therefore police should practise a zero-tolerance strategy with young perpetrators of anti-social behaviour. Experience showed that cracking down on youth for relatively minor offences exacerbated both anti-social behaviour and crime.[16]

Community-Based Crime Prevention

Community-based crime prevention emerged in the 1970s and 1980s in response to growing awareness that police could not take sole responsibility for crime in communities and a perception that much of the crime in communities was caused by social factors such as a loss of traditional values, a movement away from the church, family breakdown, and failures in education. As a result, by the mid-1980s, neighbourhood groups were engaged in everything from neighbourhood patrols to mentoring youth in recreation, neighbourhood clean-ups and gardens, and neighbourhood home improvements. In the late 1990s, crime prevention began to focus on programs to reduce crime—crime prevention through environmental design, drug abuse resistance education (DARE) programs, Neighbourhood Watch, and police–youth mentoring, to name but a few—as opposed to an overriding goal of policing or a way of doing policing (by recognizing and reducing risk factors before they lead to victimization). This movement, while not uniformly successful in reducing crime or social disorder, did usher in the era of crime prevention—an era that is only changing today as we learn more about what works and what does not work when it comes to preventing crime.[17]

CHECK YOUR UNDERSTANDING

1. What are the similarities and differences among consultation, public relations, and collaboration?
2. Why does location policing work so well? Why are more police services not using it?
3. Why is reassurance policing important for increasing public safety?
4. What does community-based crime prevention mean? Give some examples.

Problem-Oriented Policing

One of the most influential new tactics that transformed traditional policing emerged in the 1990s, initially through the work of an American professor named Herman Goldstein. He encouraged police services to do something more than simply respond to harmful incidents. He challenged front-line officers to examine what he called "clusters" of occurrences that indicated underlying problems that might be addressed.[18] Goldstein wanted police to study victims, offenders, and offences and figure out what made them occur in the first place. He sought to have police do more than enforcement: he wanted them to reach out and enlist the aid of others in the community to rectify those underlying problems proactively. Professor Goldstein called this **problem-oriented policing**: a police tactic that analyzes, and sets out to resolve, problems that underlie repeat occurrences or other patterns of offences and social disorder.

The main difficulty with problem-oriented policing as it has been practised in most places is that police and community problem-solvers oversimplify the problem. An example is the assumption that high school youth experiment with addictive substances because they are ignorant about the effects of those substances. In other words, problem-solvers have assumed that the youth are making a rational decision on the basis of information that is available to them. This assumption led police and others to invest in information programs like DARE to increase drug awareness, even though well-documented research shows that such programs do not reduce the incidence of young people experimenting with or becoming addicted to drugs. These problem-solvers oversimplified the problem in relying on education as a cure-all.[19]

Problem-Oriented Policing in Canada

SARA, PARE, and CAPRA are acronyms for problem-solving models that are most frequently used by Canadian police agencies in implementing problem-oriented policing. They are very similar in promoting a linear progression from problem specification to evaluation of results from a planned solution. Their steps are compared in Table 2.2, below.

TABLE 2.2   Comparison of Steps in the SARA, PARE, and CAPRA Problem-Solving Models

SARA	PARE	CAPRA
Scanning	Problem identification	Clients
Analysis	Analysis	Acquiring and analyzing information
Response	Response	Partnerships
Assessment	Evaluation	Response
		Assessment

---

problem-oriented policing a police tactic which analyzes, and sets out to resolve, problems that underlie repeat occurrences or other patterns of offences and social disorder

All three of these models make problem-solving look like a straightforward, linear process based on trial and error. But in truth, the roots of problems that lead to offences or social disorder are systemic in nature, non-linear, much more inclusive of many other community partners, and highly dependent on a favourable climate for policy, resource, and political changes at the community level. No simple solutions can address those needs.

IN THE COMMUNITY

Using Problem-Oriented Policing to Address Youth Violence

The SARA model for problem-solving was applied in a large municipal service where police identified clusters of youth violence occurrences in one poor part of town (scanning step). Figuring that marginalized young males needed constructive activities after school (analysis step), police used volunteer time to proactively provide coaching and mentoring in athletics (response step). The program was very successful in that it provided healthy mentoring for youth, kept youth from getting into trouble, and reduced calls for service to respond to youth violence (assessment step).

Because of these successes, the program grew and required an increasing investment by the police service. Getting officers to volunteer became a challenge—they were already overworked. But of course stopping the program was not desirable because of its positive impact on the youth and the community. The most significant problem with this program was that the original analysis of underlying issues wasn't thorough enough: it settled on a single-pronged approach using volunteers and did not consider other factors. As an experienced youth psychologist commented:

> Understanding it [youth violence] requires, among other things, a close examination of social forces that are shaping our society . . . . High levels of unemployment, changing population demographics, child poverty, stressed families, racism, sexism, prejudice against gays and lesbians, the exploitation of violence in commercial media, and the normalization of aggression as an acceptable means of handling conflict must all be factored into any discussion about youth violence and school-related problems.[20]

Fixing any of these underlying causes requires far more community partnerships and research-based interventions than a few athletic police officers volunteering their time to work with youth after school.

CHECK YOUR UNDERSTANDING

1. What is problem-oriented policing?
2. What is one of the greatest weaknesses in how problem-oriented policing has been applied by police services?
3. If police really get to the roots of the community problems they want resolved, what will be their principal roles in solving them?
4. If police cannot resolve underlying community problems, who can?

Police–Community Partnerships

The coaching and mentoring example in the previous section highlights another challenge in problem-oriented policing: developing the quality of community partnerships that are required for a collaborative effort to reduce some of the problems that underlie offences and social disorder. For example, rather than relying on a few athletic and generous police officers to volunteer their time mentoring youth, the police agency might have expanded their efforts by recruiting social service partners that could deliver sustainable athletic mentoring for the youth. The CAPRA problem-solving model shown in Table 2.2 is practised by the Royal Canadian Mounted Police. Notice that "Partnerships" is a step in their model—no doubt because they realized that police cannot take sole responsibility for resolving the social ills that lead to crime and social disorder.

Having noted these two shortcomings of problem-oriented policing as it is most often practised—oversimplified analyses and too few community partners for police—we must acknowledge that problem-oriented policing has had a profound and positive effect in transforming traditional policing. It has guided police agencies to consider that proactively addressing the underlying causes of occurrences might be more effective than relying on speedy responses to incidents. Furthermore, it has shown agencies that they are not solely responsible for ensuring public safety. Both problem-solving and partnerships remain keystones to contemporary police practices.

Decentralization and Community Engagement

With these six core tactics—public consultation, location policing, reassurance policing, community-based crime prevention, problem-oriented policing, and police–community partnerships—community policing took on a life of its own through the 1990s. It became something more than specific activities or programs—it became more of a way of doing policing, to the point where it influenced how police agencies organized and operated. Decentralization enabled front-line officers to "own the neighbourhood" and make decisions with neighbours that would help clean up the neighbourhood. Community engagement took hold—and it necessarily included community relations, community consultation, and the holding of numerous meetings with community members in order to identify their priorities, and in order to enlist their help in solving problems. Finally, it incorporated Goldstein's notion of community problem-solving—as opposed to the traditional policing tactic of speedily (and repeatedly) responding to reported incidents. All of these had the effect of opening up the police agency to involvement and scrutiny by the public. Police agencies also enrolled diverse members of the community in the challenge of ensuring everyone's safety, in partnership with police. All of these factors have made police agencies more inclusive, open, transparent, and accountable—some of Sir Robert Peel's original objectives in designing the forerunner to modern Western policing.

The Challenges That Community Policing Tactics Bring to Police Agencies

Early community involvement strategies practised by police were largely limited to public relations and consultations. One of the objectives of traditional policing is command and control—taken from the military model. Public relations and consultations did not significantly challenge police command and control. True collaboration is quite a different thing. It is a much more recent tactic embodied in that word "partnerships." Partners are supposedly equal, neither having more power in the relationship than the other. But that is a challenge for police services, which employ many of the methods of traditional policing.

It is difficult enough for police to engage community partners—not least because the traditional policing model has bred complacency among some other agencies and community members, and a natural tendency to defer to police when issues of safety and security are at stake. That is why police have to hone their capabilities in community engagement with agencies and mobilization with community assets. Even when they are successful in getting community partners to undertake problem-solving, police still have problems sharing authority, decision-making, and responsibility.

Partnerships and problem-oriented policing require decentralized authority in a police agency. Front-line officers have to have more access to resources and the authority to make decisions and apply them. For example, if a neighbourhood officer mobilizes enough neighbours to get together to discuss a community problem, the chances are good that the officer will want to attend with them, whether or not their schedule for that meeting accommodates the officer's shift schedule. The bottom line in this case is that the individual neighbourhood officer needs to have more discretion over his or her own time. Police also have to learn how and when to defer to community partners and share power with non-police agencies as well as neighbours. In more recent times, for example, at the risk mitigation tables that are springing up across Canada right now, police agencies are feeling pressure to be more collaborative (which includes sharing power in decision-making) with their community partners.[21]

These challenges will prevail and, no doubt, police agencies will continue to adapt and transform as Sir Robert's principles have taught police and community partners alike to value the concept of policing by consent. Community has a foothold in policing. If we stay with current trends in community policing, we will discover new capacities in community to resolve serious problems that trigger emergency responses if left unresolved and the unique capabilities of police to enable and support that process.

Future Transformations in Policing

Engaging Other Human and Social Support Agencies

The evolution of policing is ongoing. We can see dimly some of the outlines of future transformations. For example, while the tactic of police agencies fostering partnerships with other community organizations to resolve underlying issues will continue, more often than not, sound analysis of those underlying issues will reinforce the observation that police agencies are rarely capable of or mandated to deal effectively with them. The net result is that the principal police role is one of identifying the problems and then engaging community "partners" to deal more effectively with them. In effect, we are relying on police to leverage other agencies to do some significant problem-solving.

Evidence for this trend is emerging from Saskatchewan and Ontario. There, municipalities are regularly convening a number of acute care agencies to mitigate risk factors that will lead to harmful incidents if they are not reduced by the right mix of social services and supports. Data from a number of these initiatives are showing that police, at least initially, bring two-thirds to three-quarters of all at-risk situations to the attention of the acute care agencies and organizations. The agencies put the right blend of social supports in place to help those people who need it. But police are frequently not part of that blend; instead, they identify the problems and engage willing partners to do what they are better equipped to do.

Mobilizing Community Assets

For a long time, society has assumed that people living in marginalized conditions will only thrive if the broader community pours external resources into the marginalized ones. On the basis of that assumption, our culture has developed a whole network of human and social services that are mandated and resourced to compensate for perceived deficiencies in these marginalized neighbourhoods. Although there is no denying that external resources and supports are necessary, a parallel assumption needs to be challenged—that people living in marginalized conditions have no capacities to resolve their own problems.

The work of Kretzmann and McKnight disproved this assumption. They demonstrated that even the most marginalized neighbourhoods have individuals, businesses, and community-based organizations that can and will engage in effective problem-solving, provided that (1) they can be identified, (2) it is safe for them to problem-solve in their neighbourhood, and (3) external agencies and organizations will support them in doing so. These scholars called these particular neighbours "community assets"[22] (recall our discussion of community assets in Chapter 1). In using this term today, it is important to distinguish these "assets" from the diverse human and social service agencies that also serve the neighbourhood. In the strictest interpretation of that word, these agencies are assets too. But they are designed to do this work—that is why they exist. In contrast, Kretzmann and McKnight emphasized that even in the most broken neighbourhoods there are important assets for police to identify and work with in problem-solving. They went further with this concept by developing a neighbourhood asset inventory and prescribing asset mapping—two tools that have more recently become standard in community development circles.

Identifying community assets and supporting them to do problem-solving are roles that are particularly appropriate for police, especially where an agency is implementing location policing. There, officers have deeper insights into the attitudes and capabilities of individuals who make up the neighbourhood. They are able to discern which neighbours are ready to engage in problem-solving. Officers have a rapport with neighbours, which helps them get the neighbours focused on problem-solving. Quite naturally, officers can also make it safe for neighbours to do this work. Finally, police can also reach into the broader community to bring other agency partners into the neighbourhood in order to apply the kinds of resources and services that will support local problem-solving. Kretzmann and McKnight used the words "community mobilization" to describe the identification of local neighbourhood assets and the provision of supports necessary for them to go to work on their own neighbourhood problems. Community mobilization is beginning to emerge as a tactic of enlightened police agencies.

Expanding the Definition of "Community"

In Chapter 1, we observed that where police are responding most often, the characteristics of community are most lacking. Further, we stated that the objective of effective community policing there—starting when necessary with crime suppression—is to stimulate the social connections that create community—in other words, bring neighbours together and help and motivate them to take better care of themselves and each other. The US Department of Justice articulated a similar idea in 1994, stating: "All who share a concern for the welfare of the neighborhood should bear responsibility for safeguarding that welfare."[23] That certainly is a reference to human and social service agencies that "share a concern for the welfare" of the neighbourhood. But equally, it also includes the neighbours themselves and the businesses, community-based organizations, and other community assets that are most directly affected by crime and social disorder. That is why police mobilizing community assets is such an important part of problem-solving in this neighbourhood. It also gives us a new way to think about what we mean by "community" when we are thinking about improving everybody's safety and well-being. Those people and organizations that are easiest to engage and mobilize in problem-solving are those that are most directly affected by the risk factors that threaten people's safety and well-being. They have the greatest stake in finding constructive solutions to community problems, and they also have the most energy and resources necessary to apply to problem-solving. That is why Ontario's Mobilization & Engagement Model of Community Policing defines **community** as "every person or organization that is affected by any real or anticipated threat to peace, safety, security and well-being."[24]

All of this brings us closer to defining what we mean by "community policing":

> Community policing is … a collaboration between the police and the community that identifies and solves community problems. With the police no longer the sole guardians of law and order, all members of the community become active allies in the effort to enhance the safety and quality of neighbourhoods.[25]

Acknowledging the Social Determinants of Health

Problem-oriented policing has led agencies to consider what underlies clusters or patterns of crime and social disorder. When police agencies and their community partners do not settle for oversimplified analyses, they most often end up considering the social determinants of health (see Chapter 1). Police have very few mandates, resources, or capabilities to problem-solve when faced with deficiencies in the social determinants of health. But that does not remove them from the problem-solving partnership. It is the role of police to

- bring those problems to everyone's attention,
- mobilize neighbours and other community assets to take some responsibility for problem-solving,
- make it safe for them to do so, and
- engage a variety of other community partners in helping and supporting the neighbours in meaningful problem-solving.

---

community "every person or organization that is affected by any real or anticipated threat to peace, safety, security and well-being"; a social unit of any size that shares common values; a group of people who are connected by durable relations

The Province of Ontario is in the process of refining and producing a framework for planning community safety and well-being that encourages municipalities to look at the conditions of the social determinants of health—starting with police data on calls for service and occurrences.[26] We will no doubt see more and more agencies becoming aware of the social determinants of health and the unique roles of their officers in facilitating constructive problem-solving around them.

CHECK YOUR UNDERSTANDING

1. What is the role of police in engaging human and social service agencies in problem-solving?
2. What do we mean when we talk about community assets in a marginalized neighbourhood?
3. What is the role of police in mobilizing community assets?
4. Recognizing that our main concern is policing in order to increase safety and well-being, how would you define "community"?

CHAPTER SUMMARY

The history of community policing reflects an interesting tension between an empowered public and an authoritarian state: from Celts to kings (Ethelbert) and from citizens-in-uniform (Sir Robert Peel) to a militarized model (traditional policing). Today, we are seeing a closer blending of these approaches. It is captured in the term "community policing": police and community working together to resolve community problems that lead to crime and social disorder.

The role of police in this partnership is limited and specialized. Police can actually resolve very few of the root problems that lead to crime and social disorder; they need the active involvement of a host of agencies, organizations, businesses, and citizens to address these problems. However, police have unique capacities to make it safe for community partners to engage in problem-solving. Moreover, they have the data and communications capabilities to guide and direct community attention to crime and social disorder priorities that require their partners' attention.

REVIEW AND DISCUSSION QUESTIONS

1. Community members were largely responsible for their own safety and security in Celtic communities 1,500 years ago. What events led to the disappearance of that model and its reappearance in the 1970s?

2. What did Sir Robert Peel set out to achieve in his design for the Metropolitan Police Service?

3. What did Sir Robert mean in his seventh principle, which says: "the police being only members of the public who are paid to give full-time attention to duties which are incumbent on every citizen in the interests of community welfare and existence"?

4. What are the characteristics of traditional policing and how are they similar to or different from those of community policing?

5. Which is more effective for ensuring community safety and well-being: traditional policing or community policing? Defend your answer.

6. Is community policing a philosophy? Why or why not?

7. In responding to popular complaints about poor police–community relations, why did the police use consultation, public relations, and collaboration?

8. When and where might a police service consider using location policing?

9. What contributions did problem-oriented policing make to community policing?

10. What do we mean by the term "community assets" and what is the role of police in getting them to engage in community problem-solving?

KEY TERMS

community, 54
consultation, 44
location policing, 45
problem-oriented policing, 48
reassurance policing, 46
traditional policing, 41

NOTES

1 We rely on the Venerable Bede for the historical evidence, specifically *The Ecclesiastical History of the English People*, written around 703.

2 *Criminal Code*, RSC 1985, c C-46.

3 On or about 603, Ethelbert issued a set of edicts in 90 sections. The only surviving manuscript, the *Textus Roffensis*, dates from the 12th century and now resides in the Medway Studies Centre in Strood, Kent.

4 *Justices of the Peace Act 1361*, 1361 c 1 (Regnal 34 Edw 3).

5 *Metropolitan Police Act 1829*, 1829 c 44 (Regnal 10 Geo 4).

6 United Kingdom, Home Office, "Definition of Policing by Consent," FOI release 25060 (London: Office of the Government of the United Kingdom, 10 December 2012), online: <https://www.gov.uk/government/publications/policing-by-consent>.

7 Currently in Canada, there is new interest in "professionalizing" policing, so to avoid confusion, we will rely on the term "traditional policing" to distinguish the policing model that emerged early in the 1900s from the one that exists today.

8 Jack R Greene, "Community Policing and Organizational Change" in Wesley G Skogan, *Community Policing (Can It Work?)* (Belmont, Cal: Thomson Wadsworth, 2004) at 30-53.

9 George L Kelling et al, *The Kansas City Preventive Patrol Experiment: A Technical Report* (Washington, DC: Police Foundation, 1974) at iii, 533-35.

10 John E Boydstun & Michael E Sherry, *San Diego Community Profile: Final Report* (Washington, DC: Police Foundation, 1975) at 83.

11 Brian Whitelaw & Richard B Parent, *Community-Based Strategic Policing in Canada* (Toronto: Nelson Education, 2014) at 62.

12   Wesley G Skogan, "Representing the Community in Community Policing" in Wesley G Skogan, *Community Policing, supra* note 8 at 57-75.

13   Mark H Moore, "Problem-Solving and Community Policing" in Michael Tonry and Norval Morris, eds, *Modern Policing* (Chicago: University of Chicago Press, 1991) at 99-158.

14   Special presentation made to Toronto Police Service Command Staff by Tim Godwin, OBE, QPM; Managing Director of Policing and Justice, and Deputy Commissioner Metropolitan Police (Ret), "Safer Neighbourhoods: The Future of Policing" (Toronto: Toronto Police Service, July 2013).

15   James Q Wilson & George L Kelling, "Broken Windows: The Police and Neighbourhood Safety" (March 1982) *Atlantic Monthly* 29.

16   Robert J Sampson & Stephen W Raudenbush, "Systematic Social Observation of Public Spaces: A New Look at Disorder in Urban Neighbourhoods" (1999) 105:3 Am J Sociol 603.

17   Lawrence W Sherman et al, *Preventing Crime: What Works, What Doesn't, What's Promising: A Report to the United States Congress* (Washington, DC: National Institute of Justice, 1997).

18   Herman Goldstein, *Problem-Oriented Policing* (New York: McGraw-Hill, 1990).

19   John E Eck, "Why Don't Problems Get Solved?" in Wesley G Skogan, *Community Policing, supra* note 8 at 185-206.

20   Fred Matthews, *The Badge and the Book: Building Effective Police/School Partnerships to Combat Youth Violence* (Ottawa: Solicitor General Canada, 1995) at 23.

21   Jack R Greene & William V Pelfrey, "Shifting the Balance of Power Between Police and Community: Responsibility for Crime Control" in Roger G Dunham & Geoffrey P Albert, eds, *Critical Issues in Policing: Contemporary Readings*, 3rd ed (Prospect Heights, Ill: Waveland Press, 1997) at 278-96.

22   Jody Kretzmann & John McKnight, *Building Communities from the Inside Out: A Path Toward Finding and Mobilizing a Community's Assets* (Evanston, Ill: Centre for Civic Engagement, Northwestern University, 1993).

23   US Department of Justice, *Understanding Community Policing: A Framework for Action"* (Washington, DC: Bureau of Justice Assistance, 1994), online: <https://www.ncjrs.gov/pdffiles/commp.pdf>.

24   The model is reproduced in Figure 1.1 in Chapter 1.

25   US Department of Justice, *supra* note 23.

26   Ontario Ministry of Community Safety and Correctional Services, *Community Safety and Well-Being in Ontario: A Snapshot of Local Voices—Booklet 2* (Toronto: Ontario Ministry of Community Safety and Correctional Services), online: <http://www.mcscs.jus.gov.on.ca/sites/default/files/content/mcscs/docs/ec167634.pdf>.

PART II

Police Roles and Capabilities

CHAPTER 3

What Police Do Well, and What Police Do Poorly

An officer from the Toronto Police Mounted Unit gives his card to a child attending the Toronto Police Service 55 Division's Police Week Community Fair.

LEARNING OUTCOMES

Upon completion of this chapter, you should be able to:

■ Distinguish between the components of traditional policing and community policing
■ Explain how the effectiveness of enforcement and active and visible presence is increased by "targeting"
■ Identify the positive outcomes of effective community engagement
■ Explain why police occasionally manifest "bad manners" in their dealings with community members and their impact on fear of crime and police legitimacy
■ Provide a number of reasons why police are not particularly good at problem-solving
■ Identify and explain the appropriate role for police in community problem-solving
■ Describe how community policing has profoundly transformed the traditional policing model that emerged in the 1900s

Introduction

Chapter 2 provided a brief historical overview of the development of traditional policing and the emergence of community policing in the last quarter of the 20th century. In Chapter 3, we observe the continued evolution of Canadian policing by examining the impact of the community policing experience on the traditional policing model during the last 45 years. We begin to see that community policing is not about particular policing units, specially designated officers, or particular programs. Rather, it is about how people, other agencies and organizations, even municipal agencies, are influencing what police do and how they do it. In effect, the traditional model of policing is transforming into a community model of policing—community policing.

Factors That Influence How Police Do Their Job

The Importance of Research and Data Analysis

The discussion in this chapter stems from qualified research. This point is mentioned because it is important that readers know that the generalizations and conclusions drawn here are supported by evidence. But even more important, it is emphasized because science, in the form of qualified research and evaluations of police practices, is needed to guide new directions in policing. However, there are two major barriers to achieving the level and quality of science that the future of policing in Canada requires. The first is that Canada has very limited capabilities (compared with the United States, the United Kingdom, or Australia) to conduct applied policing research. The second is that police agencies and officers have very limited interest, knowledge, and capabilities to absorb and apply qualified research in their strategic, tactical, and management decisions. They rarely track the journals where such research is published, they rarely use consultants who know the research literature to advise them, and too few of them have research skills. In the end, they are more inclined to adopt innovations from other agencies that have tried and succeeded with them than they are to do their own research and come up with their own innovations.

In addition to the need for research, community policing (with its three components of partnerships, problem-solving, and prevention) needs data. This means that police agencies require the right data; analyzed and arrayed by the right statistical programs; interpreted by qualified researchers; and converted into policing strategic, tactical, management, and program practices by leaders who fully comprehend and value data, analysis, and evidence. Canadian police agencies are recognizing this and investing more in their crime analysis units. **COMPSTAT** (a program that analyzes and maps occurrence data, which are used to prioritize and mobilize police enforcement actions) and **intelligence-led policing** have sparked this interest and investment in many police agencies. But a lot more needs to be done there.[1] For example, crime analysis in Canadian police agencies is largely based on **uniform crime reporting (UCR)** information, which provides frequencies of types of occurrences. (The UCR system was designed by the US Federal Bureau of Investigation as a way to track the incidence of chargeable offences across jurisdictions. Subsequently it was adopted in Canada for the same purpose. Annual UCR data are rolled up and reported by Public Safety Canada.) But community policing requires many other kinds of information, including:

- data from neighbourhood or **community asset surveys** (inventories of individuals, agencies, organizations, and businesses, including their interests and capabilities in furthering safety and well-being), and
- indexes of neighbourhood or community safety and well-being (such as the well-being index developed by the City of Calgary, discussed in Chapter 1 under the heading "Community Well-Being").

We can expect to see, in the near future, growing investment by police agencies in data gathering and analysis.

The Shift from Incident-Driven to Risk-Driven Police and Community Problem-Solving

One of the most recent transformations in traditional policing also has some of the greatest potential to stimulate growth and development in community policing—a shift from incident-driven to risk-driven police and community problem-solving activities. The intelligence-led policing movement emphasizes this shift because it encourages police agencies to use intelligence in order to predict risks of crime, disorder, and other harmful or victimizing events—and thereby prepare for and attempt to prevent them. This is in

---

COMPSTAT a program for analysis and mapping of occurrence data (COMPuter STATistics) that is used to prioritize and mobilize police enforcement actions

intelligence-led policing the practice of using intelligence to identify the risk that offences, harms, or victimization will occur rather than as an investigative tool after offensive and harmful incidents have occurred

uniform crime reporting (UCR) a standard of crime reporting that counts occurrences by type and frequency; invented by the US Federal Bureau of Investigation in 1966 in order to obtain a standard of reporting across all American law enforcement agencies, it is also used in Canada and some other countries

community asset surveys inventories of individuals, agencies, organizations, and businesses, including their interests and capabilities in furthering safety and well-being

contrast to the more familiar police practice of using intelligence to investigate harmful incidents after they have occurred. There is an obvious connection between risk-driven problem-solving and the discussion of data, analysis, and interpretation. For example, besides gathering UCR data on occurrences (after the fact), agencies will have to begin to systematically gather and analyze risk data in order to prioritize problem-solving initiatives.

Methods of Officer Evaluation

Most front-line police officers in Canada continue to have their performance evaluated, in large part, on the basis of standards that emerged from the traditional model: for example, investigations closed, arrests made, and citations written. However, as this chapter points out, most of the work involved in community policing requires police behaviours that are measured in a very different way: for example, the numbers, types, and qualities of partnerships struck with other community members, and the nature and frequency of supports provided to community partners engaged in community building and crime prevention. This different way of measuring performance is supported by a 2007 publication of Canada's Police Sector Council, *A National Diagnostic on Human Resources in Policing*.[2] It details police competencies at all levels of the contemporary police agency, including the standard ones from the traditional policing model. But it also emphasizes many competencies that are more closely associated with community policing. The challenge remains for Canadian police agencies to integrate such standards in their performance measures of police officers.

A New Emphasis on Relationship Management in Policing

Community policing has brought to the traditional model a new emphasis on relationship management in policing. We have given this subject considerable attention in Chapters 1 and 2 in our discussions of police legitimacy. But the problem-solving and partnering components of community policing reinforce that relationship management will continue to evolve as a key component of the future of policing in Canada. Currently, very little attention is paid to it in police training, and the traditional model of policing continues to influence agencies to behave more like enforcers and protectors—holders of the "thin blue line"—and less like transparent partners, which is required for effective community policing.

Relationship management is vitally important in police–community partnerships and problem-solving. Some of the work of the Ontario Working Group on Collaborative, Risk-Driven Community Safety (a subcommittee of the Ontario Association of Chiefs of Police's standing committee on Community Safety and Crime Prevention) has moved this concept and language well beyond the oft-used and poorly understood word "partnerships" to "collaboration."[3] Collaboration has many interesting components—all of which will challenge police agencies and police officers—including transparency, mutual respect, shared responsibility, and shared accountability. How different those are from the recent words of a deputy chief who said, "Yes, we believe in partnerships; as long as we're in charge!" That traditional model is resistant to collaboration.

ON PATROL

Hamilton, Ontario's COAST and Mobile Crisis Rapid Response Team

On March 27, 1997, Zachary Antidormi, two and a half years old, was stabbed to death by his neighbour, 58-year-old Lucia Piovesan.

Police arrested Ms. Piovesan and charged her with first-degree murder. The investigation revealed that Ms. Piovesan had lost her son to AIDS in 1991, and she believed that his soul had been reincarnated in Zachary's body. She told police, and later psychiatrists, that she killed Zachary to free her son's spirit so that it could be reborn in her daughter's child.

A thorough investigation by police and mental health professionals during and after Piovesan's trial confirmed that she had been suffering from untreated paranoid schizophrenia for at least 25 years.

Prior to the killing, Piovesan's family and the police had repeatedly and unsuccessfully sought involuntary treatment for the woman under the apprehension provisions of Ontario's *Mental Health Act*.[4] She was never diagnosed or treated properly, nor did the mental health system consider her delusional thinking to be a credible danger to herself or others—until she killed Zachary.

In the wake of Zachary's death and similar tragedies, St. Joseph's Healthcare Hamilton and the Hamilton Police Service partnered to form the Crisis Outreach and Support Team (COAST), which consists of mental health workers and a wide range of other acute care providers, including police. Its mandate is to provide timely, coordinated responses to people in mental health crisis if they self-refer by calling the COAST hotline. Although the creation of COAST has resulted in fewer *Mental Health Act* apprehensions by police and more client diversions to appropriate health care and/or community support agencies, it was until recently inadequately funded. As a result, it could not operate around the clock, and many persons in mental health crisis could not or would not self-refer. Consequently, police officers still had to spend inordinate amounts of time in hospital waiting rooms—cumulatively thousands of hours—after making apprehensions under the provincial *Mental Health Act*. That motivated the hospital and police to create the Mobile Crisis Rapid Response Team (MCRRT) pilot project, the first of its kind in Canada.

The MCRRT differs from COAST in that mental health trained police officers are teamed with highly qualified mental health professionals and are designated as 24/7, front-line 911 responders to persons in mental health crisis.

Officers who were partnered with mental health professionals in the MCRRT pilot project apprehended 31.8 percent of the persons they encountered under *Mental*

Health Act authority. St. Joseph's Healthcare surveyed those officers, who stated that they would have apprehended, on average, about 70 percent of those persons if their mental health professional partner had not been with them. In 2015, during its first eight months of full-time operation, the MCRRT program increased its front-line responses to persons in crisis by more than 200 percent while further decreasing apprehension rates to approximately 20 to 25 percent.

SOURCES: Susan Clairmont, "Killing the Boy with the Golden Hair," *Hamilton Spectator* (13 April 2007), online: <http://www.thespec.com/hamilton>; Terry McGurk, "Mobile Crisis Rapid Response Team (MCRRT) in Hamilton" (December 2014), online: Human Services and Justice Coordinating Committee <http://www.hsjcc.on.ca/Resource%20Library/Policing/Mobile%20Crisis%20 Rapid%20Response%20Team%20(M.C.R.R.T)%20in%20Hamilton.htm>; and Uppala Chandrasekera, "First Responders: Police as Front-Line Mental Health Workers" (2009) 25:2 *Network* 18, online: <http://ontario.cmha.ca/files/2013/04/fall_2009.pdf>.

Consider the following questions:

1. The first effort to deal effectively with mental health situations that endangered people was to enhance the enforcement capacity of police officers under the apprehensions clause of the provincial *Mental Health Act*. Why was that insufficient?

2. The second effort to deal more effectively with these situations was the hospital's COAST program. Why was that inadequate?

3. The third attempt was the MCRRT. Why was it more successful? What did it require to make it successful?

What Police Do Well

Targeted Enforcement

The traditional model of policing, in place since the early 1900s, has honed and refined the capabilities of police services as a whole, and individual officers, in their roles as law enforcers. The emergence of goals and tactics like problem-solving, community engagement, crime prevention, and community policing have not in any way diminished the need for enforcement or the capacities of officers and services to deliver it.

Police in our society are uniquely empowered, through legislation, to conduct law enforcement. Their enforcement actions traditionally involve four components: gathering and analysis of information (investigation and intelligence); rapid deployment; effective tactics; and focused follow-up (usually in support of prosecutions and corrections). But the effectiveness of enforcement, both in arresting and prosecuting perpetrators and in preventing crime and reducing recidivism, depends largely on the degree to which the enforcement action is specifically targeted on

- known places where crime is most likely to happen ("hot spots"),

- known perpetrators, and
- known times when crime is most likely happen.

That is **targeted enforcement**.

Chapter 2 mentioned research that has shown that random patrols are not effective in either making arrests or preventing crime. That is largely because those patrols are not targeted on locations in which there is the highest probability of crime or social disorder, or conducted at those particular times when crime and disorder are most likely to happen. In effect, the random patrol is a crapshoot where enforcement is concerned. The same is true of rapid deployments. Rapid deployments after notification of an offence rarely increase the chances of arresting the perpetrator or enhance the quality of the subsequent investigation. On the other hand, rapid and efficient deployment of a tactical unit that is scaled to meet a known level of threat, in a specific location where that threat is most likely to occur, at the right time, shows significant levels of success at crime suppression and enforcement.

A good example is Toronto Police Service's Rapid Response Team (RRT), which is one component of that service's Toronto Anti-Violence Intervention Strategy (TAVIS). Funded by the province in 2006 (after a rash of murders that led that summer to become known as "the summer of the gun"), TAVIS deployed 18-officer tactical units to focus on violence, gangs, and gun crimes in Toronto's most violent neighbourhoods. It was targeted enforcement. By 2008, TAVIS and its RRT had seized 450 firearms, made more than 10,000 arrests, and established over 120,000 neighbourhood business and citizen contacts.

If success is measured by those criteria (firearms seized, arrests made, and information collected from neighbourhood businesses and citizens), TAVIS would have to be considered successful. By those standards targeted enforcement works; and police are very good at it. All Canadian police academies train and prepare officers for targeted enforcement—whether for traffic enforcement or, as in the case of TAVIS, guns and gangs. All Canadian police services prepare and mobilize as needed tactical units that can do what TAVIS's RRT does. Generally speaking, Canadian police services are very good at targeted enforcement.

Maintaining an Active and Visible Presence

Research has shown that random foot patrols do not suppress or reduce crime or social disorder, although they do have the effect of improving police legitimacy. But intensive, targeted foot patrols, in violent crime hot spots, can reduce violent crime levels by increasing the chances that chargeable offences or anti-social behaviour will be disrupted and, when necessary, perpetrators

---

targeted enforcement enforcement actions that are targeted on locations where offences are most likely to occur, on persons who are most likely to offend, and at times when offences are most likely to occur

apprehended, arrested, and prosecuted.[5] Similarly, motorized patrols through hot spots seem to suppress crime or social disorder if the patrol officers stop and observe the neighbourhood for at least 15 minutes.[6] Like targeted enforcement, active and visible presence of police works best when:

- it is used in locations with the highest levels of crime and social disorder,
- it is targeted on "prolific offenders" (individuals or groups with a history of frequent offending), and
- it is used when the perpetrators are most likely to offend again.

Community Engagement

Effective community engagement lies at the heart of problem-solving and crime prevention. **Community engagement** means police building ongoing, trusting, and mutually respectful relationships with neighbourhood citizens, community-based organizations, and other agencies for the purposes of resolving local neighbourhood problems that threaten safety and well-being. A good example is the police and hospital partnership that led to COAST and the Mobile Crisis Rapid Response Team in Hamilton, Ontario.

Evidence shows that where police do community engagement well, there is a reduction in public calls for police assistance, particularly those associated with social disturbances. There is less of an effect, however, on crime reduction.[7] But the most positive outcome of community engagement is increased police legitimacy, reduced fear of crime, and increased social capital among neighbourhood residents. As we saw in Chapter 1, increasing social capital is the first step in community building in high-demand neighbourhoods. Police officers who are trained and motivated to apply community engagement tactics are very effective in initiating this community-building strategy. We will review some of those community-building tactics in Chapter 6.

IN THE COMMUNITY

Engaging the Neighbours in Three High-Demand Neighbourhoods of Sudbury

The Crime Prevention Through Community Mobilization Project was launched in three Sudbury, Ontario neighbourhoods that generated 13 percent of all calls for service and absorbed the highest proportion of police

---

community engagement police building ongoing, trusting, and mutually respectful relationships with neighbourhood citizens, community-based organizations, and other agencies for the purposes of resolving local neighbourhood problems that threaten safety and well-being

resources in 2009. Targeted enforcement was followed by efforts to engage residents and community partners in social development and crime prevention. One inspired neighbour epitomized the principle of the "community asset." She motivated neighbours to help create a neighbourhood association that delivered social development programs like a homework club for children, crafts, community gardens, awareness block parties, and neighbourhood cleanups, and led to the formation of a security and safety committee—all of which fostered shared responsibility in addressing crime and social disorder. Additionally, ten groups and organizations agreed to partner in offering residents one-stop shopping in a local, multi-services centre. A one-year evaluation showed a significant reduction in calls to the police, an increased sense of well-being and safety among the residents, increased police legitimacy, and increased community pride.

Problem-Solving

Research, such as that by Herman Goldstein (discussed in Chapter 2), has shown the value of problem-solving. Where police can detect patterns of crime or anti-social behaviour, the opportunity exists to analyze why those occurrences happen, what underlies them, and what leads to repeat patterns of offensive behaviour by using problem-solving models such as SARA. Police are in the best position to begin this process by observing the repeat patterns of offensive behaviour. That allows them to probe for the root causes of these behaviours. At that point, however, it is wisest for police to identify and engage agencies, organizations, and individuals who can help further analyze root causes and begin to piece together and implement proactive solutions. Evidence shows that where police do this well, particularly in high-demand neighbourhoods, it works.[8] Police officers who are well trained in problem-oriented policing have been shown to be very effective in initiating sustainable improvements in community. But that training has to include far more than teaching SARA. It has to also teach officers that they do not have the tools to fully analyze problems to the point where effective solutions can be created and that they do have special capacities to identify and engage other agencies and individuals who can strengthen that analysis, come up with proactive solutions, and play vital roles in implementing them. Where police strike that balance well, neighbourhoods become safer.

CHECK YOUR UNDERSTANDING

1. What are the main components of traditional policing?
2. What are the major components of community policing?
3. What is targeted enforcement?

4. When is maintaining an active and visible police presence likely to be most effective in crime suppression?

5. What is community engagement and what are its most positive effects?

6. What are the principal roles of police officers in problem-solving?

What Police Do Poorly

Police are good at enforcement. It is what they are uniquely qualified, mandated, and resourced to do. But as we noted in Chapter 2, the traditional policing model, which relies on these capabilities, has in recent years changed to accommodate community problem-solving and striking meaningful and effective partnerships with other community agencies and organizations. However, problems remain. Very little police training focuses on these skills, very few police agencies have organized themselves in ways that promote and support the application of these capabilities, and very few police supervisors are good at transferring these performance expectations to front-line officers. In some respects we could say that community policing is transforming policing in ways that will be difficult for officers to fulfill.

Overreliance on Enforcement

No amount of targeted enforcement will control crime, nor will "zero-tolerance" policies or "tough on crime" initiatives achieve this goal. That is because crime is a byproduct of inadequate social policy that creates deficiencies in the social determinants of health—poverty, addictions, mental health, poor parenting, substandard housing, and social inequities. These cannot be directly or positively affected by police enforcement actions. They can only be improved by reforms in social policy. Police can do a lot to bring that about. For example, they can assemble crime and disorder data, plot the data on a map, and use presentations to raise community awareness about neighbourhood patterns of offensive behaviours that need to be addressed by enlightened policy reforms. They can use the credibility and legitimacy they enjoy to engage other, more technically qualified agencies and organizations to address these problems more effectively. While they are doing all of that, police can strive to maintain order and provide supports to those in the community who are most vulnerable. Is there a role for police in problem-solving the social determinants of safety when they lead to crime and social disorder? Yes, but not if all they do is enforcement. Are police qualified to come up with sustainable solutions to deficiencies in public policy? No, but they do have a role in drawing the attention of other agencies and individuals to the need for solutions, and engaging them in the processes of collaborating in finding needed solutions.

Bad Manners and Procedural Justice

Summarizing qualified research, criminologist Lawrence Sherman observed in 1996 that "[o]ne of the most striking recent findings is the extent to which the police themselves create a risk factor for crime simply by using bad manners."[9] He cited studies that show that recidivism rates drop if police take the time to respectfully hear the perpetrator's story about what they did and why they did it.[10] This issue has arisen most recently among Ontario police agencies and the Ontario Ministry of Community Safety and Correctional Services around the practice of street checks by police officers—known more commonly as "carding." Recall the discussion of TAVIS above. Although TAVIS and its RRT succeeded in that 450 guns were taken off the street, over 10,000 arrests were made, and 120,000 contacts were established with neighbourhood citizens and businesses, it was criticized for the manner in which they carried out those actions. Those contacts originated with Toronto Police Service's community contacts policy, which is an intelligence-gathering tool that requires stopping, questioning, and documenting individuals when no particular offence is being investigated. It was the manner in which police chose to conduct those street checks and conversations, and the demographics of whom they stopped and whom they did not stop, that backfired for Ontario police agencies. They were criticized for using "bad manners," like being overly authoritative and not listening to or respecting the people they stopped. Police legitimacy plummeted; community activists challenged procedural justice; complaints of police racism were heard; and the uproar affected other large police services in the surrounding region (in Peel Region, a citizen-filed freedom-of-information request revealed that black people were three times more likely to be stopped than whites).

What are the elements of police legitimacy? What is it composed of? Thankfully, a lot of qualified research has provided some pretty clear answers to these questions. Lorraine Mazerolle and her colleagues summarize it this way:

> [W]hen citizens perceive the police acting in a *procedurally just* manner—by treating people with dignity and respect, and by being fair and neutral in their actions—they view the police as legitimate and are more likely to comply with directives and co-operate with police.[11] [Emphasis added.]

That phrase "**procedural justice**" appears again and again in the research literature on police legitimacy. Basically, it includes four qualities, or values: citizen participation (or voice), fairness and neutrality, dignity and respect, and trustworthy motives. Procedural justice means that

- citizens, as community partners, have a voice in the actions of police or others engaged in the community safety and well-being planning process;

---

procedural justice fairness or perceived fairness in procedures

- everyone involved in the process feels that decisions are made fairly and without prejudice;
- everyone feels like they are being treated with dignity and respect by police and other community partners; and
- all community partners trust police motives and feel like their own motives are trusted by police.

An interesting question arises about whether the disrespectful actions of one police officer can spoil the community's sense of police legitimacy. Unfortunately, research on this question confirms that bad attitudes by some officers can cast a dark cloud over the whole service. Conversely, Mazerolle and her colleagues also proved that "police can gain globalized feelings of legitimacy from the public by acting in a satisfactory manner."[12]

Systemic Racism

At the time of writing, police legitimacy is threatened throughout North America and Western Europe. A spate of police shootings of unarmed citizens in America has focused a spotlight on this problem. There, systemic racism is rampant and has significantly undermined the relationship between police services and people of colour. In the words of Redditt Hudson, an ex-officer from St. Louis, Missouri:

> Institutional racism runs throughout our criminal justice system. Its presence in police culture, though often flatly denied by the many police apologists that appear in the media now, has been central to the breakdown in police-community relationships for decades in spite of good people doing police work.

Hudson went even further to explain decreases in police legitimacy:

> On any given day, in any police department in the nation, 15 percent of officers will do the right thing no matter what is happening. Fifteen percent of officers will abuse their authority at every opportunity. The remaining 70 percent could go either way depending on whom they are working with. ...
>
> That remaining 70 percent of officers are highly susceptible to the culture in a given department. In the absence of any real effort to challenge department cultures, they become part of the problem. If their command ranks are racist or allow institutional racism to persist, or if a number of officers in their department are racist, they may end up doing terrible things.[13]

Research has shown that when police legitimacy plummets, crime and social disorder increase—and vice versa. High levels of police legitimacy enhance compliance with the law and cooperation with the police.[14] People are more inclined to cooperate with police and comply with police instruction if they feel that they are treated by police with dignity, respect, and fairness. Police manners are very important.[15] Professor Sherman has concluded:

> Making both the style and substance of police practices more "legitimate" in the eyes of the public, particularly high-risk juveniles, may be one of the most effective long-term police strategies for crime prevention.[16]

Problem-Solving and Analysis

Where police do it well, problem-solving works. But, it turns out, most of the time they do not do it well. Eck listed the reasons police do not do problem-solving well in an article entitled, "Why Don't Problems Get Solved?" He listed eight answers to his question (see the box below).

Reasons Why Problems Do Not Get Solved Through Problem-Oriented Policing

- Police officers do not have the requisite analytical skills
- Police managers and supervisors do not know how to foster problem-solving
- Police agencies resist the changes needed to support constructive problem-solving
- Police workloads permit only superficial analyses
- Police too rarely involve important community partners
- Municipal agencies provide too little support
- Too little is known about the problems and what will resolve them
- The problem-solving process is too linear while most problem-solving is non-linear

SOURCE: Based on JE Eck, "Why Don't Problems Get Solved?" in WG Skogan, ed, *Community Policing: Can It Work?* (Belmont, Cal: Thomson Wadsworth, 2004) 185–206.

Eck's conclusions are well supported by research; police do not do problem-solving well. In particular, they are not particularly good at reforming fundamentally flawed social policy. Nor should they be. Social policy is not their forte. One of the biggest problems with Goldstein's problem-oriented policing was his assertion, or at least police services' assumptions, that police should be resolving the underlying causes of social disorder and crime. They are not qualified, nor do they have the time, to do that. But that does not mean that police should not engage in problem-solving. To improve police performance at problem-solving, we need to refine our expectations of what police can and should do to get problems solved.

Problem-solving remains an important component of community policing. It starts with police observations and data. For example, the first step in the SARA model is "scanning." That means looking at patterns of police occurrences in order to try to identify those that suggest underlying causes that, if properly analyzed and addressed, could be resolved in order to reduce harms, victimization, and calls for emergency assistance. That is a good role for police. They have the occurrence data. They can learn to analyze their data in order to find patterns that indicate the presence of underlying causes (like repeat occurrences). They can learn to graph and map those data in ways that will make them accessible to other agencies, including municipal agencies, and the broader public. That is a level of analysis and communication that we can and should expect of police. To play this role, police services will have to improve their ability to gather, analyze, and interpret statistical data. Then front-line officers will have to be trained to participate in that analytical process and turn their conclusions into presentations that can be shared with other agencies, organizations, businesses, and individuals in a community engagement and partnering process.

The next step for police is not further analysis of underlying causes for crime and social disorder but identification of those agencies, organizations, individuals, and offices of municipal governments that likely have greater capacities than police to analyze the root causes of problems, identify evidence-based solutions, and mobilize to resolve them. Once identified, these agencies and organizations need to be recruited to the enterprise. That is a very special role for police. It requires police community engagement skills. The In the Community feature that follows shows how a police agency can undertake this role.

IN THE COMMUNITY

There's More Fear Than Crime Downtown, Sault Police Chief Says

Crime in Sault Ste. Marie's downtown is not on the rise. However, the fear of crime is, said Robert Keetch, Sault police chief, in a report to the Sault Ste. Marie Police Service board Thursday. Certain "hot spots" in the city's downtown and "social disorder" give that fearful impression, Keetch told the board during a number-crunching presentation. "Crime statistics continue to trend downward," Keetch said, as a result of police initiatives in partnership with city council, downtown business owners, community partners and downtown residents. But still, after all the stats, there is crime, and fear of crime. "What are we doing as a police service in relation to downtown initiatives?" Keetch asked. Police continue to work on identified "hot spots" such as Station Mall (theft, vandalism). "We did a street level drug project in

2015, we did a recent break and enter project, we did a graffiti eradication project in 2015 in partnership with the downtown business improvement association and city council, we increased our bike patrols in 2015," Keetch said. "We've implemented and want to further expand foot patrols in 2016." Foot patrols, the chief said, do not prevent crime but increase police visibility and address that public fear of crime. In a social policing sense, Keetch spoke enthusiastically of police partnerships with agencies such as Superior Skills and the John Howard Society which provide job skills and aim to get people off Ontario Works. He also spoke of police partnerships with 30 community agencies at the Neighbourhood Resource Centre on Gore Street (first established in 2014 with eight agencies), which have worked with a range of troubled people, such as sex trade workers and substance abusers. Keetch also encouraged city council to keep working on the graffiti problem downtown, pointing to research which claims that if tagging is quickly painted over, the less likely it is to occur again.

• • •

Keetch's report on downtown crime covered the years 2012 to 2015. Calls for service in the area, he pointed out, decreased on a steady basis from 3,977 in 2012 to 3,640 in 2015.

• • •

"Violent types of crimes decreased over 20 percent from 2013 to 2014 and then by another 12 percent from 2014 to 2015," Keetch told the board. "Over 50 percent of the calls received in the downtown area were non-criminal in nature, such as ambulance assistance, animal complaints, fire, missing person located, abandoned or recovered motor vehicle, sudden deaths, traffic complaints, (all of which) police would qualify as non-criminal." Calls involving theft, shoplifting and mischief made up 13 percent of calls for service in the downtown area and "did not vary significantly" between 2012 and 2015. "If you look at break and enters over a four-year analysis we can see there has been a decrease across the city ... and this trend has continued in the downtown area as well," Keetch said. Social disorder calls involving liquor or unwanted or suspicious persons accounted between 27 percent and 30 percent over that period. Assault, robbery, and sexual assault accounted for about four percent of all calls received in the downtown area between 2012 and 2015, Keetch said. Duane Moleni of the Queenstown Business Improvement Area told *SooToday* after Thursday's police board meeting a revitalized downtown with more events, longer store hours and beautification, along with police initiatives such as increased foot patrols, would all combine to lead to a safer downtown. "We've got to break that (negative) perception," Moleni said.

SOURCE: Darren Taylor, "There's More Fear Than Crime Downtown, Sault Police Chief Says," *SooToday.com* (18 February 2016), online: <https://www.sootoday.com>. Courtesy of SooToday.com.

CHECK YOUR UNDERSTANDING

1. What is Chief Keetch's primary message?
2. Who are the targets for this message?
3. What police occurrence data does Chief Keetch share in order to demonstrate his message?
4. What kinds of policy and program changes did his message lead to?
5. Could police have figured out those policy and program changes?

Notice in Chief Keetch's presentation to downtown businesses, residents, and city council that he promises to continue implementing policing tactics downtown in order to help reduce fear of crime as well as continue downward trends in actual crime. That is another important thing police can do in problem-solving: maintain order and support implementation of problem solutions by doing what police do best.

In Eck's list of reasons why problems do not get solved through problem-oriented policing were two that deserve some consideration here. Front-line officers do not get sufficient support, from command or their service, to do effective problem-solving. As Eck pointed out, their schedules rarely permit sufficient time to initiate this process. Too often, the service as a whole fails to champion the value of problem-solving. It is left to the resourcefulness of enlightened front-line officers to virtually go it alone, frequently in the face of resistance from platoon mates who are stuck in reactive policing. Many agencies ask their officers to employ problem-solving while continuing to assess officer performance on the basis of traditional policing standards—like the numbers of citations written. Clearly, agencies have not developed the standards needed to evaluate officer performance in community policing—particularly problem-solving.

These kinds of barriers originate with the traditional model of policing. Police agencies train and expect their officers to react when threats to safety justify it, yet expect them to also be proactive. Officers respond reactively many times per week in the highest-demand neighbourhoods where the most problem-solving is needed. But the frequency and intensity of reactive policing there gets in the way of officers seeing the virtue of proactive problem-solving. It also leaves a certain ill will between police and the people and organizations in the neighbourhood, which makes it very hard for proactive partnerships in problem-solving to form.

This apparent conflict between problem-solving and traditional policing shows that crime cannot be resolved by treating incidents in isolation—that is, as unrelated to underlying systemic problems affecting community and society. Furthermore, we have seen that police, by themselves, cannot solve these problems. Unless and until community begins to deal with underlying systemic issues, they will continue to create crime and disorder at levels that will keep the whole criminal justice system busy, while failing to reduce the incidence of crime, the costs of criminal justice (including policing), and harms and victimization against the people who comprise community. Through effective community policing, police have the capacity to facilitate community problem-solving. It will not happen unless police initiate and support it. But it is going to take some significant transformations in how police and their agencies perceive and execute their roles for this to happen.[17]

Reducing Fear of Crime and Increasing Police Legitimacy

Reactive (traditional) policing rarely reduces fear of crime in a high-demand neighbourhood; most often it aggravates it! It reinforces what an unsafe place the neighbourhood is. Besides reinforcing fear of crime, we noted above that it can also generate some hostility between police and neighbours—even though police are there to presumably make the neighbourhood safer. Reactive policing increases fear of crime. If we add to that police who use bad manners in engaging with the public, fear of crime sharply increases and police legitimacy plummets. Those bad manners are manifest most often among officers who have to respond to repeat occurrences in high-demand neighbourhoods. For officers who chose this career because they "want to make a difference," it has to be frustrating to learn that the tactics and methods they are empowered to use do not reduce or prevent offensive behaviour. It is quite natural that their frustrations will occasionally spill over into bad manners. But they get in the way of effective community engagement for problem-solving. This is important because these are the very neighbourhoods where police need to problem-solve the most. Fear drives neighbours apart from each other—yet we have already acknowledged that social capital is what we need to develop in order to get the neighbours to start working together for the common good.

This situation in high-demand neighbourhoods creates a very complex environment in which police have to operate. Obviously, they cannot stop reacting to crime in the neighbourhood. But at the same time, they have to work on reducing fear of crime and increasing police legitimacy so that they can foster social capital among residents and local businesses and organizations.[18] Neighbourhood policing (see description of a Neighbourhood Officer Program in Chapter 2) is one approach to dealing with this complex situation. Neighbourhood officers have the greatest capacity to get to know the residents and businesses in this neighbourhood, and to get them to know the officers. These officers are able to also channel acquired intelligence to the enforcement side of the agency, as well as coach the agency in crime management meetings about those residents and businesses or other organizations in the neighbourhood that can be the most constructive partners with the police. Then, after a targeted enforcement action is taken, these same neighbourhood officers who already have some credibility in the neighbourhood can be instruments for explaining what the action was, why it was merited, and what the whole community can do to help keep it from being required again.

Community involvement in making the neighbourhood safer and solving neighbourhood problems is particularly important in disadvantaged, high-crime areas. Yet, these are the areas where trust and cooperation between members of the neighbourhood and police are most lacking. That may be why most problem-oriented policing initiatives have rarely been tried in high-demand neighbourhoods, or when tried there, have rarely shown much success. Community policing is, first and foremost, about building and sustaining trust and cooperation between police and neighbours, businesses, and community-based organizations. Only through those efforts will police realize the value of neighbours identifying priority community problems, supporting each other in problem-solving, and even intervening to help prevent offensive behaviour in the neighbourhood.[19]

Crime Prevention

Crime prevention became more important to police—as a police tactic at minimum, or goal at maximum—in the 1980s, largely in response to four factors:

1. increasing concerns in police circles about people's fear of crime;
2. the growing awareness among police—with the support of the work of Goldstein—that, in order to reduce calls for service and hopefully harms and victimization, police needed to engage in problem-solving;
3. the discovery that problem-solving by police would largely fail without the participation of community; and
4. the introduction of Wilson and Kelling's "broken windows" theory.[20]

Crime prevention matured as a police priority in the 1990s when it became one of the five mandated, core functions of all officers and all police services (see, for example, s 4(2) of Ontario's *Police Services Act*[21]). But all of this began to change by the turn of the century when police, after working diligently with crime prevention for a decade, discovered that crime prevention tactics for police officers were generally only effective when applied to targeted patrols and enforcement, hot spots, and known perpetrators and unsafe situations. Those observations were largely reinforced by qualified crime prevention research and evaluation, which has repeatedly shown that police are not particularly good at implementing either **situational crime prevention measures** (measures that target specific types of offences, like the use of double-bolt locks to prevent break and enters) or social development measures. We already noted that social development measures require major policy reforms and that police are not in that business. Additionally, situational crime prevention

---

situational crime prevention measures measures that target specific types of offences—like the use of double-bolt locks to prevent break and enters

measures may be implemented by police, but they only work in relatively safe, low-demand, neighbourhoods.

CPTED Consultation

Crime prevention through environmental design (CPTED) emerged in the early 1970s after urban planners like Jane Jacobs pointed out that architecture, building design, land use decisions, and landscaping could influence the presence or absence of crime and social disorder.[22] For example, lights on the side of an apartment building, overlooking a parking lot, make it safer for residents returning home from work on a dark winter evening to walk from their car to the building. Similarly, lowering hedgerows helps first-floor apartment owners assess whether anyone is lurking on the sidewalk, before they step out of the door.

Police agencies have championed the value of CPTED to the point where they are training and certifying officers in CPTED assessments and measures. The most positive aspect of this movement has been that police agencies have been encouraged to see crime prevention as an aspect of spatial design decisions, rather than law enforcement. In that respect, it has reinforced the notion of police becoming engaged in community problem-solving. The downside of this movement is simply that the people who are responsible for making those spatial design, layout, and planning decisions have not internalized the principles and values of CPTED as readily as have police. Furthermore, police have been slow about establishing a consultative relationship with urban planners and designers, architects, bylaw officers, and others so that they can influence design decisions. As a consequence, high-demand neighbourhoods continue to have inadequately designed buildings and spaces, and landlords and building managers continue to lack sufficient knowledge about CPTED measures and sufficient resources to implement those measures.

The DARE Program

One of the real benefits of this era of crime prevention was a growing awareness in police circles that working with the public on problems that they were having increased police legitimacy and decreased fear of crime—even if the net result was not always a reduction in crime, social disorder, or calls for police assistance. A classic example is the Drug Abuse Resistance Education (DARE) program, which was touted by its designers as a way to reduce youth experimentation with addictive substances. DARE is a police-taught drug awareness program that is used with classes in grades 4 to 9. The police who are involved in the DARE program enjoy it largely because they enjoy relating to the youth in a constructive context, and they know that later encounters with those same youth—perhaps in less desirable circumstances—might be positively influenced by the good relationships built in the DARE classroom (police legitimacy). But the research shows that DARE does not reduce youth's interest in or experimentation with addictive substances. DARE does not do what it is designed to do—but it does improve police legitimacy among youth.

The Use of Enforcement to Address Social Disorder

The broken windows theory is that social disorder leads to crime (chargeable offences) largely because it creates opportunity for crime. Therefore, if police focus on social disorder (for example, public drunkenness or youths loitering on a street corner), they would, in effect, be preventing more serious offences. The regrettable aspect of this theory is that it led police to use traditional, and rigorous, zero-tolerance enforcement tactics on social disorder calls. What they failed to recognize is that social disorder, like crime itself, is a symptom of deeper problems in society—underlying root causes, antecedents—that have to be addressed or nothing will be prevented. In effect, the best that can be expected by throwing enforcement tactics at social disorder is displacement or postponement of crime—not its prevention. Whatever causes the youth to loiter on the street corner in the first place is unaffected by move-along enforcement tactics. Such tactics will have some or all of the following effects:

- increase youth's fear and distrust of police, thus threatening any police legitimacy that may have been gained (for example, in the DARE classroom);
- make the youth more alert to the presence of police and likely to fade into the night when a patrol is spotted—only to return when the patrol moves on;
- drive the youth to "loiter" somewhere else (known in police circles as "displacement"); or
- provide a police focal point for youth angst that eventually manifests as social disorder or, potentially, more serious offences.

The most practical implication of these observations is that police should get out of the business of the direct application of crime prevention measures—particularly in those neighbourhoods where crime and disorder create the highest demand for police assistance. Rather, crime prevention should be treated by police in the same way that they treat problem-solving: identify the offences that need to be prevented; identify those agencies, organizations, or individuals that are in the best position to prevent them; and then engage and support those groups in doing the actual crime prevention work.

Acknowledging the Web of Organizations

Police are now but one of many actors in the safety and security space, which calls into question their core role and purpose and the continued prevalence of a traditional policing model that is reactive in nature, geographical in focus, jurisdictionally bound, and structured for officers qualified (at least initially) for general constabulary duties.

These traits are increasingly seen as a hindrance at a time when police are being called upon to engage in partnerships to prevent crime and to respond to the very significant challenges of international terrorism and cross-border organized crime, as well as the a-spatial challenges of cybercrime.

—Council of Canadian Academies, *Policing Canada in the 21st Century: New Policing for New Challenges*[23]

The report from which this quotation is taken will help set the future of policing in Canada. One of its conclusions is that "police no longer have a monopoly on providing public safety and security, because they are but one of many actors currently operating in that space."[24] But police agencies in general, and individual officers, are only slowly adapting to that reality. Some provinces are revising their policing legislation in order to acknowledge this web of organizations and the importance of police agencies learning how to operate as just one partner within it. If those revisions go far enough, they will force individual agencies to examine their local web; identify agencies and organizations that operate within it; foster transparent, respectful, and mutually satisfactory partnerships; and then reconfigure their own agencies to better operate within this context.

Prince Albert, Saskatchewan's multi-agency Hub model, which identifies and intervenes in situations of acutely elevated risk, is a good example of that web working together to reduce imminent harms and victimization from multiple risk factors that will lead to crime or disorder. Similar hub models are taking hold in other provinces now too. Police agencies are beginning to partner more successfully with health agencies, businesses, private security, social service providers, and municipal agencies. For example, police are partnering with banks and IT companies to fight cybercrime.

Interestingly, the web will look different in every locality. As the Council of Canadian Academies reported, the web is "neither a [national] system nor a network in the formal sense of organized and linked elements."[25] It is as variable as each location in which police and community partners are engaged in increasing community safety and well-being. That is one of the virtues of it because that means that local adaptations have the greatest potential to meet the needs and resources, and understand the constraints, of local conditions. But therein also lies the greatest challenge for police agencies. They are going to have to be responsive, creative, adaptable, and collaborative.

How different the web is from the traditional model of policing that emerged in the 1900s. In acknowledging the web, notice how close we are to acknowledging that all of community has to be partnered in the enterprise of ensuring everyone's safety and well-being. In that context, community policing takes on new meanings, none of which is more important than that of police learning how to accept their role as just one actor in that safety and security web. Of course, like other actors in the web, police have unique skills and capabilities to lend to the collective enterprise. But the overall success of the whole web will depend in large part on police and all of the other actors learning how to acknowledge each other's capabilities and responsibilities, as well as work together collaboratively. The gateway for that transformation in police agencies is through community policing.

CHECK YOUR UNDERSTANDING

1. Why are police not particularly good at problem-solving?
2. What police tactics are most effective in suppressing and preventing crime and social disorder?
3. Why are police not particularly good at crime prevention through social development?
4. What are the most appropriate roles for police in implementing crime prevention?
5. Explain what is meant by the following statement: "police no longer have a monopoly on providing public safety and security."

Impact of Community Policing on Traditional Policing

Qualified research has shown that traditional policing does little to sustainably reduce or prevent crime or disorder. But that does not mean that police should not have traditional policing tactics in their repertoire. On the other hand, community policing (comprising the practices of partnerships, problem-solving, and crime prevention) can have some strong tactical influences on traditional policing, and in so doing, can bring policing closer to the roles of other partners in the safety and security web.[26] For example, routine patrol, one of the fundamental components of traditional policing, needs to continue but is most effective when influenced by the goals of community policing. Routine patrol can be a significant part of a problem-solving strategy as well as a mechanism for community outreach designed to reduce fear of crime and increase police legitimacy. It can be used to increase police visibility and, in hot-spot policing, actually suppress crime and social disorder.

Rapid response has also been influenced by community policing. Whereas the traditional policing model required rapid response to all calls for service, community consultation with police on community priorities has permitted police to prioritize incoming calls for service and respond most rapidly to those that the community thinks merit it. Community policing has also motivated agencies to develop alternative ways for community members to report incidents to police, including online and through civilian-run call centres.

Traditional policing's recourse to arrests has also been altered by community policing. Now, arrests are one among many alternative dispositions that officers can invoke upon an apprehension. Ontario's *Youth Criminal Justice Act*,[27] for example, authorizes a range of "extrajudicial measures" that apprehending officers may implement if they conclude, after making an assessment, that these measures would be more productive than arrests. The Royal Canadian Mounted Police use what they call "Community Justice Forums" to obtain clear expressions of remorse on the part of those whose behaviours have offended others, expressions of forgiveness on the part of those who were harmed or victimized by those behaviours, and sanctions and restitution as determined by all those most directly affected by the offensive acts. Research on this model in Canada and abroad has shown that one result is a stronger sense of community (social capital and social control) among all supporters of both the offender and the victims.

Investigations too have been influenced by community policing. Some agencies, for example, are selecting for community policing roles only those officers who have a strong investigative background. This is because the challenges of problem-solving require good observation techniques, strong communication skills, and the power of rigorous analysis. Furthermore, investigations can be used to aid analysis of underlying causes and identify potential community partners to be engaged in problem-solving.

Traditional policing has always emphasized the importance of law enforcement agencies sharing important information with each other. But with the advent of problem-solving in community policing, there now exists pressure within police agencies for information sharing to include a diverse range of individuals, businesses, and organizations that are better suited than law enforcement agencies to develop and implement sustainable solutions to community problems. That puts pressure on police agencies to become a little more transparent and forthcoming than the traditional model ever permitted.

CHAPTER SUMMARY

Police employ traditional policing very well, and society benefits when that is what is required to deal with a harmful situation. But the demands of community policing—especially police engaging community partners in problem-solving initiatives—cannot be adequately addressed by rapid response, arrests, and sanctions. Police do have special characteristics that enhance their ability to initiate community policing, like specialized mandates, skills, and authorities that are largely accepted by society; general credibility and legitimacy in the public eye; and knowledge and experience with those members of community who are most marginalized and in greatest need of effective community problem-solving. But police are going to have to reorganize their agencies to support these community problem-solving activities; train their officers in striking community partnerships, community mobilization, and problem-solving; and develop new capacities to lead the community in identifying and focusing on priority risk factors.

REVIEW AND DISCUSSION QUESTIONS

1. Why does targeted enforcement work in crime and disorder apprehension, suppression, and prevention?

2. Research shows that random patrols do not suppress or prevent crime or social disorder. What tactical measures must be taken in order to increase the effectiveness of police maintaining an active and visible presence, and what are the positive spinoffs from it?

3. What are the characteristics and results of effective community engagement?

4. What are the effects of police bad manners on community policing initiatives?

5. Why are police not good at problem-solving in high-demand neighbourhoods?

6. What are the appropriate roles for police in community problem-solving?

7. Who is responsible for safety and well-being in community? Explain your answer.

8. How has community policing changed some of the conventional components of traditional policing: routine patrol, rapid response, arrests, investigations, and information sharing?

KEY TERMS

NOTES

1   J Magers, "COMPSTAT: A New Paradigm for Policing or a Repudiation of Community Policing?" (2004) 20:1 J Contemp Crim Just 70.

2   Philip Johnson et al, *A National Diagnostic on Human Resources in Policing* (Toronto: Hay Group, 2007).

3   The Ontario Working Group's work is fully reported and accessible on the Ontario Association of Chiefs of Police website: <http://www.oacp.on.ca/news-events/resource-documents/ontario-working-group-owg>.

4   *Mental Health Act*, RSO 1990, c M.7.

5   Jerry H Ratcliffe et al, "The Philadelphia Foot Patrol Experiment: A Randomized Controlled Trial of Police Effectiveness in Violent Crime Hotspots" (2011) 49:3 Criminology 795.

6   On the other hand, the suppressive effect of these patrols may not last very long once the cruiser moves on. See Christopher S Koper, "Just Enough Police Presence: Reducing Crime and Disorderly Behavior by Optimizing Patrol Time in Crime Hot Spots" (1995) 12:4 Justice Q 649.

7   K Lloyd & J Foster, *Citizen Focus and Community Engagement: A Review of the Literature* (London, UK: The Police Foundation, 2009).

8   R Tuffin, "The National Reassurance Policing Programme: A Six-Site Evaluation," Findings Paper 272 (London, UK: Home Office, 2006).

9   Lawrence W Sherman, "Policing for Crime Prevention" in Lawrence W Sherman et al, *Preventing Crime: What Works, What Doesn't, What's Promising: A Report to the United States Congress* (Washington, DC: National Institute of Justice, 1997) ch 8.

10   Raymond Paternoster et al, "Do Fair Procedures Matter? The Effect of Procedural Justice on Spouse Assault" (1997) 31:1 Law & Soc'y Rev 163.

11   L Mazerolle, E Antrobus, S Bennett & TR Tyler, "Shaping Citizen Perceptions of Police Legitimacy: A Randomized Field Trial of Procedural Justice" (2013) 51:1 Criminology 33.

12 *Ibid* at 55.

13 Redditt Hudson, "I'm a Black Ex-Cop, and This Is the Real Truth About Race and Policing" (7 July 2016), online: VOX Media <http://www.vox.com/2015/5/28/8661977/race-police-officer>.

14 A Myhill & P Quinton, *It's a Fair Cop? Police Legitimacy, Public Cooperation, and Crime Reduction* (London: National Policing Improvement Agency, 2011).

15 Mazerolle et al, *supra* note 11.

16 Sherman et al, *supra* note 9.

17 Michael S Scott, *Problem-Oriented Policing: Reflections on the First 20 Years* (Washington, DC: US Department of Justice, Office of Community Oriented Policing Services, 2000).

18 C Hale, "Fear of Crime: A Review of the Literature" (1996) 4:2 Intl Rev Victimology 79.

19 Jonathan Jackson & Ben Bradford, "What Is Trust and Confidence in the Police?" (2010) 4:3 Policing 241.

20 JQ Wilson & G Kelling, "Broken Windows" in V Kappeler, ed, *The Police & Society: Touch Stone Readings* (Prospect Heights, Ill: Waveland Press, 2006) 154-67.

21 *Police Services Act*, RSO 1990, c P.15.

22 CR Jaffrey, *Crime Prevention Through Environmental Design* (Beverly Hills, Cal: Sage, 1971).

23 Council of Canadian Academies, *Policing Canada in the 21st Century: New Policing for New Challenges* (Ottawa: The Expert Panel on the Future of Canadian Policing Models, Council of Canadian Academies, 2014) at 2.

24 *Ibid* at 11.

25 *Ibid* at 142.

26 Community-Oriented Policing Services (COPS) Office, "Spotlight on Community Policing Practice: The Role of Traditional Policing in Community Policing" (2008) 1:3 *e-newsletter* (US National Institute of Justice).

27 *Youth Criminal Justice Act*, SC 2002, c 1.

CHAPTER 4

Police Roles in Community Safety and Well-Being

The Smiths Falls Police Service, in Smiths Falls, Ontario, maintains a close connection with the community through its dedicated Community Service Officer. On May 21, 2016, the SFPS Community Service Officer, working with the local health unit and the Municipal Drug Strategy Committee, participated in the National Prescription Drug Drop-Off Day to help prevent prescription drug abuse. On that day, community members brought in over 3,350 unused or unwanted prescription medications for safe disposal by police.

LEARNING OUTCOMES

Upon completion of this chapter, you should be able to:

- Understand the common reasons why people do not report crimes in which they are victimized
- Estimate the proportion of police calls for service that do not entail chargeable offences (crimes)
- Define risk factors, and explain risk mitigation
- Define the safety and well-being web and describe who is in it
- Describe the four components of the safety and well-being framework and explain the police role in each
- Identify the principal roles of police in community policing

Introduction

More than any other chapter in this text, this one pulls together innovative thinking and successful experiments in Canadian policing over the past six to eight years. Chapter 1 introduced Ontario's Mobilization & Engagement Model of Community Policing. Rolled out by the Ontario Association of Chiefs of Police in 2010, the model introduced a number of new and key ideas that have been integrated in this text:

- Far more than a philosophy, community policing is about actions and decisions that police officers make to leverage other community actors to address the roots of crime and social disorder.
- Community policing is not one thing, done the same way in every neighbourhood; it adapts to the needs and problems of the neighbourhoods where it is applied.
- In low-demand neighbourhoods, community policing is about police supporting community actors in doing the work of making their community safer and healthier—including installing situational crime prevention measures.
- In high-demand neighbourhoods, there is a greater need for police to initiate problem-solving and sometimes provide some leadership until local leadership can be mobilized.
- Therefore, community policing starts with police officers analyzing the neighbourhoods where they want to apply it; diagnosing their problems; identifying important community actors to solve those problems; and custom designing strategies to get everyone in that neighbourhood involved.

In 2011, the Prince Albert Police Service launched its Hub model for reducing the chances that people at elevated levels of risk of harms will actually experience any. This required experimenting with a highly collaborative process of triaging harmful situations and custom designing immediate interventions that reduced risk factors. The Prince Albert experience has informed similar initiatives in Ontario, British Columbia, Nova Scotia, and other provinces.

It contributed to the work of the Ontario Working Group on Collaborative, Risk-Driven Community Safety (Ontario Working Group), which drew from the experience of Ontario municipalities and made several findings in 2014-2015:[1]

- Police spend most of their time and effort responding to non-chargeable, social disorder occurrences, which are symptoms of more profound systemic problems in community.
- Police are not particularly well qualified to deal with most of those systemic problems—or their symptoms (for example, mental health issues).

- Most police and other responders wait until a harmful incident has occurred before they respond, leading to the observation that it might be more effective to try to anticipate those occurrences by observing risk factors, and intervene before they occur.
- Focusing police efforts on assessments of risk presents a number of new possibilities—not the least, the potential for collaboration across specialized **silos** of human and social service agencies and organizations.
- If police do not limit themselves to emergency response, they can probably do more in the areas of risk mitigation, prevention, and social development—all of which will reduce harms and victimization as well as demand for emergency response.

During this period, the government of Canada, through Public Safety Canada, with support from Justice Canada and the Royal Canadian Mounted Police, asked the Council of Canadian Academies to undertake an expert panel assessment. The assessment brought together all available evidence from Canada and around the world on promising models for the future of policing in Canada. The panel, called the Expert Panel on the Future of Canadian Policing Models (the Expert Panel), drew on the experience of experts in law, criminology, business, sociology and sociological anthropology, and policing. Its work was completed and has informed this chapter significantly, particularly where it describes the "safety and security web" around which we build this chapter's contributions to our increasing understanding of community policing. We will quote and cite the panel frequently in presenting this material, so it is probably most appropriate to quote one of its summary findings at the outset:

> The safety and security web presents both the central challenge and the central opportunity for Canada's police in the 21st century. Working effectively within and through this web—rather than as isolated entities—will allow policing organizations to better respond to existing and emerging issues.[2]

ON PATROL

Neighbourhood Officer Program

In 2013, the Toronto Police Service implemented the Neighbourhood Officer Program in high-demand neighbourhoods. Assigned to a specific geographical

---

silo a metaphor for the way that many public service agencies operate with separate enabling legislation and mandates, competitive budgeting processes, and technical isolation from each other, resulting in a social service system that makes it very difficult for these agencies to collaborate

location, neighbourhood officers were primarily responsible for the integration of community and police resources in order to resolve minor crime and disorder problems. Neighbourhood Officers had to familiarize themselves with community members, build partnerships, foster good relationships between police and community members, identify potential social or economic drivers of crime and disorder within the neighbourhood, and develop local resources to build safer communities and enhance quality of life within them.

In one case a small children's park in south-central Toronto was being used by low-level drug dealers to traffic in small amounts of marijuana. The presence of the dealers scared off children and other residents, who were intimidated by the illegal activities. Businesses in the area saw a significant drop in revenues because of a loss in customer traffic. Residents were forced to travel outside of the comfort zone that their own neighbourhood had previously provided them.

Newly assigned neighbourhood officers heard numerous complaints about drug trafficking in the park. Following consultation with the community, they decided that a traditional, police-driven targeted enforcement initiative would be the best first step in addressing the problem. This would allow the police to properly identify the offenders and address the question of whether they were locals or outsiders. Police and community members took the view that local offenders might just have a stake in keeping the park safe for the area residents.

Police used traditional surveillance and undercover methods to identify and target suspected marijuana traffickers. Several individuals—mostly local residents—were arrested and charged with multiple possession and trafficking offences. They were put before the courts. Despite the relatively high number of charges, only a small amount of marijuana was seized. Prosecutors later withdrew the majority of charges related to the project, apparently balancing the interests of justice with the high cost of prosecution and minimal sentences—a strategy not uncommon throughout the province. Subsequently, traffickers returned to the children's park and their criminal activity continued.

The neighbourhood officer once again consulted with community partners. They developed a new strategy, using municipal and provincial bylaws to enforce legitimate park uses (for example, curfew hours) along with newly created legislation to curb unlawful behaviour in the park (possession or consumption of alcohol or drugs). Once again, police were responsible for enforcement initiatives but at a slower pace and unburdened by the requirements of criminal investigations. In conjunction with monetary penalties and easily enforced trespassing legislation, offenders were advised that they would eventually receive park bans lasting up to one year if their illegal behaviour did not cease.

Police, community, and local business partners educated the non-legitimate users of the park on how they were perceived by the community and that compliance with their neighbours in using the park for legitimate purposes was important. A handful of the traffickers and buyers also had kids, so the motivation to change and take accountability for their actions helped put the park back into the neighbourhood's hands. Positive change was eventually achieved, but not overnight; successes were measured in months, not days.

Consider the following questions:

1. The first attempt to deal with drug trafficking in the park used traditional policing tactics. Why was that unsuccessful?
2. The second attempt enrolled the participation of neighbours and business partners. Why was this approach more successful?
3. In the end, what was the single factor that seemed to change the drug dealers' behaviour the most? What was the police role in making that happen?

The Safety and Well-Being Web

We introduced the idea of a "web" of agencies and organizations that share some responsibility for safety and well-being in community in Chapters 1 and 3. This is where we give it a lot more attention. Without the web, we would not, and could not, have community policing. It is because members in the web have not been doing enough that social disorder (if not crime) is driving calls for police assistance upward. It is in the web that police officers find partners to help resolve community problems. It is with the web that police agencies, and individual officers, have to thoroughly familiarize themselves, in order to judiciously select the right partners for the right problem-solving initiatives.

Painting an Accurate Picture of the Prevalence of Crime in Canada: Reported and Unreported Crime

According to data from Statistics Canada's 2014 Uniform Crime Reporting Survey (UCR Survey), police-reported crime rates in Canada (that is, the number of chargeable offences per 100,000 people) continued a 40-year downward trend in 2014, dropping 3 percent from the previous year.[3] That is good news, notwithstanding that public calls for police assistance have continued to increase over that same period, owing to the demand for police response to harms and victimization from social disorder—not crime (as we reported in Chapter 1).

However, the UCR Survey does not give us an accurate picture of the prevalence of crime in Canada. Statistics Canada reported that in 2014, less than one-third of crimes were reported to police and that this figure has been getting smaller since the late 1990s (1999, 37 percent; 2004, 34 percent). The most common reasons for not reporting crime in 2009, the most recent year for which data are available, are shown in Table 4.1.

These issues led the Expert Panel to develop a graphic that depicts the distinction between reported and unreported crimes in Canada—and harms from non-chargeable offences. We have adapted it below (Figure 4.1) to emphasize that while police may not be responding to unreported crimes, they are extremely busy responding to reported crimes and the much larger, and growing, incidence of social disorder calls for service.

TABLE 4.1   **Reasons for Not Reporting Crime, 2009**

Reason	Proportion*
Not important enough	68%
Police could not do anything about it	59%
Dealt with in another way	42%
Incident was a personal matter	36%
Didn't want to get police involved	35%
Police wouldn't help	22%
Insurance wouldn't cover it	15%
No confidence in criminal justice system	14%
No items taken or items recovered	14%
Police would be biased	9%
Fear of revenge by offender	7%
Fear of publicity or news coverage	5%

* Percentages will not sum to 100 because of multiple answers by survey respondents.

SOURCE: Adapted from Statistics Canada, "Criminal Victimization in Canada, 2009," by Samuel Perreault and Shannon Brennan, in *Juristat* 30:2, Catalogue No 85-002-X (Ottawa: Statistics Canada, 2010) at 16. This does not constitute an endorsement by Statistics Canada of this product.

FIGURE 4.1   **Harms Occur from Far More Than Reported Crime**

The Increasing Number of Social Disorder Calls for Service

Police are being called on to respond to much more than just criminal offences. For example, in 2009, only 15 percent of public calls for assistance to the Ontario Provincial Police related to *Criminal Code*[4] offences; 41 percent related to traffic; and fully 44 percent of all calls for service were in this catch-all social disorder category.[5] Police obviously do enforce the law—the function for which they were established and for which we value the traditional policing model. But in the past 20 years they have also become our first-responder, generalist problem-solvers on the widest range of personal, social, and community issues. Besides fighting crime, police are increasingly being called upon to exercise discretion and make decisions in areas such as:

- social work,
- parenting,
- youth mentoring,
- health and mental health,
- social assistance,
- housing,
- school issues, and
- interpersonal relationships.

In some of these areas, police are partially trained, but in most, they are unqualified. Ontario police interaction with persons suffering from mental illness increased by 38 percent between 2003 and 2007, and police apprehensions under the *Mental Health Act*[6] increased by 35 percent during that period.[7] Our generalist, front-line officers are not trained or adequately prepared to handle these calls most effectively.[8] Such pressures are forcing police agencies to use specialized training for select officers and mobilize special units like Hamilton, Ontario's Mobile Crisis Rapid Response Team, which was explained at the beginning of Chapter 3. As discussed in Chapter 1, these are the social disorder demands that are driving policing costs to the point where municipalities are saying they can no longer afford policing.[9]

Non-Police Actors in the Safety and Well-Being Web

The safety and security web is a metaphor and a new way of looking at police in relation to the larger external environment in which all police now operate, as one of a variety of institutions fostering public safety and security. Viewing contemporary Canadian policing in this broader and more complex policing safety and security context acknowledges the new reality of a network, or "web," of multiple public and private agencies and actors operating and collaborating in various ways to produce and reproduce public and private safety and security.

—Expert Panel on the Future of Canadian Policing Models, *Policing Canada in the 21st Century: New Policing for New Challenges*

The Expert Panel, which coined the word "web," was basically acknowledging that police in Canada cannot succeed without far more effective partnerships with a whole host of other actors in community. The Expert Panel was particularly preoccupied with other actors that have roles in safety and security (like fire, emergency medical, child security, and even private security organizations). In the United States, the Office of Community Oriented Policing Services, part of the US Department of Justice, expands the web even more by including the following actors:

- *Other government agencies*: legislative bodies, prosecutors, probation and parole, public works, neighbouring law enforcement, health and human services, child support, ordinance enforcement, and schools.
- *Community members*: volunteers, activists, formal and informal community leaders, residents, visitors and tourists, and commuters.
- *Community-based organizations (non-profits)*: victims' groups, service clubs, support groups, issue groups, advocacy groups, community development organizations, and faith communities.
- *Businesses*: private, for-profit, large and small businesses, and business associations like business improvement associations and chambers of commerce.
- *Media*: print and broadcast media as well as issue-specific outlets and social media.[10]

The safety and security web described by the Expert Panel focuses primarily on crime and security issues and therefore predominantly includes the diverse array of policing and professional security agencies in its web, with a sprinkling of health and social work entities as well—like children's aid and mental health. In contrast, community policing is moving beyond "safety and security" to "safety and well-being." Community policing is about engaging the widest range of appropriate community actors that are focused on the diverse dimensions of social assistance and general well-being—the prerequisites for a safe and secure community.

Targeting well-being does not mean ignoring crime. If anything, it strengthens crime prevention. If we can reduce the antecedents to crime, we can probably reduce the incidence of crime. Furthermore, as Canadian criminologist Irvin Waller has shown in his research, police need not be involved in many crime prevention initiatives so long as they include partnerships among those actors that are most directly affected by the crimes and that have the most effective strategies for reducing crime risk factors and protecting vulnerable populations.[11] So the bottom line on the safety and well-being web is that police need a diverse range of other community actors to not only deal more effectively with social disorder issues and problems, but also prevent crimes (reported and unreported).

The safety and well-being web could, in any given situation, include different or other actors than those shown in Figure 4.2. There is no special

FIGURE 4.2   The Safety and Well-Being Web

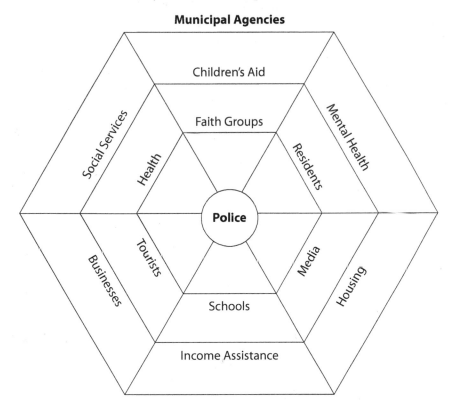

Municipal Agencies

Children's Aid

Faith Groups

Social Services

Health

Mental Health

Residents

Police

Tourists

Businesses

Media

Housing

Schools

Income Assistance

meaning in the placement of most of the actors shown in this web, except for the police at the centre and municipal agencies on the outside ring. The first and most important message in this depiction is that police are no longer the sole preventers of crime, nor the sole providers of safety and well-being in community. Safety and well-being is what the Expert Panel called a "whole-of-society affair involving multiple jurisdictions and many mandates beyond the policing system."[12] The second important message in this figure is that in order to enable the participation of other community actors, police have to do a lot of special things that are quite different from what the traditional policing model prepares them for. That includes learning how to be better partners with so many different agencies, organizations, individuals, businesses, media, faith groups, and more. Looking at initiatives like this in Amsterdam, van Steden et al. labelled this new requirement for police "team play."[13]

The third important message in this web relates to the role of municipal agencies. Most police agencies have an accountability relationship with municipal agencies. The reason municipal agencies sits on the outside ring of the web is that they have a very important role in enabling and supporting all of the team play that is expected of all of these actors within the web. '

Bancroft, Ontario, for example, municipal council unanimously passed a resolution declaring that safety and well-being for all Bancroftians is its highest priority. The council further stated that it expects all agencies, organizations, businesses, residents, tourists, etc., to do their part in supporting this goal. That resolution served police very well when it came time to call potential team players to come to the table to discuss safety and well-being priorities and strategies.

CHECK YOUR UNDERSTANDING

1. Roughly what proportion of all crime in Canada is actually reported to police?
2. Roughly what proportion of police calls for service pertain to *Criminal Code* offences? What do the balance of calls relate to?
3. What is meant by the "safety and well-being web"?
4. What are the implications of the safety and well-being web for police?

The Safety and Well-Being Framework

Eventually, in this chapter, we want to explain what police officers have to do to enable safety and well-being in community. However, at this point, it is more useful to first isolate what everyone in the safety and well-being web should be doing to make community safer and healthier. After specifying what everyone is doing together, we can more easily isolate those roles and responsibilities of police.

We will also develop a safety and well-being framework that illustrates how municipalities invest their resources to promote safety and well-being. For example, Figure 4.3 depicts a situation in which municipalities invest all their resources in emergency response. But as we have seen, emergency response is only part of the solution. We want to reallocate some of those resources to other areas—risk mitigation, prevention, and social development. In the sections below, note how, as we reallocate resources to these other areas, emergency response forms a progressively smaller proportion of the framework.

Emergency Response

The 911 call triggers an emergency response from police, fire, emergency medical services, children's aid, mental health, hospital emergency rooms, and others. The demand for emergency response by police and other first responders to deal with crime and social disorder is represented by Figure 4.3. It forms the centre of what we will call the **safety and well-being framework** (a logical

---

safety and well-being framework a logical basis for identifying and understanding the relationships among tactics for deriving community safety and well-being

FIGURE 4.3 Centre of the Community Safety and Well-Being Framework

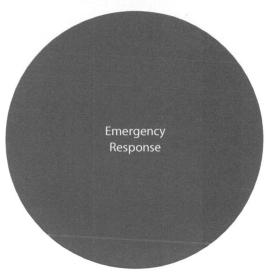

basis for identifying and understanding the relationships among tactics for deriving community safety and well-being). In the sections below, we develop this framework.

As you saw in Chapter 3, emergency response frequently draws on traditional policing skills and capabilities: rapid response, arrest where warranted, thorough and documented investigations, services and supports for victims, and follow-up. It is important to reiterate here that nothing we say in this book about community policing lessens the importance of traditional policing when and where it is required.

On the other hand, we already noted that police are receiving reports of only about one-third of all crime, and that comprises only about 15 percent of all of the public calls for assistance that police receive. All the rest of their activities deal with anti-social behaviours—most of which do not require the full range of traditional policing responses. Certainly, most of those anti-social behaviours do deserve the attention and mitigating influences of a whole host of other agencies and organizations in the safety and well-being web. The fact that police are called is only an indication that services and supports available from other agencies and organizations have not been adequately applied to that situation.

In the interests of improving the quality of emergency response to mental health situations, Vancouver operates the Car 87 program. This is a partnership between the Vancouver Police Department and Vancouver Coastal Health. It is an effort to get the most qualified people—police officers and mental health nurses—to respond to emergencies that appear to have a mental health element to them. It has been shown to have the positive effect of getting the right services and supports to people when they are in greatest need of them.

One of the key characteristics of emergency response is that it is based on harmful or victimizing incidents. Something bad has happened, or is about to happen, when someone dials 911. By the time police or other emergency responders get there, harms may well already have been inflicted on the people involved. Emergency response is incident driven, and frequently the best police can do is limit the harms or victimization to those already so affected. Therefore, it is in everybody's interests to see whether we can reduce the demand for emergency response—which, if done well, would also have the effect of reducing harms and victimization. That is our quest in developing this safety and well-being framework. What can a municipality do to reduce the demand for emergency response and, in so doing, reduce the incidence of harms and victimization for all people in the community? In effect, how can we reduce the size of the red circle in Figure 4.3? As the following sections will show, the solution involves risk mitigation, prevention of crime and social disorder, and social development.

Risk Mitigation

Risk mitigation is our first opportunity to reduce the number of 911 calls—demand for emergency response. **Risk mitigation** means efforts to identify individuals, families, groups, and locations at imminent risk of harms or victimization and customize interventions that reduce those risks before an emergency response is required.

Mitigating Risks in High School

Once a week in North Hastings High School (Hastings County, Ontario) the principal convenes a Student Success Team, consisting of five faculty and administrators (principal, vice principal, student success teacher, guidance counsellor, and special education teacher). The team's job is to triage students at risk—that is, prioritize those students who they believe need extra supports so that they can meet their own or the school's performance standards and expectations. The team focuses on more than academic achievement; it looks at issues relating to mental health, addictions, family relationships, peer relationships, and anything else that influences the student's ability to achieve success in school. In effect, the Student Success Team is mitigating risks that particular students might fail or experience behavioural or health problems.

---

risk mitigation efforts to identify individuals, families, groups, or locations at imminent risk of harms or victimization and customize interventions which reduce those risks before an emergency response is required

Risk mitigation happens at that point when harms are imminent and emergency response is inevitable unless something is done to lower those risks. **Risk factors** are negative characteristics or conditions in individuals, families, communities, or society that may increase social disorder, crime or fear of crime, or the likelihood of harms or victimization to persons or property. With risk mitigation in our emerging safety and well-being framework we are calling for interventions before a harmful incident occurs that requires emergency response from police or any other first responder (see Figure 4.4). The risk mitigation ring is coloured amber like the amber traffic light; it is the precursor to red as risk mitigation is the last chance to prevent harms before an emergency response is required.

FIGURE 4.4   Adding Risk Mitigation to the Community Safety and Well-Being Framework

By installing risk mitigation activities, we can forestall, if not actually reduce, the demand for emergency response by police or any other first responder.

Notice, in this figure, that in our effort to reduce the overall size of investment in emergency response, we are gradually working our way out from the centre of this bullseye. Our first step is to mitigate imminent harms and victimization before they happen or require emergency response. Once we protect those at imminent risk of harms and victimization, maybe we can continue to work our way out from the centre of this figure until emergency

---

risk factors negative characteristics or conditions in individuals, families, communities, or society that may increase social disorder, crime or fear of crime, or the likelihood of harms or victimization to persons or property

response (red) is only a small bullseye in the centre of a wide range of activities that make people and communities safer and healthier.

Another example of risk mitigation in the schools is an agreement among key agencies to jointly assess the potential for violence in school when a teacher or anybody else sees or hears a threat or other indicator of potential violence. Upon qualified triage of that situation, the collaborators will intervene to reduce the chances that the student(s) will act out on the perceived threat. Notice that with the addition of this risk mitigation ring of activity, we have moved from incident-driven emergency response to risk-driven anticipation of potential harms and efforts to lower that potential. If community is good at risk mitigation, it will reduce the demand for emergency response.

It is also interesting to note that with risk mitigation we have suddenly involved a whole raft of acute care human and social service providers. Risk mitigation is a bigger collaborative enterprise than is emergency response. As such, it is fraught with the challenges of collaboration, like information sharing, cooperation among front-line workers, and coordination of services. Hence, there is a need for agreement among key agencies to deal with perceived threats of violence in school. That agreement identifies not only what the model is designed to achieve, but also how the agencies will work together collaboratively.

Prevention of Crime and Social Disorder

When a community is aware of specific hazards, or vulnerable groups, they can design and install situational measures to prevent bad things from happening. **Prevention** means proactively implementing evidence-based situational measures, policies, or programs to reduce locally identified priority risks to community safety and well-being. For example, school children crossing twice daily, five days a week, at a high-speed intersection are at risk of serious harms. With that known risk, and identified vulnerable group, it does not take much to decide on situational measures to reduce the hazard by controlling traffic at that intersection.

Ontario's Ministry of Community Safety and Correctional Services highlights three components of any viable prevention tactic: (1) known risk; (2) identified vulnerable group; and (3) designated protective factors.[14] **Protective factors** are positive characteristics or conditions that can moderate the negative effects of risk factors and foster healthier individuals, families, and communities, thereby increasing personal and community safety and well-being.

---

prevention proactively implementing evidence-based situational measures, policies, or programs to reduce locally identified priority risks to community safety and well-being

protective factors positive characteristics or conditions that can moderate the negative effects of risk factors and foster healthier individuals, families, and communities, thereby increasing personal and/or community safety and well-being

If a community can identify those three ingredients—risk factors, vulnerable groups, and protective factors—it can prevent things from getting to the point where a risk mitigation intervention is needed, much less an emergency response. As Figure 4.5 shows, prevention is an important component of the community safety and well-being framework.

Notice that upon adding the prevention activity (blue) to our framework, we have significantly reduced the size of the municipality's investment in emergency response (red). But that outer red ring shows that we still have some way to go before we have reduced emergency response to a manageable and sustainable level of activity.

Assume that we are looking at a community that has decided that domestic assaults and abuse are a priority risk factor for making people safer and healthier. Women and children are the most vulnerable groups. Research has shown that the most effective protective factors are strong, resilient social networks.[15]

So the community that wants to do something about this problem has to figure out how to strengthen these social networks in order to prevent abuse of women and children. Part of that strategy includes working with women directly—for example, informing them about available social supports and encouraging them to avail themselves of them. The particular supports required will vary depending on the situation, but they could include temporary, secure shelter; health care (especially for problems associated with mental health and addictions); and safety planning (how to perceive a potential elevation in risk, where to go, who to call, what to do).[16]

FIGURE 4.5   Adding Prevention to the Community Safety and Well-Being Framework

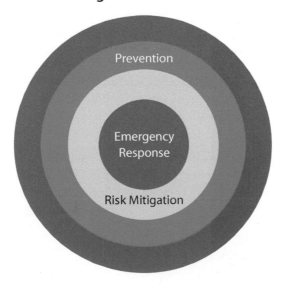

Of the range of social supports, some of the most important are informed, alert, responsive, and supportive neighbours, friends, and family members of the vulnerable women and children. In a small community, this can be a community-wide intervention in which public education is used to alert everybody about the extent and nature of the problem and the very important role that neighbours, friends, and family members can play in preventing such abuse and supporting women and children. In a larger community, programming that strengthens these social networks can be more targeted to vulnerable women and families, neighbourhoods with the highest levels of risk factors, and of course all interested and motivated individuals, groups, community-based organizations, and social and human service agencies.

Neighbours, Friends and Families

The Nova Scotia Advisory Council on the Status of Women and the Government of Nova Scotia have partnered to support the Nova Scotia Domestic Violence Resource Centre in making a well-researched and validated program called Neighbours, Friends and Families available to communities and groups that seek to address this risk factor.[17] Neighbours, Friends and Families was developed by Ontario's Western University Centre for Research and Education on Violence Against Women and Children, with support from the government of Ontario. The program has been widely implemented and proved through qualified research to reduce the incidence of violence against women and children.[18]

To mount any prevention strategy, many community members have to collaborate effectively. In fact, the farther out we move from the emergency response bullseye of our safety and well-being framework, the more inclusiveness and collaboration is required to succeed. That can be difficult in a society that organizes itself on the basis of specialization and compartmentalized human and social services. Therefore, there is an important role here for those influential actors in community—like police—who see the need for collaborative action and have the influence and leverage necessary to mobilize, engage, and support community partners that are willing to try it.

Social Development

Finally, we are ready to install the last type of community activity that will significantly lessen the amount of red (demand for emergency response) in our emerging community safety and well-being framework—social development. It is indicated by the green ring in Figure 4.6. **Social development** refers

---

social development long-term, multi-disciplinary efforts and investments to improve the social determinants of health and thereby reduce the probability of harms and victimization

FIGURE 4.6   Adding Social Development to the Community Safety and Well-Being Framework

to long-term, multi-disciplinary efforts and investments to improve the social determinants of health and thereby reduce the probability of harms and victimization.

Finally, our graphical representation of the community safety and well-being framework is complete. Overall investment in emergency response has been significantly reduced (red) while investments in the other three levels of activity have been significantly increased (amber, blue, and green).

In Chapter 1, we introduced the concept of the social determinants of health. Recall that it was defined as

> protective factors such as access to income, education, employment and job security, safe and healthy working conditions, early childhood development, food security, quality housing, social inclusion, cohesive social safety network [and] health services, which ensure equal access to all of the qualities, conditions, and benefits of life without regard to any socio-demographic differences.[19]

Social development is where the community decides that if it can no longer afford policing and other emergency responders at the level currently required, it will have to invest in resolving imbalances and inequities in the social determinants of health so that fewer people are harmed or victimized and fewer emergency incidents occur.

Social Entrepreneurship in Sault Ste. Marie, Ontario

The city selected a development company to demolish three 19th-century, red sandstone, paper mill buildings on the banks of the river in Sault Ste. Marie's downtown core. Perched at the foot of the bridge that Americans use to visit this city, this building site depicts the abandonment and decay that resulted from the death of the paper mill in the mid-1900s, followed by the restructuring and downsizing of neighbouring Algoma Steel in the early 2000s. At the same time, it shows those who could imagine something better a blank canvas that could be the centre of significant investment and rehabilitation in this northern Ontario landmark city.

The developer saw the latter. Falling in love with the iconic buildings he was asked to demolish, he noted that at the foot of the bridge between countries, these buildings and this site could be developed as a destination for tourism that would bring income and opportunity to the entire region. But, true to the core values of the private sector he represented, the developer disciplined his ambitions and designs with the requirement of profitability. If he was to repurpose and rehabilitate those buildings, then he had to find tenants whose rent revenues would make it profitable to do so.

Two years later, the first building is beautifully restored and occupied by the Algoma Conservatory of Music. Renovation of the second building is almost completed and most space is leased for visual and performing arts studios and a sound stage. The third building, uniquely shaped and structured to hold and ferment wood pulp back in its paper mill days, will house a wide variety of small businesses. Rental income for the refurbished spaces just barely affords the costs of rehabilitation. But the profit margins are sufficient to encourage the developer and his investors in their social enterprise ambitions. The net result is employment opportunities for a generation of Sault Ste. Marie residents who until now had been living in poverty, in substandard housing, and contributing to the high demand for policing and social assistance in this city.

Social entrepreneurship is the attempt to leverage solutions to social problems with the techniques of business. In collaboration with municipal social services, the developer interviewed 20 unemployed people from the highest-demand neighbourhood and selected 10 to enroll in eight weeks of learning programs financed by provincial social services. The first two weeks focused on life skills, and the balance on sewing skills. Using his commercial success, professional reputation, and business contacts, the

---

social entrepreneurship the attempt to leverage solutions to social problems with the techniques of business

developer then incorporated a sewing business called Stitch-Co. It hired seven of the newly skilled sewists (a gender-neutral term for those who can sew expertly) to manufacture marketable products for local and tourist trades. Upon distributing their first paycheques, the developer realized that employable skills, taken alone, were insufficient to help newly minted employees forge healthier pathways for themselves and their families. Most had never received a cheque and did not know how to handle it; most did not have bank accounts and did not know how to manage them; some did not have the identification documents necessary to open a bank account. Thus began a period of discovery about the ongoing social supports that people need to augment their new employment status and regular income. But with the assistance of the developer and municipal social services, these particular sewists are now fully employed, drawing paycheques, and supporting their families.

Collaboration really is the name of the game in social development. For example, collaborators in this small Sault Ste. Marie social entrepreneurship example included those listed in Table 4.2, below.

TABLE 4.2   Collaborators in the Sault Ste. Marie Social Entrepreneurship Initiative

Collaborator	Role
Private developer	Business opportunities; market assessment; production capacities; capitalization; business planning
Municipal government agencies	Policing; business start-up assistance; integration with economic development planning
Municipal social services	Social assistance for housing; family supports; employment skills development; advocacy with municipal agencies
Community-based organizations	Venues for services and supports; training; charitable status to attract resources to the initiative; family and personal mentoring; community outreach and supports
Financial institutions	Business analysis; training in financial literacy; banking services; debt service advice
University and college commerce departments	Business management training and development; business incubation and technical assistance

Collaboration is not easy. But collaboration is required if communities are going to resolve some of their more profound safety and well-being issues and problems. There is a very important role for police in getting collaboration to happen. For example, the neighbourhood from which the sewists came was the source of the greatest demand for police services, with the most crime and violence and the most social disorder, addictions, poverty, mental health issues, negative parenting, and homelessness. Adjacent to the downtown core, this neighbourhood negatively affected trade and commerce in the city. Police (and their municipal bosses) were desperate for meaningful and sustainable solutions. In that context, police saw the opportunity provided by one enlightened private property developer. Police helped the developer put together the strategy for which police advocated within city offices, including municipal social services, the chief administrative officer, and the mayor and council. Connecting the dots between the developer's social entrepreneurship scheme and crime and the costs of policing helped the city support the initiative. The collaboration grew from there.

After the success of Stitch-Co (which is a profitable company today), police again partnered with the developer, this time on a metal-recycling initiative. The initiative accepted 11 applicants with criminal records who were identified by the John Howard Society. Supported again by municipal social services, this initiative followed a similar pattern as Stitch-Co. The John Howard Society provided life skills training and the developer trained these people on the recovery of precious metal from scrap. Eight of the original 11 graduated from the program: six were employed locally and two were hired in a neighbouring town. The precious metal is sold at higher margins than typical scrap—thereby providing revenue that flows back to the partnership. Habitat for Humanity joined the collaboration and receives margins on these sales after salaries are paid. Then Habitat for Humanity reinvests in the city in the form of housing—another risk factor in any marginalized neighbourhood.

That is social development. It directly addresses the social determinants of health and is part of a long-term strategy for resolving profound community problems. It involves many community partners. But the value added from shared responsibilities and accountabilities, resources and programs, and expertise and commitment can, in the long term, reduce the demand for prevention, risk mitigation, and emergency response while building a stronger social foundation for a safer and healthier community.

This community safety and well-being framework was originally developed by the Ontario Working Group on Collaborative, Risk-Driven Community Safety. The Ontario Working Group is a collaboration too. It originated from Ontario police agencies that were motivated to work with diverse community partners in coming up with workable strategies for minimizing social harms and victimization, and reducing the costs of policing and other emergency responders. Hosted by the Ontario Association of Chiefs of Police, and partially funded by the Ontario Ministry of Community Safety and Correctional

Services, the Ontario Working Group spent a year doing theoretical research on this framework, followed by a year of research on practical applications in municipalities throughout Ontario. The results were sufficiently positive and promising that the ministry is using them to inform revisions to Ontario's *Police Services Act*[20] and developing guidelines for risk mitigation and municipal planning for community safety and well-being.[21]

CHECK YOUR UNDERSTANDING

1. What is meant by "risk mitigation"?
2. What is meant by "prevention"?
3. What is meant by "social development"?
4. What is the role of police in each component of the community safety and well-being framework?

Roles of Police

Finally, we come to the point of this whole chapter: identifying the roles of police in collaborative, risk-driven community safety and well-being—community policing. This subject was introduced by an explanation of the web of community partners that are necessary to implement the framework for community safety and well-being. As that discussion showed, beyond the demand for traditional policing, very little about the framework for community safety and well-being is about police doing risk mitigation, crime prevention, and social development. A more accurate way of looking at it would be to notice that where enforcement is concerned, police are primarily responsible for and uniquely capable to do that work. In risk mitigation, police certainly have a role, but a large number of other acute care providers share responsibilities with police. In prevention, police are certainly capable of installing situational prevention measures in low-demand neighbourhoods. But is that the best use of police resources when the people in those neighbourhoods can and should do these things for themselves? Of course, situational prevention measures do not work in high-demand neighbourhoods; social development measures are needed there. Police are not qualified to design and implement social development measures; so many other agencies and organizations are far more qualified and better resourced than police to do this work. In fact, the farther out we move from the enforcement centre of the community safety and well-being framework, the less responsibility police have to actually do the work. Rather, community policing is about police initiating, motivating, mobilizing and engaging, supporting, and facilitating the actions of so many others in community who do the actual work. In Figure 4.7, we overlay the safety and

FIGURE 4.7 **Overlaying the Safety and Well-Being Web on the Framework for Community Safety and Well-Being**

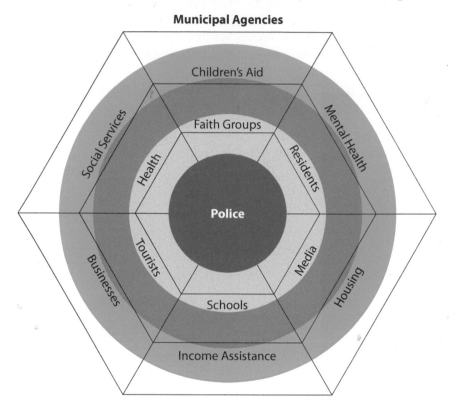

well-being web on the framework for community safety and well-being. Police appear in the centre of the web because of their significant role in emergency response. However, notice that all of the other actors in the web share responsibilities, as appropriate to their mandates, roles, and capabilities, for the three other zones of activity: risk mitigation, prevention, and social development.

The Expert Panel recognized the web of agencies, organizations, businesses, government agencies, and citizens that is needed to improve community safety and well-being. Moreover, it acknowledged that the web makes new demands on not only what police do, but how they do it.[22] The Ontario Working Group figured out what needs to be done to make communities safer and healthier. Both give us an opportunity to see community policing in a very new light. Problem-solving has to be at the heart of it, but police are not solving the problems. Partnerships are key to problem-solving—the web shows us that—but the police role is one of not only learning to be a good partner but also fostering broader and more sustainable collaborative partnerships throughout the web. The third element of community policing—prevention—continues to be important, but no more so than three other elements in the safety and well-being framework: emergency response, risk mitigation, and social development. Furthermore, police should not be doing the preventing (except where targeted enforcement and visible presence are concerned) as much as all the other community actors in the web.

It is worth emphasizing, once again, that traditional policing is a very important role for police—including in community policing. For example, the *60 Minutes* episode referenced in Chapter 1 depicted how targeted enforcement on a drug house netted weapons and arrests of serious offenders. But the action did not stop with the enforcement activity. Immediately on the heels of targeted enforcement, police officers started communicating with the public that was drawn to the action about what they could do to keep that address from becoming a harbour for crime and criminals again. In this episode one can see that even targeted enforcement is part of effective community policing or, we could say, community policing has an important role to play in effective targeted enforcement. The two are inseparable—they are not alternative policing tactics. Together, they are effective policing.

Focusing the Web on Crime and Disorder Priorities

We can theorize about the safety and well-being web and identify the kinds of agencies and organizations that should be team players in the web. But it is often more difficult to actually get that web to function deliberately and effectively in addressing crime and disorder problems in a particular community. In any given community, it is common to find actors that do not know that they have an important role to play in safety and well-being with direct impacts on crime and social disorder. This is where community policing starts: informing and motivating other team players in the web about safety and well-being priorities and their particular roles in resolving them.

One of the first challenges for police is informing everyone else in the safety and well-being web about real risk factors and vulnerable groups in the community. Most community members have an idea that drugs may be an issue in their community, or perhaps that some women experience violence from intimate partners. But that is just about the limit of their knowledge. They have no idea of the levels of these concerns, or how they stack up against other priorities like theft or traffic accidents in the downtown core. Therefore, an important first step in community policing for safety and well-being is tracking, mapping, and communicating about crime and disorder priorities in the community.

Tracking

Every Canadian police service systematically counts calls for service and occurrences by type, date, and location. These are the kinds of data that play an important role within agencies that use COMPSTAT to identify spikes in crime and hold units and command officers accountable for reducing those spikes. These data are rolled up into the Uniform Crime Reporting Survey for Public Safety Canada's annual count of crime rates. These data have been used for policing purposes, within the policing community, for a long time in order to enable resource allocation, deployment decisions, evidence of agency effectiveness, and unit performance evaluations. However, in the past ten years, agencies have been discovering the value of making such data available to other community agencies, organizations, and even the general public based on the notion that an informed public is easier to engage in problem-solving.

Data tracking, analysis, and sharing are important functions of effective community policing. Doing it for external audiences like community agencies, municipal agencies, and the public requires thinking in advance about what those audiences need to know and how they can best understand the implications of data that police collect. Most agencies collect raw frequency counts of occurrences. But sharing that with external audiences would overwhelm them in details that are not particularly meaningful. Clustering these data into a few, high-priority categories helps reduce the level of detail and direct the audience's attention to what is important. For example, a small, rural detachment of the Ontario Provincial Police provides a monthly summary to municipal council. The summary consists of only three indicators: violent crime (including counts of murder and attempted murder, sexual assault and assault, abduction, robbery, and other crimes against persons); property crime (arson, break and enter, theft, possession of stolen goods, and fraud and mischief); and drug crimes (possession, trafficking, importation, and production). In the normal course of its deliberations, municipal council has to scan only three numbers to get some sense of the safety and well-being status of their community. The Greater Sudbury Police Service also reports only three numbers, but there, social disorder is more important to municipal officials and other human and social service agencies because it is a good indicator of more profound systemic problems. So police report on violent crime, property crime, and disorder (fights, neighbour disputes, loitering, drinking, drugs, panhandling, and noise). When local decision-makers compare current totals on these three dimensions with totals in the past (say six months and a year), they can see trends that tell them something about how well they are doing at increasing safety and well-being in the community. The key point of this discussion is that every agency should think carefully about

- its audience for tracking crime and disorder data,
- what that audience needs to know in order to make good resource and program decisions, and
- how best to aggregate agency data in order to provide information that is useful to these external groups.

Most large police agencies are already doing this kind of data collection, aggregation, analysis, and communication with the broader public. It is a bigger challenge, however, for the smaller agencies, or small, rural detachments in a large distributed police agency like the Royal Canadian Mounted Police or Ontario Provincial Police. Too often, smaller units have to spend the majority of their time responding to calls for service. Although they do record the same data that every other agency records, they become servants of the centralized administration by sending those data upstream for aggregation at the command level, since they have very little capacity to do their own data aggregation and analysis locally. Then, if they ever want to make local presentations, they have to solicit analysis supports from headquarters. Frequently, that means delays and bureaucracy, which mitigate the timeliness and value of the exercise in the first place. Because they value evidence-based decision-making at all levels in their organization, the Ontario Provincial Police, in the past two years, have made hardware and software improvements at headquarters and the detachment, so that local commanders now have the technical capacity to roll up the numbers on their own activities and priorities for presentation to local, external audiences.

Another barrier to effective data tracking, analysis, and sharing is human, not technological. In large police agencies, data collection, aggregation, and analysis are conducted by qualified crime analysts. But not every agency or detachment can afford that luxury. The problem remains, even in the larger agency, of getting those analyses in the hands of officers who value data, can read data tables, and know how to apply data to police decision-making. This is an organizational and officer development challenge. It is wonderful to be able to rely on qualified crime analysts, but unless and until we get police decision-makers on the front lines and in the front office who are qualified to think about and use those data, the exercise is next to useless. Problem-oriented policing is predicated on Goldstein's original idea of looking at patterns of crime and disorder. Those patterns become most obvious through analysis of data. Therefore, data tracking, aggregation, analysis, and interpretation are essential to police and community problem-solving.

Mapping

Geographical information systems (GIS) have greatly enhanced the value of crime and disorder data that police agencies track, because they have added a spatial component to police analysis of patterns and trends. They provide an opportunity to track occurrences at many levels: community, neighbourhood, or even single street address. The map in Figure 4.8 came from the Greater Sudbury Police Service when it was mapping domestic dispute occurrences in one of its patrol zones (Zone 40).

In this map, notice that each coloured area has a two- or three-digit number that labels it. These are Statistics Canada's dissemination areas (a DA equals 400 to 700 persons). So with that information on top of the police agency's domestic dispute incidents, we can calculate the ratio of domestic disputes to the population of Zone 40 or any of these dissemination areas. That would help us determine how important domestic disputes are to a Zone 40 safety and well-being strategy. But the map also helps us locate those priorities within the

FIGURE 4.8   Domestic Disputes in Sudbury's Zone 40, in 2015

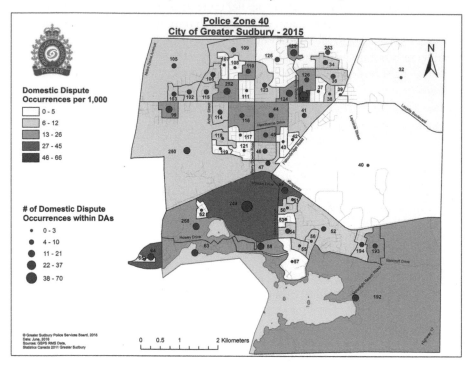

SOURCE: Map © Greater Sudbury Police Services Board, 2016 with data from: Statistics Canada. 2012. Sudbury, Ontario (Code 3552) and Canada (Code 01) (table). Census Profile. 2011 Census. Statistics Canada Catalogue no. 98-316-XWE. Ottawa. Released October 24, 2012. <http://www12.statcan.gc.ca/census -recensement/2011/dp-pd/prof/index.cfm?Lang=E> (accessed July 19, 2016).

zone. Look, for example, at dissemination area 249; obviously that is where this particular problem may be a higher priority than elsewhere in the zone.

Another advantage of using GIS of crime and disorder data on Statistics Canada Census maps is that we can add data about demographics, thus allowing us to analyze the incidence of this particular social disorder in relationship to factors like household income, numbers of children, or any other characteristics of the population that Statistics Canada has measured and recorded.

Last, and perhaps most importantly, mapping of these data really does enhance human understanding and communication about these community characteristics and problems. Some people are very good at comprehending the meaning of data that are presented in data tables; others are not. A map like this, with graphical symbols representing the incidence of domestic disputes, helps community partners and police themselves communicate with each other about priorities and programs.

GIS have been so helpful at increasing public interest in partnering with police to resolve community problems that many services now post maps online and invite anybody to view them. For example, the Edmonton Police Service offers an interactive system on its home page. Working off a Google map of Edmonton, a user can identify a neighbourhood that interests him or her, and obtain frequency and approximate locations of eight types of crime: assaults, break and enters, homicides, robberies, sexual assaults, thefts from vehicles, thefts of vehicles, and thefts over $5,000.[23]

Communicating

Finally, we come to the point of this whole discussion about data and community policing. If data are going to serve community policing, then police have to be able to communicate effectively about those data to all partners in the safety and well-being web. That is easier said than done. For example, it is usually insufficient to simply pass to members of municipal council some police-generated data tables. It is not safe to presume that all members of council can extract important meaning from data tables. The same applies to the use of maps. Colourful and interesting looking, they can also confuse those who are not accustomed to interpreting meaning from spatial information. So the rule here is to prepare presentations that give community partners the greatest chance of understanding the important patterns in and implications of the data. The presenter has to take responsibility for what other people are going to learn and understand from the presentation.

Without spending much time here teaching communications, we will look at one rule of thumb that maximizes a presenter's chances of having the desired impact on community partners. It is known in communications circles as the "rule of redundancy." It means, simply, express the key messages in different ways, repeatedly, and chances are good that recipients will understand and remember them. Usually, "repeatedly" means at least three times. So, for example, in planning a presentation, write an oral introduction that allows the presenter to tell his or her audience what the key messages are in the presentation; then make the presentation; then, upon closing, summarize the key messages again. The effect of redundancy is further enhanced if the listeners not only hear the words of the speaker, but also see the actual numbers in data tables and their spatial relationships in maps. Communication is one of the most important roles and functions of police in community policing. It deserves special development and training because, too often, police presenters presume that their only job is to express key messages. Instead, they have to learn that their primary job is to take responsibility for how those messages are understood by their audiences.

Identifying Community Actors in the Web

After police identify patterns in their data indicating the underlying problems that must be resolved by members of the safety and well-being web, they face the challenge of figuring out which community partners would, could, and should be most instrumental in problem-solving. Police roles in community policing include not only drawing people's attention to safety and well-being priorities, but attracting and engaging community partners in analyzing those problems and coming up with workable solutions.

The best way for a police service to do this effectively is to invest some effort in learning about other team players in the web. What agencies and organizations operate in the web? What are their sanctioned roles and responsibilities? What resources can they bring to community problem-solving? Who are the key contacts there? Many members of the web—for example, child security agencies—are fairly well known to police because they frequently overlap with each other in response to harmful incidents. Others are less well known. But all have to be considered potential partners in community problem-solving, so police have to make a deliberate effort to develop knowledge about them and distribute that knowledge to front-line officers and supervisors.

Publicly funded agencies and organizations are easiest to get to know because they are highly visible in neighbourhoods that are most frequently served by police, and because their mandates include some level of transparency. Community-based organizations, on the other hand, are not as well known in community—at least beyond the scope of their own outreach and programming. So police will have to work harder to find out who and where they are, what are they doing, and who to contact there.

A related challenge for police is to get all of these members of the safety and well-being web to understand and value the role of police in community problem-solving. Just as police agencies too often rely on traditional policing for their primary identity, the broader public, including other human and social services agencies, too frequently assume that police are only good for enforcement actions. Therefore, increasing transparency of the police agency, conducting outreach efforts with community partners, and engaging in regular and constructive communication (for example, using social media) with everyone in the community about the potential for collaboration with police on community problem-solving will strengthen the effectiveness of community policing.

Engaging Other Agencies and Organizations

If police data have highlighted a community problem that needs to be resolved, and police know which human and social service agencies and organizations would be most instrumental in helping resolve it, then it remains to engage them in the process of collaborating for community safety and well-being. If the police agency has invested significantly in developing the necessary rapport with these other agencies at both the front line and command levels, it may not be much of a challenge to engage them in community problem-solving. On the other hand, it more often occurs that sufficient rapport has not been developed; police and other agencies have too rarely partnered before, and when a problem looms that needs collaboration, the engagement process has to start from scratch.

At this point, it is appropriate for police to strategize about how to engage other agencies and organizations. They need to identify the agencies to be engaged; discern at which level police have good contact and rapport with them; anticipate how they may react when first approached to collaborate in community problem-solving; and develop an approach that will be most successful.

IN THE COMMUNITY

Using the Deputy Mayor to Leverage Engagement

When police in North Hastings (Ontario) saw patterns of theft in the down-town core, they asked the deputy mayor to invite businesses to attend at city hall in a meeting to discuss the problem. They also asked the local business improvement association to sponsor and promote the consultation. The deputy mayor sent a letter to business owners asking them to attend, and the association went door-to-door reinforcing the invitation. The net result was two meetings with good attendance among businesses. The businesses went on to play a large role in significantly reducing theft in their establishments. They applied crime prevention through environmental design to their stores, trained floor staff on how to confront suspected thieves, and supported a police investigation that demonstrated that theft of high-end products supported the drug trade.

Mobilizing Assets in High-Demand Neighbourhoods

It is quite a different challenge to get neighbours and residents of high-demand neighbourhoods mobilized to help out with community problem-solving. In the most marginalized neighbourhoods, these people are not likely to attend a meeting just because they receive a form letter from the deputy mayor or see a tri-fold brochure slipped under their apartment door by a social service agency. Chapter 1 reviewed some of the reasons why people in these neighbourhoods do not know and trust each other, and are not working well together. Therefore, the approach to mobilizing them, again, has to be strategic. Police have to ask themselves: "What will most likely get these people to meet in order to consider working together?" This is a place where the popular credibility and legitimacy of police provide the most effective mobilization strategy. In Waterloo, Ontario, police used recruit officers who were just back from basic constable training to canvass door-to-door in the neighbourhood. Sudbury police, working in a major drug neighbourhood, used their uniformed auxiliary to do the same. Turnout at the follow-up meetings, in both locations, was excellent.

Mobilization in high-demand neighbourhoods requires a number of special techniques, which will be expanded upon in Chapters 5 and 6, because it is in these neighbourhoods that people are most vulnerable and police have to respond most often. Furthermore, it is in these neighbourhoods that the most systemic issues (like poverty, addiction, mental health, and ignorance) require the largest investments from community partners in the safety and well-being web.

Creating and Supporting Partnerships

Presuming that police have helped the community identify the priority problems that need to be solved, and mobilized and engaged community partners to address them, it remains to support the partnership's initiatives. If police have fulfilled their community policing roles well, then, in general, they will also experience diminishing responsibility for implementation of problem-solving actions. But just being present to support those initiatives and provide encouragement to all players is very important.

The principal exception to that generalization relates to the primary role of police—that is, ensuring everyone's safety during problem-solving activities and initiatives. In the most marginalized, high-demand neighbourhoods, this may require targeted enforcement actions at the outset of problem-solving. That is because it is next to impossible to mobilize people who are afraid of perpetrators that operate in their neighbourhood. However, in any initiative it can mean providing security and oversight while neighbours and other community partners do the problem-solving work.

Collaborating

Collaboration is not something that agencies and organizations do easily, because our society has organized them around technical specializations, provided them with different enabling legislation, and virtually set them up to compete for diminishing public resources. However, experience with risk mitigation strategies has shown that the value added from collaboration exceeds the value of each agency's services offered in one-off relationships with beneficiaries of those services. This is a classic example of the whole being greater than the sum of its parts.

One approach to stimulating appropriate levels of collaboration is building on other collaborative initiatives that operate in the community. For example, the City of Toronto launched a collaborative risk mitigation initiative focused on hoarding and homelessness, based on experience with 15 agencies that have been collaborating to reduce acutely elevated levels of risk in one of that city's most marginalized and violent neighbourhoods.

A second step in fostering collaboration is finding specific champions and spokespersons among agency partners. The initiative will be most successful if it is promoted by two or more champions from different sectors, but with equal levels of credibility and legitimacy in the community. Collaboration is toughest to sell if it has only one spokesperson, no matter how persuasive he or she is. It will not get off the ground if it is only mandated, but no local spokesperson believes in it or will stand for it.

The final step in increasing and improving collaboration is, perhaps, the most difficult one of all: developing a strong basis for productive relationships among all of the team players. That only happens when knowledge and information about each agency's roles, resources, and commitments are openly and fully exchanged, thereby allowing partners to identify each other's roles in relationship to their own and learn to trust each other's competence to deal with the issues that will arise through the collaboration. Most partners in the safety and well-being web will expect police to be the least forthcoming and transparent. That is a good place for police to call for transparency and demonstrate how it is achieved. This is an area where police leadership and support for the ongoing initiative are key to the success of the whole enterprise.

Roles of Others in the Web

We have written a lot about the role of police in community policing. We can summarize their role as follows:

- Police must develop and sustain a level of legitimacy with the community they serve, which permits them to positively influence all the actors in the safety and well-being web.
- Police must track, analyze, map, and communicate to other partners in the web the priorities for community problem-solving.
- Police must know who all of the players are in the web, and understand and identify their resources, capabilities, mandates, and roles in community problem-solving.
- Police must develop the relationships and techniques needed to engage other human and social service providers in the web, and mobilize citizens, neighbours, and community-based organizations in the highest-demand neighbourhoods.
- Police must learn to support ongoing problem-solving initiatives of the team players in the web.
- Police must improve their capacities to collaborate with other community partners by increasing transparency, sharing responsibility and accountability, and framing and communicating common goals and support, equally, with every other partner in the enterprise.
- Police must constantly be ready to exert their unique mandate and capabilities in traditional policing in order to ensure that every other aspect

of community policing has a chance to succeed, and that all community partners are safe and secure in the process.

The roles of other agencies and organizations in the web are, of course, unique to their mandate, resources, capabilities, and practices. Whereas police have to discover those so that they will be more effective in leveraging them to meet the needs of community problem-solving, police do not necessarily have all of the leverage that may be required to get some of those players to "team play." That is where municipal government agencies come in. As the Expert Panel has emphasized:

> Police cannot initiate change on their own if the institutions and organizations in the wider safety and security web are not flexible. An effective transition by police to new models must therefore happen in concert with changes made by other actors, and it must be supported by governments.[24]

If nothing else, this chapter is about police no longer being seen, or held accountable, as the sole providers of safety and well-being in the community. Community policing is about community taking responsibility for its safety and well-being—in which enterprise police have unique and special roles to play, as do all other community partners. This model of community policing, as the panel reported, requires police to "acknowledge, adapt to, and leverage the specialized capabilities and resources in the safety and security web."[25] Municipal agencies are a key resource to help police do that leveraging.

With community policing becoming a whole-of-society strategy for achieving safety and well-being, police will occasionally need help in getting other team members to play. It is in this context that the Canadian Association of Chiefs of Police coined the phrase "higher order directive and imperative."[26] That is a role for municipal agencies, which oversee everything that happens in the community. Remember the case, above, of police asking the deputy mayor to invite local businesses to attend at city hall to talk about the problem of theft in their stores. That letter is, virtually, a higher-order directive and imperative for those businesses to come meet with police to talk about this problem. You may recall the earlier example of the Bancroft town council passing a resolution that says they expect everybody in Bancroft to do their part to develop and sustain safety and well-being for all. That is a higher-order directive and imperative that police can effectively use to leverage reluctant actors in the web to join the team play.

Both examples demonstrate the role of municipal agencies in enabling effective community policing. Both require good rapport and communication between police and municipal agencies. But that communication and rapport lies at the heart of community policing. Our frequent, earlier reflections on research relating to police legitimacy reinforce this point again and again. Police must develop and sustain excellent relationships with all of the community if community policing is going to succeed. We will close this chapter with another quote from the Expert Panel:

> As the complexity of police responses to crime grows, so too will the reliance upon resources, knowledge, and capabilities external to most police services. This type of resource interdependency ultimately requires police to become more adept at managing partnerships towards strategic goals and to become more open to shared roles in delivering safety and security in a cost-effective manner.[27]

CHAPTER SUMMARY

For community policing to succeed, all the team players in the safety and well-being web have to do the work of risk mitigation, prevention, and social development. Police can be the initiators and catalysts for the whole process, but before emergency response is required, non-police agencies, organizations, businesses, residents, and municipal agencies have to do most of the work. As indicated in the previous section, role clarity among all the team players is paramount for the success of community policing. Community policing is the work, and the result, of all of these team players contributing what they can to resolving community problems. Our understanding of community policing has to move beyond the old notions that it is simply something that police believe (for example, a philosophy) or do (for example, get out of their cruisers and relate to the people). If it is going to be anything meaningful, community policing has to resolve community issues with the net result that community people are safer and healthier.

REVIEW AND DISCUSSION QUESTIONS

1. Explain the difference between reported and unreported crime levels and the approximate proportion of each to which police respond in the average community.

2. Provide at least three common reasons why people do not report crimes in which they are victimized.

3. Give an approximate estimate of the proportion of police calls for service that do not entail chargeable offences.

4. Define risks and risk factors, and explain risk mitigation.

5. Define "protective factors." Provide a few examples.

6. Explain what is meant by social development.

7. Explain what social entrepreneurship is. Provide an example.

8. Define the safety and well-being web and describe who is in it.

9. Describe the four components of the safety and well-being framework and explain the role of police in the framework.

KEY TERMS

prevention, 100
protective factors, 100
risk factors, 99
risk mitigation, 98

NOTES

1   Hugh C Russell & Norman E Taylor, *New Directions in Community Safety: Consolidating Lessons Learned About Risk and Collaboration* (Toronto: Ontario Working Group on Collaborative, Risk-driven Community Safety and Well-being, Ontario Association of Chiefs of Police, April 2014), online: <http://www.oacp.on.ca/Userfiles/StandingCommittees/Community Policing/ResourceDocs/OWG%20New%20Directions%20in%20 Community%20Safety.pdf>.

2   Expert Panel on the Future of Canadian Policing Models, *Policing Canada in the 21st Century: New Policing for New Challenges* (Ottawa: Council of Canadian Academies, 2014) at xi.

3   Statistics Canada, "Police-Reported Crime Statistics in Canada, 2014," by Jillian Boyce, in *Juristat* 35:1, Catalogue No 85-002-X (Ottawa: Statistics Canada, 2015).

4   *Criminal Code*, RSC 1985, c C-46.

5   Ontario Provincial Police, *2011 Annual Report* (Orillia, Ont: 2012).

6   *Mental Health Act*, RSO 1990, c M.7.

7   J Durbin, E Lin & N Zaslavska, *Impact Study Final Report: A Study of Hospital Emergency Service Use, Crisis Service Delivery and Police Response After Mental Health System Enhancements* (Toronto: Health Systems Research and Consulting Unit, Centre for Addiction and Mental Health, 2010).

8   Canadian Mental Health Association, *Study in Blue and Grey: Police Interventions with People with Mental Illness: A Review of Challenges and Responses* (Vancouver: Canadian Mental Health Association, BC Division, 2003).

9   C Murphy, "Securitizing Canadian Policing: A New Policing Paradigm for the Post 9/11 Security State?" (2007) 32:4 Can J Sociology 449.

10 Community Oriented Policing Services, "Community Policing Defined" (Washington, DC: US Department of Justice, 2014), online: <http://www.cops.usdoj.gov/pdf/vets-to-cops/e030917193-CP-Defined.pdf>.

11 Irvin Waller, *Smarter Crime Control: A Guide to a Safer Future for Citizens, Communities, and Politicians* (Lanham, Md: Rowman & Littlefield, 2014).

12 Expert Panel on the Future of Canadian Policing Models, *supra* note 2 at xiv.

13 R van Steden et al, "The Many Faces of Nodal Policing: Team Play and Improvisation in Dutch Community Safety" (August 2013) Security J 1.

14   Ministry of Community Safety and Correctional Services, *Crime Prevention in Ontario: A Framework for Action* (Toronto: Ministry of Community Safety and Correctional Services, 2012) at 8-9.

15   World Health Organization, *WHO Multi-Country Study on Women's Health and Domestic Violence Against Women* (Geneva, Switzerland: World Health Organization, 2005).

16   See e.g. the Arizona Coalition to End Sexual & Domestic Violence website at <http://www.acesdv.org>.

17   Nova Scotia Domestic Violence Resource Centre, "Safety Planning for Women Who Are Abused," online: <http://nsdomesticviolence.ca/sites/default/files/publications/NFF_Safety_planning_for_women.pdf>.

18   Western University, "Neighbours, Friends & Families," online: <http://www.neighboursfriendsandfamilies.ca>.

19   Community Safety and Crime Prevention Committee, "Definitions of Words and Concepts That Are Important in Promoting Community Safety and Well-Being" (Toronto: Ontario Association of Chiefs of Police, 2016).

20   *Police Services Act*, RSO 1990, c P.15.

21   All of the Ontario Working Group documents and reports may be accessed on the Ontario Association of Chiefs of Police website: <http://www.oacp.on.ca/news-events/resource-documents/Ontario-working-group-owg>.

22   Expert Panel on the Future of Canadian Policing Models, *supra* note 2.

23   Edmonton Police Service, "Edmonton Police Service Neighbourhood Crime Map," online: <http://crimemapping.edmontonpolice.ca>.

24   Expert Panel on the Future of Canadian Policing Models, *supra* note 2 at xiv.

25   *Ibid* at xii.

26   Institute for Strategic International Studies, "Full Circle Community Safety: Changing the Conversation About Community Safety" (Ottawa: Canadian Association of Chiefs of Police, 2012).

27   Expert Panel on the Future of Canadian Policing Models, *supra* note 2 at xv.

PART III

Mobilization and Engagement

Problem-Solving and Problem-Oriented Policing

Officers from the Ottawa Police Service's Marine, Dive, and Trails Unit participate in the Great Canadian Shoreline Cleanup, an initiative spearheaded by the Vancouver Aquarium and the World Wildlife Fund. The purpose of the initiative is to remove items that present a hazard to swimmers and boaters in the Rideau Canal.

LEARNING OUTCOMES

Upon completion of this chapter, you should be able to:

- Explain what problem-oriented policing is, and how it relates to community policing
- Define and explain the four elements of the SARA problem-solving model
- Explain why the CAPRA problem-solving model is better suited than SARA for community policing
- Explain why police often oversimplify problem analysis
- Define community cohesion and its relationship to violence in high-demand neighbourhoods
- Explain the asset principle in community building
- Define a mobilization moment and explain its role in community policing

Introduction

Part III of this text, Mobilization and Engagement, is where we begin to get down to the mechanics of community policing. How is it actually done? What does it look like on the ground? Who does what to whom, and why? In this first chapter of Part III, we return to the topic of problem-solving and explore in greater depth the SARA, PARE, and CAPRA problem-solving models we introduced in Chapter 2. We discuss what we have learned about problem-solving through well over 20 years of problem-oriented policing. We also closely examine the logic models that underpin problem-solving of any kind—whether done by police or by others.

All of us engage in problem-solving of one kind or another on a daily basis. For most of us it is a relatively automatic process—that is, we do not spend a lot of time taking apart how we go about solving problems. We just do it! Now of course if the solutions we choose do not work, we may begin to question how we are going about solving our problems. Sometimes that review of our internal problem-solving process can lead to improvements that will give us a better solution next time. For example, we may decide we do not know enough about the problem to come up with an optimal solution, so we may decide to consult someone who is more experienced with it. That is the spirit in which we approach this chapter of the text. We want to examine how problem-solving is done in the context of community policing.

This chapter benefits from some very detailed examples of community problems that were solved by police and their community partners. We will tie our ideas about problem-solving processes to these very real, tangible examples. Through it all, we hope the reader will discover that nothing we say here is really new to anyone; most of us have already mastered problem-solving to an appreciable degree. So notwithstanding some scholars' tendencies to put labels on problem-solving and make it sound mysterious or specialized, it is really rooted in common sense. The challenge for police is to apply it to the process of solving community problems in partnership with a host of other actors from the safety and well-being web that we discussed in Chapter 4.

IN THE COMMUNITY

A Good Program but a Bad Solution

Many kids living within the boundaries of Toronto Police Service's 32 Division in the early 1990s really did not have much to do after school—except perhaps bow to peer pressure and run with youth gangs. To address this growing problem, Toronto Housing Authority and Toronto youth workers partnered with Lawrence Heights area teachers to develop a hockey program for at-risk kids attending grades 5 to 8. The targeted youth attended an after-school mentorship session with city workers where the workers would encourage discussions about respect, loyalty, teamwork, and friendship. Toronto police officers volunteered as mentors and coaches for the kids at a local arena where a weekly hockey game did its best to reinforce the kids' classroom sessions.

The efforts of city staff and police volunteers became known as the "Junior Blues Hockey Program," and the initiative fit well with the police service's efforts to bolster what they believed was the essence of community policing in marginalized neighbourhoods. Unfortunately, community support and interest in maintaining this partnership approach to the Junior Blues waned over the next ten years. Toronto Housing Authority and Toronto youth workers had other projects to run and besides, the Toronto Police Service was doing a fine job juggling resources and staffing to keep the initiative going. Or were they?

Analysis conducted in the summer of 2011 by supervisors overseeing the 32 Division Community Response Unit found that its officers, who were responsible for community initiatives and events for the entire community and not just Lawrence Heights, were contributing an inordinate number of staffing hours to keep the Junior Blues program going—so much so that it became necessary to commit on-duty time to maintain the program. The Toronto Police Service concluded that its commitment to the Junior Blues was unsustainable. Police efforts to recruit human resources and funding from new community partners were unsuccessful and the Junior Blues program was cancelled.

In 2013, community members in the Lawrence Heights area requested that the Junior Blues be brought back to life. Based on lessons learned and a critical analysis of what the police role could sustainably be, the Toronto Police Service took the lead in reinventing the program (but not running it) by:

- mobilizing human resource and financial commitments from the City of Toronto, including the donation of free ice time for weekly games;

- engaging community leaders within the Lawrence Heights neighbourhood to sustain ongoing program leadership and financial support;

- partnering with ProAction Cops & Kids for significant funding contributions to buy and maintain program equipment and storage space;

- securing flagship support from the Toronto Marlies AHL hockey team, which provided tickets and transportation to Marlies games two or three times per season; and

- recommitting its own members to a sustainable level of support for the initiative rather than assuming complete responsibility for it.

Consider the following questions:

1. What was the problem that this police partnership sought to resolve?
2. What solution did the partnership come up with?
3. Why was that solution unsustainable?
4. What adjustments would make it more sustainable?

A Review of Problem-Solving as It Relates to Policing

Police are problem-solvers. They go where people are facing problems or creating problems in order to resolve them. One of the main messages about community policing that we have been repeating in this text is about how limited the traditional policing model is for sustainable problem-solving. That presents police with a choice: they can either keep responding to repeat occurrences of the same problem, or investigate the problem in greater depth in hopes of finding some resolutions that will decrease those occurrences and in the process reduce harms and victimization and demand for police assistance.

Building on Problem-Oriented Policing

We introduced Professor Herman Goldstein's concept of problem-oriented policing in Chapter 2. The basic idea behind problem-oriented policing is that rather than continuing to respond to harmful incidents, police should look for patterns among those incidents to identify underlying problems. By solving these problems, police can reduce the incidence of harm and the demand for police assistance. Numerous police agencies throughout Canada, the United States, and the United Kingdom have applied Goldstein's principles and practices, with varying degrees of success. But their experiences have provided many lessons learned, which fit well in this text on community policing. They fit because at its root, community policing is about the efforts of police and all of their community partners in the safety and well-being web to solve the problems that create risks of harm and victimization. Among other things, Goldstein's problem-oriented policing achieved a significant redirection of police investment from merely fighting crime to solving problems, including problems that do not derive from criminal behaviour or chargeable offences.

Goldstein and his collaborators and followers make a distinction between problem-oriented policing and problem-solving. They see problem-oriented policing as bigger; it includes problem-solving behaviour, but it also influences how an entire police agency is organized, resourced, and managed. Problem-oriented policing could be considered a model for delivering policing services. In fact, one of Goldstein's collaborators, Michael S. Scott, founded and became chief of a police agency that has been described as a problem-oriented police service (Fort Lauderdale, Florida). Scott is worth noting in this context because he also completed an extensive analysis of the first 20 years of problem-oriented policing in the United States, Canada, and other countries. Throughout this chapter, we will refer to his observations about what has been learned about police and problem-solving.[1]

Identifying the Problem and Determining Whether It Falls Within the Mandate of Police

One of the best indications of underlying problems in a community is repeat occurrences. Chronic or recurrent incidents indicate patterns that will repeat without **profound interventions**—meaning interventions that involve more than just incident response and enforcement. Upon recognizing such patterns of incidents, the question arises as to what are the most appropriate interventions and who should implement them. Consider these questions as you read the On Patrol feature below.

ON PATROL

Partnering with Transit to Reduce Late-Night Noise

Police responded at 2:30 a.m. on a Friday night to a downtown street corner on which several storefronts and a bus stop were located. Above the storefronts were several apartments. The residents above the storefronts complained of disturbances, loud shouting, laughter, and disputes. Police encountered nine bar patrons waiting for a bus after being turned out when the bar closed at 2:00 a.m. Police advised them to quiet down and maintain the peace until their bus came to take them out of the city centre. The same thing happened on most Friday and Saturday nights, until the residents above the storefronts on that corner got angry and started demanding meetings with the chief of police in order to obtain more effective enforcement.

Police investigated the bar in collaboration with liquor licensing and bylaw officials to see whether they were over-serving or violating any other rules for their establishments; they were not. Police asked bar management to cooperate with police in advising patrons, at closing time, to be more mindful of the needs of local residents who were trying to sleep. But the problem persisted—to the point where police routinely deflected a two-officer patrol unit to attend at this street corner shortly after bar closing time every Friday and Saturday night. To ensure order and keep the noise down, officers had to stay with the bar patrons until their bus arrived.

Unsatisfied with this solution, police began to get creative. Recognizing a pattern of occurrences that argued for more profound solutions than advising inebriated patrons to keep the peace, police asked the bus company to reschedule the route so that the bus showed up as close to 2:00 a.m. as possible. The bus company was unable to reschedule the bus because of implications for other stops on the route. Undeterred, patrol officers invited a bus route supervisor for a Friday night ride-along so that he could experience the problem first-hand and help problem-solve.

---

profound interventions interventions that go deeper than incident response and enforcement

After the bus picked up that night's bar patrons, officers and the supervisor brainstormed solutions. The supervisor suggested they move the bus stop to the next block, in front of a two-storey bank building and a parking lot where any disturbances at the bus stop would be less likely to be heard by sleeping residents in the neighbourhood. The problem was solved.

Consider the following questions:

1. Do you think that twice-weekly dispatch of a two-officer patrol unit to attend at this corner for half an hour between 2:00 and 2:30 a.m. was a reasonable use of police resources and time? Explain.
2. How did police know that something more than simple enforcement was required to resolve this problem?
3. What was the role of community partners in resolving this problem?
4. What did it take to get community partners engaged in productive problem-solving?

Goldstein and Scott emphasize that police should limit this kind of analysis and problem-solving to those harmful behaviours or incidents that are of concern to police and that comprise a legitimate component of police business. Their point is that communities have many problems that need solving, but it is only appropriate for police to take the initiative and apply themselves to those problems that fall within their mandate. These include problems that threaten people's safety and security and that, if left unresolved, would require emergency response by police and other acute care providers (for example, mental health workers, children's aid, emergency medical services, or the fire department).

That same rule—solve only those problems that relate to police business—applies to the planned interventions to resolve them. Recall the example from the beginning of this chapter about the Toronto Police Service organizing a hockey program for at-risk youth. Their analysis of the crime and disorder issues created by the youth suggested that an after-school program would help the kids in a number of ways. By choosing to organize a program, police responded appropriately because troubles with youth are certainly within the police mandate and their responsibility. However, police launched the program using the volunteer and in-service time of officers and other police resources to deliver these services. That is where they strayed from the principle of doing things that relate to police business. Police are not in the business of athletic mentoring for youth, and they cannot sustain such an initiative. Their solution to this problem only worked when they figured out that other community partners had to be mobilized and engaged to manage and sustain the solution. Scott sums up this idea in the following passage:

> Under a problem-oriented policing approach, the police would recognize how functions like moral education, youth recreation and charity are integral to public safety, but would not see their role as one of

providing these services directly ... . The key for the police is first, to establish some sense of ownership or responsibility for a community problem and if the problem falls within the police mandate, either address it themselves, broker ownership to some other entity or, in some instances, merely refuse to accept ownership.[2]

This is where problem-oriented policing and community policing are complementary. Problem-oriented policing encourages police to identify and analyze problems that relate to the police mandate of providing safety and security for communities. Community policing provides police with some of the tools that are needed to enlist other community actors from the safety and well-being web in the processes of analyzing and resolving those community problems.

Tackling Gang Violence in London's (UK) Boroughs

The Metropolitan Police in the London borough of Waltham Forest piloted a problem-solving strategy for reducing gang violence. Gang violence has been a persistent problem for communities in this borough and in other London boroughs. The Metropolitan Police maintain a database on 250 active criminal gangs in London, 62 of which they classify as "high harm" gangs that commit two-thirds of all gang-related crime. In 2011, this group was responsible for 22 percent of all serious violence, 17 percent of all robberies, 50 percent of all shootings, and 14 percent of all rapes in London.

Called "Operation Connect," this strategy very clearly differentiated the roles of police and other community actors. Operation Connect started when police invited human and social service agencies to meet in order to discuss the gang violence problem in Waltham Forest. Hosting and chairing the discussion, police asked each agency representative to list on a piece of paper 100 names of those gang members in Waltham Forest who were most likely to be violent again. Then police shared their own list, at which point all of their guests realized that everyone in the meeting knew about the same people and shared common concerns about their inclination to be violent. Then police asked the human and social service providers to design customized services and supports for each of the 100 designated gang members should those individuals be convinced to leave gang life forever.

Armed with those custom-designed lists of services (plus all of their requisite tactical gear), police made direct contact with each of the 100 gang members and gave them a simple choice. They could choose to leave gang life forever and immediately become eligible to receive all of the social supports, or they could reject that offer, at which point the police promised relentless enforcement. The supports that gang members were offered included significant social investments, including finding a new place to live for the gang member and vulnerable members of his or her family, education, addictions treatment, employment assistance, counselling, and health care. In the pilot, half of the original 100 gang members chose to leave gang life and received these supports, yielding within the first year of the pilot a 25 percent reduction in gun crimes, a 13 percent decrease in robberies, and 5 percent decrease in knife crimes.

While active gang members were being engaged by police, members of the local borough council implemented an anti-gang program for young people who were vulnerable to the appeal of gang affiliation. The pilot was so successful that the Met replicated it in the rest of London's boroughs.

SOURCE: Adapted from Metropolitan Police, "Operation Connect Targets NE Gangs" (16 September 2011) *Total Policing*.

Consider the following questions:

1. Did police stick to their own role and mandate in solving this problem? Explain your answer.
2. How important were the Met's community partners in getting half of the violent gang members to choose to leave gang life forever?
3. What was the role of police in engaging these community partners?

The two most significant take-aways from Operation Connect are that police recognized the pattern of gang violence (persistent repeat occurrences) and chose to tackle the roots of the problem. But at the same time, they recognized that their mandate and capabilities did not extend into the realm of social services and supports. Accordingly, they limited their role to engaging other agencies and making direct contact with the gang members while increasing enforcement actions against those gang members who chose to remain engaged in their criminal activity. Obviously, the police understood the sociological and psychological roots of the gang violence problem. But they also clearly limited their own investment and involvement to those actions that were appropriate to the police agency, while leaving the balance of the work to other agencies in the safety and well-being web.

The Assess-Plan-Act Sequence of Problem-Solving

How do you decide what to wear when you get out of bed in the morning? If you are like me, you first think about what you are going to be doing during the day, who you are going to be seeing, and what you want those people to think about you. If, for example, you are going to spend the best part of the day in classrooms, then you will certainly want to wear something comfortable; but you may also want to wear something that expresses your own sense of style, while not straying too far from style standards and values shared among your classmates. In contrast, if you have a job interview or an important meeting today, maybe you will want to be a little more buttoned-down than you would be if you spent most of the day studying. The point of this example is that deciding what to wear first thing in the morning is a lot like identifying and analyzing problems to be solved through community policing. You have to assess the circumstances of your day, try on some looks, examine them in the mirror to see if they fulfill your expectations, and if they don't, try another look until you get the right result.

One reason for using the dressing analogy is to simply demonstrate that problem-solving does not require expert knowledge—all of us engage in problem-solving on a daily basis. But in the context of community policing, we want to unpack problem-solving a little more and break it down into a logical, stepwise process. The Ontario Use-of-Force Model depicts just such a breakdown in the bullseye of Figure 5.1.

FIGURE 5.1 Ontario Use-of-Force Model

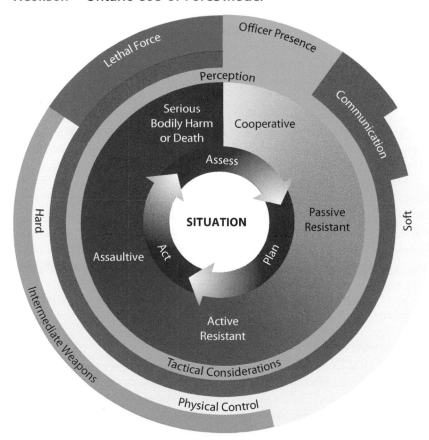

SOURCE: MA Hoffman, C Lawrence & G Brown, "Canada's National Use-of-Force Framework for Police Officers" (2004) 71:10 The Police Chief 125. Canadian Association of Chiefs of Police. Used with permission.

The bullseye shows that when officers arrive at the scene of a call for service, they have to immediately assess the situation for any threats to the people or property at the scene, or to themselves. Some of that assessment process commenced at the point where the officers received the call from dispatch to attend the scene—based on whatever information about the situation that dispatch picked up in the call for service.

That assessment guides officers in planning their approach to dealing with subjects at the scene. If, upon arrival, they do not detect any significant threats, they may choose to use communication tactics to defuse any problems or disputes in the situation. If, on the other hand, there are some real threats of violence toward officers, anyone else at the scene, or property, officers may rapidly escalate to harder forms of physical control over the situation. That is the assess-plan-act sequence of problem-solving. In this case, it has been applied to the problem of deciding how much force to use in a given situation.

A modified version of that bullseye appears in Ontario's Mobilization & Engagement Model of Community Policing, as shown in Figure 5.2. That bullseye is almost the same as the one used in the Ontario Use-of-Force Model; the only difference is that whereas the Use-of-Force Model presumes that police are doing the assessing, planning, and acting, the community policing model says that those functions are to be carried out by community members and police working in partnership. The difference between these two bullseyes reflects the differences between problem-oriented policing as conceived and promoted by Goldstein and Scott, and community policing. In the Use-of-Force Model, police are doing the assess-plan-act. Similarly, in problem-oriented policing, police are principally responsible for identifying and analyzing the problem to be resolved; and they limit their efforts in resolving the problem to those actions that fit the policing mandate.

In contrast, Ontario's community policing model stresses primary roles for actors in the safety and well-being web who work with police to ensure safety and well-being for all. As Scott said, "Problem-oriented policing primarily emphasizes the substantive societal problems the police are held principally responsible for addressing," like safety and security, whereas "community policing primarily emphasizes having the police engage the community in the policing process," like public consultations for establishing policing priorities.[3]

One of the first things police and community partners assess is whether they are dealing with a problem in a relatively high- or low-demand neighbourhood. In fact, that assessment process will probably be quite different in these two neighbourhoods. In a high-demand neighbourhood (a red zone neighbourhood), police will most likely not discover many neighbourhood partners to share this responsibility with them. In a low-demand neighbourhood (a green zone neighbourhood), police will probably find many community members who have already thoroughly assessed the problem and have some proposed solutions. You will recall in Chapter 1 that this distinction led the architects of Ontario's community policing model to distinguish between mobilization in the high-demand neighbourhoods and engagement in the low-demand neighbourhoods.

FIGURE 5.2   Ontario's Mobilization & Engagement Model of Community Policing

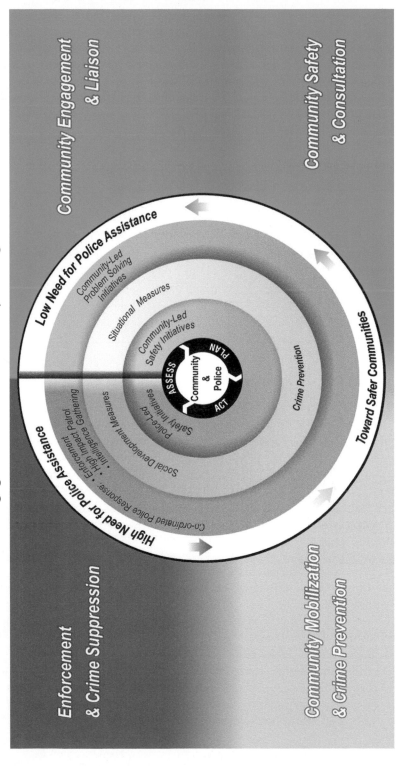

To summarize, community policing benefits significantly from problem-solving techniques and practices learned through the problem-oriented policing movement. Community policing is definitely about solving problems. But community policing differs from problem-oriented policing to the extent that it emphasizes the roles and responsibilities of everyone in the safety and well-being web working in partnership (including police). Further, community policing focuses on police leveraging all of those partnerships to address the community's priority problems.

CHECK YOUR UNDERSTANDING

1. What is problem-oriented policing?
2. How does problem-oriented policing differ from community policing?
3. How can police identify problems that would benefit from problem-oriented policing?
4. Communities have many problems and police cannot solve them all. Whether applying problem-oriented policing or problem-solving in general, police should limit their involvement to what kinds of problems and solutions?

Standard Planning Models and SARA, PARE, and CAPRA

During the Second World War, British and American engineers developed a logical, step-wise process for inventing and producing new technologies. Known as "technology assessment," their process has become the mainstay for contemporary planning models used in many areas, including community planning and social development. It is this process that is reflected in the common-sense approach to choosing what clothes to wear every morning when you wake up, and it forms the basis of the assess-plan-act sequence of problem-solving that we have just covered. Technology assessment has the following standard steps:

1. Analyze the problem to be resolved.
2. Develop some objectives and benchmarks for the final solution to the problem.
3. Examine alternative solutions and pick the solution that is most likely to achieve those objectives.
4. Apply the chosen solution.
5. Evaluate whether the chosen solution meets the objectives and benchmarks.
6. If necessary, try another solution to see if it will work better. Repeat the process until the best solution is discovered.

Problem-solving in community policing relies on these same standard steps, although some of them may be combined or they may be labelled differently.

Community policing and problem-oriented policing in Canada have adapted the technology assessment approach to problem-solving. Most agencies claiming to do problem-oriented policing teach their officers SARA. Recall from Chapter 2 that SARA stands for Scanning, Analysis, Response, and Assessment. If we apply the SARA approach to our earlier analogy of deciding what clothes to wear, each step in the process might look something like this:

1. Scanning: "I want to wear the right clothes for what I'm going to do today."
2. Analysis: "What am I going to do today and who am I going to be seeing?"
3. Response: "I should pick something buttoned-down for that job interview—maybe a suit."
4. Assessment: "Now, to look in the mirror and see if that works!"

Another version of that same sequence of steps is PARE: Problem identification (what should I wear?), Analysis (what will I do today and who will I see?), Response (I've got a job interview, so a suit might be best), and Evaluation (how do I look in the mirror?).

The RCMP added two steps to this same sequence to create the CAPRA problem-solving model. These added steps make their approach particularly useful in a community policing context. Each step is described below.

1. Clients: identify people with a stake in the problem or the solution to the problem
2. Acquiring and analyzing information: acquire and analyze relevant information to help resolve an incident and to investigate possible offences
3. Partnerships: engage others in the safety and well-being web to help solve the problem
4. Response: choose a solution
5. Assessment: see if the solution works

The most common approach among Canadian police agencies is SARA, so we will review it in detail. But we will also expand on CAPRA because in some ways it is better suited than SARA for community policing.

SARA

SARA emerged in 1987 as a proposed problem-solving approach to be applied by problem-oriented policing agencies.[4] It was designed to complement Herman Goldstein's problem-oriented policing as applied in controlled experiments on crime reduction in Newport News, Virginia.

SCANNING

This first step involves recognizing that there is a pattern of occurrences suggesting an underlying problem or problems that need to be resolved before the occurrences will decrease. Applied to problem-oriented policing, these would be problems that are of concern to the public, but also fit within the mandate of police. Scanning also includes an effort to summarize the consequences of these problems, because knowing the consequences helps establish some objectives and benchmarks for problem-solving. Notice that in completing this first step, we still do not know what created the problem or problems in the first place. So we cannot, upon completion of scanning, say much about proposed solutions. Scanning merely helps us isolate the problem and set up some acceptable standards for resolving it.

Scanning a Drug House Problem

This scenario, based on a true story,[5] will be presented in four parts to correspond with SARA. In this part, you will be presented with the facts of the problem. In later parts, you will be guided through the analysis, response, and assessment of the response to the problem. Consider each part and the questions following each part before moving to the next.

Irate neighbours of a single street address in Southwestern Ontario demanded that the chief of police train and empower them to patrol their own neighbourhood. This neighbourhood of early 20th-century brick homes, within walking distance of the downtown core, was slowly being bought up and restored by young couples. But a particular two-storey home, owned by an absentee landlord, threatened the whole neighbourhood because of the high incidence of drug use and attendant crime and disorder (drug trafficking, sex trade activity, and disturbances) that occurred there. Police admitted that this single address had accounted for 16 percent of their calls for service, per year, over the past 15 years. Citizens' demands for more rigorous enforcement forced police to examine these patterns and consider underlying problems. Police knew that the home was a base for drug using and dealing. Users would phone their dealer and arrange to meet a "mule" (a person who assists a dealer by delivering drugs to buyers and returning the money to the dealer) at the address. Frequently, the mule was an addicted woman who would provide sexual favours at the address in exchange for some of the drug.

Scanning disclosed that the house was occupied by five tenants—all of whom suffered from mental health and addictions issues and were in the care of various provincial and federal social assistance programs. Frequently, these drug and sex exchanges would take place within the confines of one of the five apartments. Police told stories of chasing various dealers, users, sex trade workers, and others into the house and having them disappear somewhere inside.

The five tenants of this house were incapable of policing their own living spaces, much less the whole house. There was no responsible supervision in the house; no secure ingress or egress; no smoke or carbon monoxide detectors; no fire suppression systems; no phones; and no locks on the five tenants' apartment doors. The landlord, who lived in a nearby suburb, received direct payments from the rent portion of his tenants' monthly social assistance allotments. As a consequence, there was no accountability mechanism between the landlord and the tenants. (Rent money usually gives a tenant some leverage for demanding safe and healthy living conditions from landlords.) Upon further scanning, police discovered that this address was listed on municipal records as a licensed lodging house. The landlord paid a fee to the municipality every year to renew that licence, and the renewal was supposed to be contingent upon, among other things, annual inspections by bylaws officials for safety and other standards. These inspections had not been done.

CHECK YOUR UNDERSTANDING

1. What is the pattern of occurrences that led police to scan for deeper, underlying problems?
2. What underlying problems were disclosed when police applied scanning at this address?
3. From the police standpoint, what should be the objectives of problem-solving at this address?
4. From the standpoint of other agencies, what should be the objectives of problem-solving?

ANALYSIS

There is an obvious blurring between scanning and analysis in the SARA model. Once we dive into trying to understand the conditions that underlie a pattern of occurrences, it is not easy to say when scanning stops and analysis begins. However, drawing a clear line between scanning and analysis is not important. What is important is to continue analyzing deeply enough that we can be fairly sure that our proposed solutions will have the desired effect and that they will be sustainable. Analysis includes discovering all of the actions and conditions attendant to the problem; deciding what kinds of data and information are needed to get to the roots of the problem; and examining how the problem and the underlying conditions have been dealt with to date. Usually, through this process, we will also discover other agencies, organizations, and people with some connection to the problem and its roots. These parties will need to be brought into the scope of the analysis and the proposed solutions.

Analyzing the Roots of the Drug House Problem

A police constable took some of the irate neighbours with him to visit the municipal bylaw office that issued the lodging house licences. The constable called for the meeting and introduced the neighbours. The neighbours described in detail the problems they had been experiencing with this drug house over the years. After some protracted discussions and a little soul-searching, the municipal bylaws officials admitted that the lodging house licence was renewed without inspecting the house, principally because the bylaw officer responsible for inspections was afraid to attend there. The constable immediately arranged an inspection blitz of the address with police, fire department, and bylaws officials attending at the same time. As well as all of the safety and security infractions, they discovered an attic trap door above a closet on the second floor. This was the space into which people fled when police responded at this address. The attic was the classic "drug den," with drug paraphernalia and mattresses thrown about the floor on which users could more comfortably cater to their addictions.

With a list of bylaw infractions, the constable and citizens once again met with municipal officials and discovered that current lodging house bylaws permitted the city to order a landlord to correct the infractions, and if they refused to do so, the city could file civil charges against the landlord, shut down the house, make the corrections, and charge the landlord for all of those costs on his annual tax bill. Of course, in order to shut down the house, the city would have to come up with alternative housing for the five disabled and dysfunctional tenants.

The constable arranged for some new recruit officers to canvass other addresses around the drug house to see if they could get other neighbours involved. They interviewed neighbours on both sides of the drug house. A small mom-and-pop grocery operated on one side; a 90-year-old widow lived on the other. Owners of the first-floor grocery, who had a small baby and lived upstairs, complained to police that drug dealers, users, and sex trade workers were regularly using the pay telephone affixed to the side of their building to arrange drug deals and solicit; so they had the phone company remove the phone. That only led to various unsavoury and intimidating people coming into the store and demanding to use the proprietor's behind-the-counter phone. So they asked the phone company to come back and re-install the exterior phone.

The 90-year-old widow claimed she was a prisoner in her own house. She was afraid of the five tenants who were her neighbours. She said whenever she walked to the grocery to get a newspaper or a bottle of milk, one of the tenants, who was schizophrenic and was frequently off his medications, would confront and threaten her. So she stopped going there.

This particular tenant seemed to be primarily responsible for much of the disorder at this address. So the constable and his team of irate neighbours visited the mental health care provider to find out what kind of supervision this tenant should be under. They discovered a situation much like that involving the lodging house bylaw inspector. The social worker who was supposed to be supplying and supervising the administration of medication for the schizophrenic tenant was afraid to attend this address. So she gave the tenant money and asked him to use public transit once a month to come to her office, across town, in order to pick up his medication. Quite obviously that system was not working.

CHECK YOUR UNDERSTANDING

1. How had problems at this address been dealt with up to the time the police decided to apply SARA to try to resolve them?
2. What were the consequences of these past efforts to deal with the problems at this address?
3. What did the analysis reveal about the role of social service agencies and organizations in addressing the problems?
4. What was the police constable's role in engaging these agencies and organizations, and what was the role of the irate neighbours?

There are some important points to note about the above analysis. First, consistent with a community policing and problem-oriented policing approach, police focused only on those issues and actions that were appropriate to their role and mandate. Safety and security were their responsibility, and they applied SARA in order to increase safety and security. Second, only moderate effort was required to apply SARA; it required just one enterprising constable and a few new recruits to do this work. Granted, the constable had to have good investigative skills, but most experienced officers do. Third, this officer used his influence as a police officer to get in the front door of those agencies and organizations that needed to be engaged to deal more constructively with this problem. Finally, he did not need to carry the arguments with other agency people because he relied on the interests and concerns of the irate neighbours to express their anger, frustration, fear, and discomfort caused by the disturbances at this address. That is good community policing.

RESPONSE

The response step involves choosing viable solutions to the underlying problems. The challenge for police agencies is to stick with those measures that are appropriate to the police agency and engage and support other actors in the safety and well-being web sufficiently so that they do their part too.

Responding to the Drug House Problem

Police mounted surveillance on the drug house. That led to the arrest of a small-time drug dealer who forced his girlfriend into the sex trade to support his own drug habits and chosen lifestyle. The same operation shut down some mid-level suppliers of crack cocaine, who were operating out of a house eight blocks away from the drug house.

Accompanied by the constable, irate neighbours demanded that the municipality charge the landlord with bylaw infractions, shut down the house, retrofit it, and pass the costs on to the landlord on his tax bill. The city refused because it did not have alternative housing for the five disabled tenants. So the constable arranged a meeting for the neighbours with a social service agency that provided temporary shelter for women. There were no women tenants in the drug house, but this particular agency was the only one in the temporary shelter business that agreed to help police and neighbours with this problem. Once again, the officer booked the meeting and made introductions; the neighbours carried the arguments and provided the explanations. The agency agreed to help by reaching out to all other agencies in the region that provided any kind of temporary housing, and convene them to discuss the problem. At the meeting, temporary housing officials agreed to divide the five tenants among themselves. That made it possible for the neighbours to go back to the city and ask that it retrofit the house and act against the landlord. The city responded by finding and installing a responsible housing supervisor; installing hall phones on both floors; installing steel doors and door frames on all apartments (with locks); securing ingress and egress; and installing smoke detectors, alarms, and fire-suppressing equipment. The landlord was required to pay the costs and fines.

One of the biggest systemic flaws that underpinned the problem of this drug house was a weak lodging house bylaw. That led a couple of the irate neighbours to research such bylaws from other, neighbouring municipalities and draft a new one for this city. The constable and neighbours engaged a local councillor to sponsor the motion, and a new, more stringent bylaw was passed by city council.

CHECK YOUR UNDERSTANDING

1. What solutions were implemented by police?
2. What solutions were implemented by other actors in the safety and well-being web?

3. What was the principal role of police in getting all of these other agencies, organizations, and individuals to play a constructive role in problem-solving?

ASSESSMENT

The assessment step involves comparing outcomes of the applied problem resolution to the objectives and benchmarks set out in the scanning step. There are many ways to do that, depending on the nature and scope of the problem. But without going into details about quantitative and qualitative data assessments here, it is important to note that comparing outcomes to expectations is important for everyone involved in the solutions, not least because frequently, adjustments have to be made in order to maximize outcomes. Further, desirable outcomes need to be sustained and only constant monitoring and assessment can inform actors in the safety and well-being web when something else has to be done to keep everyone safe and healthy.

Assessment of Solutions to the Drug House Problem

Police cleared five drug dealers from the wider neighbourhood. Addicts no longer reside at the residence. The house and grounds meet all municipal property standards. Neighbours have a good and helpful relationship with tenants at this address, who need various kinds of personal supports and social assistance. Neighbouring residences and the street itself have strengthened their security (called **target hardening** in crime prevention language) with improved street lighting and motion-sensitive residential lighting. Living conditions for the tenants have improved markedly. Police calls for service to this address have decreased by 75 percent. But police still look in on the address from time to time, to monitor what is going on and to see whether any new supports are needed to sustain these positive outcomes.

CAPRA

CAPRA stands for Clients, Acquiring and analyzing information, Partnerships, Response, and Assessment. You can see the parallels to SARA, where CAPRA's Acquiring and analyzing information comprise SARA's Scanning and Analysis. But the RCMP adds two new elements to this problem-oriented policing model: Clients and Partnerships. That makes it more suitable for community policing than either SARA or PARE.

As mentioned in Chapter 1, community policing is all about developing social capital in a neighbourhood that is marginalized. Chapter 2 reinforced

---

target hardening efforts taken through situational measures to strengthen the security of people, places, or things the observation that the traditional model of policing, which revolves around enforcement, has proved inadequate to either develop or sustain community safety and well-being. However, traditional police tactics are necessary in an emergency situation where there are significant threats to personal safety or property. But enforcement is insufficient for building a community that takes good care of itself. For that, the neighbourhood needs social capital: people in the neighbourhood connecting with each other and respecting each other sufficiently to recognize common goals for safety and well-being, and working together to resolve any emerging community problems.

As a consequence, community policing is about connecting people to each other, mobilizing those who are afraid to deal with community problems or are distracted by their own issues, engaging a wide variety of human and social service agencies to address issues collaboratively, and basically reweaving the social fabric, which is everybody's safety net when there are problems in the community. That is why the RCMP's use of Clients and Partnerships adds so much value to the standard planning model. With CAPRA, they are acknowledging the importance of social capital, social cohesion, and collaboration. If police do not acknowledge the importance of those qualities, then they too often end up owning the problem and being held accountable for the solutions. If that is not bad enough, any solutions the police bring usually end up being unsustainable because the community does not own them. This creates a vicious circle of repeat occurrences with significant levels of harm and victimization, to say nothing of the cost to society and the criminal justice system.

IDENTIFYING THOSE WHO ARE MOST AFFECTED BY THE PROBLEM

As CAPRA suggests, identifying key actors in the safety and well-being web surrounding any community problem starts right at the outset of scanning and analysis. One of the most useful rules of thumb is to look for those individuals, families, businesses, organizations, and agencies that are most directly affected by the problem. These include the victims, people who care about the victims, and those who are in a position to help resolve the problem. All of them are affected by the problem; hence all of them are essential to finding sustainable solutions.

Take a look at those who were most directly affected by the drug house problem examined earlier in this chapter. At the outset, you may recall, a group of angry neighbours of that drug house confronted the chief of police with a demand that they be trained and equipped to patrol their own neighbourhood—with the implication that they thought police were not doing a good enough job at that. We can make two important observations about this group. First, they are profoundly affected by the crime and disorder associated with the drug house in their neighbourhood. Second, they are connected to each other and they are addressing the problem. In other words, there already exists, at least among these neighbours, a degree of social capital and community cohesion that the police can build on to find more permanent solutions to this problem.

Rather than be defensive when these angry neighbours confronted the chief, police judiciously solicited their cooperation in finding more permanent solutions to the problem. That was followed by police using some new recruit officers to canvass other addresses around the drug house to see if they could get other neighbours involved. That helped too. Remember the story of the 90-year-old widow who felt imprisoned in her own home? Officers found a neighbour, down the street and around the corner from her address, who worked across town in a seniors' home. She was very familiar with the kinds of personal and social issues some seniors face. So it took very little effort to get her to agree to assist this particular senior whenever she felt like she needed some support in going to the grocery store for her bottle of milk or newspaper. That is social capital triggered by police; notice how it made a vulnerable senior safer in a potentially dangerous environment.

The irate neighbours were key to resolving this problem. Look how police relied on them telling their own stories about the drug house in their neighbourhood to leverage a whole raft of other agencies and organizations, including four or five temporary housing agencies, municipal agencies and bylaws officials, mental health officials, social assistance workers, and a municipal councillor.

Analyzing the Neighbourhood

An important part of scanning and analyzing the problem to be resolved is the process of learning about the neighbourhood. Who lives, works, and plays there? Are they aware of the problem? What do they think about the problem? Are they willing to get involved in problem-solving? If a bunch of neighbours come to police and demand that their problems be addressed, that analysis is relatively easy—as in the case of the drug house neighbourhood. With the notable exception of the drug house, that was an upwardly mobile, middle-class neighbourhood. So that case did not require a lot of effort by police to analyze the neighbourhood and figure out where the neighbourhood assets were. The job is a little tougher in a high-demand neighbourhood where people are less inclined to worry about anything other than their own personal problems, and where there is very little community cohesion.

Sources of Useful Data and Information

There are a lot of ways to find out useful things about the neighbourhood in which there is a significant community problem to be resolved. Patrol officers who are called to the neighbourhood will certainly have a useful perspective. However, it is important to realize that their impressions may be more negative than those of others because usually these officers are not called to the neighbourhood unless someone has been harmed or victimized and offences have been committed. Hence, it is also useful to consult other officers who may have a different perspective on the neighbourhood.

In the drug house example, police used new recruit officers to canvass homes near the house, in order to get other neighbours' perspectives. But another approach would be to use what sociologists refer to as **gatekeepers**. These are local community members such as grocers, faith leaders, municipal councillors, school administrators or teachers, community activists, and others who make it their business to know what is going on in the neighbourhood. Often, they are aware of who in the neighbourhood could be a useful asset in resolving community problems.

Just as police have some knowledge about the neighbourhood because they are frequently called for assistance there, front-line workers from human and social service agencies that work in the neighbourhood have a tremendous amount of useful information that can be brought to bear on problem-solving. However, obtaining their information requires that the police develop a rapport and relationship with these front-line workers and their supervisors in their home agencies, which supports this kind of information exchange. Developing such relationships is a sound investment in productive community policing.

Police Data and Other Social Service Data

Police data on calls for service and occurrences can reveal a lot about a neighbourhood. But of course it requires a qualified crime analyst to get the most meaning out of that data. You saw in Chapter 4 how those data, turned into a map, can help police and other agencies focus on elements of a neighbourhood that deserve extra attention and investment in problem-solving.

Human and social service agencies also have databases about neighbourhoods. These databases often include the levels of demand for assistance, types of assistance provided, demographics of client populations, and other parameters, which can tell a lot about the nature of problems to be solved, as well as the experiences of agencies that should probably be engaged in the problem-solving process. Therefore, it is prudent for front-line patrol officers to establish a relationship with front-line workers from other agencies when they encounter them in the neighbourhood. Similarly, it is helpful if command officers take some responsibility for outreach to executives of those same agencies in order to talk about opportunities to collaborate on problem-solving, as well as encouraging front-line workers from all agencies to become acquainted with one another and look for opportunities to work together on behalf of the community.

---

gatekeepers a term sociologists use to refer to community members who know the most about what is going on in a neighbourhood, and on whom others can rely for that kind of information

Crime and Disorder

Crime and disorder in a community, as documented by police, certainly indicate that the community has problems that need to be resolved. In the end, however, crime and disorder are merely symptoms of more profound problems in a community. Think back to the problem of the noisy, inebriated people disturbing the peace at 2:00 a.m. on a downtown street corner. The traditional policing response would be to insist they keep the peace, and if they did not do that, hold them accountable. The more fundamental problem, and the source of a solution, has to do with the decision to put the bus stop in front of a bar in the first place. That was not good route planning. But it was easy to fix once police and the bus company figured that out.

A similar problem occurred in Toronto in an area known as the "Entertainment District," so known because of its nightlife and many night clubs. The problem came about as a result of a planning decision. Municipal council had noted that the area was undergoing a period of high-rise condominium construction that was expected to take five to six years, and voted to allow entertainment establishments to be set up in order to bring more life and income to this old warehouse district. The resulting bus stop problem occurred in spades on Queen Street West. In fact, it took three Toronto Police Service divisions and all the tactical and specialized units to patrol that area, three nights per week, when thousands of inebriated young people exited the clubs at closing time. Significant harms (shootings, stabbings, assaults, etc.) prevailed all because of a bad land use planning decision made by council and supported by land use developers and entertainment club owners. The traditional policing response could not make this area safer or reduce these harms and victimizations. It required changes and enforcement in liquor licensing and entertainment density bylaws—a public policy strategy—to fix this problem.

There are three key lessons to be learned from these anecdotes. First, crime and disorder are the indicators of problems, but not the roots of problems. Second, traditional policing is not a significant deterrent or a sustainable solution to these more profound problems. Third, police need to scan and analyze the problem far more deeply, and do more than simply look for quicker, more efficient ways to do enforcement. They have to look past their own roles and responsibilities for safety and security to the more profound roots of crime and disorder in the first place. When they do that, they will no doubt discover at least two things: first, the most viable solutions may not include much of a role for police, and second, a whole host of other actors in the safety and well-being web need to be brought into problem-solving.

Using SARA to Resolve a Booze Can Problem

The city of Toronto has vibrant entertainment districts and nightlife. Hundreds of liquor licensed clubs and lounges are found throughout the city, and the Toronto Police Service often has its hands full enforcing regulatory compliance and the requisite runoff of issues related to alcohol abuse—like excessive noise, unruly and intoxicated persons, and violence.

In the late 1990s and early 2000s, police saw a rapid increase in illegal and unlicensed after-hours clubs, more commonly known as "booze cans." Popping up all over the city, they catered to an all-night crowd that didn't know when to call it quits. Widespread problems associated with booze cans, including violent crime, significantly increased demands on police.

Specialized plainclothes units identified booze can locations and applied various tactics to shut them down. Undercover officers would enter the premises, learn as much as they could about the operation, purchase and consume liquor, and then help prepare *Provincial Offences Act*[6] search warrants to support a follow-up raid, the seizure of liquor, and the laying of applicable *Liquor Licence Act*[7] charges. But these efforts were time consuming and, in some cases, dangerous. Analysis of the management and locations of booze cans revealed that an operator charged one night would simply absorb losses related to liquor seizures and relatively minor *Liquor Licence Act* fines and set up shop in another leased location the next night. Profits far outweighed the risks of running an illegal after-hours club.

Toronto police eventually rethought their enforcement strategies by using the SARA model of problem-solving. Rather than simply targeting the operators of these leased booze can locations, police partnered with Toronto Fire Services, City of Toronto bylaw officials, and the insurance industry to crack down on the landlords who leased their properties for these illegal purposes. Police conducted undercover operations, seized liquor, and charged booze can operators under the authority of the *Liquor Licence Act*. Toronto Fire Services addressed compliance relating to municipal and provincial fire codes, including overcrowding standards. City bylaw officials addressed business licensing and anti-smoking and property insurance standards. Finally, the insurance industry, in partnership with financial institutions, worked to terminate insurance and mortgage agreements for the most egregious offenders.

Landlords eventually took notice and became increasingly hesitant to support the operation of these illegal clubs. The booze cans became a thing of the past as their potential profits no longer outweighed the risks of engaging in illegal business.

Consider the following questions:

1. Initially, police tried traditional enforcement; how well did that work?

2. What made their second strategy more effective?

3. How did SARA help police come up with a better solution?

Types and Levels of Risks

We introduced the idea of risk, or risk factors, in Chapter 4. Recall that we defined risk factors as negative characteristics or conditions in individuals, families, communities, or society that may increase social disorder, crime or fear of crime, or the likelihood of harms or victimization to persons or property. Obviously then, any attempt to reduce crime, social disorder, or fear of crime and social disorder, much less the actual harms or victimization that result from them, has to reduce those risk factors. That means it is necessary to first identify the predominant risk factors that people in the neighbourhood are experiencing. In the drug house case, the biggest risk factor for the neighbours was the house itself because of all the offensive behaviours that took place there. But behind offensive behaviours lie more risk factors that are closer to the roots of the problem, such as addictions, mental health issues, and anti-social behaviour stemming from negative life experiences. In introducing the concept of risk factors, Ontario's Ministry of Community Safety and Correctional Services gave examples such as those in Table 5.1.

In doing the neighbourhood analysis, police could simply look at the offensive behaviours that occur in and around the drug house and they might come up with some strategies to reduce those offensive behaviours through improved enforcement. But a deeper analysis shows the kinds of risk factors

TABLE 5.1 Examples of Risk Factors

Individual	Family/Peers	Community	Society
Behavioural problems	Abuse	Crime in area	Cultural norms supporting violence
Poor educational achievement	Few economic resources	Few social services	Social disorganization
Poor mental health	Neglect	High poverty concentration	Negative media messaging
Prior criminal behaviour	Negative parenting	Poor housing	
Racism/ marginalization	Poor peer influences		
Victimization/ abuse	Parent/sibling criminality		

SOURCE: Ministry of Community Safety and Correctional Services, *Crime Prevention in Ontario: A Framework for Action*, completed in partnership with the Ontario Association of Chiefs of Police (Toronto: Ministry of Community Safety and Correctional Services, 2012) at 9. Courtesy of OACP.

listed above in the ministry's table. There is not much that police can do about those. So many other agencies have to be involved in solving this problem. An even deeper analysis shows more profound risk factors surrounding the drug house. These included the municipality's failure to enforce a lodging house bylaw, which was weak to start with, and a mental health agency's failure to fulfill its mandate to provide medication for the schizophrenic tenant and supervise its administration. As these examples show, effective community policing and problem-solving has to dive as deep as possible into analysis of the problem.

Vulnerable Groups

Analysis of the problem also involves identifying vulnerable groups—that is, those individuals, families, and groups that are most vulnerable to the harms and victimization that come from the risk factors. Clearly, the irate neighbours of the drug house perceived themselves as vulnerable to what was happening at the drug house. Further analysis of this community problem also showed that the young couple with a baby who owned the grocery store were vulnerable to risk factors at the house. So was the 90-year-old widow next door. Were there any other vulnerable people?

What about the five disabled and dysfunctional tenants of the drug house? Because their home had no secure ingress or egress, bad people were constantly coming through there for a variety of harmful and illegal purposes. The schizophrenic tenant who went off his medications because his social worker would not deliver them or supervise their administration was vulnerable—and of course, in turn, he made others vulnerable. What about the municipality itself? Start with the costs of policing. The drug house accounted for 16 percent of all calls for service in that part of town, making the municipality and all of its taxpayers financially vulnerable. A good problem analysis will identify all of these vulnerable groups in some detail in order to give the problem-solving strategy a good sense of priorities and desirable outcomes.

Avoiding Linear Problem-Solving and Oversimplification

In his report, Scott said, "A thorough problem analysis, at a minimum, means fully describing the problem, describing the multiple and often conflicting interests at stake in the problem, calculating the nature and costs of the harm arising from the problem, and taking inventory of and critiquing the current responses to the problem."[8] He pointed out that police problem analysis is most often flawed because of four factors: insufficient time, insufficient expert guidance on the problem, oversimplified problem-solving models, and insufficient consultation with local informants about the problem. SARA and CAPRA can be grossly oversimplified. For example, both of them suggest that problem-solving is a linear process—scan, analyze, respond, and assess. But real problem-solving does not work that way. We have already seen that finding the roots of the problem requires successive deep dives from superficial symptoms (like crime and disorder) to underlying dysfunctions (like health issues or anti-social behaviour), to failures in public policy. In that sense, problem-solving is not a simple, straight-line process. It is more iterative; it moves back and forth, and around and around.

In their studies, Cordner and Biebel have been quite critical of problem-oriented policing, largely because of oversimplified problem analysis by police officers. They make four key points:

- Crime analysis is only the starting point. Officers doing this work have to look at other sources of data such as that from other agencies, observations of other officers, and even field interviews.
- Problem analysis has to include diverse sources of information—particularly those sources that are knowledgeable about and have experience with the problem.
- Oversimplified analysis comes from basing analyses on anecdote, hearsay, or routine observations of other officers or neighbours.
- In high-demand neighbourhoods, police need to talk more with residents and neighbours. That is an opportunity to not only get their perspective on the problem but also pull them together into a coalition of like-minded community assets who identify in each other a common goal to support problem resolution (building social capital).[9]

In summary, police are most effective at problem-solving when they avoid linear thinking and oversimplification. Community policing requires a deeper level of analysis and problem-solving, and police can do this kind of work.

Mobilizing Assets in High-Demand Neighbourhoods

The most significant community problems that cause crime and disorder, and require the most investment in problem-solving, occur in high-demand neighbourhoods. Applying problem-solving models in high-demand neighbourhoods is quite different from applying them in low-demand neighbourhoods—like the drug house neighbourhood, which, other than that single street address, was a middle-class neighbourhood. Low-demand neighbourhoods like that one have neighbours who are already well connected with each other—like those irate neighbours who banded together to demand more police enforcement.

Sociologists call that **community cohesion**: strong and positive relationships between people who may have different backgrounds, tackling community problems together and developing a positive climate for community building. In high-demand neighbourhoods, community cohesion rarely exists, so it has to be developed. That is a good job for community policing and it is essential for effective problem-solving. Examining data from over 380 Chicago neighbourhoods, Sampson, Raudenbush, and Earls identified a strong connection between the presence of community cohesion in a neighbourhood and the absence of family violence, assaults, and disputes between neighbours.[10] In Chapter 1, we introduced the concepts of social control and social capital. Community cohesion completes the trio, as shown in Figure 5.3.

Of course this figure, like SARA or CAPRA, can grossly oversimplify the process of community building. Here it looks like a straightforward, linear process. But experience will demonstrate that even this process not only takes a long time, but also occasionally suffers from fits and starts, and has to re-cycle on itself in order to achieve the desired ends. So treat this graphic as a schematic of a process only, not a prescription for speedy problem-solving.

The Asset Principle and the Role of Police

Researchers Kretzmann and McKnight have been working in the community-building movement for a long time, and they have concluded that "[c]ommunities can only be built by focusing on the strengths and capacities of the citizens who call those communities 'home.'"[11] Their research and experience in community building led them to conclusions that fly in the face of common prejudices and misconceptions that high-demand neighbourhoods are cesspools of human deficiency. They discovered that most people in high-demand neighbourhoods have some capacity to make better decisions for themselves and their neighbours if it is safe for them to do so, and if they are supported in doing so. This idea that even in the most broken neighbourhoods, there are

FIGURE 5.3　**Building Community in High-Demand Neighbourhoods**

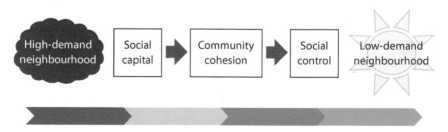

---

community cohesion strong and positive relationships between people who may have different backgrounds, tackling community problems together and developing a positive climate for community building people, agencies, organizations, and groups that can and will make good decisions for themselves and their neighbours, and will engage constructively in community problem-solving, is known as the **asset principle**. Kretzmann and McKnight coined the phrase "community assets" to get community builders to see the residents and neighbours in highly marginalized neighbourhoods in a more positive and constructive light. Ontario has adopted this concept in its Mobilization & Engagement Model of Community Policing.

Finding those community assets can be challenging because too often, in the most marginalized neighbourhoods, people are preoccupied with their own problems, they may be reluctant to reach out to their neighbours, they may be afraid of crime and social disorder in their neighbourhood, or, for any of a host of other reasons, they avoid broadcasting what they could do for the neighbourhood. But as reported in the Mrs. Robertson story in Chapter 1, street-wise and experienced police officers are particularly good at finding community assets—even in the most broken neighbourhoods.

Once found, community assets may face personal obstacles to getting involved in community building. They may truly doubt that they have anything to offer the enterprise; they may have relied on social assistance for so long that they think they cannot do anything better for themselves and their neighbours; and they may truly believe the prejudice and misconception that only the generosity and charity of more privileged people will save their neighbourhood. These are some of the personal obstacles that community policing has to overcome. The best way to do that is for police officers to constantly refuse to do things for people, but support them in doing things for themselves.

Mobilization Moments

We have mentioned a number of times in this text that a high priority for police officers is making a high-demand neighbourhood safe enough for community assets to step up and become involved in developing social capital and community cohesion. In a gang-ridden neighbourhood, for example, even the best community assets will think twice about engaging other neighbours in cleaning up the neighbourhood if they fear retribution from gangs. So police need to do what they do best—using the best of the traditional policing model—to make it safe enough for community assets to mobilize.

Experience in red zone neighbourhoods in Ontario and elsewhere has shown that community policing projects are best started with a major enforcement blitz. That happened at the drug house. The first step—after the citizens persuaded the police to invest in a more effective and sustainable strategy—was surveillance by the drug unit, followed by a bust that removed five

---

asset principle the idea that even in the most broken neighbourhoods, there are people, agencies, organizations, and groups that can and will make good decisions for themselves and their neighbours, and will engage constructively in community problem-solving

neighbourhood drug dealers who were using that address as a base for their business. Another example is found in the *60 Minutes* video "Counterinsurgency Cops: Military Tactics Fight Street Crime" cited in Chapter 1.

Enforcement measures like these are excellent ways to begin to mobilize community assets in high-demand neighbourhoods. We call them "**mobilization moments**" in Ontario's Mobilization & Engagement Model of Community Policing. That is because police get a lot of people's attention when they engage in an enforcement action, and getting people's attention in a high-demand neighbourhood is the first step in identifying assets and demonstrating to them that police will not only make it safe for them to engage in community building, but continue to keep it safe and support them in their efforts.

Asset-Based Community Development

The rest of the process of community building in high-demand neighbourhoods follows the principles of what Kretzmann and McKnight called "asset-based community development." They have founded an institute and run workshops on this subject.[12] Additionally, there is a vast technical literature on it. In Canada, the Tamarack Institute for Community Engagement offers technical advice, courses, research, and workshops on the subject.[13] In the next chapter of this text, we offer some concrete techniques for mobilizing community assets in high-demand neighbourhoods and promoting asset-based community development.

Supporting Problem-Solving Partnerships

In this chapter we have established that police have a very important role in identifying problems to be solved and analyzing them in order to not only ferret out their roots, but also identify risk factors, vulnerable groups, and individuals, agencies, and organizations that should be enlisted in the problem-solving process. We have also discovered that if police do a deep enough analysis of the roots of the problem, they will probably also discover that they do not have a primary role in problem-solving. But they have an important supporting role to play.

Enforcement, Safety, and Security

Enforcement always has to be considered a high priority for police in high-demand neighbourhoods. It is obvious that enforcement is needed to ensure that people are abiding by the law and living peacefully. But equally important, community assets cannot be reasonably expected to get to know each

---

mobilization moment a brief moment in time during which police draw neighbours' attention to a community problem through their enforcement actions

other, work together, develop community cohesion, and tackle some of the neighbourhood's more profound problems if it is not safe for them to do so. Safety and security is one of the foundation stones for effective community policing, and police are uniquely qualified to deliver it.

Outreach, Representation, and Engagement

Remember how the constable found Mrs. Robertson and how, upon being guided to her door by an 11-year-old boy, the officer got Mrs. Robertson to open the door and consider his overture for her involvement in a community-building initiative? That is effective outreach. Police are particularly good at it and they have a lot of experience with it. They also have learned to be assertive and respectful at the same time. Further, their uniform helps a lot: Mrs. Robertson probably would not have been as inclined to open her door and listen to the same overture if it had been delivered by a stranger who was not a police officer—no matter how well qualified that stranger was to do that work.

When it comes to engaging a wide range of community agencies and organizations, police, once again, have a knack for getting the attention of executives and decision-makers of those agencies in ways that people who are not police officers cannot. Think back to the constable's role in getting an audience with municipal officials in the drug house case or arranging a meeting with officials from temporary housing agencies. To get those appointments the constable only had to identify his agency, and the earliest possible appointment with those executives was given to him.

Also notice that once the officers leveraged the audiences, the irate citizens carried the discussions about the community problem and the agencies' roles in helping resolve it. The officer did not have to do the talking on behalf of the group. Two lessons come from that point: first, it is important that the officer not dominate the discussion because effective mobilization and engagement means fostering a relationship between the community assets and the helper agencies; and second, notwithstanding that first lesson, it is important for the officer to continue to be present during those discussions (if relatively silent) because his or her presence reminds everyone that police want this problem fixed, and they expect everyone else to engage in the problem-solving process.

Presence and Encouragement

As community assets in high-demand neighbourhoods begin to connect with each other, share in problem-solving, and engage with external agencies and service providers, police presence and encouragement are vital. It does not have to be a large presence; remember that it was only one constable who worked with the irate neighbours to solve the drug house problem. On the other hand, it is important that the officer(s) providing that presence and encouragement be the same one(s) who helped start the initiative, identify assets, mobilize them, and engage agencies. It does not work to constantly rotate other officers through the problem-solving process. That is one of the adjustments that police agencies have to make in order to have effective community policing initiatives. After all, this work is all about building and maintaining effective relationships: among community assets; between community assets and human and social service agencies; and between police and community assets, as well as other agencies. That is not possible if the personnel keep changing.

Technical Consultation and Advice

Occasionally police can be a source of technical information and advice that will assist a community-building initiative. **Crime prevention through environmental design (CPTED)** is a good example. Other situational crime prevention measures may also be within the purview of some officers who have received crime prevention training. When police have technical information that could serve the project, they can switch from some of their other roles (enforcement, safety, outreach, representation, support, presence, and encouragement) to an active role in guiding the initiative toward some of its objectives and outcomes.

Monitoring Effects on Crime and Disorder

Finally, because police data on calls for service and occurrences may have been the original stimulus for a community-building initiative, monitoring those occurrences throughout the initiative can also help police and community partners discern whether they are having any appreciable impact on crime and disorder. A caution, though: public calls for police assistance frequently increase at the start of such an initiative in a high-demand neighbourhood. That is because active police presence and increased police legitimacy encourage people to report more often when they have a concern. Therefore, it is important for police to not only monitor these data, but also engage in further analysis about what they mean and their implications for the direction and outcomes of the project.

Of course, other agency partners also track data that pertain to their own agency's roles and services in the initiative. So there is another opportunity to monitor data in order to inform the direction and outcomes of the initiative.

---

crime prevention through environmental design (CPTED) a wide range of spatial, architectural, and physical measures applied to buildings and grounds in order to strengthen their security and the security of people who use them

CHAPTER SUMMARY

Problem-solving in high-demand neighbourhoods needs to be initiated by police. This is because the neighbourhood would not have a high demand for police assistance if other agencies or problem-solving initiatives were reducing crime and disorder. So it comes down to police launching problem-solving initiatives. But that does not mean that police have to come up with the solutions to the community's problems. Therein lies a trap for too many police agencies. One way to avoid that trap is to stick to the business of policing. Another is to recognize, early in the scanning and analysis stages of problem-solving, that a whole host of other agencies and organizations, individuals, and groups do have mandates, resources, roles, and responsibilities that can help solve community problems. Then it becomes a community policing job to mobilize and engage them in applying themselves more productively to the problem-solving process.

REVIEW AND DISCUSSION QUESTIONS

1. What is problem-oriented policing, and how does it relate to community policing?

2. Define and explain the four elements of SARA.

3. What do the "C" and "P" in the RCMP's CAPRA problem-solving model stand for? Describe each.

4. Why is CAPRA a more suitable problem-solving model than SARA for community policing?

5. From what sources can police obtain data and information to analyze a given community problem?

6. Why do police often oversimplify problem analysis?

7. What is community cohesion, and how does it relate to violence in high-demand neighbourhoods?

8. What is the asset principle in community building?

9. What is the role of police in applying the asset principle to community policing?

10. What is a mobilization moment, and what is its role in community policing in a high-demand neighbourhood?

KEY TERMS

asset principle, 153
community cohesion, 152
crime prevention through environmental design (CPTED), 156
gatekeepers, 146
mobilization moment, 154
profound interventions, 129
target hardening, 143

NOTES

1   Michael S Scott, *Problem-Oriented Policing: Reflections on the First 20 Years* (Washington, DC: US Department of Justice, Office of Community Oriented Policing Services, 2000).

2   *Ibid* at 6.

3   *Ibid* at 98.

4   William Spelman & John E Eck, "Problem-Oriented Policing," *Research in Brief* (Washington, DC: National Institute of Justice, January 1987) at 2.

5   Jeff Outhit, "Former Crack House Gets Clean Bill of Health," *The Record* (18 November 2000) B8.

6   *Provincial Offences Act*, RSO 1990, c P.33.

7   *Liquor Licence Act*, RSO 1990, c L.19.

8   Scott, *supra* note 1 at 59.

9   G Cordner & E Biebel, "Problem-Oriented Policing in Practice" (2005) 4:2 Criminol & Public Policy 155.

10   Robert J Sampson, Stephen W Raudenbush & Felton Earls, "Neighbourhoods and Violent Crime: A Multilevel Study of Collective Efficacy" (1997) 277 Science 918.

11   Jody Kretzmann & John McKnight, *Building Communities from the Inside Out: A Path Toward Finding and Mobilizing a Community's Assets* (Evanston, Ill: Centre for Civic Engagement, Northwestern University, 1993) at 21.

12   *Ibid.*

13   Tamarack Institute for Community Engagement, "How We Work," online: <http://www.tamarackcommunity.ca/howwework>.

CHAPTER 6

Transformative Community-Building Practices

A talking circle is held at the Centre d'artistes Vaste et Vague in Carleton-sur-Mer, Quebec, as part of the Nasgwa'tatijig (Mi'kmaq for "sharing equally") project. Participants discussed avenues for pursuing communication and engagement between the Indigenous and non-Indigenous residents of the area.

LEARNING OUTCOMES

Upon completion of this chapter, you should be able to:

- Identify the highest-priority goal of transformative community-building practices
- Explain what asset-based community development and appreciative inquiry have in common, how they complement each other, and why they are important for community building in high-demand neighbourhoods
- Understand why community circles are an important technique for fostering social cohesion, and the importance of their format, venue, and rules of discourse for community building
- Explain management by consensus and why it is important for community building
- List the important distinctions between community justice and justice as it is handled by the formal criminal justice system

Introduction

We are about halfway through this text on community policing. This is where we turn the corner from history, theory, and principles of community policing in order to begin to figure out how effective community policing is actually applied. This chapter will leave you with some useful tools to put in your community policing toolkit—particularly for use in high-demand neighbourhoods.

One of the most important principles to remember when applying community policing tools is that in so doing, you are trying to get people and agencies—indeed, everyone in the safety and well-being web—to connect with each other and work together to solve community problems. Your principal role is to create environments where they can do that, coach and support them, and above all, respect them and refuse to do things for them that they have to learn to do for themselves if they are going to solve community problems.

As a consequence, community policing is less about police making speeches to the community—as is done when police are interviewed by the press—and more about police getting community members to talk among themselves and to each other. In some ways, community policing resembles parenting an adolescent. The parent can tell the adolescent what all of their decisions should be, in which case the adolescent will not learn to make good decisions and will also blame the parent for any failings in the decisions they do make. Or the parent can coach and support the adolescent as they struggle to make their own good decisions—always supporting them, of course, if the initial decisions they make are the wrong ones.

This is also the chapter in which we use a community policing perspective to re-examine the meaning of "justice." Here, in our examination of the practical tools for community policing, we once again examine the distinction explained in Chapter 2 between justice as imposed by the state and justice as derived by community members, among themselves. This is not a discussion about which approach is right and which is wrong, or which works and which does not. Rather, it is an introduction to methods that officers may use to derive justice in a community, whether or not the standards of justice imposed by the state are met. The discussion is based on the presumption that if any members of the community feel unfairly treated by other members (including police), it will be next to impossible to foster community cohesion; without community cohesion, community members cannot solve community problems.

IN THE COMMUNITY

Improving Bad Relations with the LGBTQ Community

The Toronto Police Service's historical relationship with the lesbian, gay, bisexual, transgender, and queer/questioning (LGBTQ) community has been tainted by ugly instances of homophobia and transphobia. One of the worst occurred on February 5, 1981 in a takedown that Toronto police officers called "Operation Soap." Officers targeted gay bath houses, arresting more than three hundred men. Shortly afterward, thousands of Torontonians protested in the streets. That night served as a rallying call to the LGBTQ movement in Canada. Since then, Canadian policing agencies have worked to address homophobia and transphobia in police culture and behaviour and to improve relations with the LGBTQ community, with the Toronto Police Service now at the head of the pack. Among its other initiatives, the service developed the *Toronto Police Service Style Guide: A Guidebook to Fair & Equitable Language*, which helps officers learn the appropriate language to use when working with the LGBTQ community (for example, using "gay" rather than "homosexual") so that they are "attentive and responsive to discrimination." Toronto police also rely on LGBTQ community consultative committees in order to be proactive in community relations, crime prevention, education, and communication initiatives.

Police agencies throughout Ontario have made a commitment to bias-free and inclusive policing for all community members, with a special pledge to the LGBTQ community. The Ontario Association of Chiefs of Police (OACP) created a diversity committee with the mandate to develop best practices in policing LGBTQ communities in order to heal and move beyond a historical relationship that has been marked by discrimination and harassment:

> The goal of the project is to bring perspectives from police services, openly serving LGBTQ police personnel, and LGBTQ community organizations throughout Ontario together with cutting-edge research, legislation, and case law in an effort to improve the quality of policing in Ontario.[1]

The initiative engaged the LGBTQ community through liaison committees that consult with community organizations to review police practices. While the LGBTQ community has long been marginalized and discriminated against by the enforcement community, Ontario has made significant efforts to not only create policy for best practices, but also work collaboratively with LGBTQ communities so that all members of the community are treated with respect and dignity.

Consider the following questions:

1. Up to this point in the text we have talked about "community" in terms of high-demand or low-demand neighbourhoods. How does the LGBTQ community fit into this discussion? What makes them a community that is worthy of discussion in a text on community policing?

2. What techniques did police use in order to obtain assistance from the LGBTQ community in changing the way police relate to its members?

3. What other special groups and communities do you think would benefit from this approach to community engagement and community policing?

A Review of Community Policing Principles

Before detailing some on-the-ground community policing techniques, it is helpful to review some of the principles on which they are based. While all of the following principles have been explained in the first half of this text, we will briefly review them here.

In high-demand neighbourhoods, where police have to respond most often, there are the fewest characteristics of community. Recall that we have defined "community" as people with shared values for safety and well-being and enduring relationships that permit them to collaborate in resolving any community problems.

What is most lacking in high-demand neighbourhoods is social control. Hence, police are called to exert that control from outside the neighbourhood.

Therefore, one of the most important goals of community policing in high-demand neighbourhoods is to develop a community's internal capacity to exert social control.

In order to foster the development of internal sources of social control, police have to have good relationships with people in the neighbourhood— known as police legitimacy.

Social control grows out of social capital—that is, people in the neighbourhood connecting with each other, discovering common values for peace and security, and collaborating in developing the protective factors that yield peace and security.

Ultimately, those protective factors are the same as what is known in the health sector as the "social determinants of health." For a sustainable peace in the neighbourhood, people need the following protective factors, among others:

- sufficient income for their needs,
- quality housing,
- care that keeps them healthy,
- the ability to raise their children without violence and coercion,
- levels of education that help them excel in life, and
- social acceptance and inclusion.

Those are significant challenges in high-demand neighbourhoods.

Deficiencies in any of the social determinants of health are the roots of most crime and social disorder problems that police encounter in high-demand neighbourhoods. Those deficiencies have to be remedied if crime and social disorder are going to diminish. That means police and communities need a problem-solving strategy to go about resolving them.

At the same time, police agencies need to remember that these problems go well beyond what police are mandated, resourced, and trained to resolve. When engaging in problem-solving, police must limit themselves to the business of policing.

However, a lot of other agencies, organizations, groups, and associations are in the business of dealing with the social determinants of health, so there is a role for police in engaging them in this problem-solving enterprise. Recall Kretzmann and McKnight's conclusion from Chapter 5: "Communities can only be built by focusing on the strengths and capacities of the citizens who call those communities 'home.'"[2] Therefore, while many agencies are needed to help resolve problems in high-demand neighbourhoods, first and foremost, police must mobilize community assets in those neighbourhoods.

Mobilizing community assets means developing social capital and community cohesion in order to bring those assets to the fore and meld them into a mobilized force for growth and development in the community—a primary goal of community policing in high-demand neighbourhoods.

With that last point, we are right back where we started this logical sequence of community policing principles. True enough, community policing is often a circular process—much as we indicated in unpacking those apparently linear planning models, SARA and CAPRA. Reality teaches that none of this work is linear: it does not progress in a straight line from one phase to another.

Asset-Based Community Development

In our review of community policing principles, above, we repeated Kretzmann and McKnight's important, research-based conclusion: "Communities can only be built by focusing on the strengths and capacities of the citizens who call those communities 'home.'" That means that community policing starts with the neighbours in high-demand neighbourhoods. Of course it will expand to include external agencies and organizations that have mandates, resources, technologies, and specialists to help in community building. But the whole exercise has to be anchored in the positive energies, capacities, and relationships of the neighbours who live, work, and play there. That is why they are called "assets."

Asset-based community development is diametrically opposite a needs-based model of community development and problem-solving. Think back to the story of Mrs. Robertson in Chapter 1. That group of five parents from the neighbourhood was being led by a Family and Children's Services social worker who asked the neighbours to itemize all the "needs" in their community, all the bad things that the parents wanted to fix, and all that was wrong about the community. As Mathie and Cunningham point out:

> [T]he consequences of a needs-based, problem-solving approach can be devastating: leadership that denigrates the community by emphasizing the severity of problems in order to attract resources; and people in these communities internalizing a view of themselves as incapable of initiating positive change, leading to a pervasive feeling of hopelessness.[3]

We had examples of those negative effects in the Mrs. Robertson story. Recall how the social worker told the constable that no one in that neighbourhood of 250 single-family dwellings was qualified to provide child care for the children of the five parents who were gathering to do good work in their own neighbourhood ("leadership that denigrates the community"). She said that because she needed to spend $900 out of her agency budget. The truth is that if she did not spend that by the end of the fiscal year, her budget for the next year would be cut by that amount based on the assumption that she could not use the funds ("emphasizing the severity of problems in order to attract resources"). When one of those parents was asked if he thought there was anyone qualified to provide child care, he, a successful father of two young children, agreed with the social worker ("people in these communities internalizing a view of themselves as incapable of initiating positive change"). This is how neighbourhoods become further weakened by the well-intended efforts of external agencies and organizations that pour resources and advice into the neighbourhood. As Mathie and Cunningham concluded, the neighbourhoods "become further weakened by a reliance on outside institutions to solve their problems, and perversely those institutions develop a vested interest in maintaining this dependency."[4]

Asset Inventorying

Asset-based community development starts with the notion that even the most marginalized, high-demand neighbourhood has within it numerous human assets that can be identified and mobilized to productively engage in strengthening the neighbourhood under the right conditions. This approach does not deny that there are needs and problems in the neighbourhood that need to be solved urgently. It does not mean that all our efforts to understand problem-solving strategies do not work. But it does say that community policing and community building will be much more successful if police build on what is good about that neighbourhood—especially those individuals, families, associations, groups, networks, and social relationships that already show significant capacities to make a positive difference and demonstrate some degree of community cohesion.

In contrast to listing a neighbourhood's needs, then, asset-based community development focuses on inventorying the neighbourhood's assets. An **inventory of community assets** is an important resource for community

---

asset-based community development a community development approach that takes the stance that even the most high-demand neighbourhood has human assets that can be mobilized to strengthen the neighbourhood

inventory of community assets a bank of information about the assets in a neighbourhood, including its physical assets, community groups or associations, and human assets, that can be drawn on for resources to achieve neighbourhood improvement and problem-solving building. It includes human assets, such as Mrs. Robertson. In her case, the inventory would include Mrs. Robertson's name and contact information, along with a list of her interests in community building, her skills and abilities, her availability, and her commitment. More generally, an inventory of human assets includes five types of information:

- minimal personal information for contact purposes;
- skills, whether learned at home, on the job, or in a community, including which ones the person considers their most valuable skills;
- community experience and interests;
- workplace experience and interests; and
- culture and arts skills.

An inventory of community assets also includes local groups or associations in which neighbours come together to pursue a wide range of activities. Examples include a church congregation's ministry group or a local Optimist Club, such as the one in the story about the woman who asked the Optimists for funding for children's summer programming in a high-demand neighbourhood (Chapter 1). They could be there for religious, cultural, civic, recreational, or other purposes. In the case of local groups or associations, the asset inventory includes:

- the name of the group;
- a description of its members;
- its contact information;
- its purposes;
- when and where it meets; and
- the range of skills and abilities, interests, and commitments it has to offer the neighbourhood.

An asset inventory also includes physical assets in the neighbourhood, such as

- common rooms in social housing;
- playgrounds;
- places of worship;
- schools;
- parks; and
- community facilities, such as a local basketball court.

An inventory of physical assets would also include information about how to access these resources, their hours of operation, contact names, and telephone numbers.

Finally, an inventory of community assets includes local businesses—like the grocery—or offices of social services that work in the neighbourhood. The asset inventory becomes, then, a resource base on which to draw in order to achieve any neighbourhood improvements. It also has the very real but subtle effect of demonstrating to everyone—especially these neighbours—that far from a cesspool of human deficiencies, their neighbourhood is a fount of resources that can be tapped for neighbourhood improvements and problem-solving.

Building such an asset inventory is an excellent early project for mobilized neighbours. After all, it is most important that the neighbours know what their own assets are, so why not have them go through the process of discovering them? It becomes an initiative that can pull neighbours together in an effort that will foster social capital among them. It is a start of community capacity-building. Kretzmann and McKnight's *Building Communities from the Inside Out* includes a format for developing such asset information and arraying it.[5] But experience has shown that each neighbourhood will probably do a better job of it if they invent their own way of developing an asset inventory. Usually, it will require some form of interviewing and recording information, but it need not be an onerous job.

Steps in Asset-Based Community Development

Researchers Mathie and Cunningham offer a linear and logical series of steps for asset-based community development that is not unlike SARA or CAPRA.[6] They suggest that the process of asset inventorying comprises the first two steps of these problem-solving models; the remaining steps, which build on that experience and the resulting inventory, consist of

1 • interviews, walkabouts, and other research to learn about past or current successful neighbourhood initiatives and to identify community assets;

2 • developing the comprehensive asset inventory on which the neighbourhood will draw to complete various initiatives;

3 • mobilization of core groups of people to apply themselves to various neighbourhood initiatives;

4 • initiation of community activities that require no external resources or assistance; and

5 • progressive scaling up of these activities as links to external services and resources are tapped for investment in neighbourhood community building.

In all of these activities, one rule of thumb addresses the broad community policing goal of developing social and community cohesion in high-demand neighbourhoods. It is the rule of inclusion: all initiatives and efforts should be as open and inclusive as possible. So, for example, in Mathie and Cunningham's step involving the "mobilization of core groups" it is important to not exclude anyone who would like to be part of that initiative. In more functional, low-demand neighbourhoods, picking a couple of community leaders to drive some initiative is a source of efficiency in community building; it allows others to focus on other initiatives. But where community cohesion is lacking, the highest priority has to be placed on getting people to relate to each other—about anything—so that they can begin to discover in each other shared values for the neighbourhood and complementary energies and resources to resolve community problems.

Appreciative Inquiry

Appreciative inquiry is an organizational development technique that works well in high-demand neighbourhoods, not least because it builds on what is good about the neighbourhood, rather than focusing on what is wrong with it. In that respect it meshes nicely with asset-based community development.

The technique is based on the idea that the types of questions we ask tend to either focus people's attention and energies or diminish them. So if they are negative questions, like "What are all your needs that you'd like to focus on here?" then the energy to work on them will rapidly diminish. Kinni said that "focusing on dysfunctions and problems can actually cause them to multiply or become intractable."[7] Much like asset-based community development, the principal idea is to build community in high-demand neighbourhoods by relying on what works there instead of inventorying everything that is wrong with the neighbourhood. In that sense, it is the opposite of problem-solving, where we start by singling out a problem that we want to solve. We compare the problem-focused approach and appreciative inquiry in Figure 6.1.

Bushe labels the four steps of appreciative inquiry with D-words, making them easier to remember, and offers the following descriptions:

- Discover: participants discuss core strengths, or positive characteristics, of whatever brings them together;
- Dream: participants talk about what improvements they would like to see in the thing that brings them together;
- Design: participants develop concrete plans to achieve the improvements they would like to see; and
- Deliver: participants implement their plans for making improvements.[8]

---

appreciative inquiry an organizational development technique that advocates building on what residents already experience as positive characteristics of their neighbourhood

FIGURE 6.1 **Comparing Problem-Focused Development and Appreciative Inquiry**

Problem-Focused Approaches	Appreciative Inquiry
Basic assumption: Development means solving problems!	*Basic assumption*: Development is an opportunity to build on the best!
Steps:	*Steps:*
1. Express felt needs and identify the problems to be solved (Scanning)	1. Express and value the best of what already exists (Identifying)
2. Analyze possible causes of the problems (Analysis)	2. Imagine what improvements might look like (Imagining)
3. Choose and implement preferable solutions (Response)	3. Talk about what could be done to improve things (Planning)
4. Evaluate outcomes and adjust solutions (Assessment)	4. Innovate and keep striving for the desired outcomes (Achieving)

SOURCE: Adapted from Theodore Kinni, "The Art of Appreciative Inquiry," *The Harvard Business School Working Knowledge for Business Leaders Newsletter* (September 2003).

IN THE COMMUNITY

Community Cleanup

It was a cold February night, and the constable stood at the self-locking door of the Cloverdale Public School gym. He was there to admit neighbours who wished to attend the 7 o'clock meeting the police had called "to talk about your neighbourhood." Uniformed police auxiliary had canvassed this high-demand neighbourhood to ensure that everyone knew about the meeting. But that was only after police had gone to the superintendent of schools in order to obtain access to this meeting space because the school principal had rejected the idea of such a meeting. He had said that parents from the Cloverdale neighbourhood wouldn't come and that "they don't care about their kids; they don't care about their neighbourhood; they don't care about education; and I won't have them in my school!" However, there was no other centrally located space in Cloverdale that would comfortably accommodate the number of people that the constable guessed would attend, so it was necessary to contact the superintendent of schools.

Seven o'clock rolled around and about 30 people were sitting, silently, in a circle in the gym, waiting for the constable to join them. One went to the door to retrieve the constable, but he stalled, saying, "I think I see someone else coming." Sure enough, out of the gloom waddled two ten-year-old boys in big boots and oversized hand-me-down hockey clothes. The constable opened the door for them and one little boy's soprano voice said, "Hey mister, I hear there's a meeting 'bout our neighbourhood; can we come?" The officer paused as if thinking about the question and then asked them, "Are you between the ages of 0 and 100?" When they assured him they were, he ushered them into the gym, where they sat, side by side, among a circle of adult strangers.

The constable sat and welcomed everyone, thanking them for responding so positively to this police-initiated call for a discussion. He then took a beanbag out of his cargo pants pocket and said: "I'm going to start this beanbag around the circle; whoever holds it can speak, and the rest of us will listen. If you don't want to speak, just pass the beanbag on. Let's start by hearing your answers to the following question: 'What do you like about Cloverdale?'"

It turned out that a lot of these people liked a lot of things about this high-demand neighbourhood. But that did not prohibit them occasionally mentioning something they did not like. Finally, one person complained about all the trash that was strewn throughout the neighbourhood and a lot of the others in the circle nodded. So when it came his turn to speak, the constable said, "What would you like to do about that trash?" and passed the beanbag along.

Then ideas about a spring cleanup began to percolate through the group: maybe get some soil from the city to put in windowsill flower boxes, ask a garden centre to donate or offer significant discounts on spring flowers, arrange a potluck afterward, etc. Finally, the beanbag came to one of the ten-year-old boys. He stood up—probably because he thought he couldn't be seen among all these big people. He announced, "I'm pretty good with markers and so are my friends. We could do posters for the spring cleanup and that way everyone in Cloverdale would know that they can come and help!"

That is exactly what happened. By springtime the local promotion with children's posters was so successful that outside agencies, the municipality, and people in an adjacent low-demand neighbourhood were all figuring out how they could support the initiative. A construction company donated dumpsters for the trash; Cloverdale youth were organized and supervised by municipal public works in preparing flowerbeds where neighbours wanted them; a hardware store donated the garden tools; a plant nursery donated pansies and other flowers; the municipality landscaped street corners and a cul-de-sac; people from the low-demand neighbourhood raised funds to rent a jumping castle for little kids—and Cloverdale got cleaned up.

CHECK YOUR UNDERSTANDING

1. What was the role of police in this initiative?

2. What can we learn from the story of the police having to go to the superintendent of schools to obtain access to the school gym for an evening?

3. When the constable asked the two little boys if they were between the ages of 0 and 100 years, what point was he trying to make? Explain your answer.

4. What type of questions did the constable ask the people at the meeting, and what impact did that have on the whole initiative?

In the context of our earlier discussion about problem-solving models, including SARA and CAPRA, it is important to note that the constable in this Cloverdale example used neither of them. Rather, he proceeded on the premise of asset-based community development, grounded in the assumption that everyone in this neighbourhood had something worthwhile to contribute and if he just brought them together in an environment in which they could discover those assets in each other, probably something good would come out of it.

The second thing the constable did that was so important in this neighbourhood initiative was recognize that these neighbours did not know each other. They were not cohesive in any sense. Further, he knew that while he could have suggested a spring cleanup or any of a host of other projects, if anything constructive was ever going to come from the neighbours, they had to have a way to discover it in each other and build social capital. The constable knew that his job was to create an environment in which these neighbours could begin to develop enduring relationships—the cornerstone of community building.

The third thing he did, which generated so much creative and constructive energy from these people, was to simply ask them two positive questions: "What do you like about Cloverdale?" and "What would you like to do about that trash?" That is appreciative inquiry. Notice that the first question leads all the neighbours sitting in that circle to say good things about their neighbourhood; of course, that allows all those neighbours, listening to each statement, to begin to see positive qualities in each other as well as their neighbourhood. It gives all of them positive access to each other. Also notice that such positive statements did not prohibit the expression of negative ones. If anything, the series of positive statements encouraged these neighbours to get creative when someone expressed what turned out to be a common concern about trash in the neighbourhood.

Choosing the Most Appropriate Approach

So, does our discussion of asset-based community development and appreciative inquiry suggest that problem-solving models like SARA and CAPRA do not work? Not at all. It is all about what police apply them to and how they go about applying them to problems in high-demand neighbourhoods. Think back to the Toronto Police Service challenge with booze cans (Chapter 5). They applied the SARA problem-solving model successfully to their enforcement problems. Scanning allowed them to recognize that every time they busted a booze can, it sprang up somewhere else. That pattern of repeat occurrences indicated to police that their enforcement strategy was not solving the problem. Their analysis exposed a handful of other partners in enforcement and a more effective point of leverage—landlords rather than booze can operators. Using the problem-solving model, they solved that problem.

In the Cloverdale example, it would have been just as easy for the constable, after neighbours exposed their concerns about trash, to gently guide them through the logic of SARA or CAPRA if they had not already found a desired solution. But notice the difference in approach between these two examples. If effective enforcement is the problem, then applying a problem-solving model is a job for police and their enforcement partners. If the neighbourhood has a problem that the neighbours want to solve themselves, then it is very important that the police not apply a problem-solving model for them; rather, police should coach them in doing it for themselves. Remember that the fundamental goal in the latter case is not getting trash cleaned up; it is getting people to connect with each other to share responsibility for neighbourhood improvements. So it is important that no helper agency (police, social workers, community developers, anybody) dominate the problem-solving process in the neighbourhood.

Challenges in Facilitating Social Capital

In the most marginalized neighbourhoods, it is important for police to use mobilization methods that help the neighbours connect with each other. That assertion is based on the assumption that the neighbours already have an acceptable relationship with police—or at least with those officers who are trying to work with them. If they do not, then of course establishing some police legitimacy has to be the first priority.

So, presuming that neighbours' relationships with police are sufficiently positive to launch some mobilization efforts, what can police do to get them in touch with each other? The first thing to notice is that the standard outreach or consultation strategy that police use is not appropriate. This is no place for the classic, police-driven, town hall meeting. Remember, this is not about police talking to neighbours; this is about neighbours talking to each other—as facilitated by police. That is one reason why community policing is less about police learning public speaking skills and more about police learning public listening skills.

Police officers are taught to be assertive; to control the discussion; to instruct people on what to do and how to do it. So in some respects, refraining from doing that with neighbours in high-demand neighbourhoods can be a challenge for good police officers. But that is exactly what is required when community policing focuses on fostering social capital and community cohesion. Officers need to be present and confident—thereby signalling that it is safe for neighbours to try to get to know one another—but not particularly assertive and certainly not domineering.

Mere police presence stabilizes the social dynamics in order to give neighbours a chance to reach out and hear each other. For that same reason, the police uniform is important because it makes it very clear that police are present and will keep everybody safe from any threats to relationship building. A police presence defuses tensions or disputes that may arise over the simplest subjects. But beyond mere presence, police have an opportunity to create a whole environment in which the neighbours will find it easiest to speak to each other, and hear each other. Increasingly, police have been using community circles to create that environment.

Community Circles

Community circles is a name for one technique that is useful for getting neighbours in touch with each other in order to begin to foster social cohesion around neighbourhood improvement projects and community problem-solving. This technique is ancient; it has been used for centuries around the world where there are Indigenous people who have sustained their capacity to hold their communities together. In North America, it is frequently known as the "talking circle" process. Many First Nations communities in Canada use it today for a variety of purposes. It has also been adapted in many places around the world for the purposes of achieving justice where members of a community feel they have been wronged by other members of that community. In that context, it is known as "restorative justice." We will take another look at the talking circle process toward the end of this chapter when we discuss techniques for dealing with disputes in community groups.

Format for the Community Circle

The community circle format is one in which everyone is welcome (inclusive) and everyone has an equal opportunity to speak and be heard by everyone else (voice). Everyone in the community circle has equal status with everyone else. There is not even a designated chairperson. Yet it is a very tightly controlled exchange that is designed to keep people on the topic at hand, keep them behaving respectfully toward each other, and keep the exchange efficient and goal oriented.

---

community circles a technique for facilitating communication and social cohesion that ensures that all participants have equal status and equal opportunity to speak; also known as talking circles, family group conferencing, community justice circles, or restorative justice circles

All of that control is in the process that the community circle uses, not in the power of one designated chairperson or expert facilitator or community leader—much less a police officer. (The process is discussed in greater detail under the heading "Rules of Discourse for the Community Circle," below.) This format is about neighbours discovering that they all have an equal stake in whatever the group decides to do and that everyone's ideas are valued. There are no winners and losers here, as happens when majority opinion dominates group decisions.

Venue for the Community Circle

The success of the community circle depends in large part on the space in which it is held and how that space is set up. This is one of those techniques that benefits from good research and preparation. The constable in the scenario about the spring cleanup in Cloverdale had to go to the superintendent of schools in order to gain access for an evening meeting of neighbours in the local public school gym. He did the right thing. There was no other space in Cloverdale that could comfortably accommodate the number of people he guessed would attend the meeting. If he had been forced to find another venue, it would have taken him outside the neighbourhood—for example, to a municipal community centre. A community centre has lots of space but two significant drawbacks for these particular neighbours: (1) it would be too far away and would prohibit people without transportation from getting there and (2) it would be a space with which few of these neighbours would be familiar or feel comfortable, largely because their personal issues (disability, poverty, single-parenting pressures, etc.) meant they would not have used the centre in the past, would not be familiar with it, and would not feel comfortable there in the future. So it would be foreign territory for them—not exactly conducive to friendly get-togethers. The chosen venue for a community circle has to have the following characteristics:

- It must be central to all participants and easily accessible.
- It must be sufficiently large to accommodate everyone comfortably.
- It must permit deliberations without external interruptions.
- It must have good lighting and temperature control.
- It must have accessible washrooms.

Set-up for the community circle is also critical. In fact, the desired set-up further limits the choice of venue. For example, police would want to avoid using a school classroom or an auditorium because the furniture typically is designed for people to sit in rows facing the front of the room. That is not the effect police want to create in a community circle. It is much better to use a layout that gives every neighbour a clear line of sight and the ability to hear every other neighbour, and in which there is no focal point for the discussion. That is why the circle is the best layout for this purpose. So the first task is to move any furniture in the room out of the way and set up a big circle of comfortable chairs—enough to accommodate all of the expected participants. It is always a good idea to have some extra chairs at the back of the room for latecomers to pull into the circle.

The chairs should be set up with sufficient space between them so that people's elbows do not bump each other. People should feel comfortable and not crowded, but also somewhat close to each other, as if they were in someone's living room. Tables should not form any part of the circle. The community circle is not like a goal-oriented workshop, where six people might be seated at a table for group work; rather, people should feel somewhat exposed to each other. Perhaps surprisingly, this improves listening behaviour. Of course, some people will arrive with bags or purses, or maybe kid's toys if they are bringing a little one, and in colder weather, coats and other articles of clothing. So the venue should have a safe place for the neighbours to put them. Tables pushed to the back of the room can serve that purpose. Alternatively, people can be invited to put their bags and purses under their chairs so that they are readily available and close to their owners.

All of this set-up requires that police arrive early enough to see to all the details. The goal is to have the neighbours come into a space where they get the sense that someone is in charge and has all the details worked out. Most people find that reassuring. Mind you, some people will feel nervous about taking a seat in a circle with a bunch of strangers watching. But that nervousness will be diminished when people experience the rules of discourse, and their proximity to each other will enhance their ability to see, hear, and begin to trust and respect each other. (The rules of discourse are discussed under the heading "Rules of Discourse for the Community Circle," below.)

It is also important for police to be at the door to welcome people, give them directions to the meeting room, tell them where to put their things, invite them to find a place to sit in the circle, and in all respects act like a host who is there to ensure everyone is safe and has a good time.

Police should continue to greet arrivals at the door right up to start time, and then start the meeting on time. Starting on time, being on time, being set up, and adjourning on time are all important acts of discipline that will influence the whole group to abide by those same standards as they begin to work together on community problems. It is a simple way to show respect for everyone who is involved in this collective enterprise.

When the meeting is about to start, everyone should be comfortably seated and there should be only one empty chair in the circle. The officer can announce that the empty chair represents all those people from the neighbourhood who should be at the meeting, but could not make it. It is just a gentle reminder that this group is setting out to serve the whole neighbourhood—not just themselves. If latecomers arrive, stop the discussion, welcome them, and ask them to drag a chair into the circle. Bring them up to speed about what is going on and the rules of discourse; then resume the discussion where it left off.

Rules of Discourse for the Community Circle

Even before the discussion starts, this choice of venue and room layout will have begun to have subtle but profound influences on the neighbours, most of whom probably have never spoken to each other before the meeting. For example, sitting in a circle, there is no opportunity for the shy or frightened participant to hide in the back of the room. That is sending the message that everyone is expected to participate. Sitting in the circle sends the strong message that everyone at the meeting is equal. There is no speaker's podium, no head table, no gavel, no symbol of higher authority. Everyone is respected equally. Everyone's ideas are equally important. When the group first comes together, there will likely be very little talking in the circle before start-up. Only people who arrived together and know each other might be chatting while waiting for the meeting to commence. That is all right. It gives people a chance to look around, see if they recognize anyone, and consider how they are feeling about what is about to happen.

When the meeting is ready to start, a chosen guide will remain seated and make opening remarks, including laying out the rules of discourse. Note that we have avoided using a word such as "facilitator" or "chairperson" to describe this person's role, which might suggest someone who controls the flow of the discussion, imposes an agenda, interrupts or challenges speakers, or otherwise controls the proceedings. A guide, by contrast, is someone who gently offers a sense of direction and leaves it up to the individuals in the circle to make their own choices about whether they want to go in that direction or not.

If police called the meeting and are hosting it, then an officer may lay out the rules of discourse. On the other hand, if the officer is aware that one of the neighbours knows the rules and is willing to lay them out, that works too. It really does not matter who does it because it is the rules of discourse that control the discussion, leaving all of the people free to participate openly and unhindered by any responsibility to control things. For the sake of this text, we will assume that it is the officer who calls the meeting, greets people at the door, and lays out the rules of discourse. Sample rules are provided in the box below.

Rules of Discourse for a Community Circle

1. The guide makes a simple welcome statement like: "Hello, my name is _____. I want to thank you all for coming here today!"
2. "We're here to share our ideas about living here in [name of neighbourhood]." (*This sentence tells everyone why they are all there.*)

3. "We're going to use a talking circle format for our discussion." (*This sentence is aimed at those who may be more accustomed to tables and chairs or auditorium seats, and find the circle format a bit odd.*)

4. "We want to make sure that everybody gets a chance to speak, and that everyone gets a chance to hear everybody else." (*This statement tells everyone what is expected of them.*)

5. "Here's how it will work. I'm holding a beanbag." (*The guide holds the beanbag up for everyone to see.*) "Whoever holds it can talk as long as they want. During that time all the rest of us will be quiet and listen carefully to what the speaker is saying."

6. "When I am done speaking, I will pass the beanbag to the next person, and they can speak as long as they hold it."

7. "No one has to speak; if you don't want to speak, simply pass the beanbag along."

8. "Now, I want to reinforce two things for you to consider when you get the beanbag: only tell your own point of view—your own story—and remember, our time here is limited and everyone deserves a chance to speak, so don't dominate the air time—be considerate of others."

9. "We'll use this method for many of our meetings. Notice that there's an empty chair in the circle. That chair is for the people who we know should be here but can't for various reasons. We have to remember that what we say and do here is for them as much as it is for us."

10. "We'll start every meeting by introducing ourselves to each other and then addressing the question before us. Feel free to use only your first name if you prefer."

11. "Let's start by answering the question: 'What do you like about [name of neighbourhood]?' Since I'm holding the beanbag I'll tell you I don't live here but from what I've seen, I like [say something positive about the neighbourhood]. And now I'll pass the beanbag."

After the rules of discourse have been laid out, the direction of the discussion is determined primarily by the comments of the neighbours as the beanbag goes around the circle. Occasionally, when the beanbag comes back to the person who asked the first question, he or she can ask another question that moves the discussion toward some concrete outcomes. That is what the constable did in the spring cleanup example when he sensed that people were interested enough to answer the question: "What would you like to do about that trash?"

Sometimes the discussion takes on a life of its own, without the gentle nudging of another question from the guide, as in the real example described in the box below.

Community Problem-Solving in Social Housing

While starting a community mobilization initiative in a high-demand neigh-bourhood, officers began to pick up frequent and believable reports about illegal behaviour by a building superintendent who managed 75 single-family social housing units. This man had been managing these units for 15 years and seemed to be fairly rigid and unresponsive to the tenants' requests, even for routine maintenance, particularly if they came from people of colour. Police heard he was responsible for illegal evictions when some tenants tried to set up a tenant's association, sexual offences against women and girls, and trafficking in marijuana and pharmaceuticals out of his recreational vehicle. Non-coercive interviews with the superintendent certainly exposed his bad attitudes toward all of his tenants—but especially toward people of colour. So police commenced an investigation including surveillance.

Meanwhile, two constables went door to door, inviting the neighbours to a community conference on a Saturday morning. This neighbourhood had for years dominated calls for service and there were no indications that the neighbours were inclined to do anything to make things better for themselves. So police knew they had to facilitate social capital and com-munity cohesion.

Forty neighbours showed up for the meeting. They were of all ages and many ethnicities, and few of them showed signs of knowing each other. One constable welcomed the people and explained the rules of discourse. Then he started the beanbag around with the question: "What do you like about living here?" People began to hear good things about their neigh-bourhood, and most of them agreed with those positive comments. After about 20 such statements, the beanbag came to an approximately 30-year-old white, blonde mom who had brought her four-year-old son and five-year-old daughter with her. She announced: "I really liked living here some years ago, but I had to move away. Then I had my kids and I've just moved back because I wanted to bring them up here." Looking around the circle you could see that people were interested in her story. She continued, "But I have a problem. You see, when I leave my apartment, say to go to the com-mon laundry room, the super comes out and walks too close beside me, bumping his hip into mine. And twice when I got into the laundry room and put my basket down, he tried to hug me and kiss me on the lips!"

She stopped talking, but continued to hold the beanbag. Everyone was staring at her—many with shock and anger on their faces. You could have heard a pin drop; the silence was prolonged, and profound. Finally, the other police constable violated the rules of discourse and addressed her from across the circle, "If you'll come down to the station and make a statement, we will investigate that." She challenged him directly, "But I'll get evicted!" An uncomfortable silence followed until the young mother passed the beanbag along. Comments the rest of the way around the circle were about how disturbed the people felt about what this mother was going through and how powerless they all felt to do anything about it.

Finally, the beanbag landed in the lap of an 18-year-old black youth. Police had been warned that he was having behavioural and educational problems in high school. This youth had come to the meeting unaccompanied. Hunched over, he held the beanbag tightly, with his chin in one hand and his elbow on his knee. He looked very angry. Silence, again, prevailed. Finally, he broke protocol and raised his eyes to look across the circle directly at the mom, and said, "Do you know where I live?" Everyone looked surprised by that outburst. The mom responded, "Well, no!" The youth replied, "Well I'm going to write down my unit number for you; you should come see my mom; she can help you." He reached under his chair for his backpack to pull out a pen and paper. Then he stopped in mid-pull, and pointing at all the people in the circle, looked at the woman and asked, "Do you know where all these people live?" Again, she protested, "Well no, of course not!" The youth started writing on his paper and said, "I'm going to pass this paper around and I want everyone to write their name and unit number down." He looked at the mom again and said, "And then you can walk anywhere in our neighbourhood safely."

It was an "aha" moment for everyone in that circle. Body language and smiles said that everyone agreed with this young man's approach to this mom's problem with the superintendent. Apparently the constable who had asked the woman to file a complaint with police was inspired by his idea too, because when the beanbag came to him he once again addressed the mom. He said: "Would it be all right with you if we, the police, went to the super and told him we know what he's been doing and we are watching him?" He should have known what her reply would be: "Can you guarantee I won't be evicted?" This time he answered, "No, but if you are, we'll help you fight it." Again, people's smiles in the circle indicated they liked that answer and police legitimacy just went up a notch!

But this officer was not done; apparently the young man's inspiration was catching. The officer said, "What if I go to the super and tell him that not only the police know what he has been doing, but everyone else in this room knows also; and police and all the neighbours are watching him too?" The people were out of their chairs with joy, solidarity, and the rightness of these solutions to a very harmful community problem.

Meanwhile, police surveillance on this individual continued. In fact, police watched as this individual, after reigning over marginalized tenants for 15 years, moved away from this neighbourhood one month after this community circle.

Consider the following questions:

1. What elements of traditional policing did you see in this example? What elements of community policing did you see? Compare and contrast them in terms of their effectiveness in finding a solution.
2. Identify the community assets involved in this discussion.
3. What were the tangible indicators that this community circle was having the desired effect of facilitating social capital and community cohesion?

It is often asserted that the barriers to community building in marginalized neighbourhoods are racism, sexism, and ageism. But note in this example that the solution to the problem was proposed by an adolescent black male to an approximately 30-year-old white female. Note also that the solution came from a youth whom the school board had flagged to police as "marginal." In the context of asset-based community development, look what a community asset this young man was. Finally, note that all of this happened because police created a safe environment in which a community circle could be held, laid out the rules of discourse, and gently guided the neighbours in discussing and finding solutions to problems in their community. As a result, a group of people came into that room as strangers, but over the course of an hour and a half discussion, left the room in solidarity with a solution to a significant community problem.

Management by Consensus

Many of us are accustomed to group decision-making, whether it is in a business meeting, a club, or an association. In a business meeting, decisions are usually ultimately made by an authority. That is, the boss asks for opinions and then makes the decision for the whole group. In clubs or associations, the process more often is based on majority opinion. That is, people suggest different approaches, a vote is held, and the most popular opinion prevails.

Neither of those approaches works very well in high-demand neighbourhoods. Or, more accurately, decisions in high-demand neighbourhoods can be made in those ways, but they will not have the desired effect of creating the kind of solidarity and social cohesion that occurred in the story about the building superintendent. In contrast to the community circle, the authoritarian decision-making process is based on a power differential: the boss has all the power and authority. With **majority rule**, the majority has the power to

---

majority rule a decision-making process in which a decision or outcome that gains the greater share of votes (that is, a majority) is the decision that is chosen as final

make decisions; in other words, there are winners and losers. Neither of those approaches to group decision-making is conducive to community cohesion and, in a high-demand neighbourhood, community cohesion is the priority objective of police. In contrast to these approaches, consensus-based decision-making does generate community cohesion as well as good decisions.

Meaning of "Consensus"

Unanimous agreement about the best decision is not necessary to achieve **consensus**. The word does not mean that everyone thinks the final decision is the best one they could come up with. What it means is that everyone is willing to support the decision as the best one in the current circumstances. Consensus emerges out of everyone's consideration of what is in the best interests of the whole group. If a person can live with the emerging decision, in the interests of the whole group, they will sacrifice their preferred alternative in favour of the cohesive effect of agreement to proceed with what they might otherwise consider a suboptimal decision. Consensus really means that no one disagrees with the chosen solution to the extent that they would block the whole group from going forward with it.

Goals of Management by Consensus

Management by consensus works well in high-demand neighbourhoods because it supports community cohesion. Management by consensus seeks agreement. That is quite unlike majority rule, which is based on an adversarial discourse. Management by consensus strives to foster collaboration and cooperation, as opposed to competition.[9] Like the community circle, management by consensus encourages inclusiveness, voice, and participation.

Outcomes of Management by Consensus

If the discourse has been truly inclusive—that is, it has voiced all of the diverse opinions and points of view—then decisions that result from management by consensus are usually those that best address everyone's needs. Those are the best decisions for holding the group together and the easiest to implement effectively. Finally, decisions derived this way strengthen relationships in the group and generate the kind of collaborative spirit that is necessary for community problem-solving.

---

consensus a decision-making process that prioritizes the decision or outcome that all persons involved are willing to support as the best one in current circumstances

Stages in Management by Consensus

Management by consensus can be done in many ways, but most of the approaches rely on some form of the following six stages:

- Discussion of the problem and options for solutions: In this opening stage, participants get a firm grip on the problem they want to solve, and then begin to lay out the qualities of desirable solutions.
- Development of a proposed solution: At some point, a desirable solution will begin to percolate to the top of the discussion and the group can shift to a detailed development of that solution.
- Call for consensus: At some point, it will become obvious that a lot of the participants are ready to accept the proposed solution. This is an opportunity to see if consensus has emerged.
- Deal with concerns: Frequently, the first call for consensus will uncover some people's concerns with the proposed solution. This is a good time to have those concerns clearly voiced.
- Modify the proposed solution: Having heard concerns about the proposed solution, the group makes modifications with the aim of producing a solution that everyone will accept.
- Call for consensus: Participants are asked if they are now ready to support the modified, proposed solution.

Figure 6.2 shows how those stages relate to each other in the total flow of a consensus-based discussion.

FIGURE 6.2 **Flow of Discussion in Management by Consensus**

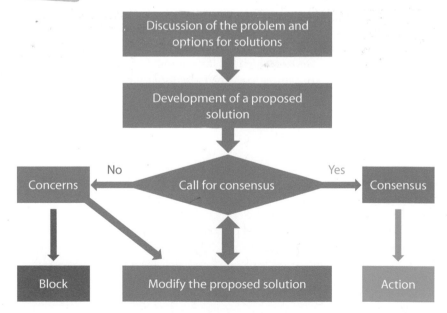

Notice that at the bottom of the figure there are only two possible outcomes when problem-solving with management by consensus: "Block" and "Action." If consensus is achieved, then the group can act on their proposed solution. If consensus is not achieved, then any action going forward is blocked—for the whole group. Management by consensus is about what the whole group is going to do. Of course, participants can shift between the call-for-consensus and modify-the-proposed-solution stages as often as they need to and have time for, and that may just permit them to achieve consensus eventually.

Key Roles in Management by Consensus

Just like any group decision-making process, management by consensus works better if some people play specialized roles. We are going to use the word "guide" as we did in our discussion of community circles, because this import-ant role is significantly different from the roles we may be more familiar with, like director, chair, president, facilitator, expert, or consultant. In fact, once the people in the group understand the role of the guide, anyone can do it. Some groups find that it is useful to pass that role around between meetings so that everyone shares responsibility for helping the whole group make good decisions.

The guide's job is to help the participants work their way through the sequence shown in Figure 6.2. One of the talents this person has to rely on most is listening. The guide has to listen carefully to the flow of discussion so that he or she can tell when it is time to shift between stages in the discussion. For example, when the guide begins to hear repetitive comments about the problem and alternative solutions, it is probably time to suggest that the par-ticipants piece together a proposed solution. Then, when that proposed solu-tion seems to be fully fleshed out, the guide has to sense when it is time to call for consensus. If someone has concerns about the proposed solution, it is important for the guide to help them express what their concerns are and then shift the discussion to ways in which the large group may accommodate those concerns through modifications to the proposed solution.

Achieving Consensus

1. One person agrees to guide the meeting.

2. The guide commences the community circle by offering a question for everyone to consider—for example, "We're here tonight to decide if we should mount a project to deal with loitering and litter." The guide then passes the beanbag to the next person.

3. The guide listens carefully to how people address this question, in order to discern whether there is an emerging consensus or a direction the group appears to be heading in.

4. By the time the beanbag gets back to the guide, some emerging consensus may be evident. The guide tests this by saying something like: "I'm beginning to get the sense that folks would like to focus on the litter problem and perhaps have a weekend neighbourhood cleanup project that includes outreach, sharing food, and maybe even some games for kids like a treasure hunt. Is that what you're saying?" The guide then passes the beanbag.

5. In the next round, either that idea will be rejected and another will take its place, or the people will begin to develop that idea in more detail so that by the time the beanbag gets back to the guide, the solution is fleshed out.

6. The guide summarizes the more detailed idea and, if he or she feels the group is ready to make a decision, asks: "I'm getting the sense that this group would like to go ahead with this idea. Is there anyone present who is opposed to this idea and does not want the group to go ahead and implement it?" The guide then waits for any dissenters to speak up.

7. If there is even one person who is so steadfast in their disagreement that they would block the whole group going forward, the guide will ask the whole group: "How do you think we can address his (her) concerns?" In seeking an answer to this question, the guide must consider whether to pass the beanbag or to simply mediate a spontaneous discussion in which participants suggest ways of addressing the dissenter's concerns. After the suggestions have been made, the guide asks the dissenter, "Would that make you feel better about going ahead with this plan?"

8. Finally, toward the end of the meeting, the guide reviews what has been accomplished: "We have come a long way here tonight. We have agreed to [description of actions agreed to]. We should probably put some point people on this. Who will take charge of [description of task]? Who will take charge of [description of task]? What will be our deadlines for these tasks?"

9. The following points are recorded:
   a. the problem that people set out to resolve,
   b. the tasks to be undertaken,
   c. who is responsible for each task,
   d. when the tasks should be completed, and
   e. the time of the next meeting.

Another important role in management by consensus is that of a timer. This is a person who keeps track of the total time for the meeting, estimates the amount of time needed for each stage of the discussion, warns people when they are running out of time, limits the air time of domineering speakers, and alerts people to elapsed time so that runaway discussions do not eat up the remaining time and derail the whole exercise. It is a delicate and important job.

The third important role in management by consensus is that of notetaker. In a more conventional meeting, this person might be called "secretary" or "recorder." But again, we use a new word for this position in order to differentiate it from those more familiar roles. In the first place, unlike an elected or appointed secretary in a club or association, the notetaker has no authority; they are not part of an executive body that runs the organization. They just take notes. Second, they take far fewer notes than a secretary or recorder would take in the more conventional setting. Conventionally, a club secretary takes the minutes of a meeting. These can be notes about who said what, to whom, etc. They can get quite detailed and they are rarely useful—with the exception of legal proceedings, where some of that information can be helpful to adversaries before the court.

For management by consensus, the only notes that the whole group needs are those that answer the following questions:

- What is the problem they set out to solve?
- What is the agreed solution? (Or if there was no consensus, the notes indicate only that.)
- What are the actions that follow from that agreed solution?
- Who is supposed to take those actions, and by when?

These notes are designed to help everyone keep their eye on the targets, take responsibility for actions, and meet deadlines. As with the positions of guide and timer, anybody in the group can take notes. Again, from time to time it is useful to give everyone experience with these roles because it helps to build cohesion and a sense of fully shared responsibility.

Methods in Low-Demand Neighbourhoods

Throughout these discussions of asset-based community development, appreciative inquiry, community circles, and management by consensus, we have focused on high-demand neighbourhoods. That is because they are where most of the crime and social disorder are; where police respond most often; and where there is the least community cohesion or capacity to resolve community problems. For effective community policing, it is important to remember that the first goal of all of these methods is to get the neighbours in touch with each other and foster a climate in which they can share some responsibility for resolving community problems. If that is not achieved, then police and other external agencies will continue to be held responsible for finding solutions to community problems—and that is not sustainable.

Alternative methods for group decision-making, with which we all are more familiar, are designed to get decisions made efficiently (in short order and with the least amount of effort)—not develop community cohesion. They work fine in low-demand neighbourhoods because there is already a foundation of social cohesion in these neighbourhoods. Most conventional decision-making processes have the following four components:

- Chair: designed to control the whole discussion, including the topics discussed, the persons allowed to speak, and the decisions made.
- Agendas: designed to control the ideas and topics to be discussed. Developed before the meeting, they prohibit the discussion from straying to topics that were not anticipated by those who designed the agenda—another form of control in the discussion.
- Majority rule: designed to force decisions as quickly as possible around the assumption that what the majority wants is good enough for the minority.
- Minutes: designed to document all that was said, and by whom, with the intent to hold individuals **accountable** and facilitate any follow-up action that might be required.

CHECK YOUR UNDERSTANDING

1. Compare and contrast the role of the guide in a community circle or management by consensus with that of the chair in a conventional decision-making process.
2. What are the differences between taking notes in management by consensus and taking minutes in a conventional problem-solving discussion?
3. Why are community circles, appreciative inquiry, and management by consensus more useful for application to community problem-solving in high-demand neighbourhoods than in low-demand neighbourhoods?

Community Justice

Community justice, called "restorative justice" in some literature, involves a major shift in how we think about and resolve disputes in the community, including criminal offences. Conventional approaches treat criminal acts as offences against public laws. In contrast, community justice treats criminal acts as offences against people in relationships in the community. Conventional approaches presume that it is the job of the state to extract reparations from, and mete out punishment to, those who offend against the laws of the land.

---

accountable accepting responsibility for one's actions

In contrast, **community justice** presumes that justice involves people who breach community relationships and people who are offended by those breaches. It is the community's job to manage a collective process for deciding on reparations and preventing re-offending—the dual purpose of these approaches being to maintain the cohesiveness and integrity, as well as safety and security, of the community.

Goals and Characteristics of Community Justice

Community justice brings together the offender(s), the victim(s), and the community to address the offence. The primary goals of community justice are to

- hold the offender(s) accountable for the impacts of their actions on the people and the community;
- restore (where possible and desirable) the relationship between the offender(s), victim(s), and the broader community; and
- reintegrate the offender(s) into the community for the purposes of healing the community, healing the offender(s) and victim(s), increasing community safety, and reducing the incidence of such offences.

Community justice strategies have four defining characteristics:

- they treat all offences seriously because offences threaten the peace, safety, and well-being of relationships in the community;
- they encourage community members to learn the impacts of their actions, take responsibility for those impacts, and stand accountable to the community for those impacts;
- they focus on providing a safe, democratic, and non-stigmatizing environment for repairing the damages caused by crime and anti-social behaviours and for reducing further occurrences; and
- they strive to be as inclusive as possible in order to maximize community cohesion.

Community Justice as Another Way to Look at Crime

Community justice is an alternative way to look at crime; it focuses on the harms done to the community and the community's collective response to it. It is in direct contrast to retributive justice and the conventional criminal justice system, which focuses primarily on the guilt and punishment of the offender. Community justice is a problem-solving process whereby all involved

community justice an approach to justice that addresses offences by focusing on the harm done to the broader community and the community's response to the offence; goals include accountability, healing, restoration of relationships, reintegration of the offender into the community, and reducing future offences

parties participate in a dialogue about the offence, its effects, and its implications for the future of the community. Community justice deals with crime and anti-social behaviour in their social contexts and involves the victim(s), the offender(s), their respective social support systems, and the community. It incorporates a variety of approaches and may be applied at the pre-charge, post-charge, pre-sentence, post-sentence, pre-incarceration, and even post-incarceration stages of the criminal justice process.[10]

Community justice strategies are well suited for disputes in the community—whether or not such disputes ever escalate to the point of chargeable offences. In that sense, community justice strategies are yet another tool in the community policing toolkit. Their greatest strength is their capacity to restore community cohesion after it has been ruptured by disputes, anti-social behaviour, or crime. They work. Sherman and Strang conducted randomized trials in which community justice practices were applied to violent crimes and property crimes. They concluded that these strategies

- substantially reduced repeat offending for some offenders;
- doubled the offences brought to justice as diversion from criminal justice;
- reduced crime victims' post-traumatic stress disorder symptoms and related costs;
- provided both victims and offenders with more satisfaction with justice than criminal justice;
- reduced crime victims' desire for violent revenge against their offenders;
- reduced the costs of criminal justice, when used as diversion from criminal justice; and
- reduced recidivism more than prison for adults or as much as prison for youths.[11]

Is Community Justice Soft on Crime?

Skeptics of community justice assert that it is "soft on crime." This is largely because they remain wed to the notion that punishment is the only appropriate response to offensive behaviour—notwithstanding mounting evidence that punishment more often exacerbates offensive behaviour. These critics fail to recognize that

- research has shown that punishment rarely deters crime;
- punishment is not synonymous with accountability;
- sincere remorse, apologies, reparations, and efforts to avoid re-offending are synonymous with accountability; and
- the burden, for an offender, of being held accountable to victims and members of their own community is far greater than most conventional forms of punishment meted out by the courts.[12]

Community justice has a greater impact on healing victims as well as offenders, strengthens the community's capacities to manage the behaviour of its members, and yields lower rates of recidivism.[13]

Community Justice and Classroom Bullying

The school liaison officer was called to the public school for the fourth time to deal with Tim, an 11-year-old boy who had assaulted a classmate, Kyle, in the schoolyard after school. The officer had tried everything with Tim—being his buddy to get him to talk about his problems; attempting to scare him straight by putting him in the back of a patrol car and informing him that he could be charged as a juvenile when he turned 12 years old; talking to his mother and asking her to exert more influence on Tim—but nothing worked. So he turned to the school board's social worker for advice. She recommended using a community justice conference, which she volunteered to run.

The first step was preparation. The social worker and officer interviewed Tim and his mom. She was white; he was mixed race, and his father was black. The first thing the social worker and officer established with both the mom and her son was that Tim had assaulted a classmate in the schoolyard. The social worker explained to the officer, "If they contest that the incident happened at all, then we won't use community justice." Both mom and Tim admitted that it happened. The team explained the community justice process and asked if they would cooperate; they said they would. The team asked them to select a few close friends and supporters of Tim to accompany him in the community justice meeting.

Then they interviewed Kyle (a dark-skinned black boy who was larger than Tim) and his single mom. This interview was not an easy one. Kyle's mom was angry because Kyle was being constantly picked on by Tim. She felt the school administration was refusing to deal with it. She wanted Tim to be expelled or face some other serious punishment, and complained that "this community justice thing is just another whitewash by the school board, which refuses to deal with these issues!" The team patiently explained the community justice process and asked if she and Kyle would support it; they reluctantly agreed that they would. The team then interviewed key participants in the school: the principal, the vice-principal, Tim's teacher, and Kyle's teacher. They discovered that both teachers had a good rapport with the boys.

The day of the community justice conference arrived. A vacant classroom, well away from the hurly-burly of the busy school, was set up for the meeting. All furniture was pushed back to the walls and 13 chairs were arranged in a circle in the middle of the room. A name was placed on each chair so that the people, upon arriving, would know where to sit. Boxes of facial tissues were distributed under every other chair. The meeting was attended by the school social worker and the police officer; the vice-principal and the two teachers; two school friends of each of the boys; and the boys and their moms.

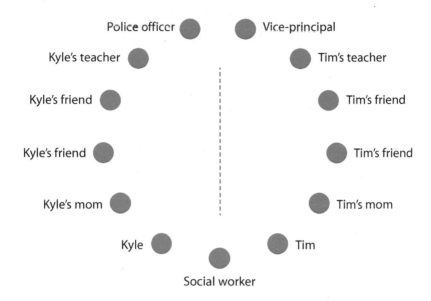

The day before, the social worker had explained to the officer: "Note that Tim, his mom, and his supporters will sit on my right, and Kyle, his mom, and his supporters will sit on my left. That is a deliberate effort to distinguish the two sides of this dispute. You and the vice-principal will be opposite me. You're just there because you want this dispute to be resolved; you are not taking sides. Nor am I. So the three of us will sit on the ends of the dividing line between the two sides." The officer asked, "Do you want me to come in uniform?" She replied, "You are a police officer! So, of course, wear your uniform. But leave your police enforcer at home, and bring your compassion and understanding." The officer asked, "Why will those other kids be there, and those teachers?" The social worker replied, "For real, sincere remorse to occur, Tim has to have his supporters there. If he is isolated, away from all those who love and care for him, it is much harder for him to lower his defences and consider the impact of his own actions. And for forgiveness to occur, Kyle needs his supporters too."

The community justice forum began when the social worker asked Tim to explain what happened. Looking defiantly at her, with his harms folded across his chest, Tim said, "I jumped on Kyle." The social worker asked, "How do you feel about that?" He replied, "I guess it was stupid!" She asked, "Why do you think that?" He answered, "'Cause if I hadn't done it, I wouldn't be here!" She asked, "How do you think Kyle felt about that?" He blurted, "I dunno!" She said, "Well, let's find out."

The social worker turned to Kyle and asked him, "Kyle, will you please tell us about what happened that day?" He did, in some detail. She asked, "How did you feel about that?" He replied at some length about the pain he felt, his fear of Tim, and his shock because he could not figure out what he had done to deserve it. The social worker thanked Kyle and asked his mom to describe what all of this meant to her. Predictably, Kyle's mom related her concern for her son, her anger that it happened at all, and her dismay that the school had not effectively stopped Tim's well-known bullying behaviour before this time.

Continuing around the circle on Kyle's side, the social worker asked Kyle's friends to tell her what they thought about the incident. They described their concern for Kyle, said they did not like to see him hurt, and vowed to stick with him to be sure it did not happen again. Moving on, the social worker asked Kyle's teacher to give her perspective. She expressed concern that anyone would pick on Kyle because she had always found him to be a gentle, loving, and considerate boy. She felt confident he had done nothing to justify such treatment, and said that while she would like to help and support Tim, his behaviour was making it awfully difficult for her to do so.

Finally, the social worker came to the police officer; she asked him to give his perspective. He sat silently for a moment, as if trying to figure out what to say. A large man, with a stern countenance, his silence and the expression on his face made it look like maybe he was going to be angry. But that is not what came out of his mouth! Slowly, quietly, he said, "I can't help but go back to when I was these boys' age, in school in Montreal. Every day after school, an older boy would wait for me and beat me up. I could never run fast enough to get away from him. Finally, I had to pretend that I enjoyed helping my teacher by staying after school to tidy the classroom and clean the blackboards. Meanwhile, I kept watch out of the windows to make sure this guy had left the school grounds before I headed home! To tell you the truth, I think it was that experience that had the strongest influence on my choosing to become a police officer." The people sitting in the circle looked stunned by the officer's story. The social worker let it sink in a bit, as if waiting to see if the officer had anything more to say, before asking the vice-principal for her perspective.

The vice-principal looked and sounded sad. She talked about how she took her job very seriously; about how school should be a place where all children felt safe; and how she felt like she was failing in her chosen career because she could not prevent Tim's aggressive behaviour. The social worker next prompted Tim's teacher and Tim's two friends. All three expressed support for Tim; they liked him; they saw good traits in him; they wanted him to succeed. But each, in their own way, expressed how disappointed they were in him that he continued to bully Kyle.

Then the social worker asked Tim's mom to speak. She had arrived with a blonde toddler, Tim's half-sister, in her arms. Tim's mom looked distraught and overwhelmed. She spoke quietly but unwaveringly, as if, while struggling with all that she had on her plate, she was determined to deal with this issue as best she could. She expressed her love for Tim, even guessed that his behaviour reflected some inner struggle of his that she did not fully understand and certainly did not know how to address with him. She reflected that maybe her current common law partner, the father of the little girl in her arms, was too harsh with Tim, saying, "He's never liked or accepted Tim; he's always yelling at Tim and he blames me for having Tim in the first place. I don't know what to do about that. Tim needs a good father figure, but his own dad is long gone!" She talked about her struggles to make ends meet; about how she had very little help and could not even get to medical appointments because she had no vehicle, no one to help with her daughter, and not enough money for public transit. She closed her statement by repeating that she loved Tim and would do anything to help him get through this negative phase in his development.

The social worker waited, very patiently, to see if Tim's mom had anything more to say. Then she looked at Tim, who by this time was sitting very still with his hands folded in his lap, shoulders slumped forward, and head down, looking at his hands. She asked Tim gently: "Tim, is there anything you would like to say?" He sat still and silently, until the movement of his shoulders showed that he was silently weeping; he mumbled something under his breath that no one in the circle could hear. The social worker asked, "What did you say?" He raised his head halfway, still not looking at anyone, and repeated, "I'm sorry!" She asked him, "Tim, is there something you would like to say directly to Kyle?" Tim looked up at Kyle with tears rolling down his cheeks, and said, "Kyle, I'm sorry I jumped on you; I won't do it again!" The social worker let that hang in the air for a moment, then turned to Kyle: "Kyle, is there anything you would like to say to Tim right now?" He replied: "That's all right, Tim; I guess it didn't hurt as much as it scared me!"

By this time, Tim's mom was quietly crying too. The social worker turned to Tim and asked, "Tim, what do you think you can do to repair the hurt caused when you jumped on Kyle?" Tim thought for awhile, and then offered, "I guess I could stay inside during recess so that he won't be afraid I'll do it again." She turned to Kyle and asked, "Kyle, would that be helpful?" Kyle replied, "I guess so." Then the social worker asked, "Does anybody else have a good idea about how to repair the damages this incident has caused?" Tim's mom spoke up: "I'll bring my daughter and we'll be here at the end of the school day to walk Tim home." Then the vice-principal spoke up and offered: "So that Tim won't have to sit alone in a classroom during recess, we could give him a job working with the janitor in the basement, cleaning the gum off the bottom of desks." The social worker asked, "Does everybody think that'd be a good idea?" Tim and everybody else agreed. Finally, Kyle's mom spoke up: "I think all these things will help. I want to thank Tim for his apology and I'd like to offer to transport his mom to her medical appointments whenever she has them." The social worker asked Tim's mom, "Would that be helpful?" She was silently weeping again, but looked at Kyle's mom and through a small smile said, "Thanks."

The social worker asked, "If no one has any more suggestions, let's plan to meet here again in three months and see how things are going. Is everyone in agreement with that?" Everyone agreed, and the social worker adjourned the meeting by inviting the group to have a drink and cookies that were set up at the back of the room. As they went for their refreshments, Tim stayed close to his mother, as Kyle did to his. Kyle's mom approached Tim's mom and gave her a hug, saying something under her breath that others could not hear. Tim's mom wept again as Kyle's mom held her. The four boys who were supporters of Tim and Kyle ate their cookies and acted like 11-year-old boys at recess. The police officer walked up to Tim and held out his hand for a handshake. Then putting his hand on Tim's shoulder, he invited Tim to accompany him over to Kyle. The officer said something only the boys could hear and the two boys also shook hands nervously. The vice-principal joined them and thanked both boys for being so helpful in the meeting.

One month later, the school liaison officer was invited back to the school to attend a convocation celebrating the work of outstanding students. What struck him most about the event was the image of Tim and Kyle, sitting side by side, way up at the top of the bleachers, sharing laughter and acting like good friends. When the officer mentioned that to her, the vice-principal replied, "That's nothing! You'd never guess what happened two weeks after our meeting! Kyle came to me and asked if he could work with Tim and the janitor during recesses, scraping the gum off desks. The janitor says he likes both boys and that they're working very well together. I just hope we've got enough gum chewers here to keep that going for awhile!"

Consider the following questions:

1. How did the dynamics of social cohesion change throughout this example?

2. What was behind the social worker's comment to the police officer: "You are a police officer! So, of course, wear your uniform. But leave your police enforcer at home, and bring your compassion and understanding."

3. Do you think the expressions of remorse and forgiveness were sincere? How could you tell?

4. Compare the community justice approach used in this scenario with the approach used in a courtroom. What might have happened in a courtroom if these boys were a little older?

Community justice forums like this are just one of many alternative dispute resolution processes that work in most communities. Others include various forms of mediation and arbitration. Some of them are more adversarial than others, so in picking an approach to a particular dispute, police must assess how important it is to restore community cohesion—then pick an approach accordingly. One of the best Canadian texts to consult on these issues is Susan Sharpe's *Restorative Justice: A Vision for Healing and Change*.[14]

CHAPTER SUMMARY

Community policing is, most certainly, about justice. However, police and members of the community have to think a little more broadly about what that word means. It means that everyone involved in an initiative feels like they are being treated fairly, that they are part of the solutions to community problems, that they are valued in the processes of problem-solving, and that they are contributing positively to the whole community.

Throughout this text we have reinforced the idea that where police and other first responders are called most often, they are required to compensate for deficiencies in a community's internal sources of social control. Asset-based community development and asset inventorying, appreciative inquiry, community circles, management by consensus, and community justice strategies share in common the goals of strengthening social cohesion and the community's internal capacities to exert social control. They are essential tools for effective community policing. These are tools for transforming a high-demand neighbourhood into a lower-demand neighbourhood.

REVIEW AND DISCUSSION QUESTIONS

1. What is the highest-priority goal of asset-based community development, asset inventorying, appreciative inquiry, community circles, management by consensus, and community justice forums?

2. Explain what we mean when we apply the phrase "community assets" to high-demand neighbourhoods.

3. If a neighbourhood has many problems to solve, why would police start that process by getting neighbours to talk about the positive qualities of the neighbourhood?

4. If appreciative inquiry starts out by focusing on what's good about a neighbourhood, how can police ever get neighbours to solve community problems?

5. What does "inclusiveness" mean? Why is it an important characteristic of all of the community policing tools we have discussed?

6. Why is the talking circle format ideal for many of the transformative community-building practices we have discussed?

7. What are important roles for police in applying these community policing tools?

8. In management by consensus, how does a guide know when consensus is beginning to emerge in a group?

9. What are some differences between the characteristics of community justice and criminal justice?

10. How do all these transformative community-building practices relate to community policing?

KEY TERMS

accountable, 185
appreciative inquiry, 167
asset-based community development, 164
community circles, 172
community justice, 186
consensus, 180
inventory of community assets, 164
majority rule, 179

NOTES

1   Kyle Kirkup, *Best Practices in Policing and LGBTQ Communities in Ontario* (Toronto: Ontario Association of Chiefs of Police, 2013).

2   Jody Kretzmann & John McKnight, *Building Communities from the Inside Out: A Path Toward Finding and Mobilizing a Community's Assets* (Evanston, Ill: Centre for Civic Engagement, Northwestern University, 1993) at 21.

3   Alison Mathie & Gord Cunningham, "Who Is Driving Development? Reflections on the Transformative Potential of Asset-Based Community Development" Occasional Paper Series No 5 (Antigonish, NS: Coady International Institute, October 2003) at 2.

4   *Ibid*.

5   Kretzmann and McKnight, *supra* note 2.

6   Mathie & Cunningham, *supra* note 3 at 3.

7   Theodore Kinni, "The Art of Appreciative Inquiry," *The Harvard Business School Working Knowledge for Business Leaders Newsletter* (September 2003).

8   Gervase R Bushe, "Appreciative Inquiry: Theory and Critique" in D Boje, B Burnes & J Hasard, eds, *The Routledge Companion to Organizational Change* (Oxford, UK: Routledge, 2011) 87.

9   T Hartnett, *Consensus-Oriented Decision-Making: The CODM Model for Facilitating Groups to Widespread Agreement* (Gabriola Island, BC: New Society, 2011).

10 Margaret Shaw, "Bringing the Community into Ontario Justice: Restorative Justice and Its Implications for Policing" (Address to the Police Conference on Community Justice: Strengthening Community Responsibility, Orillia, Ontario, October 1998).

11 Lawrence W Sherman & Heather Strang, *Restorative Justice: The Evidence* (London, UK: The Smith Institute, 2007).

12 Heather Strang, *Repair or Revenge: Victims and Restorative Justice* (Oxford: Clarendon Press, 2002).

13 John Braithwaite, *Restorative Justice and Responsive Regulation* (Oxford: Oxford University Press, 2002).

14 Susan Sharpe, *Restorative Justice: A Vision for Healing and Change* (Edmonton: Mediation and Restorative Justice Centre, 1998).

CHAPTER 7

Collaborating with Other Agencies and Organizations

FOCUS Rexdale situation table participants discuss a situation of acutely elevated risk as Police Constable Laura Langdon (in purple) takes notes at the June 22, 2016 meeting.

LEARNING OUTCOMES

Upon completion of this chapter, you should be able to:

- Explain why police and other community agencies need to collaborate
- Itemize what skills and capabilities police bring to a cross-sectoral collaboration
- Identify typical barriers to effective cross-sectoral collaboration
- Itemize the kinds of measures that are useful in overcoming barriers to effective collaboration
- Explain what police need to consider when thinking about whether they should join a cross-sectoral collaboration
- Identify steps in pulling together a cross-sectoral collaboration

Introduction

This chapter shifts our focus from the high-demand neighbourhoods in which we have spent so much of this text to the agencies and organizations that serve them. That is because the problems that police seek to resolve in those neighbourhoods require so much of the knowledge, resources, and program specialization that exists among all the agencies and organizations that populate the safety and well-being web described in Chapter 4. Consequently, police have to figure out how to obtain access to those agencies and organizations and engage them in community problem-solving in high-demand neighbourhoods.

Notice that this shift in focus takes us from mobilization of community assets in high-demand neighbourhoods to engagement of community organizations, agencies, businesses, and municipal bodies. Both are jobs for community policing, but the community policing tactics are significantly different in each. This chapter is about those differences.

Our discussion also signals a significant transformation in policing, moving police agencies further and further away from the traditional model described in Chapter 2. Think back to our discussion of traditional policing for a moment. Traditional policing was based on the military experiences of the 19th century. Police represented a self-contained unit that possessed all of the skills and capabilities it needed to achieve the ends it set out to achieve. But as we have emphasized in previous chapters, no police agency can possess all the skills and capabilities that are needed to resolve the significant problems that create crime and disorder in high-demand neighbourhoods. As a result, police need to partner with other agencies and organizations, and that creates significant challenges for police and other agencies alike.

For example, under the traditional model, police were not subject to close public scrutiny and could get away with withholding information under the guise of investigating crime and maintaining standards of evidence. But under today's more collaborative model, that will not work. Now police agencies are expected to be more transparent, share responsibilities, be more accountable, and even occasionally defer to the preferences of other agencies and specialists.

All of these changes reinforce the idea first expressed in the introduction to Chapter 1 that community policing is not static—it is alive and constantly changing. In that sense, this snapshot in time does not represent all that community policing can ever be. Unlike in the traditional model, community policing is always evolving—much as communities grow, change, and adapt to changing circumstances.

Why Should Police Collaborate?

Much of this text has focused on the reasons police and other agencies and organizations need to collaborate more often. We have noted that solving the problems police encounter requires more than what police alone can bring. For that matter, solving most of these problems requires more than what any single agency can bring. As Spezza and Borbely have said: "Multi-field collaboration can utilize an expanded array of strategies, resources, and capabilities to create outcomes one agency cannot accomplish alone."[1]

In earlier chapters, we emphasized the role of the social determinants of health, which underpin so much social disorder and crime—for example, access to income, access to education, employment and job security, safe and healthy working conditions, early childhood development, food security, quality housing, social inclusion, cohesive social safety network, and health services. Pick any one of them and ask yourself, "What single agency can effectively deal with this determinant all by itself?" Rhys and Entwistle call these "**wicked issues**," by which they mean community problems with many different roots that reach into different sectors of specialization.[2] They state that the reason no single agency can resolve wicked issues is that most agencies, including police, have narrow and specific mandates, authorities, roles, resources, and accountability:

> For local service providers, neither their mandate nor their powers usually extend beyond quite specific contingencies identified by higher levels of government. Although individual agencies may develop considerable expertise within their mandated area, many pressing social problems— or wicked issues—cut across or fall between these boundaries.[3]

At a minimum, then, problem-solving with wicked issues requires at least coordination in service delivery between and among a number of agencies. Coordination includes things like scheduling service delivery between agencies so that professionals from their respective agencies do not get in each other's way. Coordination also includes informing other agencies when one is about to implement an intervention so that they may consider the impacts of that intervention on their own services.

But collaboration requires much more than coordination. It requires that agencies get together to develop common goals. It requires that they share responsibility for planning all of the appropriate interventions, whether or not their own agency is involved in each of those interventions. The advantage of collaboration is frequently unanticipated. As Selsky and Parker point out, "[W]hen actors from different sectors focus on the same issue, they are likely to think about it differently, to be motivated by different goals, and to use different approaches."[4] That is what we call the **value-added** of collaboration— the extra capabilities that become possible when people work together. It goes back to the old adage that "the whole is greater than the sum of the parts." When specialists from a variety of agencies get together to consider solving a community problem, they bring different kinds of knowledge and levels of

---

wicked issues problems that have many causes that fall into different sectors of specialization

value-added extra capabilities that become possible when people work together

experience to the discussion. That stimulates everyone to look at the problem in new ways and consider solutions that had never occurred to them before.

IN THE COMMUNITY

High-Risk Case Coordination Protocol Framework

Some social problems are so complex that agencies have to break down their silos and collaborate in order to find resolution. One such problem is domestic or intimate partner violence. In 2010, Nova Scotia created the Domestic Violence Action Plan, which brings together 16 government agencies (including education, health, justice, Aboriginal affairs, immigration, labour, municipal relations, and seniors) to protect the safety of persons at risk of intimate partner violence. People working in the field of domestic violence had been striving for comprehensive case coordination for a long time. When one agency identified a person at substantial risk of harming their intimate partner, that agency sought to notify others and mobilize a concerted package of supports and services that would reduce those risks. In the past, this communication and collaboration was stymied by provincial privacy protection legislation and common practices among social service providers.

To remedy this, the Domestic Violence Action Plan convened the Department of Justice, including police, victim services, and court services, with partners from the Department of Community Services, such as child welfare, transition houses, and men's intervention programs, and created the High-Risk Case Coordination Protocol Framework. Now, when a high-risk case is identified, information must be shared so that all of the agencies can take collaborative action. The goal is to increase victim safety, reduce risks, and avoid duplication of files.

One way to determine who is "high risk" is with the use of the Ontario Domestic Assault Risk Assessment (ODARA), which is a 13-item assessment tool that estimates the chances that a person (usually, but not always, a man) who has assaulted his or her intimate partner (usually, but not always, a woman) will do so again. ODARA also assesses how that perpetrator's risk factors compare with those of other known abusers. When a victim is administered ODARA in order to assess the chances they will be victimized again by the same perpetrator and receives a score that is "high risk," a domestic violence case coordinator at a Nova Scotia police agency is notified and case planning begins. This is called "proactive referral" because the process is designed to begin before another incident of violence can occur. Although the High-Risk Case Coordination Protocol Framework has not yet been evaluated, police officers from across the province are hopeful that collaboration will lead to improved safety for victims of intimate partner violence and the reduction or elimination of intimate partner homicide.

SOURCE: Department of Justice, *Inventory of Spousal Violence Risk Assessment Tools Used in Canada*, online: <http://www.justice.gc.ca/eng/rp-pr/cj-jp/fv-vf/rr09_7/p4.html>.

Consider the following questions:

1. What makes domestic violence a problem that requires collaboration among many agencies?
2. If human and social service providers realized that domestic violence requires inputs from many agencies, what kept them from reaching out to each other and working together?
3. If the Nova Scotia High-Risk Case Coordination Protocol Framework works, what will be the impact on police agencies?

Collaboration and Goal-Setting

Collaboration simply means two or more social or human service organizations working together to realize mutually derived and valued goals. Collaboration is the opposite of competition. The key to this definition is the phrase "mutually derived and valued goals." That implies that the agencies start working together in order to determine the goals that will drive both of them forward, together. It is that kind of work that forces police partners to dive a little deeper into understanding the problems they want to resolve.

Collaboration does not allow police to simply be content with the goal of preventing a particular crime or reducing the incidence of some form of social disorder. For example, presume that a police service wishes to reduce officers' wait times in hospital emergency rooms when they apprehend someone who is manifesting symptoms of a mental health problem. That goal requires that officers collaborate with mental health agencies. But once the officers begin to unpack that problem with experts in mental health, they soon realize that there are more profound goals that need to be achieved, like getting mental health clients more direct access to higher-quality mental health services, quicker, so that the situation does not escalate to the point where police are called to intervene in the first place. That is the goal that drove the development of Hamilton, Ontario's Mobile Crisis Rapid Response Team in which officers partner with qualified social workers to deal with these kinds of situations (discussed in Chapter 3). That will certainly reduce the total amount of time that police officers spend in ER waiting rooms. But consider how much more it accomplishes in serving the needs of the mental health client—a goal that may not have occurred to police officers if they had not collaborated with mental health professionals in the first place.

---

collaboration two or more social or human service organizations working together to realize mutually derived and valued goals

Differences Between Sectoral and Cross-Sectoral Strategies

Collaboration is tough enough within sectors, where the collaborators already share many similarities—say, when a municipal police service chooses to collaborate with the RCMP. Both collaborators come out of the justice sector; both thoroughly understand policing; both have similar perspectives on the problems they want to resolve together. But those similarities do not mean that it easy for them to collaborate effectively. Most police services, for example, can relate stories about investigations during which they felt that they were competing with other police services with which they were supposed to be collaborating. Too often those investigations have been hampered when competitive tendencies led to dysfunctional behaviours like withholding from partner agencies intelligence and information that would have moved the investigation along much quicker. Collaboration at the best of times, even between agencies within the same sector, is not easy.

Cross-sectoral collaboration can be even more challenging. **Cross-sectoral collaboration** means two or more agencies from entirely different technical sectors working together to achieve shared goals. A good example would be a police officer and a social worker responding together to a person presenting mental health symptoms. The important distinction here lies in the word "sector." Generally speaking, a **sector** is composed of organizations with specific expertise, mandate specialization, and resource allocation. For example, police operating in the justice sector have expertise in applying the *Criminal Code*; they are mandated to enforce that law with very special capabilities that almost no one else in Canada possesses; and they are given resources that are dedicated for that work. How different that sector is, then, from the health sector, in which specialized agencies are empowered by provincial health legislation to promote health as well as treat disease, and are given dedicated resources for that purpose.

This chapter is really about cross-sectoral collaboration. Officers need to know when and how to collaborate with specialists from other sectors because the wicked issues that bring officers back to high-demand neighbourhoods time and time again require inputs from diverse agencies and organizations that operate in the safety and well-being web described in Chapter 4. At that point, it becomes a job for police to engage those partners from other sectors in the problem-solving enterprise already started with neighbourhood assets. That is cross-sectoral collaboration.

---

cross-sectoral collaboration two or more agencies from entirely different sectors, working together to achieve shared goals

sector a group of organizations with specific expertise, mandate specialization, and resource allocation

Spezza and Borbely have pointed out some significant differences in the characteristics of problem-solving within sectors and across sectors. Adapted from their work, Table 7.1 summarizes these differences.

TABLE 7.1   A Comparison of the Characteristics of Problem-Solving Within and Across Sectors

Within Sectors	Across Sectors
Scaling up one agency: Authorities that provide mandates and resources presume that the resolution of wicked issues can be achieved by simply scaling up the most appropriate agency. For example, if crime is rampant, pour more resources into policing.	*Involving multiple agencies*: Authorities that provide mandates and resources acknowledge that wicked issues can only be resolved through systemic reform that is achieved through the concerted efforts of agencies from a variety of sectors.
Government withdrawal: Once mandates are given and resources are provided, governments largely disconnect themselves from operations.	*Government engagement*: Governments closely monitor the collaborative and stand by to leverage partners, resources, and operations whenever and wherever it is appropriate.
Resources for one, best agency: Similar agencies within the sector (like police agencies within the justice sector) compete for limited funds to do their work. Funders grant these moneys based on assumptions about which competing agency will provide the best outcomes.	*Resources for the best collaborative*: Funders (like provincial governments) recognize that wicked issues require diverse types of expertise. As a result, they provide financial support for cross-sectoral collaboratives that promise the most effective combination of expertise.
Competition: Human and social service agencies jealously guard operational goals, data, information, and strategies in order to enhance their competitive position for limited resources.	*Collaboration*: Human and social service agencies work together to find common goals to achieve mutually desired outcomes, in order to attract shared resource supports.
Evaluating one agency: Evaluation of project outcomes focuses on the inputs, processes, and results of a single agency.	*Evaluating the collaborative*: Evaluation starts with performance criteria that are derived by all partners and ascribes outcomes to the whole collaborative.

SOURCE: Adapted from Carolynn Spezza & Christina Borbely, "Cross-Sector Collaboration" (2013) 9:10 *Prevention Tactics* at 1, online: <http://www.cars-rp.org/wp-content/uploads/2014/08/PT09.10.14.pdf>.

One of the places that this analysis takes us is to the observation that if local collaboration is as important as evidence is beginning to show it is, then authorities that enable and fund these collaboratives have to get behind the effort with more cross-sectoral mandates and resources.

ON PATROL

A Drug Intervention in a Low-Demand Neighbourhood

Police dispatch received the call from the hospital emergency room administrator at 8 o'clock Sunday morning: "We had a problem Saturday night that I think you guys will probably want to follow up on. Ten kids from the same high school were brought here last night. All of them OD'd on heroin!" The drug unit investigated and found 10 distraught and contrite high school students, 20 shocked and frightened parents, and 1 frustrated school principal, who said, "I've got one scumbag in my school who is responsible for all of this. You guys take care of him and I'll handle the rest of it!" Police commenced investigation of the principal's suspect while continuing to interview the parents of the ten students. What they discovered suggested that the problem was bigger than one high school drug dealer.

All of these youths lived in an upper-middle class suburb and were sons and daughters of double-income parents, making them latchkey kids. The parents were dedicated, hard-working professionals who invested significant amounts of time and energy in their jobs. Most left home early in the morning (before school buses picked up their kids) to drive to the downtown core for work, and returned very late in the afternoon. They wanted to be good parents and felt somewhat guilty for not spending more time with their children. So they used some of their earnings to give their kids the latest technology and cars as soon as they were eligible. The parents all denied having any idea that their children were experimenting with drugs, much less struggling with potential addictions. In fact, most of the parents claimed to not even know how to identify whether their child had a drug problem.

One father admitted to unwittingly paying off his son's drug dealer, on the front porch of his own home, three times. The dealer, getting no satisfaction from his user, had shown up at the youth's house at suppertime and rung the doorbell. Suppertime was the only time the family had to spend together during the week, so dad resented the interruption and insisted on answering the door. When the dealer asked for his son, dad explained that suppertime was not a good time to reach him and asked why the dealer needed to see him. The dealer replied, "He borrowed money from me and I need him to pay it back." Dad said, "How much?" and upon getting a figure, forked over the cash. Returning to the dinner table, dad chastised his son, who promised to be more responsible in the future. But this occurred three times!

At this point in the investigation, the drug unit asked for help from community policing officers because they realized that the level of naiveté exhibited by these parents indicated bigger problems in the whole school population. Officers convened an evening conference at the school, sending invitations to everyone in the school community. Expecting 70 to 100 people to attend, they were overwhelmed when 700 people showed up. Police arranged in advance for the ten youths to tell the school community what they had done and for their parents to relate their experience and feelings about the whole matter. That led to a very lively discussion about the problem of drugs in the school, the ignorance of both youth and parents, the ability of youths with driver's licences to access drugs in the city, and the school administration's avoidance of the whole issue.

This meeting stimulated police to reach out to a local addictions professional who operated a not-for-profit addictions treatment and counselling agency in the basement of a local shopping mall. Initially, this woman (accompanied by one officer) met with these ten youths and their parents. By this time, all of them were highly motivated to more effectively tackle the problem of drugs and addictions in their high school. One of the youths, who worked on the school newspaper, agreed to write and publish a series of articles about drug experimentation and addiction to discourage other students from using drugs.

The 20 parents decided to meet weekly to support each other in doing things that would help their children grow up safe and healthy. They started by soliciting the addiction specialist's help in putting together a brochure about how to recognize drug and addictions problems in high school youths. They printed hundreds of copies of the brochure and distributed them widely throughout their suburb and in the high school. But then they moved on to other subjects that were important to their kids, like safe sex, sexual assault (including a discussion of "No means no!"), how to get summer employment, preparing for exams, prospecting for post-secondary education, dealing with body image problems and eating disorders, and safety for newly licensed drivers. Each initiative was led by concerned parents working together in collaboration with subject matter experts from a wide variety of agencies and organizations in the surrounding community.

The incident involving the ten youths who overdosed on heroin occurred in 1999. That organization of double-income parents who cared enough about their kids to support each other in ensuring their kids grew up safe and healthy exists to this day in that suburb. Of course, the members have changed as the kids have grown and families have come and gone. But what started out as a serious community heroin problem has turned into a huge youth development asset in that suburb and school community.

Consider the following questions:

1. Was this just a police problem, as the school principal implied? Explain your answer.

2. What factors contributed to the kids' drug abuse?

3. Why do you think 700 members of the school community showed up for that evening meeting? What does that say about the scope of the problem?

4. What is the role of cross-sectoral collaboration in this story?

5. What was the role of the police in initiating cross-sectoral collaboration?

6. What would you guess is the role of police in the ongoing parent group that continues to work with subject matter experts on ways to ensure youths grow up safe and healthy?

Police Experience with Collaboration

Most police agencies have some experience with collaboration. Often it occurs around discrete problems, with a defined target audience, and goals that originate with police—for example, a safe-driving campaign targeted at new drivers, in a partnership among police, high school administrators, and Mothers Against Drunk Driving. We can learn something about such experiences, what makes them work, and some of the problems with them, by looking at an Australian survey of such initiatives.

In 2007-2008 the Australian Institute of Criminology (AIC) surveyed 229 community-based crime prevention initiatives.[5] Police were involved in 69 percent of them, the highest level of involvement by any stakeholder. A little over one-quarter of them were delivered by government (27 percent); the balance were initiated or led by a variety of agencies like health, social services, sports, media, youth, businesses, charities, and community-based organizations (not-for-profits). This sample gave the AIC an opportunity to find out just exactly what police bring to such collaboratives and what were some of the challenges that partners experienced in working with police. Table 7.2 defines the roles of police at three stages of the projects: planning, implementation, and evaluation.

Morgan reported that police were involved in these projects for some or all of the following reasons:

- Police provide a credible, and therefore persuasive, presence.
- Police are gatekeepers to the whole criminal justice system.
- Crime and social disorder reduction and prevention are something police know about.
- Police control a highly specialized workforce.

Morgan found that police were helpful on the projects if

- partners saw some value in engaging them,
- the collaborative's leadership had a positive relationship with police,
- police had an obvious and unique role to play,
- police brought some resources to the initiative, and
- police demonstrated an interest in becoming involved.

On the other hand, these 229 community-based crime prevention initiatives also exposed some of the challenges community collaboratives faced when working with police agencies. These challenges were found in three areas: agency alignments, staffing, and operations.

Agency Alignments

Sometimes it was easier to get a police agency to "partner" in name only. That is, they would add their name to a partnership proposal or agreement but fail

TABLE 7.2 **Police Contributions to Community-Based Crime Prevention Projects**

Planning	Implementation	Evaluation
Demonstrating project support; lending credibility to the project; supporting funding proposals; promoting the project to the community.	Advising persons and organizations on personal safety.	Steering, with other partners, project management and evaluation.
Informing and advising project partners about crime, police actions, and prevention.	Referring community members for specific services and supports (like victims' services).	Offering crime data and analysis to support evaluation.
Offering crime data and analysis for project planning.	Providing officers to implement solutions.	
Consulting with communities on problems to be resolved.	Implementing proactive problem-solving initiatives to support the work of the coalition.	
Recommending specific actions and solutions.		
Engaging third parties to join the collaborative.		

SOURCE: Adapted from Anthony Morgan, "Police and Crime Prevention: Partnering with the Community" in Judy Putt, ed, *Community Policing in Australia*, Research and Public Policy Series No 111 (Australian Institute of Criminology, 2010) 54 at 59. Copyright Australian Institute of Criminology.

to demonstrate real commitment to the partnership by taking an active role in it. Differing agency structures and understandings of the problem to be resolved by the collaborative provided a stumbling block for police participation. Often, this problem stemmed from differing ideas about the causes of crime and social disorder, with police having one point of view and other agency partners having quite a different one. The hierarchy of police agencies also created challenges for community partners—particularly when support for the initiative existed among front-line officers but not among senior command.

Staffing

A frequent challenge for collaboratives that included a police agency related to their tendency to constantly rotate police personnel through the initiative—whether for short-term replacement purposes (when an officer went on holidays, had a shift change, or was assigned for training) or for long-term reassignment. This seriously jeopardized continuity of police inputs and efforts. Other times, police would assign someone to liaise with the initiative as their representative, but would not assign officers to attend committee or team meetings and share in project decision-making and implementation. A third staffing problem that was frequently faced by community-based collaboratives was a reduction in force in the police agency—usually accompanied by the withdrawal of officers from a crime prevention initiative so that they could be reassigned to general duties.

Operations

Cross-sectoral collaboratives frequently take a lot of time and effort to form, organize, and become operational. Too often, that time and level of effort are not anticipated or planned for in project documents or partnership agreements. That often jeopardizes the capacity of police and other agencies participating in this most important piece of the work. Additionally, while police data and analysis may have led to the formation of a crime prevention collaborative, police frequently found it difficult to sustain quality data and analysis to inform regular, systematic problem analysis and monitoring of solutions.

Barriers to Effective Collaboration

Police agencies are not the only partners that create barriers to effective cross-sectoral collaboration. Other agencies in the partnership may create barriers as well. That is not surprising, and certainly the point is not to place blame at the feet of those agencies that find it difficult to collaborate. After all, many have been legislated, mandated, and resourced to operate in a virtual silo. Cross-sectoral collaboration is a relatively new idea for many human and social service providers—and certainly for police. So it is appropriate for us to take a look at some of the common barriers that most new collaboratives encounter at the outset.

Core Differences Among the Partners

Three core differences between potential partners in a cross-sectoral collaboration frequently create barriers to effective problem-solving. The first is strictly a function of the fact that the partners, by definition, come into the collaboration with different responsibilities.[6] For example, police have responsibility to enforce the laws of the land, whereas health agencies have responsibility for health and healing. Those core responsibilities can create conflict. For example, when a mental health client is disturbing the peace or threatening to hurt himself or others, the first priority for police is the safety and security of all involved, even if that requires restraint and detention of the person; whereas the first priority for a mental health worker might be to de-escalate tensions and emotional stresses the individual is feeling. Such barriers need to be acknowledged early in the life of the collaborative, and partners need to have clear and frank discussions about where barriers exist and how to effectively work through them together.

The second core difference is that agency partners from different sectors often have differing perspectives on the problem they are setting out to resolve. Police may see a young gang member from an abusive home as a budding career criminal, whereas a social service provider may see this person as someone needing treatment and support after a life of abuse and rejection from more acceptable community groups. It is important to note that both perspectives are valid, so the discussion about differing perspectives should never be reduced to "Who's right and who's wrong?" Rather, to allow the collaborative to proceed effectively, such perspectives need to be discussed, their holders need to work hard to see the other's point of view, and together they need to decide what concerted actions would satisfy both points of view while achieving the broader goals of the collaborative. In this case, police could take enforcement actions that stop harmful gangland behaviours while the social service provider could figure out what social supports would help the individual avoid falling into those old behavioural patterns again.

The third core difference among partners in a cross-sectoral collaborative relates to differences in interpretation and understanding of policies and legislation.[7] Consider a new collaborative of human and social service providers that comes together to identify people at acute risk of harm or victimization. It plans an intervention to reduce those risks before anyone gets hurt or requires an emergency response. But early in the forming stage, the partners present differing interpretations of privacy legislation. This becomes a barrier for the whole collaborative because minimal private and confidential information needs to be shared between the agencies that will be planning the intervention—like the name and age of the person who is the subject of the intervention. In one such collaborative in central Ontario, the mental health agency has absolutely refused to participate based on its interpretation of its own provincial enabling legislation, which it says prohibits the sharing of any privacy-protected information with anyone else unless a warrant is issued. This stance flies in the face of provincial privacy legislation, which enables the sharing of private and confidential information under conditions of potential harm to self or others, and with the appropriate measures of effective information management.[8] But the mental health agency is holding out—jeopardizing the potential of the whole collaborative.

However, it is important for the parties to not place blame on the mental health agency or accuse it of being unreasonable and obstructing what would otherwise be a real boon to this community. The collaborative needs to identify and work through these differences. The backstory on this particular case is that the whole mental health sector in Ontario recently came under criticism on this issue when a Canadian wanting to cross at the Canada–US border was stopped by border officials.[9] The officials saw on their computer database some indication that the individual had previous mental health issues. That health information should not have appeared on the border agency's database. That was privacy-protected information that had been inappropriately, if not illegally, shared between agencies. At the time of writing, Ontario's *Mental Health Act* was being revised to address this and other problems. But a local mental health official had chosen to interpret these events as applying to his own sector and as a prohibition against sharing any privacy-protected information, at any time, with anybody outside of his sector.

Tensions and Suspicions

It is relatively easy to isolate the kinds of core differences that exist among partners to a cross-sectoral collaboration. It is harder to put one's finger on the subtler, but potentially more damaging, tensions and suspicions that frequently operate between and among agencies. One of the most common tensions arises over issues, perceived or real, of power and control in the collaborative. Most of the agencies coming into a collaborative are accustomed to being entirely in control of their own policies, procedures, decisions, actions, and resources. But as soon as they invest in a true collaborative, those become shared functions (depending on how well the collaborative comes together). That necessarily implies that all partners to the collaborative lose some of their autonomous power and control, and that can create tensions between partners.[10] Think back to the Mrs. Robertson story in Chapter 1. The Family and Children's Services social worker who was leading those five parents in a discussion about making improvements in the community bore the title "Community Development Specialist." When the police officer interrupted her efforts to hire child care from outside the community in order to enable these five parents to do community development work, this social worker felt threatened. She complained to her boss, "Police are just trying to take over community development from us!" That, of course, is not what the officer was trying to do, but in this situation, the perception was more important than the reality. In situations such as this, the goal is to bring perceptions and reality into alignment. Therefore, it is important for budding collaboratives to voice and discuss such tensions.

Another barrier to effective cross-sectoral collaboration is suspicion about why some partners want to join in the first place.[11] A common suspicion levelled at police agencies is that they are collaborating only to get more intelligence and information that would strengthen their investigations. There is no amount of denial that will reduce that suspicion, but it docs help to at least air it in early discussions about the involvement and roles of all agencies in the partnership. The best way for police to effectively defuse this suspicion is to contribute positively and collaboratively (transparently, equitably, and fully) with all community partners.

A related source of tension in the collaborative is concern over any agency's real commitment to the common cause. You can see how this would run parallel to suspicion about an agency's true motives for joining the collaborative in the first place. For example, if partners thought that police were joining only in order to get better intelligence on targets of their investigations, then they would also doubt the police agency's commitment to the collaborative's shared goals. As with most of the other barriers already identified, this one is best dealt with up front, during discussions that lead to articulation of the common cause—the goals of the collaborative. If all agencies are investing equally in those deliberations, the chances are good that all of them will invest equally in resourcing and supporting their implementation.

Structural Shortcomings

Finally, there can be structural shortcomings that create barriers to effective collaboration across sectors. One of those is inadequate knowledge or training on the issues underlying the problem that a community is setting out to resolve. The social determinants of health are a good example. All health agencies, and most social work agencies outside the health sector, have received training and information about those determinants over the past 50 years. But the social determinants of health have entered the consciousness of some enlightened police officers only in the last 10 years. They certainly have not been incorporated into core police training or even training for specialist community policing officers. You can imagine how such a structural difference would influence the differing perspectives that agencies bring to their analysis of the same problem.

A second structural challenge for collaboratives relates to available technologies.[12] For example, most computer systems are not compatible between agencies in different sectors. Databases certainly are not. So when a group of agencies wants to work together and monitor the effects of their work on target communities and individuals, they face a significant challenge in figuring out how to do that efficiently. We introduced this challenge in Chapter 1 in our discussion of municipalities that fostered collaboratives to create one index of well-being that could be applied to many neighbourhoods. Such indexes have to be created out of different databases that are maintained by diverse agencies operating in relative isolation from each other. That is a huge technical challenge.

A third structural barrier for most collaboratives is resource limitations and fragmented funding.[13] When collaboratives come together and begin to recognize the potential impact and value-added that a coalition brings to problem-solving, they also realize that resources dedicated for this purpose are far too few to produce optimal outcomes. Furthermore, those resources are usually dispersed among some—never all—partner agencies. So some agencies end up contributing more resources from their siloed funding window; others contribute only in kind. Such fragmented funding can not only threaten to fail the needs of the consortium, but also instill tensions and suspicions about commitment among the partners. This problem will prevail until higher levels of government acknowledge the value of cross-sectoral collaboration and enable and resource it with that goal in mind.

CHECK YOUR UNDERSTANDING

1. Give two examples, each, of useful roles and functions that police can bring to planning, implementing, and evaluating cross-sectoral collaboratives.

2. Name at least two of the most common problems that collaboratives have with police partners.

3. List six common barriers to cross-sectoral collaboration.

What's Needed to Make a Collaborative Work?

With all these potential barriers and pitfalls, how can a group of agencies put together an effective cross-sectoral collaborative? It all starts with legitimacy and trust. Recall our earlier emphasis that police efforts to engage in community problem-solving will not work if the police do not enjoy a level of legitimacy in the community. It is legitimacy that permits neighbours to trust police when officers begin to mobilize and engage people who, up until that moment, have not had much to do with each other. Trust, stemming from legitimacy, does not happen overnight. Neither is it a static state. That is, even if trust is not quite established yet, it can be developed. But first and foremost, potential partners to a collaborative have to respect each other for what they do, and how they do it (legitimacy). And that goes for police as well as others.[14]

Once a base level of mutual respect and legitimacy among potential partners in a collaborative has been achieved, the foundation of an effective cross-sectoral collaborative can be laid. It then remains for agency representatives to

- engage in strategic planning for the collaborative;
- develop goals and activities for the collaborative with which each member can agree;
- communicate often and thoroughly with all partners;
- draw on available expertise around specific issues as they come up; and
- spread responsibility for funding and other resources as broadly as possible among all partners.[15]

Collective Impact

"Collective impact" is a term that has grown in significance since 2011, as more and more agencies and organizations discover that they can be so much more effective in resolving the kinds of wicked issues that plague high-demand neighbourhoods if they work together and share goals and accountability. **Collective impact** means working together, across sectors, to resolve large-scale social problems with shared goals, responsibilities, and accountability. Collective impact implies cross-sectoral collaboration. So this is quite different from the effects of two police agencies coordinating and cooperating in an investigation. Collective impact forces us to consider how a police agency, with its unique mandate, knowledge, capabilities, technologies, and specialized personnel can effectively develop mutual trust, shared goals, collective responsibilities, and accountability, and pool resources with partner agencies from other sectors.

Kania and Kramer framed this concept in 2011 when they said that collective impact "requires a systemic approach to social impact that focuses on the relationships between organizations and the progress toward shared objectives."[16] They laid out five conditions for effective cross-sectoral collaboration:

- a common agenda;
- a shared measurement system;
- mutually reinforcing activities;
- continuous communication; and
- the presence of a backbone organization.

IN THE COMMUNITY

FOCUS Rexdale—Collaborating to Reduce Emergency Calls for Assistance

In response to a high demand for services, and repeat occurrences in the Rexdale neighbourhood of northwest Toronto, executives from the City of Toronto, United Way Toronto, and the Toronto Police Service met to consider whether, and if so how, they could collaborate in order to improve community safety and reduce crime there. They examined Prince Albert, Saskatchewan's efforts to do the same thing using their "Hub model" (mentioned in Chapter 3). Prince Albert's successes encouraged Toronto's three agencies to convene ten community partners in a discussion about how, together, they could "provide a targeted, wrap around approach to supporting individuals,

---

collective impact working together, across sectors, to resolve large-scale social problems with shared goals, responsibilities, and accountabilities

children, youth and families that are experiencing heightened levels of risk involving anti-social behaviour as well as victimization."[17]

They called their collaborative "FOCUS Rexdale." FOCUS is an acronym for "Furthering Our Communities—Uniting Services." This large team meets weekly, for about 90 minutes, to identify individuals in Rexdale who are at acutely elevated risk of engaging in criminal behaviour or being victims of crime or anti-social behaviour and who "if left untended [will] have an extremely high probability of requiring targeted enforcement and/or other emergency responses." They then work together to bring other agencies to the table, designate appropriate agencies to intervene in those situations, and plan and implement the intervention. The diverse skills of participating community partners provide FOCUS Rexdale with the capability to design and implement the best, most relevant, and most appropriate intervention that will reduce risk factors in any situation. A community partner originates a referral to FOCUS Rexdale, and after agreeing that it merits the group's intervention, a lead agency is identified and collaborates with the originating community partner to share information and begin the intervention process. All community partners commit to providing an initial response within 48 hours.

From 2013 to 2015, FOCUS Rexdale responded to 302 situations. The Toronto Police Service brought 68 percent of them to the table. Over that period the most frequent risk factors identified were mental health, housing, criminality, and domestic violence. FOCUS Rexdale provides a model for community collaboration and service coordination. Furthermore, it collects data that can be used to advise all local service agencies about the needs of the most vulnerable members of the community to assess where the focus should be.

Consider the following questions:

1. The City of Toronto, United Way Toronto, and the Toronto Police Service are large, well-endowed agencies that have learned to collaborate effectively. What measures do you think helped them learn how to do this? Explain your answer.

2. Those three large agencies leveraged a bunch of other agencies to participate at the FOCUS Rexdale table. Why did it take these three agencies to get others to participate?

3. Most situations are brought to the FOCUS Rexdale table by the Toronto Police Service. Does this imply a new trend in community policing? Can police referrals help address the underlying factors in crime and victimization?

Common Agenda

FOCUS Rexdale (Toronto) emerged out of the collective effort of over ten agencies, which found a common agenda in the goal of reducing risk factors for people who were under imminent threat of harm or victimization. That condition has become known as a **situation of acutely elevated risk**: a situation negatively affecting the health or safety of an individual, family, group, or place where there is a high probability of imminent and significant harm to self or others. The contributing risk factors cut across multiple human service disciplines.

Collective impact is about a shared vision, among all collaborative partners, for social change. It is a vision that includes common understanding of the problem to be resolved and a joint approach to solving it with mutually agreed tasks. Notice in that statement how the common agenda actually forces partners to address some of the potential barriers to cross-sectoral collaboration that we identified earlier—for example, different understandings of the problem and different approaches to it. Collective impact requires that police agencies sit down with potential cross-sectoral partners, compare their respective understandings of and approaches to the problem, and come up with an approach that all partners can champion. In the case of FOCUS Rexdale, the common goal is to reduce risk factors for people (individuals, families, or groups) or locations (a single address, business, park, etc.) where circumstances have elevated the chances of imminent harm or victimization. All of the agencies around that table share that common goal; it is what brings them together. And that goal tells all the partners at the end of the year whether the collaborative is doing a good job.

Shared Measurement System

This is about ways that the collaborative's successes will be assessed and reported to all partners and their broader, external constituencies. A shared measurement system follows naturally from development of a common agenda. The latter derives goals toward which all members of the collaborative are striving. That is followed by discussions among all partners about how they will know when and how well those goals are achieved. That, in turn, sets up the discussion of criterion measures, or indicators of success, instruments for observing them, and systems of analysis for reporting on the overall successes of the coalition. The shared measurement system helps all partners remain focused on the common goals. It also gives all partners the same tools for holding each other equally accountable for common outcomes.

Shared measures means measures (or criteria for evaluating the initiative) that all partners agree are meaningful and to which all partners have some data to contribute. In the case of FOCUS Rexdale, shared measures include:

- the types of risk factors on which partners choose to intervene;

---

situation of acutely elevated risk a situation that negatively affects the health or safety of an individual, family, group, or place where there is a high probability of imminent and significant harm to self or others

shared measures measures (or criteria for evaluating the initiative) that all partners agree are meaningful and to which all partners have some data to contribute

- the agencies that bring the situations of acutely elevated risk to the attention of their partners at the table (for example, at least in the beginning, the Toronto Police Service brought most of the situations to the table);
- the lead and partnering agencies that plan and implement the interventions (the Toronto Police Service participated far less often in interventions);
- the disposition of the intervention (for example, whether or not another intervention is necessary); and
- the impact of the interventions on the people who received them.

Mutually Reinforcing Activities

This characteristic stems from the observation by Kania and Kramer that "multiple causes of social problems, and the components of their solutions, are interdependent." It follows that if the causes of problems are interdependent, then so are the activities required to resolve them. Further, all partners should be engaged in the activities in which they excel, and those activities will not be the same in all agencies. For example, police excel at maintaining order and, by their mere presence, reassuring people that it is safe for them to express themselves and seek to be heard by others. When the plan of action for the collaborative calls for that function, police should provide it. But when other kinds of activities at which other agencies excel are required, then quite obviously the collaborative's plan of action should not assign those activities to police. As Kania and Kramer say, "The power of collective action comes not from the sheer number of participants or the uniformity of their efforts, but from the coordination of their differentiated activities."[18]

At FOCUS Rexdale, the agency picked to lead planning and implementation of an intervention is usually the one that has the most positive experiences and strongest rapport with the clients being served. Other agencies that are partnering in the intervention are picked for the qualities of the services they can bring to the intervention. For example, police are most often included if there are any questions about safety that must be considered in the intervention.

Continuous Communication

It takes time and continuous communication for agencies, and representatives of those agencies, to develop enough mutual trust, respect, and confidence in each other to collaborate effectively on common goals. For example, FOCUS Rexdale is Toronto's first **situation table**. A situation table is simply a regular

---

situation table   a regular meeting of front-line workers, from a variety of human services agencies and sectors, who work together to identify individuals, families, groups, or locations that are at an acutely elevated risk of harm, and customize multi-disciplinary interventions to mitigate those risks

meeting of front-line workers, from a variety of human services agencies and sectors, who work together to identify individuals, families, groups, or locations that are at an acutely elevated risk of harm, and customize multi-disciplinary interventions to mitigate those risks. FOCUS Rexdale convened once weekly for almost a year before the partners felt confident enough to handle their first situation of acutely elevated risk. What were they doing in all those meetings if they were not handling acutely elevated risk situations? They were learning to trust and work with each other. That required thorough discussion about their collective goals, their different approaches to clients, the processes the collective would adapt, and the language they would use to describe their work (with each other and with the broader public). The process also required a lot of training and practice so that they all felt competent in their own right, and confident in their partners. Today, three years later, that situation table hums like a well-oiled machine. But that level of effective collaboration does not come quickly or easily. It takes continuous and ongoing communication.

Backbone Organization

Collective impact research has shown that one of the most frequent reasons cross-sectoral collaboratives fail is that there is insufficient investment in the staff and administration required to make them succeed. That led Kania and Kramer (and others) to suggest that each such collaborative requires a special organization just to support the collaborative—a **backbone organization**. The backbone organization is one of the collaborative's agencies that agrees to undertake some of the administration, supervision, and oversight required to support the collaborative. This special organization includes people and processes for planning, managing, handling resources, scheduling, reporting, and carrying out the wide range of administrative activities needed to complete tasks efficiently and effectively.

One of the notions behind the idea of a separate backbone organization is that partnering agencies do not have the time or resources to add administration of the collaborative to their regular duties. Sometimes that may be true, in which case the collaborative must, early in its strategic planning, figure out just exactly how this work will get done. For example, FOCUS Rexdale uses three chairpersons from three agencies, plus one person to do administration, whose time is donated by one partner agency. Additionally, it operates with a steering committee composed of senior executives of the three founding partners (the City of Toronto, United Way Toronto, and the Toronto Police Service). On the other hand, a collaborative formed in a rural Ontario municipality to fight the problem of domestic violence might house the administration in a partnering agency whose core mandate most closely relates to the

---

backbone organization an agency in a collaborative that agrees to undertake some of the administration, supervision, and oversight required to support the collaborative

problem—for example, child and family services. But in this case, it is important to note that the home agency would also source separate funding to support a part-time position that would be dedicated to providing backbone administrative services to the collaborative.

1. What is included in a "common agenda" for a cross-sectoral collaborative?
2. Why is it difficult for a cross-sectoral collaborative to develop a "shared measurement system"?
3. What are "mutually reinforcing activities" in a cross-sectoral collaborative?

How to Pull a Collaborative Together

Cross-sectoral collaboratives will likely become increasingly popular vehicles for dealing with wicked issues, largely because most sectoral agencies, like police, are increasingly acknowledging that they cannot have the desired level of impact on their own. That leads to an important question for police: should they join a collaborative that another agency is promoting or should they take the initiative in forming a collaborative? After that decision is made, there arise two other significant challenges: attracting other key agencies to the collaborative and, once all partners are there, defining what the collaborative is going to do and how.

Deciding Whether to Create or Join a Cross-Sectoral Collaborative

In deciding whether to create or join a collaborative, police (or any other potential partner) need to find answers within their own agency to a standard set of questions. Morgan, in thinking about whether police in Australia should join community-based crime prevention initiatives, has provided some guidance.[19]

Criteria for Deciding Whether to Join a Cross-Sectoral Collaborative

1. Do police have a good understanding of the problem the collaborative is setting out to resolve?
2. What are current police activities and priorities pertaining to this problem?
3. Is there any evidence that the collaborative's proposed resolutions will work?

4. What will be the benefits to police if they join the collaborative?

5. What resources will police need to provide if they join the collaborative, and are they sufficient?

6. What are the likely consequences if police choose to not join the collaborative?

7. Does the community expect police to participate in the collaborative?

8. What other issues influence the decision whether police should join the collaborative?

9. Who in the police agency has authority to make this decision, and do they have all the information they need to make the right decision?

Adapted from Anthony Morgan, "Police and Crime Prevention: Partnering with the Community" in Judy Putt, ed, *Community Policing in Australia*, Research and Public Policy Series No 111 (Australian Institute of Criminology, 2010) 54 at 62.

A good place to start this decision-making process is with a look at the problem that such a collaborative is organized to resolve. What is the problem? What are its effects? Has there been a thorough analysis of the roots of the problem? Is this problem important to the police agency?

If the problem is important to the police agency, then the next question is: what police actions or initiatives have dealt with this problem in the past? How effective were they? Would they have been more effective if police had enjoyed inputs and supports from other agencies addressing the same problem?

Anybody considering joining a collaborative has to have some confidence that doing so will increase everyone's chances of resolving the problems that bring them together in the first place. So it is important for police and other potential partners to know whether there is any evidence that the activities of the proposed collaborative will be effective. Once that is established, police can then carefully consider whether the collaborative initiative will benefit police in any way. Will it reduce demand for police assistance? Will it help police respond more effectively? Will participation enhance police legitimacy with the public they serve?

That series of questions about the benefits to police of participating can then be followed by a consideration of costs to the police agency. What police resources will be required if police join the collaborative? Are they sufficient? That last consideration has to be made carefully because most collaboratives underestimate resource requirements, and police, in particular, underestimate the level of effort for select officers who will be needed to support the collaborative.

Against all of those considerations, police should ask themselves what the downside will be if they choose not to join the collaborative. Would it reduce the collaborative's chances of being effective? Or, more likely, would it reflect badly on the police agency itself—thereby threatening police legitimacy?

The decision to join or not join a collaborative should not be made by police acting in isolation from the broader community they serve. Are there expectations in the community that police should, or should not, participate?

Finally, police should answer the general question whether there are any other variables they should consider in making this decision. For example, relationships with other agencies might be significantly harmed by this decision. It is even possible that police capabilities in other initiatives might be adversely affected by this decision.

Answers to all of these questions can be put together in a short briefing package for command staff, who have to make the final decision. These answers not only give them the basis for decision-making, they also inform command about expectations if they decide to join the collaboration. That becomes very important when front-line officers start working with the collaborative and occasionally need backup from the front office.

Bronstein has provided a much briefer checklist of questions for when an agency is considering joining a collaborative. Her first criterion, applied to a police agency, is whether the proposed work of the collaborative meshes well with the professional role and capacity of police. The second is whether the structural character of the agency (hierarchical and authoritarian) will work well with the collaborative. The third is whether the agency has experience in partnering with other agencies that would suggest they can be effective in the proposed collaborative. The final consideration concerns the personality and capabilities of those individuals who will be asked to participate in the collaborative, including their ability to understand and trust each other.[20]

Promoting the Idea to Partners

Having decided to join or initiate a cross-sectoral collaborative, it remains to attract the right partners to join the enterprise. Usually that is a fairly straightforward process of promoting the collaborative to prospective partners. But it has to be done at a couple of different levels in their organizations. So it is usually helpful to start out by anticipating a couple of potential partners who will most likely become champions of the whole idea and promote it to them first. Then it is possible to share with others the burden of attracting new partners.

Another approach is to start with a partner with which the police service already has a successful partnering experience and build on that experience. Either way, the job of promoting the collaborative and engaging other agencies to become partners becomes easier. The list of potential partners is divided among the best promoters, who contact the potential partners. It works best if the original overture is made at levels in the potential partnering agencies that correspond to the levels of those who are promoting the idea. If they can get their counterparts onside, then it is easier to enlist their help in also reaching the decision-making executives in those agencies.

It is never too early to convene potential partners in a general information meeting, at which point the idea of the collaborative can be laid out. But in addition to that, it is helpful to share some information about the problems the collaborative should address, the police agency's experience with those problems, some of the proposed strategies the new collaborative might wish to consider, and the kinds of agencies—including names of specific ones—that would be optimal working in this way with others. Such information meetings also allow agencies to learn more about each other and what each can offer the consortium.

Eventually, each potential partner agency will have to get approval at their executive levels. There are a couple of ways to do that but the final choices should be informed, and certainly approved, by those lower-level workers who are already engaged in forming the collaborative. One way to get executive-level approval is to write up a brief description of the collaborative idea—much like the write-up that was prepared to obtain police command-level approval—and ask each partnering agency front-line representative to send that briefing note up their own hierarchy with a request for approval. Another approach is to select a couple of executive-level people who are already known to support the idea and ask them to conduct outreach to their counterparts in other agencies. A third approach is to invite a number of executives from each of the potential partners to a general meeting at which the whole idea is laid out and discussed so that the executives can make their participation and resource decisions.

Defining the Collaborative

Once most of the partners have expressed interest in the idea of the collaborative, the focus shifts to defining the partnership and how the partners will work together. Their first job is to define the collaborative:

- What problem is it going to tackle?
- What results is it going to strive to achieve?
- Who are its members?
- What skills, capabilities, and resources do the members bring?
- What tasks need to be completed, and by whom?
- Who is going to provide administrative backup for the collaborative?
- How often will the collaborative meet?
- How will the collaborative communicate among its own members and the broader constituent community?

These are just a few of the questions that need to be answered at this initial stage. And of course, during this process, collaborative members will learn a lot about each other. Hopefully this work will also lead to greater confidence, trust, and respect among the partners.

FIGURE 7.3 **Profile of Partners**

Partner	Issue Importance	Organization's Goals	Expertise	Strengths	Desired Outcomes	Data	Benefits

SOURCE: Adapted from Prevention Institute, "Collaboration Multiplier: Enhancing the Effectiveness of Multi-Field Collaboration," online: <https://www.preventioninstitute.org/sites/default/files/uploads/Collaboration%20Multiplier.pdf>.

A California group known as the Prevention Institute recommends starting this work by profiling the collaborative's members under a series of headings (see Table 7.3). Each heading is described below.

- Partner: the proper, full name of the partnering agency or organization
- Issue importance: why this issue is important to this particular partner
- Organization's goals: this agency's goals as they relate to the problem the collaborative is setting out to resolve
- Expertise: the knowledge, experience, and expertise this partner brings to the enterprise
- Strengths: other capacities, skills, training, funding, or other resources this partner brings to the enterprise
- Desired outcomes: outcomes this partner would like to see
- Data: data related to outcomes that this partner routinely collects and which it can bring to the collective enterprise
- Benefits: the benefits to this partner of participating in the collaborative

This spreadsheet, then, becomes a basic identifier of all the partners to this collaborative. It can be updated as partners change and it can be posted or distributed to all partners so that as much transparency as possible is encouraged in these relationships.

The next job for this group of potential cross-sectoral collaborative members is to define their collaborative. What is it? What does it do? What are its values? How does it work? Strategic planning tools are helpful for this task. But basically it comes down to getting everyone's agreement on the reason the collaborative exists in the first place and the ways in which it will work. This work, too, can be turned into a core document that informs all partners, and members of their broader constituency, about the purpose and work of the collaborative. The box on the next page provides an example drawn from the FOCUS Rexdale collaborative in Toronto.

Mission, Vision, and Values of FOCUS Rexdale (2012)

FOCUS Rexdale is not, nor does it strive to be, an agency!

- It is not registered or incorporated
- It has no budget, finances, or bank account
- It keeps only the barest of files, with no identifiers of the people it serves
- It has no paid staff or director

FOCUS Rexdale is a regularly scheduled meeting (once weekly for 90 minutes)

- The meeting is guided by one of three chairs who share that responsibility
- Participants come from a variety of agencies and organizations
- All are supported by their respective agencies to participate in *FOCUS Rexdale*
- All participants behave during these meetings according to the opportunities and constraints provided by their home agencies' enabling legislation, mandates, and administrative protocols

FOCUS Rexdale meeting participants share common values and beliefs:

- Rexdale is, can be, and should be a safe, secure, and healthy place in which to live, work, and play
- Rexdale is blessed with a diverse blend of individuals, organizations, networks, and agencies which have significant resources, capacities, skills, attitudes, and abilities to strengthen and sustain Rexdale
- Everyone who desires to strengthen and sustain Rexdale will be more successful through cooperation and coordination with each other

FOCUS Rexdale participants meet in order to:

- Identify persons, families, groups, or places that are at significant risk of some form of crime, disorder, or victimization; and to
- Compile and immediately deliver a custom blend of resources, capacities, or capabilities that can reduce those risks before harms or victimization become a reality

The Mission of *FOCUS Rexdale* is to:

- Reduce the incidence of emergencies to persons, groups, or places in Rexdale
- Strengthen the capacity of the Rexdale community to sustain safety, security, and well-being for all

SOURCE: FOCUS Rexdale, "Mission, Vision, and Values" (4 July 2012) (Internal document).

CHECK YOUR UNDERSTANDING

1. Name four things a police service should consider in making a decision whether or not to join a collaborative.

2. Describe a couple of strategies for promoting the collaborative among potential partners.

3. What kinds of information about the partners and the collaborative will all partners want to obtain and develop in the initial stages?

The Value-Added of Collaboration

This chapter has emphasized that cross-sectoral collaboratives are important because the community problems that police and other agencies are called upon to resolve have diverse roots that cut across areas of specialization and that wicked issues cannot be solved by any one agency. But more than that, collaboratives often come up with solutions that none of the agencies, acting singly, would have thought of. This is what we mean when we talk about the value-added of collaboration.

Often, partners in such collaboratives begin to experience significant transformations in how they look at those problems and in particular their own agency's role in resolving them. Working with professionals from other sectors helps them pick up new perspectives on the problem. They develop new ways of thinking about the problem and new approaches to the problem. New ways of thinking about the problem, combined with cross-sectoral problem analysis and brainstorming on optimal solutions, frequently generates creative new solutions.

Those creative new solutions are possible because partners in the collaborative are learning from each other. Research has shown that this is one of the most significant outcomes of successful cross-sectoral collaboratives.[21] Sometimes that learning is about the technical subject matter associated with the problem the collaborative is trying to resolve. But these transformations also include agencies learning more about each other. The first-year process evaluation of FOCUS Rexdale looked at the relationships among the collaborative's members. One of the most consistent findings was that agency representatives learned a great deal about each other, including information about

- the range of services each agency could and was willing to provide;
- the resources the agency could bring (like funding, expertise, and personnel); and
- the agency's values associated with the problem and its clients and constituents.

For example, one of the social service agency respondents to a survey in that evaluation said, "I never even imagined that police felt about this problem the same way we do, and I certainly did not think they would be so willing to work with us!"

Collaboration and Its Impact on Knowledge-Based Policing

One of the most profound changes that emerges from cross-sectoral collaboration may be the fostering of a significant transformation in policing, a transformation that will continue the evolution of community policing from how we know it today. Williamson labels this transformation knowledge-based policing.[22] In essence, Williamson says that as human and social service agencies collaborate, they exchange information, data, and knowledge through their personal and intermediate technology networks. Those exchanges not only enlighten all partners' perspectives on the problems they are working on but also create a rich knowledge base from which new solutions can be developed. Williamson points out that this new knowledge does not rest solely in the hands of those who govern but rather is distributed through the vast networks created by cross-sectoral collaboratives, without regard to hierarchy of governance or privilege of authority to make program decisions. Each person in that network represents a node that can influence outcomes—meaning that each node has equal access and opportunity to make decisions. Policing must adapt to this eventuality, much as the health sector has striven to adapt to the emergence of Internet health information websites.

We will spend the next two chapters reflecting on these transformations, the meaning of knowledge-based policing, and where it is going to take community policing.

CHAPTER SUMMARY

The whole idea of cross-sectoral collaboration grows out of the awareness that problems in the community that lead to calls for police or other emergency assistance stem from a variety of root causes that exceed the capacities of police or any other single agency to resolve. If we truly want people to be safer and healthier, then we have to collaborate to reduce the risk factors that threaten them in the first place.

The requirement for cross-sectoral collaboration sets up many challenges for police and other agency partners. Police have to learn to work more productively with other agencies, and those agencies have to learn to work more productively with police. More than that, police—our first responders when people are threatened with imminent harm—have to learn how to engage agency partners in development and prevention activities that will reduce the need to call police in the first place.

Effective engagement of other agencies by police requires a threshold of police legitimacy among those agencies. That means that other agencies have to see police as just one more specialized agency that shares equally and equitably in the challenges of resolving community problems. That means that police have to see themselves in the same light—as just one more specialized agency that must work equally and equitably with a host of others. When those transformations are achieved, community policing takes on whole new meanings and the potential for community safety and well-being is increased.

REVIEW AND DISCUSSION QUESTIONS

1. Why do police and other community agencies need to collaborate?
2. What special skills and capabilities do police bring to a cross-sectoral collaboration?
3. List some of the typical barriers to effective cross-sectoral collaboration.
4. What kinds of measures are effective in overcoming those barriers?
5. What do police need to consider when deciding whether to join or create a cross-sectoral collaborative?
6. What are some steps to take in pulling together a new collaborative?
7. What are some steps a new collaborative can take in establishing itself?

KEY TERMS

backbone organization, 215
collaboration, 199
collective impact, 211
cross-sectoral collaboration, 200
sector, 200
shared measures, 213
situation of acutely elevated risk, 213
situation table, 214
value-added, 197
wicked issues, 197

NOTES

1 Carolynn Spezza & Christina Borbely, "Cross-Sector Collaboration" (2013) 9:10 Prevention Tactics at 1, online: <http://www.cars-rp.org/wp-content/uploads/2014/08/PT09.10.14.pdf>.

2 Andrew Rhys & Tom Entwistle, "Does Cross-Sectoral Partnership Deliver? An Empirical Exploration of Public Service Effectiveness, Efficiency, and Equity" (2010) 20 J Public Admin & Research Theory 679.

3 Rhys & Entwistle, *ibid*.

4 John W Selsky & Barbara Parker, "Cross-Sector Partnerships to Address Social Issues: Challenges to Theory and Practice" (2005) 31:6 J Mgmt 851.

5 Anthony Morgan, "Police and Crime Prevention: Partnering with the Community" in Judy Putt, ed, *Community Policing in Australia*, Research and Public Policy Series No 111 (Australian Institute of Criminology, 2010) 54 at 66.

6 Lisa Pinkney, Bridget Penhale, Jill Manthorpe, Neil Perkins, David Reid & Shereen Hussein, "Voices from the Frontline: Social Work Practitioners' Perceptions of Multi-Agency Working in Adult Protection in England and Wales" (2008) 10:4 J Adult Protection 12.

7 Sue Richardson & Sheena Asthana, "Inter-Agency Information Sharing in Health and Social Care Services: The Role of Professional Culture" (2006) 36:4 Brit J Soc Work 657.

8 See e.g. Ontario's *Freedom of Information and Protection of Privacy Act*, RSO 1990, c F.31, s 42(1); *Municipal Freedom of Information and Protection of Privacy Act*, RSO 1990, c M.56, s 32; and *Personal Health Information Protection Act, 2004*, SO 2004, c 3, Schedule A, s 40(1).

9 See "Canadians Mental-Health Info Routinely Shared with FBI, US Customs," CBC News, online: <www.cbc.ca/news/canada/windsor/canadians-mental-health-info-routinely-shared-with-fbi-u-s-customs-1.2609159>.

10 L Hodgson, "Manufactured Civil Society: Counting the Cost" (2004) 24:2 Crit Soc Policy 139.

11 M Warner & R Sullivan, eds, *Putting Partnerships to Work* (Sheffield, UK: Greenleaf, 2004).

12 Richardson & Asthana, *supra* note 7.

13 Pinkney et al, *supra* note 6.

14 S Waddell, "New Institutions for the Practice of Corporate Citizenship: Historical, Intersectoral and Developmental Perspectives" (2000) 105:1 Bus & Soc'y Rev 107.

15 Pinkney et al, *supra* note 6.

16 John Kania & Mark Kramer, "Collective Impact" (2011) 9:1 Stanford Soc Innov Rev 36.

17 Scott McKean, "FOCUS Rexdale—Furthering Our Communities, Uniting Services" (Brief description of FOCUS Rexdale for use with partnering agencies and the public, Office of Community Development, City of Toronto, 6 September 2012).

18 Kania & Kramer, *supra* note 16.

19 Anthony Morgan, *supra* note 5.

20 Laura R Bronstein, "A Model of Interdisciplinary Collaboration" (2003) 48:3 Soc Work 303.

21 Selsky & Parker, *supra* note 4 at 859.

22 Tom Williamson, ed, *The Handbook of Knowledge-Based Policing: Current Conceptions and Future Directions* (Sussex, UK: John Wiley, 2008).

CHAPTER 8

Collaboration, Information, Knowledge, and Risks

Police officers from the Belleville Police Service and the Ontario Provincial Police, along with representatives from community organizations, Highland Shores Children's Aid, and the Hastings-Quinte EMS, attend a Belleville Community Hub situation table meeting on August 8, 2016.

LEARNING OUTCOMES

Upon completion of this chapter, you should be able to:

- Explain how cross-sectoral collaboration generates new knowledge about the social drivers of crime and anti-social behaviour
- Define what communications nodes are in the community safety and well-being web
- Explain how provincial privacy protection affects collaboration across the communications nodes in the community safety and well-being web
- Outline six steps in implementing a community-based, risk-focused program
- List three primary roles for police agencies in community-based, risk-focused programs, and explain how police legitimacy relates to all of them
- Explain three ways in which shifting from incident-based, response-driven interventions to community-based, risk-focused programs will further transform policing

Introduction

A funny thing happens when organizations start working together, like they do at FOCUS Rexdale. As Chapter 7 concluded, they start learning from each other and, through that process, they develop new knowledge about the problems they are trying to resolve. New knowledge helps them co-produce new and more creative solutions than would ever have been possible with agencies working in silos!

When police agencies join such cross-sectoral collaboratives, another funny thing happens. Recall from Chapter 2 that from the very earliest days, sovereignty over the governance of security was asserted and maintained by the state (by King Ethelbert in the 7th century)—taking that responsibility away from the community. In the 19th century, police took on that role, becoming an arm of the state. Ever since, police have guarded their sovereign role over the governance of security. This is one factor that led the London Met, in its reassurance policing model (Chapter 2), to mobilize, train, and uniform up to 17,000 civilians. They called these civilians Police Community Support Officers, and put them under the direction and control of sworn officers. By putting more boots on the ground, they effectively undermined the efforts of many organizations to privately contract security services, which would have threatened the sovereignty of police over the governance of security.[1]

But as Maguire pointed out, mobilization and engagement of community members, the fundamental building blocks of community policing, have led to many more community members co-producing solutions to crime and disorder problems. Co-production necessarily leads to police relinquishing some of their sovereignty over the governance of security.[2] A good example is provided in the following On Patrol feature. Essentially, police bring a security problem to the table and other, more appropriate agencies pick it up and resolve it.

ON PATROL

A Youth and His Mom at Acutely Elevated Risk of Harms and Victimization

Police responded to an emotional distress call. A 16-year-old male was arguing with his mother and when the argument became heated, the mother called police. The youth then threatened self-harm. Police apprehended him and transported him to hospital, where he was assessed by emergency room staff and deemed unlikely to harm himself or others on the basis of the symptoms he presented. He was released to return to his home.

However, police were still concerned. With the consent of his mother, police brought this situation to their local situation table. There, experts from ten agencies agreed that this was a situation of acutely elevated risk to the youth, his mom, and potentially others because of his mental health problems, his mom's history of being unable to control the situation, and the youth's history of conflict in the family and at school. The public health school nurse led planning for an intervention to reduce this family's risk factors. She inquired about the youth at school and learned about past efforts to help him and his mother by referring them to other agencies. The school nurse then spoke to the youth about risk factors and appropriate services and supports. She planned an integrated, multi-disciplinary, collaborative intervention for the youth and his mom. The local community health centre agreed to partner with the school nurse. Police asked if either of them wanted police to attend at the intervention and they were told they were not required.

The local community health centre and the school nurse coordinated initiatives by a parenting support group, the high school counselling department, the youth's favourite homeroom teacher, and the coordinator of an after-school athletic program for the youth. These efforts included frequent monitoring of how things were going at home for these two. Further, the help team agreed to remain open to inviting other service providers to join the effort if circumstances merited it.

Consider the following questions:

1. What would have been the most likely outcome of this call for police assistance if police had not brought this situation to the situation table?
2. Why do you think so many agencies had to become involved in supporting this mom and her son?
3. What was the role of police in getting all those agencies to help out?

Chapter 4 introduced the concept of the community safety and well-being web—that web of agencies, organizations, businesses, and individuals who care about what is happening in the community and who have significant capacities to promote safety and well-being in the community. Chapter 7 introduced the idea of cross-sectoral collaboration into that mix. Here, in Chapter 8, we want to further understand what happens when all of these community actors begin to co-produce solutions to community crime and disorder problems. They all come to the task with slightly (or significantly!) different perspectives on the problem because they all come from different disciplines and have different types of expertise. When they begin to share these perspectives, information flows fast and furious throughout the web, challenging some actors' points of view, enlightening others', and blending into a totally new orientation to the problem and an opportunity for new and better solutions. Therein lies the hope that community policing—the empowering of all community actors to take more responsibility for resolving community problems—will yield more effective and sustainable solutions to the root causes of crime and social disorder.

This chapter focuses on the knowledge that emerges when agencies collaborate to learn more about risk factors and install protective factors. Recall from Chapter 4 that protective factors are positive characteristics or conditions that can moderate the negative effects of risk factors and foster healthier individuals, families, and communities, thereby increasing personal and community safety and well-being. This chapter is about police learning to discover and apply that knowledge through community policing. Scholarly work relating to policing and risk management focuses almost exclusively on the police priorities of investigating, apprehending, and prosecuting those who violate laws. While that is certainly appropriate to the traditional role of police, they have also to take on a wide range of duties and responsibilities to help people who manifest risk factors that may put them in jeopardy of committing crimes or creating social disorder, or of being victimized or harmed by those who do. Where community policing is concerned, we are interested in police acting as catalysts or agents for community members (including the widest range of agencies, offices of government, businesses, and other organized agents) becoming more familiar with such risk factors, and acting collaboratively to either mitigate them or install protective factors so that those offences, harms, and victimizations never occur.

Police Are Information Specialists

On average, a police officer in Canada records one indictable crime occurrence a week, makes one indictable crime arrest every three weeks, and secures one indictable crime conviction every nine months.

Richard V Ericson & Kevin D Haggerty, *Policing the Risk Society* (Toronto: University of Toronto Press, 1996) at 19

That passage was written in 1996. Those rates may have changed since then, but one is still left to wonder: "Well then, what are they doing with all the rest of their time?" Shadgett explored that question in 1990, when he demonstrated that police officers spend most of their time generating, distributing, receiving, forwarding, and storing vast amounts of information pertaining to

- crime and criminals, social disorder, and the anti-social behaviour of individuals;
- the locations where these crimes and anti-social acts occurred; and
- the actions police took.

Shadgett found that

officers spent an inordinate amount of time either accounting for their work or preparing for the time when they would have to account for their work. Very little crime fighting in the popular sense was really going on. Indeed, one of the most common jokes around the police office, heard almost every day, was the statement, "Well, I'm gonna go out and fight crime."[3]

Until the advent of intelligence-led policing, most of this information was generated in support of investigations—intelligence gathered after the occurrence of some criminal or anti-social incident. But upon the development of COMPSTAT and intelligence-led policing (Chapter 3), copious amounts of new information about neighbourhoods, street addresses, people, and events were added to the mix as police services sought to better predict where crime and disorder might happen, and prepare to address it.

Where does all this information go? Through the 1990s, most of it stayed within justice circles—meaning police agencies, the courts, and associated offices and agencies. That began to change in the 2000s when police began to partner more constructively with other agencies and organizations—outside the justice community. By 2010, cross-sectoral collaboratives like FOCUS Rexdale began to emerge to deal with significant safety and security problems in highly marginalized neighbourhoods. The information and knowledge that police generated and used percolated throughout the community safety and well-being web, with two main effects: it reduced the police monopoly on safety and security information and it empowered community partners to be more effective in co-producing, with police, more constructive and sustainable solutions to significant community problems.

Figure 8.1 shows the effect that such information sharing has had throughout the community safety and well-being web. Scores of new **communications nodes**—connections between and among agencies and organizations that allow new information to flow among them—have been created. Information and knowledge about safety and security are no longer the sole domain of police or other justice and security agencies. All of the other actors in the community safety and well-being web now can become full participants in the process of achieving safety and well-being for everyone in the community.

This leads us to the topic of the role of information and knowledge in community policing. Here, the goals are less about fighting crime and more about community problem-solving among a web of stakeholders—all of whom use information technology and rely on more or less accurate knowledge about their intended targets and desired outcomes.

As we saw in Chapter 7, modern information and communications technologies no longer rest solely in the hands of those who govern. Agencies have access to modern information and communications technologies that they use to disseminate knowledge, data, and information through their own professional and personal networks. Each person in that network represents a node that can influence outcomes—meaning that each node has equal access and opportunity to make decisions. Policing must adapt to this eventuality.

---

communications nodes connections between and among agencies and organizations that allow new information to flow among them

FIGURE 8.1 **Information, Knowledge, and Communications Nodes in the Community Safety and Well-Being Web**

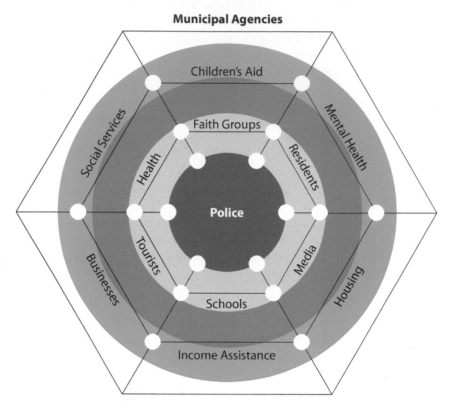

New Knowledge and a Shift to Risk-Based Intervention

With information about safety and security becoming more widely accessible among all community actors, new knowledge about problems and how to deal with them has emerged from the collective. This presents police with the opportunity to use this knowledge, including knowledge of risk factors, to intervene where appropriate rather than wait for harmful incidents to occur. Recall Nova Scotia's High-Risk Case Coordination Protocol Framework (Chapter 7), which was designed to reduce the incidence of domestic violence. Under the framework, any agency can trigger that protocol if it identifies a situation of acutely elevated risk where a person is under imminent threat of harm or victimization. When that level of risk is identified, a case coordinator in the police agency is informed. They then pull together the appropriate agencies to plan the appropriate mix of services and supports. This protocol was made possible because the government of Nova Scotia removed barriers to information sharing among the agencies. Today, those communications nodes are open and flowing, thus enabling police and all other agencies to receive information about potential victimization, obtain knowledge about the risk factors, and plan an intervention that prevents domestic violence.

Williamson calls this **knowledge-based policing**: using information technology like social media and collaborating with partners from other sectors to obtain new knowledge about the social drivers of crime and anti-social behaviour and then intervening by managing risk.[4] He concludes:

> It is not that knowledge-based systems have been absent from policing … but the mindset has been focused narrowly on arrest and conviction within a traditional punitive retributive paradigm of justice which falls short of the broader goal of managing risk.[5]

Monitoring Levels of Risk

Once police and other actors in the safety and well-being web move away from an exclusive focus on incident-driven response, they have vastly expanded potential to notice risks that suggest an intervention is needed to avert a crisis. The communications nodes in the safety and well-being web permit partners to obtain, from each other, information about individuals, families, or locations at risk, acquire knowledge about risk factors, and coordinate proactive interventions to avoid crises.[6] That is exactly what is happening at FOCUS Rexdale's situation table (Chapter 7). Although most situations of acutely elevated risk are brought to the FOCUS Rexdale table by the Toronto Police Service, other agency partners have begun to feel more confident in doing that too. Each of the ten or so agencies has different professional skills that inform the ways they assess levels of risk. Further, each has knowledge about those risk factors that they can share with the collaborative to create the most effective intervention. Like Nova Scotia's High-Risk Case Coordination Protocol Framework, FOCUS Rexdale has protocols in place that permit partners at the table to share privacy-protected information across the nodes that exist among them. That information is needed by all community partners to mount a collaborative intervention. In many respects, FOCUS Rexdale is a microcosm of the community safety and well-being web.

The communications practices and protocols that apply to situation tables all across Ontario, and in many other provinces, have been codified and are available online. The Ontario Provincial Police Service, in partnership with Wilfrid Laurier University, has designed and posted a free three-hour e-learning

---

knowledge-based policing using information technology like social media and collaboration with partners from other sectors to obtain new knowledge about the social drivers of crime and anti-social behaviour and then intervene by managing risk

package. The package is accompanied by video material and free downloads of useful documents, including a comprehensive list of 103 risk factors that situation tables most often encounter and a comprehensive manual that explains what a situation table is and how it works. This package may be accessed at <http://www.wlu.ca/academics/faculties/faculty-of-human-and-social -sciences/centre-for-public-safety-and-well-being/situation-table.html>.

Information Sharing and Privacy Protection

The police contribute to the security efforts of various institutions by communicating knowledge of risk relevant to each of them. These institutions, including the police, are … bound … by communication rules, formats, and technologies that connect them to each other in time and space and provide them with the immediate knowledge of risk that becomes the basis for action.

Richard V Ericson & Kevin D Haggerty, *Policing the Risk Society* (Toronto: University of Toronto Press, 1996) at 44

The "communication rules, formats, and technologies" that connect all the actors in the community safety and well-being web are composed of policies, procedures, and protocols that will vary from agency to agency but that, for the most part, dictate the standards, terms, and conditions of communication between and among agencies' front-line workers. They can have a profound effect on the behaviour of these workers at a collaborative table like FOCUS Rexdale.

Another important source of communication standards that has a profound impact on how well cross-sectoral collaboratives share information and co-produce creative resolutions to community problems relates to the issue of privacy protection. Both privacy protection and individual agency policies affecting communications standards of front-line workers are grounded in provincial legislation. For example, the way that police handle information about crime, social disorder, offenders, victims, and occurrences is largely prescribed by legislation that varies from province to province. The same is true for all of the other public, human, and social service agencies. Additionally, there is separate provincial legislation that deals directly with the handling of the personal and confidential information of people who are receiving the services of cross-sectoral collaboratives.

Until recently, both sources of communications and information-sharing guidelines and restrictions meant that front-line workers either withheld information about their clients from anyone not working for their own agency or disclosed such information only with the consent of their clients. These are the kinds of barriers that had to be overcome among community agencies in

Nova Scotia to create the High-Risk Case Coordination Protocol Framework and those in Ontario to establish situation tables like FOCUS Rexdale. These are the kinds of barriers that will have to be broken down everywhere before cross-sectoral collaboratives can be as successful as research is beginning to show they can be.

CHECK YOUR UNDERSTANDING

1. What are the implications for community problem-solving of all the communications nodes that are created in a cross-sectoral collaborative?
2. What are some of the communication challenges among collaborative partners created by the communications nodes in the community safety and well-being web?

Community-Based, Risk-Focused Programs

Community policing is all about community members engaging in solving community problems and proactively implementing measures to reduce risk factors, or at least introduce protective factors in order to prevent harms and victimization. Community policing has always implied mobilizing neighbours in high-demand neighbourhoods, but engaging other agencies has been a challenge since the late 1990s. Generally, agencies do not want to bend their priorities, expend more resources, absorb more responsibility, and assume greater accountability just to accommodate police requests for assistance. By 2010, that resistance to engagement began to break down as incontrovertible evidence began to mount in all sectors that the core, social determinants of health underpinned most crime and social disorder and, consequently, all agencies in all sectors had a hand in making improvements.

Risk-Focused Justice Agencies

As noted earlier, police have been risk-focused for a long time, only their focus has largely been targeted on enforcement, offender management, and effective prosecutions. In other words, police attention to risks is usually offender-based, not community oriented. The same is true of other justice agencies. For example, corrections agencies are risk-focused for the purposes of designing rehabilitation programs and reducing recidivism. However, most of the justice agencies withhold information about risks and risk-focused initiatives from each other, including from police agencies. Effective networks among justice agencies are rare because "criminal justice agencies generally work largely independent of each other, often at cross-purposes, often without coordination, and often in an atmosphere of mutual distrust and dislike."[7]

Role for Police in Community-Based, Risk-Focused Programs

Well-researched successes in community-based, risk-focused programs have shown a significant role for police. Such programs are based on the idea that with networks of collaborators comes a growth in communication, information, intelligence, and the technologies that drive them. These combine to increase community actors' knowledge about the risks and probability of harm and victimization. On the basis of this knowledge, collaborators can work to reduce those probabilities by risk management—that is, mitigating risks or introducing protective factors. Community-based programs are driven by the increased interest and focus on risks—as opposed to offences. Identifying risks requires information; recognizing which risks predict harmful outcomes requires knowledge; and that information and knowledge come from a variety of agencies—all looking at the same problem but through different lenses of professional specialization.

There are three primary roles for police in such community-based collaboratives:

- identifying community problems,
- engaging community agencies, and
- liaising with community members.

Because they are emergency responders, police are the first to recognize when not enough has been done by other human and social service providers to avoid a crisis. They need to share that information with those other agencies so that the collective can consider what new approaches can be taken to avert repeat occurrences. Police can do this by using police data and their own specialized information networks.

Engaging and supporting community agencies to acknowledge these problems and examine them through their own specialized lenses goes back to our discussions of Ontario's Mobilization & Engagement Model of Community Policing in Chapters 1 and 5. This is a special job for police, not least because they have evidence (occurrence data) that they can present to agencies to show that the measures taken to avert harms and victimization have been insufficient. But it also falls to police agencies to do this engagement work because in Canada, police are generally respected and viewed as credible.

Liaising with community is a broader outreach and information-sharing role that police can do, not only with community partners in resolving the problem but also with community members who are not involved in finding solutions but care about the problem and the collaborative's progress. Again, this falls to police because they are a credible source of information. It remains, of course, for police to become proficient in this information-sharing and communications role.

However, as we learned in Chapter 1, police will not succeed in any of these three roles in community-based, risk-focused programs if they have not built and sustained high levels of legitimacy in the community they serve. All of their successes in this work can only be built on a foundation of police legitimacy.

Elements of Community-Based, Risk-Focused Prevention Programs

The health sector has been experimenting with and refining community-based problem-solving models for a long time. Building on health models, Williams and his colleagues designed a framework for reducing and preventing violence among youth.[8] Their model is general enough that we can adapt it to community problem-solving. It has six steps, as shown in Table 8.1.

TABLE 8.1   Six Steps in Community-Based, Risk-Focused Problem-Solving

Steps	Explanation
1. Identify and analyze the problem to be resolved	This is about learning everything there is to learn about the problem to be resolved: its origins, scope, impacts, and history. Most often the analysis requires inputs from agencies that have different specializations and perspectives on the problem.
2. Identify risk and protective factors	These factors are key to figuring out what can be done to resolve the problem. They are best derived through empirical analysis of community members and community experience.
3. Design an intervention	This is a planning process, only it involves diverse agencies that have specialized experience and knowledge about the problem, as well as risk and protective factors.
4. Implement the intervention	This involves targeting the right individuals, families, groups, or locations with the planned actions, in the most appropriate settings, in order to reduce the chances that risky situations will turn into crises.
5. Evaluate implementation	This is about measuring both short- and long-term outcomes of the intervention. Its purpose is not only to inform modifications of the current intervention but also to guide future ones in different settings.
6. Disseminate the results	This step ensures that the community learns from the problem-solving process. But it also informs more profound changes—like policy reform—that can prevent the problem from recurring.

SOURCE: Adapted from K Williams, N Guerra & D Elliott, *Human Development and Violence Prevention: A Focus on Youth* (Boulder: Center for the Study and Prevention of Violence, University of Colorado, 1997) at 25.

This is a very logical problem-solving model. It should remind you of SARA, PARE, and CAPRA in many respects (Chapters 5 and 6). By the same token, it shares one of the same weaknesses as those problem-oriented policing models—namely, problem-solving is never that simple. For example, the Williams model looks like a straightforward, linear process in which step one is followed by step two, etc. But the reality is that problem-solving frequently involves false starts, U-turns, start-overs, speed-ups, slow-downs, and unintended results—all of which is manageable if police and their community partners are committed to managing them together.

Applying the Williams Model to a Youth Violence Problem

Recall the On Patrol scenario in Chapter 2 about youth violence and "swarming" behaviour in school. Police responded by forming a Street Crime Unit whose strategy was to

- embed members in select schools where this problem was prevalent;
- establish a rapport with students there (police legitimacy);
- obtain more accurate and timely information about potential violent behaviour and real victimization; and
- try to inform and educate students about the problems with their violent behaviour.

As the scenario reported, Toronto police found this unit to be very helpful. In the context of this chapter, it is important to note that the Street Crime Unit is an offender-based initiative that is targeted not only on more timely interventions on real or potential violent behaviour but also on more timely supports for victims of youth violence.

Below, we apply the steps from Williams's community-based, risk-focused approach to the same youth violence problem to see where it takes us.

1. *Identify and analyze the problem to be resolved:* The problem is youth violence. But we need to dive deeper than that. Who is being violent, from which schools, and how often? Who are they picking on, from which schools, and how often? How serious are the harms and victimization resulting from these assaults? What other agency specialists can provide us with more information about both victims and perpetrators, and about this problem in general? Obviously, school personnel can be helpful—but which ones? If we can learn the names of particular violent students, then we can probably narrow this list of school informants down to specific teachers or coaches who work with them, perhaps a guidance counsellor or school social worker, and maybe a vice-principal in charge of student discipline. Further, there may be other agencies we can consult, like children and family services, other social services, or people from public health who know the youths or their families.

The point is that we have to learn everything we can about the problem, from as many different sources as possible, each with its own area of expertise and specialized knowledge. If there are many occurrences, then this investigative process needs to apply to most of them. This work is best done by officers who are good at investigations. This first step in the model is an excellent one for police to implement. It is only through such thorough investigating that we can begin to understand enough about the problem that we can do the research that is needed to identify risk and protective factors. But although police can do this work, it is important for them to include representatives of other specializations in their investigation (like health, schools, psychologists, family supports, etc.) and not rely on police sources alone.

2. *Identify risk and protective factors*: With this step we are beginning to look for potential solutions to the problem. For example, Saner and Ellickson completed a large study of 4,500 grade 12 students and high school dropouts in California and Oregon in 1996 that revealed risk and protective factors against school violence. Gender and deviant behaviour were key among the risk factors, meaning that males were more likely than females to engage in violence, and young people who were using or selling drugs or engaging in other anti-social behaviours were more inclined to be violent in school. Further, the study showed that these risk effects are additive—that is, the more of them a person has, the higher the probability that they will be violent. There were also some differences for males and females. Females were more influenced by family conflicts and disputes, violence, and unresolved emotional harms and disruption, whereas males were more influenced by other deviant behaviours (drugs, stealing, etc.). Weak bonds with school and family were strong predictors of serious violence for males.[9]

Note that this study was published in the health sector (*Journal of Adolescent Health*), not policing or criminal justice. The health sector has understood the importance of risk and protective factors for well over 30 years. Risk and protective factors are only beginning to make inroads in policing and justice. It also pays to note that while problems like adolescent violence may be mysteries to police officers, they are not necessarily mysteries to professionals working in other sectors. For example, recall how Toronto police turned to a psychologist to help them understand swarming behaviour. That is an excellent strategy for learning about risk and protective factors: turn to experts who are familiar with research on this question in the scientific literature or who may be able to conduct research on it.

A more recent study in 2003 supports the Saner and Ellickson findings reported above but adds the finding that students who have hostile attitudes toward school will not ask for help from school personnel. As a result, they may become isolated while in school, thereby increasing their risks of acting out in violent or anti-social ways. The researchers concluded:

> If researchers can identify the sources of victimization risk at school, then policy makers can more effectively focus attention on correcting risk factors that actually bear some relationship with victimization in the school setting.[10]

3. *Design an intervention*: Without knowing enough details about the Toronto swarming problem, let us presume for the sake of this narrative that most of the perpetrators were males, and few of those males were engaged in other anti-social or illegal behaviours (like selling drugs). Of course, in the real world, we would want to check out those assumptions. But for the sake of this text, we will focus on the risk factors associated with low academic orientation (young males who do not enjoy school or learning and are not performing well there), and weak school and family bonds. It remains then to design some interventions to address these issues.

   The first step in doing that is to be sure that the right community partners have been pulled together to do this work. Clearly, that would include school personnel, but it would also have to include specialists from youth support and family services organizations. In 2004, Margaret Shaw from Canada's International Centre for the Prevention of Crime reviewed police-initiated crime prevention programs in schools from around the world. One such program in Quebec provides an example of the kinds of community partners that might be drawn together to address the youth swarming problem. Quebec's Programme d'intervention en milieu scolaire (PIMS) is a collaborative of school administrators, principals and staff, school bus drivers, psychologists, youth workers, students, parents, and police. Launched in 1987 in response to drug trafficking in the schools, PIMS proved to be useful and was replicated throughout the province of Quebec. Eventually, it was also expanded to address issues of bullying and violence. With all of these partners engaged in proactive problem-solving focused on individual youth and their families, police can remain in their traditional role of sharing information about crime and social disorder as they encounter them, plus questioning suspects, searching school properties, and making arrests when necessary. At the same time, they can support all of their partners in the design and implementation of efforts to improve young males' orientation to school and home life.[11]

4. *Implement the intervention*: One of the important measures that Williams discovered is that of targeting the strategy on those youth and families who are most likely to manifest these particular risk factors. In other words, the intervention will be more effective if the collaborative

identifies who is most likely to be violent and customizes the intervention to meet their specific needs. Sometimes, this proves a challenge for police because it is hard to predict who is most likely to be violent and police are more accustomed to responding after harm or victimization has occurred. Again, that is where relying on community partners can be helpful. Many of them, like those from the health sector, have been working with risk factors far longer than have police. They are more experienced at predicting who is most likely to be violent again.[12]

5. *Evaluate implementation*: We are going to talk in greater detail about evaluation in Chapter 11 of this text. For now, it will suffice to point out a few basics. The first step is, from the outset of planning the intervention, getting the team to consider how they would evaluate whether the intervention is working or not. Part of that process is about being precise, when goals are being set out for the intervention, in determining what variables need to change, and benchmarking them. A whole other, but related, issue is how the collaborative will measure these variables. A third issue is when the collaborative can expect to see the results of the intervention. Many times, results are not apparent until well after the intervention has started; sometimes, meaningful results do not appear for a year or more.

Finally, there is the issue of who can or should do the evaluation. Too often, program people turn to an outside source of evaluation in the belief that outsiders can or will be more "objective" in doing the evaluation work. We will say more about objectivity in Chapter 11, but for now, suffice it to say that objectivity comes from research designs, not from people. In other words, a member of the collaborative can perform a credible evaluation, but only if they make good methodological decisions. And the last thing the intervention needs is an outsider who appears to be "objective," but in fact is unaware of the dynamics at play in the intervention.

Reflecting on evaluation of a gun violence reduction initiative in one neighbourhood of Los Angeles (in 2003), Tita and his colleagues published an important evaluation result that should emerge out of all such initiatives, including the initiative to curb youth violence in schools:

> Perhaps the most important success of the program was the success of the working group—using data analysis and with collaboration from many different agencies—in achieving a well-designed intervention. ... Through the working group process, individual organizations were able to design a collaborative intervention and contribute resources sufficient for the initiative. ...
>
> Each organization had unique resources that, when pooled ... , made it more effective in curbing violence than it could have been alone.[13]

6. *Disseminate the results*: This is where the whole community stands to benefit a lot from this collaborative's work on school violence. It is essential to share with the wider community why this team came together (the problem), what was done (the intervention), and how well it worked (the evaluation). Of course, this information would be shared without sharing private or confidential information about any person, family, group, or location. The purposes of dissemination are many, starting with simply letting people know that a serious problem has been recognized and some qualified people are investing in resolving it effectively. But a whole other set of information needs arise with other people, in other communities, who may be faced with similar problems and who would benefit significantly from learning how well this solution worked.

CHECK YOUR UNDERSTANDING

1. What are the differences between an offender-based approach and a community-oriented approach to identifying and managing risk and protective factors?
2. What does research show about risk and protective factors for adolescent school violence?

Risk and Protective Factors Transforming Policing

The quality of policing in communities can be improved, much as criminal investigations can be improved, through the acquisition and targeted dissemination of new knowledge about crime and anti-social behaviour, and the people who perpetrate them or are victimized by them. Risk and protective factors compose some of that new knowledge, which is beginning to pervade policing and justice circles. A group of Canadian police officers, sponsored by the Canadian Association of Chiefs of Police (CACP), travelled the world in 2012 in order to find out how other police services, in other countries, are dealing with some of this new knowledge. Their research revealed

> a very notable shift in the focus of community safety in many countries, with less emphasis being placed on … incident-driven and response focus … . This does not mean shifting police into pure "prevention" mode, rather, it acknowledges that even our approaches to intervention and suppression can be directed more effectively by risk factors.[14]

Below, we examine how focusing on risk and protective factors transforms our understanding of prevention, community intelligence, and policing itself.

Prevention

In their examination of community policing, Ross and Pease concluded, "If policing is to be effective it must be proactive and predictive, and if it is to deploy effectively it must have the tools to make accurate forecasts."[15] The traditional model of policing tries to meet these expectations through the use of confidential informants and other intelligence initiatives. That is, by those means, police seek to better anticipate where an offence might occur and at least be there to block it, if not pre-empt it altogether with timely, targeted enforcement. But quite obviously, the persistence of crime is an indication that traditional policing tactics are not sufficient. Police need to improve their capacity to predict crime and anti-social behaviour.

Knowledge of risk factors may just give police the edge they need. In an upcoming publication of the International Association of Law Enforcement Intelligence Analysts, Ratcliffe says, "a prediction of the future is often what decision-makers crave in their role as risk managers with responsibility to manage resource allocation."[16] Ratcliffe based that generalization on a logical construct that makes the connection between knowledge of risk factors and what we in policing have come to know as "crime prevention." Recall Herman Goldstein's concept of problem-oriented policing from Chapter 5. He contended that police should look for patterns of crime or anti-social occurrences and let those patterns (like repeat occurrences) inform ideas about where police and community members should look for underlying causes. Ratcliffe starts with a similar notion of "patterns" but he suggests looking for patterns among risk factors—long before crime or anti-social behaviour leads to occurrence data. With awareness of patterns among risk factors, Ratcliffe is suggesting that police really have a chance to be proactive in addressing crime and anti-social behaviour. We depict the logic of his ideas in Figure 8.2.

In effect, Ratcliffe is suggesting that if police can learn to recognize risk factors, then they can predict who is likely to get into trouble; and if they can do that, they can proactively intervene to prevent their getting into trouble. That sheds a whole new light on prevention insofar as it suggests that instead of focusing on perpetrators, victims, and offences, police should start to recognize those negative characteristics or conditions in individuals, families, communities, or society that may increase social disorder, crime or fear of crime, or the likelihood of harms or victimization to persons or property. If police can do that, then they can prevent harms and victimization, which, after all, is the purpose of crime prevention in the first place.[17]

FIGURE 8.2 **The Relationship of Patterns of Risk to Prevention**

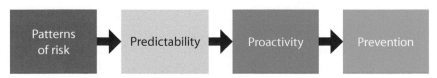

Community Intelligence

Intelligence-led policing really put the spotlight on crime analysis as a weapon for police to use against crime and anti-social behaviour. But it also had the effect of demonstrating to officers that effective policing has to involve many other actors in the community safety and well-being web. Few officers, or police services for that matter, championed this learning by opening themselves up to more effective community collaboratives and coalitions. But some did, and where they did, evidence began to show that policing became more effective.[18]

The Met's use of thousands of Police Community Support Officers brought new sources of information and intelligence into the intelligence-led framework as they were charged with contacting diverse community members and obtaining a fuller awareness of the root causes of threats to safety and security in the community. Neighbourhood officers, like those used in high-demand neighbourhoods in Toronto, do the same thing (Chapter 2). The result is what could most accurately be called community intelligence—to differentiate it from police intelligence. **Community intelligence** is information about community dynamics that originates with community members and is used by community members to improve their own social control over issues like crime and social disorder.

Have you heard the old saying, "Knowledge is power"? A similar idea applies to community intelligence. Those people who have the most knowledge about an issue that concerns a community are usually the ones in whom a community invests most to resolve that issue. That is a reasonable approach to problem-solving. After all, a community would not want people who are largely ignorant about the roots of a problem to be put in charge of resolving it. The interesting thing with community intelligence is that it significantly increases everyone's knowledge quotient in the safety and well-being web. And when people obtain useful knowledge, they feel empowered to act on it for the betterment of their community. That brings us to our last point in this chapter: how knowledge of risk and protective factors is transforming policing.

Community Policing

We talked at the beginning of this chapter about the erosion of police sovereignty over security. That has resulted from three factors:

- an acknowledgment in the broader community that police alone are unable to ensure a sustainable peace in the community;

---

community intelligence information about community dynamics that originates with community members and is used by community members to improve their own social control over issues like crime and social disorder

- a recognition that the social determinants of health underpin most of the real threats to safety and security and police are not specialists in those areas; and
- the experience of police officers collaborating effectively with many community partners.

Now we can add a fourth factor: all members of the community safety and well-being web becoming vastly more knowledgeable about crime and social disorder, perpetrators and victims, and their own specialized capacities as well as responsibility for applying their knowledge for the good of the community—community intelligence.

All of these factors have taken the emphasis off *police* and put it on **policing**, meaning community members' exertion of social control for the purposes of preserving order and preventing harms and victimization from crime or anti-social behaviour. Note that in this context, "policing" does not mean enforcing the law, investigating criminal occurrences, or arresting and aiding in the prosecution of criminals. Those obviously are duties and responsibilities for which only sworn police officers are uniquely qualified and empowered. Further, those are duties and responsibilities for which traditional policing tactics are best suited. Rather, with the use of the word "policing" we are talking about everything else that police officers now find preoccupies up to two-thirds of their time and attention.

Also notice that in talking about the role of community members in policing we are not excluding police officers; they are members of the community too. By using the word "policing," we are simply acknowledging that it takes a whole community to ensure everyone's safety and well-being. Police officers have very specialized roles and responsibilities in doing that, as do human and social service agencies, government agencies, businesses, community-based organizations (not-for-profits), and citizens. Innes and Roberts sum up this idea:

> As an approach this seeks to recognize that the public police are not monopoly suppliers of social control at the neighbourhood level. Indeed, on a day-to-day basis the management of social order in a neighbourhood may have little to do with policing, but results from the regulatory arrangements performed by communities themselves, together with interventions performed by a plethora of other agencies and organizations.[19]

This broader concept of policing opens up a whole new set of considerations about how modern communities enable and control the goals of policing. For

---

policing community members' exertion of social control for the purposes of preserving order and preventing harms or victimization from crime or anti-social behaviour

example, current police enabling legislation is probably sufficient for governing the police but it is grossly insufficient for governing this broader concept of policing. As police find themselves increasingly engaged with a wide array of other community actors, even the various pieces of provincial legislation covering the governing of police may have to be altered and expanded. The governance of policing would have to accommodate concepts like community intelligence and risk and protective factors, neither of which are covered in current legislation governing the police.

So once again we find ourselves, in thinking about community policing, setting our sights on a moving target. Policing continues to evolve and we need all of the infrastructure that supports it to learn and evolve with it in order to realize the greatest return on our investment in community safety and well-being.

CHAPTER SUMMARY

Collaboration stimulates all partners to learn from each other because they each bring different expertise about the problems they wish to resolve and they have different perspectives based on their different experiences with the problem. All of that differential information flows throughout the intricate communications web that exists in any cross-sectoral collaboration. The net results are a new knowledge about the problems and solutions in which the collaborative can begin to understand and use risk and protective factors in the co-production of creative and effective solutions.

That new knowledge also enables community-based, risk-focused problem-solving in which police have at least three important roles: identifying problems to be resolved, engaging partners in the collaborative effort, and liaising with community as the problem-solving work unfolds. There are at least six steps in community-based, risk-focused problem-solving: problem identification; identification of risk and protective factors; intervention design; implementation; evaluation; and dissemination of information to the community.

Use of risk and protective factors in community-based problem-solving will vastly improve community efforts at prevention of harms and victimization from crime and social disorder. It will strengthen community intelligence about problems and their potential solutions. But most importantly, it will strengthen the community's hand in exerting more social control in those high-demand neighbourhoods, and on those community problems, that presently preoccupy so much police time and resources.

REVIEW AND DISCUSSION QUESTIONS

1. How does cross-sectoral collaboration generate new knowledge about the social drivers of crime and anti-social behaviour?

2. What are communications nodes in the community safety and well-being web and how do they affect collaboration?

3. Why has it taken police so long to focus on risk and protective factors when other sectors like health and social services have recognized their importance for well over 30 years?

4. How does provincial privacy protection affect collaboration across the communications nodes in the community safety and well-being web?

5. What are three primary roles for police agencies in community-based, risk-focused programs? Explain how police legitimacy relates to all of them.

6. What are six steps in implementing a risk-focused, community-based program? Explain each one.

7. What are three ways in which shifting from incident-based, response-driven interventions to community-based, risk-focused programs will further transform policing?

KEY TERMS

communications nodes, 231
community intelligence, 244
knowledge-based policing, 233
policing, 245

NOTES

1   Les Johnston, "Neighbourhood Policing and Community Engagement: Police Community Support Officers in the London Metropolitan Police" in Tom Williamson, ed, *The Handbook of Knowledge-Based Policing: Current Conceptions and Future Directions* (Sussex, UK: John Wiley, 2008) at 369.

2   M Maguire, "Policing by Risks and Targets: Some Dimensions and Implications of Intelligence-Led Crime Control" (2000) 9:4 Policing & Soc'y 315.

3   P Shadgett, *An Observational Study of Police Patrol Work* (Master's Thesis, Centre of Criminology, University of Toronto, 1990) at 36, 42, 72.

4   Williamson, *supra* note 1 at 6.

5   *Ibid* at 1.

6   Richard V Ericson & Kevin D Haggerty, *Policing the Risk Society* (Toronto: University of Toronto Press, 1996) at 41.

7   A Braga & C Winship, "Creating an Effective Foundation to Prevent Youth Violence: Lessons Learned from Boston in the 1990s" (26 September 2005) *Rappaport Institute Policy Briefs* at 4, online: <https://www.innovations .harvard.edu/sites/default/files/brief_tenpoint.pdf>.

8   K Williams, N Guerra & D Elliott, *Human Development and Violence Prevention: A Focus on Youth* (Boulder: Center for the Study and Prevention of Violence, University of Colorado, 1997) at 25.

9   Hilary Saner & Phyllis Ellickson, "Concurrent Risk Factors for Adolescent Violence" (1996) 19:2 J Adolescent Health 94.

10 Christopher J Schreck, J Mitchell Miller & Chris L Gibson, "Trouble in the School Yard: A Study of the Risk Factors of Victimization at School" (2003) 49:3 Crime & Delinquency 460 at 477.

11 Margaret Shaw, "Police, Schools and Crime Prevention: A Preliminary Review of Current Practices" (Discussion paper for the International Centre for the Prevention of Crime, 2004), online: <http://www.crime-prevention-intl.org/ fileadmin/user_upload/Publications/2005-1999/2004.ENG.Police__Schools _and_Crime_Prevention_A_Preliminary_Review_Of_Current_Practices.pdf>.

12 Williams, Guerra & Elliott, *supra* note 8.

13 G Tita, KJ Riley, G Ridgeway, C Grammich, AF Abrahamse & PW Greenwood, *Reducing Gun Violence: Results from an Intervention in East Los Angeles* (Santa Monica, Cal: RAND Corporation, 2003) at 49.

14 Institute for Strategic International Studies, *Full Circle Community Safety: Changing the Conversation About Community Safety Economics and Performance—A Handbook and Guide in Support of New Multi-Agency Metrics for Community Safety* (Ottawa: Canadian Association of Chiefs of Police, 2012).

15 Nick Ross & Ken Pease, "Community Policing and Prediction" in Williamson, *supra* note 1 at 319.

16 Jerry H Ratcliffe, "Intelligence-Led Policing: Anticipating Risk and Influencing Action" (In press publication of the International Association of Law Enforcement Intelligence Analysts, 2016) at 2.

17 JH Ratcliffe, "The Structure of Strategic Thinking" in JH Ratcliffe, ed, *Strategic Thinking in Criminal Intelligence*, 2nd ed (Sydney: Federation Press, 2009).

18 TC O'Shea & K Nicholls, *Crime Analysis in America* (Full, final report to the Office of Community Oriented Policing Services, US Department of Justice, Washington, DC, 2002) at 212.

19 Martin Innes & Colin Roberts, "Reassurance Policing, Community Intelligence and the Co-Production of Neighbourhood Order" in Williamson, *supra* note 1 at 242.

PART IV

Knowing What to Do, and Seeing if You Did It

CHAPTER 9

Community Safety Planning

Swan Valley Communities That Care (SVCTC) hosts a community planning training event as the first step in creating a community action plan for the healthy development of Swan Valley, Manitoba children and youth.

LEARNING OUTCOMES

Upon completion of this chapter, you should be able to:

- Summarize the meaning of and distinctions among the four components, or rings, of the community safety and well-being framework
- List and explain six principles for planning community safety and well-being
- Outline and explain the process of planning for community safety and well-being
- Explain how the culture of specialization makes it difficult for community partners to collaborate
- Explain five special roles for police in planning for community safety and well-being
- Explain why police legitimacy is so important for the success of planning for community safety and well-being

Introduction

We are nearing the end of this text on community policing. Therefore, we are now equipped to look back at how community policing used to be interpreted, and see how far we have come here, in moulding it to accommodate the needs of communities today. The concept of community policing has been around for over half a century, but it has taken on different meanings during that time. One of the common threads over the years has been the idea that community policing provides police some way to tap into community members' knowledge, attitudes, and resources that can help police do their job better. Looking back over the years, we can see some differences in how police interpreted community policing and sought to involve citizens. One of the earliest strategies was to simply convene groups of citizens or community members and ask them what they thought police priorities should be. However, this turned out to be ineffective because police often then went ahead and established their own priorities without regard to citizens' opinions of them.

Subsequently, police tried to tap into community intelligence by making it easy for citizens to call police to report fears, incidents, knowledge of potential incidents, etc. This has had the effect of significantly increasing calls for police assistance, and in turn, necessitating a triage system that allows police to prioritize those calls before mobilizing a response.

Remembering the recent work of the Expert Panel on the Future of Canadian Policing Models (Chapter 4), we now see that community policing has morphed into a strategy for getting all community members to take far more responsibility for safety and well-being than they ever did before. In the words of criminologists Julie Berg and Clifford Shearing:

> Finally, there have been arrangements that encourage members of the public to get directly engaged in policing. For a while this idea was regarded with considerable suspicion by the police as likely to challenge their monopoly of policing but it has, especially under the impact of neo-liberal encouragements to [enable the public taking more responsibility], gained increasing acceptance.[1]

Below, we lay out a process by which the whole of the community takes very seriously its challenges in providing safety and well-being for all. But here, we depart slightly from Berg and Shearing's concept of community challenging the police "monopoly of policing." Rather, we assert that the whole of community is increasing its involvement, responsibility, and accountability for safety and well-being, leaving it to police to struggle with relinquishing some of their sovereignty over safety and security. In effect, we are saying that today "community policing" has become primarily about "collaborative safety and well-being."

Planning a Community-Wide Strategy to Reduce Conflict in the Drug Trade in Surrey

Surrey, British Columbia, one of the fastest-growing communities in Canada, is rich in diversity and struggling with rapid growth. For the past 40 years, waves of immigrants have emigrated to the city from many places including Vietnam, Hong Kong, Honduras, El Salvador, Fiji, and, most recently, Somalia. This has resulted in a number of rival gangs competing for space and influence in the city. Between January and April 2016, Surrey experienced a total of 40 shootings related to low-level, gang-related drug dealing. City officials and the RCMP have been working together to combat this rash of shootings. However, they face a number of issues, including an unwillingness on the part of the victims and bystanders to provide information to police. In one recent incident, a young victim refused to answer questions about what happened, saying, "Maybe bullets fell from the sky," while another said, "Don't you worry about it. No need for you cops to be here."

Between January and April of 2016, at least one homicide was connected with the conflict. At the time of writing, no arrests had been made in relation to the shootings, which led residents to complain that they did not trust the ability of the police and city officials to protect them. Current strategies to end the gun violence include an increase in the number of police resources dedicated to investigating low-level conflict in the drug trade, with assistance from the public.

In an effort to engage the public, three specific initiatives were undertaken. The first focused on at-risk youth, who have been identified as a key part of the problem associated with this conflict. For this initiative, a hotline was created for parents who are concerned that their children are at risk to join a gang or may already be involved in criminal activity. This telephone resource, which is offered in a number of languages, puts parents in touch with youth officers and counsellors who can offer more resources and professional interventions. For the second initiative, a police task force was created to directly tackle the criminal activities associated with this conflict. Finally, for the third initiative, the City of Surrey began a series of consultations with the public on general community safety issues. These will lead to the creation of a public safety strategy, with the end goal being to address issues such as the low-level drug conflict proactively. A key component of this strategy is to engage the public in the process of making Surrey a safer community, but as noted above, the turf wars among gangs and organized crime make this a continuing challenge.

Consider the following questions:

1. What other kinds of measures do you think will help Surrey RCMP reduce criminal violence?

2. What are some reasons for involving the broader public in the process of developing strategies to make Surrey safer?

3. If you participated in a community consultation, what measures would you suggest to improve safety in Surrey?

SOURCES: Adapted from Tom Zytaruk, "No Charges Laid Yet for Pulling Triggers in Surrey's 2016 Shootings," *Surrey Now* (8 June 2016), online: <http://www.thenownewspaper.com/news/382245091.html#.V1rx1U5lxt0>; Nancy Macdonald, "The Fight to Staunch a Street War in Surrey," *Maclean's Magazine* (14 April 2016), online: <http://www.macleans.ca/news/canada/surrey-violence-continues-despite-rcmp-surge>.

Review of the Community Safety and Well-Being Framework

In Chapter 4, we introduced the four elements of a framework for achieving community safety and well-being: social development, prevention of crime and social disorder, risk mitigation, and emergency response. That framework is based on the notion that, for the most part, crime and anti-social behaviour result from insufficient access to the social determinants of health. For example, a person who is experiencing poverty and mental health challenges may act out in ways that are harmful to himself, herself, or others. Therefore, social development initiatives should be planned to increase everyone's access to the social determinants of health.

In this short section, we will review the characteristics of all four elements of the community safety and well-being framework. This will lay the groundwork for a discussion of how communities plan to achieve each component and what the most appropriate police roles in that planning process are.[2]

Social Development

By investing in social development, prevention, and risk mitigation, we are trying to reduce the demand for and costs of emergency response. If the red circle represents a community's investment in emergency response, then we can reduce those demands and costs by investing more in social development—represented by the green ring, above. Social development includes projects and activities that increase people's access to income, higher levels of education, employment and job security, quality health care, and all the other prerequisites of a good life, without regard to any socio-demographic differences. But we must ask: which social determinants of health are lacking in any given community? What particular initiatives, projects, or investments are required to improve social development and reduce crime and social disorder? Those are some of the questions we will have to answer when it comes time to plan for social development.

Prevention

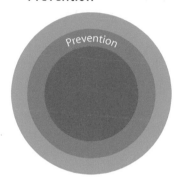

Prevention focuses on proactive measures that are designed to keep bad things from happening in the community. But in order to do them well, we have to find answers to three questions:

1. What are the known risk factors?
2. Who in the community is vulnerable to them?
3. What protective factors can we install to protect those who are vulnerable from known risks?

Prevention is based on the practical observation that even the most effective social development work will miss some risk factors. But we can still keep them from creating harms that require emergency response. Notice, however, that in adding this blue ring of prevention, we have significantly reduced the size of the emergency response circle—symbolic of reducing the demand for and costs of emergency response.

Risk Mitigation

Even with the largest investment in social development, and prevention measures, some risk factors may still exist, or can occur anew, which put people at imminent threat of harm or victimization. Risk mitigation refers to a community's systems for acknowledging when risks become so threatening that it becomes necessary to rally all community resources to immediately reduce those risks and thereby prevent the anticipated harms. Situation tables like FOCUS Rexdale perform this function. Similarly, school communities may use risk mitigation strategies to address imminent threats of violence.[3]

The risk mitigation ring is amber, like the amber traffic light—it is the precursor to the need for emergency response. In other words, if a community does not nip acutely elevated risks in the bud, then harms become imminent and emergency responders will be required. Still, by adding risk mitigation to prevention and social development, we have significantly reduced the demand for and costs of emergency response. More significantly, we have reduced the incidence of harms and victimization to people in the community. Fundamentally, the community is safer and healthier.

Emergency Response

One of the most significant differences between emergency response and the other three components of the community safety and well-being framework is that emergency response is reactive. That is, police and other emergency responders get involved after something bad has happened to someone. On the other hand, all of the other three components of the framework—risk mitigation, prevention, and social development—are proactive measures designed to prevent crime and social disorder.

Emergency response is incident-driven; the other three components are risk-driven. That means that understanding and anticipating risk factors is fundamental to implementation of these three parts of the framework. And that is where planning comes in. The first step in the planning process is observing the most immediate risk factors and then organizing social development, prevention, and risk mitigation initiatives to reduce the risk and prevent harm.

CHECK YOUR UNDERSTANDING

1. What are the similarities and differences between risk mitigation and prevention?
2. What are the similarities and differences between prevention and social development?
3. What is the most significant difference between emergency response, on the one hand, and risk mitigation, prevention, and social development, on the other?

Principles of Planning

Recall from Chapter 4 the findings of the Expert Panel on the Future of Canadian Policing Models. After a worldwide search for promising ideas and a review of research by world-class scholars, the Expert Panel acknowledged that safety and security are no longer the sole domain of police and other emergency services personnel:

> The safety and security web is a metaphor and a new way of looking at police in relation to the larger external environment in which all police now operate, as one of a variety of institutions fostering public safety and security. Viewing contemporary Canadian policing in this broader and more complex policing safety and security context acknowledges the new reality of a network, or "web," of multiple public and private agencies and actors operating and collaborating in various ways to produce and reproduce public and private safety and security.[4]

Expert Panel members specializing in policing, justice, criminology, sociology, psychology, and a host of other pertinent disciplines have recognized that all people, agencies, and organizations in a community share equal levels of responsibility and accountability for safety and well-being. That leads to two significant questions:

1. When will police agencies acknowledge this new reality and adapt their methods and styles of operating with other community partners accordingly?
2. When will all the other, non-police members of the community acknowledge this new reality and take up their new responsibilities to ensure the safety and well-being of everyone in the community?

Those two questions inform three fundamental principles for planning community safety and well-being:

1. The highest authority in the community should publicly announce its commitment to the initiative and charge others to join.
2. Effective communication among the partners and with the public is key.
3. Collaboration among agencies, organizations, businesses, community groups, and individuals is essential.

Additionally, our whole shift from incident-focused emergency response to risk-focused mitigation, prevention, and social development gives us three further principles for planning community safety and well-being:

4. Planning must be risk-focused.
5. Planning must be asset-based, and it must include all assets in the community.
6. Planning must be data-driven and evidence-based.

We review these six principles of planning community safety and well-being below.

1. The Highest Authority in the Community Should Publicly Announce Its Commitment to the Initiative and Charge Others to Join

This first principle for planning community safety and well-being stems from the premise that this initiative requires community-wide participation. The Expert Panel called it a "whole-of-society affair involving multiple jurisdictions and many mandates beyond the policing system."[5] Planning on this scale requires dedication and inputs from every agency, organization, and group, and from many citizens; yet, it is not always easy to get them to participate. Therefore, it helps to have the highest authority in the community mandate community safety and well-being planning. Planning requires vision, leadership, commitment, and, occasionally, the voice of authority. In a high-rise social housing unit, that highest authority might be composed of landlord and building managers plus officers of the tenants' association. In a neighbourhood, it might be the local municipal councillor and representatives of homeowners and businesses. In a municipality, it might be the municipal mayor and council. At the county level, the county warden, chief executive officer, and heads of departments may compose that authority. The point is, such a charge has to come from somewhere and the higher the level of authority that issues the charge, the more authority there is to lend to the whole exercise.

2. Effective Communication Among the Partners and with the Public Is Key

With so many local actors involved in planning and implementing strategies for community safety and well-being, it becomes paramount that everyone understand what they are trying to do as a group and what their individual roles and responsibilities are. That calls for excellent communication throughout the exercise. As a result, the collaborative must get serious about thorough, accurate, clear, and timely communication from the outset.

The collaborative must also decide how that information will be communicated, keeping in mind that communications and communicators can come in many forms and voices. If they choose to use the local press, they must ensure that press representatives appreciate the value of this exercise and take the time to understand why it's being undertaken as well as the press's role in advocating for and supporting it. Then there is the approach of using articulate and charismatic spokespersons. Each local initiative will, no doubt, have at least one partner that is adept at communication, so it would only be appropriate to expect more communications to emanate from that partner. Social media is also extremely useful for an enterprise such as this. The point of this principle is simply that the collaborative must get serious about effective communication early in the game.

3. Collaboration Among Agencies, Organizations, Businesses, Community Groups, and Individuals Is Essential

There is no more profound requirement in a whole-of-society initiative like this than collaboration. As we have noted in previous chapters, all of these agencies, organizations, businesses, community groups, and individuals have to be able to work productively together, notwithstanding their different mandates, resources, knowledge, and expertise, styles of operating, and goals and preferences. That is a huge challenge, not least because we naturally tend to organize our communities and all these actors in vertical silos with discrete roles and resources. We tend to think of them as separate entities with different technologies and specializations. They are also usually set up to compete with each other for scarce public resources. So it becomes doubly difficult to get them to work together collaboratively, at the level required by community-wide planning. Therefore, collaboration becomes our third principle for community safety and well-being planning.

It is important to note that collaboration becomes more and more of a challenge the farther out we move from emergency response to social development in the framework. Notice, for example, that in emergency response, very little collaboration is required among the few agencies responding to an incident involving harm. Police, fire, and emergency medical services are the most common collaborators at the scene of these incidents, and collaboration usually consists of a set pattern of exchanges among them. But as soon as we move out to the amber ring of risk mitigation, the number of actors increases significantly. We find at least ten acute care agencies, whose members meet regularly, often weekly, to collaborate in identifying people at acutely elevated risk of harms, and to plan an immediate, coordinated intervention to reduce those risks. Collaboration gets even more complicated in the social development realm (green ring). There we need inputs from all agencies and organizations: school boards, public health, economic development, public works, and more. Many of these are agencies with little or no experience collaborating with each other. You can see the challenges inherent in this principle of effective planning for community safety and well-being.

4. Planning Must Be Risk-Focused

Police used to mobilize only when an incident occurred that required emergency response. That works fine in the red circle of our community safety and well-being framework. But the other three-quarters of the framework requires something quite different. There, police and all other community partners have to do a better job of anticipating probable incidents, based on knowledge and appraisal of risks that precipitate such incidents. Police must work to prevent harms and victimization by identifying and addressing risks.

Many community agencies and groups have information about real risks, and obviously police can draw on occurrence data. But all other human and social service providers also have information about the prevalence of risks in the community. Schools have a good idea of the risks that their students' families face daily. Workplaces know what risks employees face. This fourth principle is basically requiring that all partners in community safety and well-being planning share risk information so that, in the end, the plan for community safety and well-being focuses on the highest priority threats.

5. Planning Must Be Asset-Based, and It Must Include All Assets in the Community

An enterprise like community safety and well-being planning should be undertaken with the most capable, articulate, experienced, committed, and progressive people and organizations in the lead. Usually those organizations and individuals are known by everyone, so it is not difficult to identify and mobilize them. However, experience in numerous communities has shown that too often other valuable community assets (individuals, organizations, agencies, groups, businesses, etc.) get overlooked. That is not acceptable for a whole-of-society enterprise. Hence, it is useful, early in the planning process, to begin to develop an asset inventory. The inventory lists those individuals, organizations, and groups that have the most to offer community safety and well-being planning in various priority risk areas.

One area of community assets that is too often overlooked in an endeavour like this is the marginalized neighbourhood. Most often, people think of well-resourced agencies when they think of "community assets," and indeed, those agencies are certainly assets. But it turns out that even in the most marginalized neighbourhoods, there are individuals, groups, and organizations that have a lot to offer a community-wide exercise like safety and well-being planning. Hence, this fifth principle emphasizes: do not forget the people in greatest need of improvements in their social determinants of health. They are assets too.

6. Planning Must Be Data-Driven and Evidence-Based

This sixth planning principle is all about data and evaluation. Obviously, human judgments are required throughout the planning and implementation enterprise. But this principle emphasizes that human judgments will be better if they are informed by the best science available. That science comes into play at two main points in the process: at the outset of planning, when community members are selecting priority risk areas to focus on; and upon implementation of the plan, when people need to see some evidence about whether or not the plan is working as it is expected to work.

What constitutes data-driven and evidence-based planning will be different in each of the four components of the framework: social development, prevention, risk mitigation, and emergency response. For example, in the emergency response circle (red ring), we are accustomed to benchmarking and evaluating numbers and types of occurrences, clearance rates, types and scope of injuries, harms, and victimization—and that is about all. But when we move to risk mitigation (amber ring), the scope broadens to include well over a hundred risk factors, demographics of vulnerable individuals, agencies selected to intervene, and dispositions of interventions. Way out in the social development arena (green ring), we are concerned about everything from average annual income, to high school completion rates, to numbers and demographics of people on various forms of social assistance. Measurement becomes more complicated the farther out we move from the centre to the outer perimeter of the framework. Some guidelines for appropriate measures for all four components are in the public domain and may be sourced through the Ontario Association of Chiefs of Police.[6]

CHECK YOUR UNDERSTANDING

1. Why is it advisable to start the community planning process by having the highest authority in the community publicly announce its commitment to the initiative and use its authority to influence others to do the same?
2. What does the risk-focused principle mean?
3. What does the asset-based principle mean?
4. What does the data-driven, evidence-based principle mean?

An Action Plan to Address Violence Against Indigenous Women and Their Overrepresentation in the Justice System

Indigenous women have been overrepresented and underprotected in the justice system for decades. Aboriginal women are three times more likely than non-Aboriginal women to be victims of violence. Kim Pate, executive director of the Canadian Association of Elizabeth Fry Societies, says:

> They are women who are often already marginalized by virtue of their race, class, and sometimes disability if they have disabling mental health issues or intellectual disabilities. ... We know that the rates of violence ... against indigenous women are particularly high, and they are also more likely to not have had support in addressing that violence.

An RCMP inquiry into murdered and missing women between 1980 and 2012 found that 16 percent of murdered women in Canada were Aboriginal. A new action plan was put in place following public outcry. The plan takes a proactive, restorative approach to addressing one of the highest-risk populations in Canada. It focuses on the creation of productive relationships through expansion of community-based initiatives. They include enhanced training for First Nations police officers with an emphasis on investigating violence in relationships; coordinated community programs designed to break the cycle of intergenerational violence; greater support for Aboriginal victim services; transition services; and opportunities for training and job skills to empower First Nations women.

"The plan recommends continued emphasis on missing and murdered indigenous women, engaging in productive relationships with indigenous communities, and utilizing the First Nations Policing Program as an essential service to reduce the number of indigenous people in the criminal justice system," Perry Bellegarde, the National Chief of the Assembly of First Nations, said at the Canadian Association of Chiefs of Police conference. The plan is about reducing and preventing risks of further violence and harm for indigenous women.

SOURCES: Kristy Kirkup, "Examine Police Behaviour in Missing, Murdered Indigenous Women Inquiry, Advocates Say," *The Canadian Press* (3 May 2016), online: CBC News <http://www.cbc.ca/news>; Rachel Cain, "How Canadian Police Are Improving Their Relationship with Indigenous Peoples," online: ThinkProgress <https://thinkprogress.org/how-canadian-police-are-improving-their-relationship-with-indigenous-peoples-26ac2eccbcb5#.k5gj1rv8r>; and Royal Canadian Mounted Police, *Missing and Murdered Aboriginal Women* (2015), online: <http://www.rcmp-grc.gc.ca/wam/media/455/original/c3561a284cfbb9c244bef57750941439.pdf>.

Consider the following questions:

1. Should police be the lead agency in efforts to reduce the risk of violence for Aboriginal women? Why or why not?
2. Do you think this action plan will reduce the risk of violence for Aboriginal women?
3. Is there anything missing that you would want included in the action plan?

Roles of Community Partners

One of the nice things about a community-wide initiative like planning for community safety and well-being is that it benefits from a wide range of skills, experiences, and capabilities that are offered by a diverse range of community partners. Of course, all of them have to work well together, and sometimes that can be a challenge. But when they do, the whole community benefits.

Appropriate to Their Mandate, Resources, Expertise, and Capabilities

One of the ways to work toward that benefit is to ensure that each community partner is properly slotted into activities and given responsibilities that correspond to its roles and specializations as an independent agency. To the extent possible, people should not be slotted into unfamiliar duties.

That means that it will be important to have a good sense of the capabilities, resources, and responsibilities of all community partners. That requires a deliberate effort to get to know all of them—a good job for police. Officers with good investigative skills are very efficient in ferreting out the information needed for something like the project's asset inventory. It is relatively easy for police to obtain access to any agency's leadership, and agency executives are generally open about sharing information with police officers about their own agency, and its goals, mission, vision, resources, staffing, activities, and responsibilities.

Collaboration

Collaboration may prove to be a challenge for some agencies. As of this writing, Ontario has close to 65 risk mitigation, situation tables operating in local municipalities across the province. Yet every one of them will report that some local human and social service agencies are finding it difficult to join this worthy enterprise. Reasons for these difficulties vary with the agencies. Some school boards, for example, hold fast to the notion that they can resolve any high-risk situation that they face within the school community. There is almost a sense from some school boards that they do not want any other agencies involved in any problems that reside within the school community. Some mental health agencies are having difficulties collaborating too. They cite the need to protect the privacy and confidentiality of persons in their care, and their executives raise the issue of corporate liability should any breach of privacy and confidentiality occur in the process of collaborating with others. Very few situation tables in Ontario have hospital emergency staff helping in the risk mitigation process. Many of them claim that they are already overworked and simply do not have time to attend one more 90-minute meeting every week.

Collaboration is not easy; indeed, it is far easier to operate as a separate agency. Each agency has its own enabling legislation, standards, and mandate; a clear, limited, and discrete range of programs and services; and the expectation that no other agency in the community is similarly mandated, resourced, or expected to deliver the same services. Each agency is accountable only to its own enabling legislation and provincial oversight bodies. There is comfort in those limits, and things become less comfortable when those limits are challenged the way they are in collaborative planning for community safety and well-being.

Planning for community safety and well-being means that all community partners have to share responsibilities and accountabilities for the plan, the planning process, and the plan's implementation. If any single component of the plan has problems, all of the community partners have problems and they have to work together, again, to resolve them. Part of the reason that this resistance to collaborating exists is because over the years provincial and federal agencies have organized our human and social services network in silos of specialization—each mandated by separate legislation yet funded out of the same, too often shrinking, pool of public resources. Too often that legislation fails to enable collaboration across vertical silos. Too often that legislation fails to protect agencies from liabilities that an expanded mandate to collaborate would bring. On the other hand, current research and practices in collaborative, risk-driven community safety and well-being are informing all of us that problem resolution will require collaboration, and collaboration will require a significant redevelopment of the way we mandate and organize human and social services in the public sector.

One of the organizational tools most agencies have used to protect their resources, staff, mandates, programs, and prerogatives is the aura of specialization and expertise they can claim as a way to set them apart from other agencies and organizations. For example, the use of specialized acronyms signals to others, "We're special; no one else can understand what we do!" Yet transparency is what is needed to further effective collaboration. Police are just as bad at this as the health sector, school boards, children's aid, and others. Although in the case of police, this tendency is reinforced by the monopoly that police have protected over the sovereignty of community safety for a couple of centuries. As that monopoly breaks down, police and other agencies will learn that their effectiveness is actually improved through judicious transparency. That means being more open about policies, programs, and practices and inviting specialists from other sectors to share in the responsibilities and accountabilities required to make everyone in the community safer and healthier.

That transparency problem comes down to the issue of agencies judiciously and responsibly sharing more information with each other and communicating more often, in straightforward language that does not require agency specialization to understand. It helps if all agencies can also appreciate the commitment, resources, and technical specializations of other agencies. It is only through recognizing their partners' strengths that they can invite their partners to acknowledge their own. In that sense, collaboration has to be a reciprocal process, and one in which police are involved.

Advocacy and Support for the Planning Process

All community partners have an important role to play in advocating, community-wide, for the safety and well-being planning process. A good plan has inputs from every sector in the community, especially those that too frequently do not have a voice in public issues and problem-solving. The wider the appeal, the larger the community investment, and the better the quality and quantity of planning and implementation. Each community partner has its own natural constituency. Therefore, each partner is a channel to reach those constituencies and solicit their involvement in planning for community safety and well-being.

Roles of Police

This chapter has been about planning for community safety and well-being. We have talked about the planning process, community partners, and some of the unique challenges that come from a community-wide initiative like this. But now it is time to focus on the role of police in planning for community safety and well-being. This chapter on planning is in this text on community policing because police have a number of very special roles to play in the whole process. It is safe to generalize that if police are not intrinsically involved in the whole process, it will not work.

Priority Problems

Police, more than any other agency or organization, have their fingers on the safety and security pulse of the community. They know where people at risk of harms and victimization reside. They know the types of occurrences that are symptomatic of shortcomings in the social determinants of health. They spend much of their time responding to those occurrences. Yet police are not good at openly sharing this kind of information with the community at large. That has to change, because if community members are not aware of these problems, they cannot, and will not, take responsibility for resolving them.

Hence, one of the first jobs for police is initiating the whole community safety planning process by sharing with the highest authority in the community (for example, the mayor, municipal administration, and city council) the highest priorities for making the community safer and healthier. This information comes right off the data that police are already tracking on occurrences, locations, and trends. Most often, it is this kind of information that will move the local powers-that-be to mandate a planning process for community safety and well-being. In that sense, the police can, and should, be the starting point for the whole planning process.

That means police will have to figure out how to communicate clearly about these occurrences to people who are not steeped in police jargon. This is a place where police can practise some of those principles of collaboration discussed above. They can start out by using plain language to describe the most significant problems the community safety plan should focus on immediately. Second, they can use a data analyst to develop some trends data on these occurrences so that municipal councillors can see for themselves how the frequencies of these occurrences change over time, in different seasons, in different parts of town, etc. But it is not enough to dump a data table on a naive council; it is more important to provide an oral presentation that helps councillors interpret what they are seeing. All of this can be a communications challenge for police; but it is the challenge that gets the whole planning ball rolling and it is well worth it.

Which problems should police bring to the council for immediate attention in the community safety planning process? There are a couple of ways to answer this question. One of the more obvious ones is that police should focus everyone's attention on those community problems that create the most harm and victimization. Each community needs to act first on those problems that put people in the most danger. For example, in a large city, organized crime

and gang violence associated with drug trafficking may be the most important threat to safety and well-being. But in a small rural municipality the
most important problem may be high summertime traffic flow through the
downtown core as a result of people travelling to and from their cottages. If
that is the greatest source of risks to people's health and safety, then obviously
this municipality's community safety and well-being plan ought to have a
major section devoted to traffic flow and situational safety measures.

But a second criterion is those problems that are costing the municipality
the most in terms of staff time, infrastructure costs, monitoring, and administration. Police are part of the municipality's costs of governance. So what
occurrences are eating up most of the police time in responding to calls for
service? The municipality pays directly for that police staff time. An examination of occurrence data may reveal that addictions and mental health problems contribute most to these costs. They are usually two-officer calls, and too
frequently they require both officers to transport individuals to hospital
(which in a rural area can be quite far away) and stay with them in hospital
until the individual is seen by qualified health personnel and released,
detained for further treatment and observation, or transferred to another
health care facility. We saw earlier in this text how some police services have
saved the municipality money by mobilizing an officer and psychiatric social
worker or other mental health specialist to these kinds of calls. The point of
this example is that police need look only at their own occurrence data to have
a good idea of what priority problems to recommend to council's attention in
a community-wide planning process.

Community Partners

Once priority problems have become clearer, it is time to assess which potential community partners need to be drawn into the mix to do some of the
safety planning work. This is another place for police to play a specialized role,
and it raises a series of questions. What specialized agencies and public organizations have a role to play? What about roles for private sector businesses? Are
there community organizations (not-for-profits) that have information,
experience, or community intelligence that would inform planning and problem resolution? What individuals care about these issues and can be brought
to the table to help figure out how to resolve them?

That brings us back to the point made earlier about police taking on the
role of developing a solid base of information about all potential community
partners. Police do not necessarily have to do all the work, but they are
good candidates to take charge of developing the community asset inventory.
Then, through judicious outreach and recruitment of community partners for
this exercise, police can gradually help everyone learn about each other
and, ultimately, select the most appropriate partners to help resolve specific
problems.

Once identified, those community partners need to be recruited for the exercise of community safety and well-being planning. It helps, of course, to have a mandate for planning from the highest authority in the community, but that is not enough. Armed with that mandate, someone has to reach out to the selected agencies—initially at the executive level—and recruit them to the exercise. Police are perfect for this role. As an organization that specializes in crime and social disorder, they are credible to all other agency representatives. As one of the few local agencies with the duties and responsibilities of keeping everyone safe and secure, police are appreciated—that is, their legitimacy is high, thereby making an appeal from police more persuasive. It is easier for agency executives, who may find it difficult to collaborate on a community-wide initiative like this, to respond positively if they are invited by police than if they are invited by an executive of another agency, or even a member of municipal council.

The same is true when it comes to recruiting community assets from marginalized neighbourhoods. Whether they are individual residents in social housing, or community-based organizations (like churches offering after-school activities for local children), these assets are invaluable to a community-wide planning exercise, and police have the capacity to reach them and persuade them to participate. Once so mobilized, it also falls to police to help these community assets weave their way into the broad, community-wide planning partnership. Many of these assets do not have a good understanding of the roles of other community partners, like social service agencies. Many of them may not have the best relationship with such agencies. Hence, it is doubly important for police to stand by in support of these local community assets as they find their own strengths in the collective planning process.

Collaboration

We spent a lot of time, above, talking about the importance of collaboration for community partners engaged in planning for community safety and well-being. But as alluded to earlier, the same generalizations apply equally to police. In fact, it could be argued that collaboration is a greater requirement for police than it is for almost any other agency. That is because police are kicking off this planning exercise based on what they see every day in responding to calls for service. It is because police have the broadest public legitimacy of any agency—at least in those municipalities where they have worked to develop and sustain that legitimacy. But it is also because, traditionally, police have been the least transparent of any agency—protecting their sovereignty over safety and security. We have already observed that worldwide, communities are being invited back into the safety and well-being web. Police are no longer the sole actors; in fact, we have seen how community safety and well-being will only be achieved if everyone in the community takes their share of responsibility for it.

Consequently, we need police to model the collaboration process for other agencies and community partners who may have some difficulty doing it. Police can model the process by

- demonstrating transparency and openness;
- fostering partnerships with other agencies and facilitating new partnerships between other agencies;
- leveraging collaboration across the board by advocating for it with community partners;
- mediating between agencies, some of which may find it difficult to join the collaborative; and
- facilitating an open negotiation among all partners about each other's roles in planning for community safety and well-being, as well as the process for doing this work.

Advocating

Police are invaluable to planning for community safety and well-being. Community needs their initiative; their data and information about risk factors; their credibility on the issues that need to be resolved; the openness they can model in dealing with all community partners; and their capacity to reach everyone in the community to promote the planning exercise. Advocacy is, in many respects, their most important job and it continues throughout the planning process. Even when the plan is completed, police have a huge role in advocating for its implementation and helping all other actors in the community do their own part at putting the plan to work.

Traditional Policing

In all this talk about planning for community safety and well-being, we must never lose sight of the invaluable role of traditional policing. We saw earlier in this text that traditional policing absorbs about 15 percent of a police agency's time and resources. Notwithstanding those small numbers, it is traditional policing that secures everyone's safety as the community begins to grapple with some of its priority crime and social disorder problems. If, for example, a community chooses to tackle domestic violence as a priority problem for long-term investment with a goal to reducing such incidents, police still need to respond quickly when such an incident occurs. A program to reduce such incidents is laudable—particularly if it works. It would be wonderful if a given community safety and well-being plan, once implemented, actually reduced the demand for traditional policing below 15 percent. But one domestic dispute is too many, and a community safety plan that focuses on them is not a licence to relax our vigilance for the safety and well-being of community members.

CHECK YOUR UNDERSTANDING

1. What is the role of police in helping the community identify priority risk factors?
2. What is the role of police with respect to other community partners in community safety and well-being planning?
3. What is the role of police in collaborating with other community partners?
4. What should police do to support collaboration among the whole planning team?
5. How does traditional policing fit in the process of community planning for safety and well-being?

The Planning Process

There are lots of planning models that can be applied to community safety and well-being. In fact, most municipalities have lots of qualified planners on staff because planning is the soundest basis for making all kinds of investment and operational decisions in both the public and private sectors. Planning uses the same logic that applies to SARA, CAPRA, and PARE: decide on some goals, research and select some ways to achieve them, assess your results, and make adjustments accordingly.

One of the things that makes planning for community safety and well-being unique is the sheer number of agencies and organizations that have to be involved. They are the strength of this planning framework, but they are also one of the biggest challenges because most of our institutions are accustomed to working, largely, alone (aside from very limited partnerships for service delivery purposes).

Directive from the Highest Authority in the Community

At the outset of the planning process, the highest authority in the community should issue a directive stating that all agencies are expected to participate in community safety and well-being planning. That will require deciding who that person or body is—for example, municipal council and the mayor may be excellent choices. The mandate to plan for community safety and well-being should be clear in this directive. But it also helps if the directive specifies that all agencies, organizations, businesses, citizens, and community groups are expected to collaborate to promote the greater good. With that, it becomes easier to recruit partners for the planning exercise.

One municipality used a unanimous resolution of the municipal council for this purpose. It declared that community safety and well-being was the council's highest priority and that the council expected everyone to participate in planning for it. But it also laid out a three-year planning cycle, which was helpful because it virtually extended the mandate into periodic revisions of the plan that emerged from this effort.

The directive should be used to recruit appropriate agencies, executives, and citizens to form a working group that will drive the planning exercise. These individuals should be carefully chosen. They should understand and value planning as a process, and it helps if they are fairly diverse in terms of their technical specialization and agency alignment (for example, a police leader and individuals from social and human services, municipal agencies, business, and a neighbourhood association).

Priority Problems to Be Resolved

The first job for the newly appointed working group is to identify the priority safety and well-being challenges that the community needs to resolve most urgently. A few should be chosen that can be dealt with on a priority basis. After all, in three years' time, a renewal of the plan will permit re-examination and specification of priority problems. Not everything needs to be resolved at once.

This is one of the first places where the data-driven principle of planning comes into play. The way to figure out priority community safety and well-being problems is to examine data provided by a range of agencies and organizations. Police have occurrence data, GIS maps of those occurrences (discussed in Chapter 4), and data on trends (for example, whether certain types of occurrences are increasing or decreasing). But data from other first responders also need to be examined. Then, the working group can move outward in our community safety and well-being framework and ask the same questions of a sample of acute care providers who work in the risk mitigation business (mental health, children's aid, women's support groups, etc.). Finally, they can go all the way to the outer ring, social development, and ask people like school board representatives, business executives, and social and economic development agencies what they think the immediate safety and well-being priorities should be. Make sure to include inputs from citizens, neighbourhood groups, and individuals who have, in the past, shown some interest in community safety and well-being. It is especially important to include community assets who reside in marginalized neighbourhoods.

To illustrate this planning process, we will presume that the working group decided that mental health and addictions issues are far too prevalent in this community, and they want this first plan to address those.

Priority Task Groups

For each priority safety and well-being problem that the working group decides to include in this first plan, a small task group of people (not the same people as already serving in the working group) should be assigned to do the research that is necessary to plan. They should be picked for their knowledge and experience with the issues pertaining to their assigned priority problem, and they should have good access to information about it. In our mental health and addictions example, the working group should be sure to appoint people from those sectors who understand these problems.

The first job of each priority task group will be to identify the pertinent risk factors, vulnerable groups, and protective factors associated with the problem they are setting out to resolve. This will, most likely, require some thorough research on their part. What do research scholars say about the problem? What have other municipalities done to resolve similar problems? What would be practicable in this community context? What is realistic to expect in the way of outcomes?

In our mental health example, the task group will specify that children, youth, families, and individuals with mental illness are the vulnerable groups they want to serve in this community safety and well-being plan. They will also identify the following risk factors for mental health and addictions problems:

- negative parenting
- domestic violence
- social isolation
- stress factors

The term "stress factors" refers to any circumstantial stressors, like tension in a relationship, losing a job, difficulties meeting expenses, or child-rearing challenges.

Finally, the task group will do sufficient research on these risk factors and the mental health and addictions problem so that they can, with some confidence, list specific protective factors they want to install through this community safety and well-being plan; for example:

- social networks
- family supports
- recovery supports
- physician screening for mental health and addictions disorders

Drawing Up the Plan

With a focus on the protective factors, the task group can specify desired outcomes of the plan, strategies for achieving those outcomes, and the kinds of measures they will use to see if the plan is working as specified. The following table shows how all of these plan components can be brought together. Notice that the plan covers options in all four zones of the community safety and well-being framework.

TABLE 9.1 Sample Community Safety and Well-Being Plan: Mental Health and Addictions

Vulnerable Groups
- Children and youth
- Seniors
- Families
- People with mental illness

Risk Factors
- Negative parenting
- Domestic violence
- Social isolation
- Circumstantial stress factors

Protective Factors
- Family supports
- Social networks
- Physician screening
- Recovery supports

	Social Development	Prevention	Risk Mitigation	Emergency Response
Outcomes	• Less stressed children and youth • Stronger social networks • Improved mental health	• More physician screening • More access to treatment • Increased youth recreation	• Reduced emergency room visits • Reduced drug-related problems • Reduced family crises	• Shorter emergency room response times • Increased access to qualified health workers
Strategies	• Parenting education • Youth mentoring • Health promotion	• Link physicians to treatment • Recreation programs for youth	• Identify addictions and mental health thresholds for intervention • Multi-agency interventions	• Provide advocacy for addicts • Develop crisis response teams
Measures	• Quality of life • Stress levels • Affiliation rates	• Physician referrals to treatment • Treatment enrollments	• Access to treatment • Family supports	• Time in emergency room • Access to treatment • De-escalation of emergency room stressors

Example of what a community safety and well-being plan might look like if it was designed to reduce problems with mental health and addictions.

SOURCE: Hugh C Russell, "Framework for Planning Community Safety and Well-Being" (Animated PowerPoint presentation for the Ontario Working Group on Collaborative, Risk-Driven Community Safety and Well-Being, 5 February 2014), online: Ontario Association of Chiefs of Police <http://www.oacp.on.ca/news-events/resource-documents/ontario-working-group-owg>. Courtesy of OACP.

CHECK YOUR UNDERSTANDING

1. Outline and explain the process of planning for community safety and well-being.

Police Legitimacy

Much earlier in this text we defined police legitimacy and made a number of comments throughout subsequent chapters about how important it is for police effectiveness in whatever they are trying to do. That is, high police legitimacy makes traditional policing more efficient and more effective. As well, it is essential for the effective implementation of community policing.

Mazerolle and her colleagues reviewed qualified research on the subject of police legitimacy and concluded that it is especially important because it ensures individuals' compliance and cooperation with police and police partners. Further, compliance and cooperation are motivated by the individual's view of police as legitimate, rather than by any fear of consequences should they not cooperate or comply. In that sense, the researchers point out, police legitimacy becomes an important social value that can, and should, be used to win and sustain public compliance and cooperation with broad social causes like planning for community safety and well-being.[7]

The bottom line is that the capability of police to get all other members of a community to take better care of themselves and each other, and to work collaboratively toward the goals of increased community safety and well-being, is highly dependent on the police acting, at all times, respectfully, fairly, without prejudice, and inclusively. And that is a standard that police can set for all other community partners as well.

CHAPTER SUMMARY

Communities will become safer and healthier if they make deliberate efforts to construct a community safety plan. Any such plan should cover four areas of safety and well-being activities: social development, prevention, risk mitigation, and emergency response. The most effective planning process starts with the most authoritative voice in the community mandating the plan. The next step is identifying priority risk factors derived from police occurrence data and data from other human and social service agencies.

As part of the planning process, diverse community partners are drawn into the planning exercise based on their expertise, resources, and commitment to the broad goals of increasing community safety and well-being. Police are invaluable to this whole exercise, even though their direct actions and planning responsibilities may be less than those of other community partners. But police cannot positively influence the process if they do not enjoy a solid level of legitimacy in the communities they serve.

REVIEW AND DISCUSSION QUESTIONS

1. Summarize the meaning and distinctions among the four components, or rings, of the community safety and well-being framework.

2. List and explain six principles for planning community safety and well-being.

3. Outline and explain the process of planning for community safety and well-being.

4. Explain five special roles for police in planning for community safety and well-being.

5. Explain why police legitimacy is so important for the success of planning for community safety and well-being.

NOTES

1 Julie Berg & Clifford Shearing, "Integrated Security: Assembling Knowledges and Capacities" in Tom Williamson, ed, *The Handbook of Knowledge-Based Policing: Current Conceptions and Future Directions* (Sussex, UK: John Wiley, 2008) at 394.

2 Hugh C Russell & Norman E Taylor, "Framework for Planning ... Community Safety and Well-Being" in *New Directions in Community Safety: Consolidating Lessons Learned About Risk and Collaboration* (Toronto: Ontario Working Group on Collaborative, Risk-driven Community Safety and Well-being, Ontario Association of Chiefs of Police, April 2014), online: <http://www .oacp.on.ca/Userfiles/StandingCommittees/CommunityPolicing/Resource

Docs/OWG%20New%20Directions%20in%20Community%20Safety.pdf>
[*New Directions*].

3   Manitoba Education, Citizenship and Youth, *When Words Are Not Enough: Precursors to Threat—An Early Warning System for School Counsellors* (Winnipeg: Manitoba Education, Citizenship and Youth, 2005). Or access the British Columbia version of the same document at <https://www.bced.gov.bc.ca/ sco/resourcedocs/words_not_enough.pdf>.

4   Expert Panel on the Future of Canadian Policing Models, *Policing Canada in the 21st Century: New Policing for New Challenges* (Ottawa: Council of Canadian Academies, 2014) at 33.

5   *Ibid* at xiv.

6   Hugh C Russell & Norman E Taylor, "Performance Measures for Community Safety and Well-Being" in *New Directions*, *supra* note 2.

7   Lorraine Mazerolle, Emma Antrobus, Sarah Bennett & Tom R Tyler, "Shaping Citizen Perceptions of Police Legitimacy: A Randomized Field Trial of Procedural Justice" (2013) 51:1 Criminology 33.

CHAPTER 10

Applying Risk Analysis to Violent Extremism

United States Ambassador Pamela Hamamoto, Permanent Representative to the United Nations in Geneva, speaks at an international round table focusing on multi-sectoral, community-led approaches to the role of women in countering violent extremism. As part of her remarks, Ambassador Hamamoto called upon stakeholders to support and implement community-level programming aimed at increasing community resilience to radicalization: "For our efforts to be effective, they have to be driven by local knowledge and responsive to concerns of those local communities where violent extremism is a problem."

LEARNING OUTCOMES

Upon completion of this chapter, you should be able to:

- Explain six sequential steps in a community problem-solving model
- Distinguish between lone attackers and violent extremists, and explain which of these two we see most often in Canada and the United States
- Distinguish between four levels of radicalization on the road to martyrdom
- List and explain two behavioural risk factors for each level of radicalization
- Explain why police cannot and should not deliver countering violent extremism (CVE) programs
- Explain the role of community policing in countering violent extremism

Introduction

By intent, design, and necessity, a police service is a reactive agent in the maintenance of peace and social order. When faced with the prospect of violent extremism like that carried out by social deviants in Orlando, Paris, Nice, Ottawa, Boston, Sydney, Peshawar, and Istanbul, police services must, first and foremost, possess reactive strategies to safeguard the public.

That priority, however, makes it difficult for this particular social agency to understand, value, and develop proactive strategies that reduce the requirement for emergency response in the first place. Police must develop the capacity to see beyond the demand for tactical response; recognize the risk factors that lead to anti-social, illegal, or harmful behaviour; and guide and enable all other agents in fostering community growth and development in ways that ultimately minimize the requirements for police-led emergency response.

This chapter continues the discussion of risk analysis that commenced in Chapter 8. But here, risk analysis is applied to the problem of violent extremism with three purposes in mind:

- to reflect that community policing applies to even the most severe threat to safety and security;
- to show the value of applying risk analysis to a community problem; and
- to encourage officers and police services to do the background research and analysis that is required to effectively deal with any kind of community problem.

This chapter is about the proactive measures that police are uniquely qualified to take in order to help communities protect themselves from the ravages of violent extremism. We have chosen this topic because violent extremism is a worldwide preoccupation of safety and security professionals.

Many communities are threatened by different kinds of violence, and some of it is extreme—like that which has happened to Canada's murdered and missing Aboriginal women (Chapter 9). In this chapter, however, we focus on violence perpetrated by individuals who claim to adhere to an ideology that requires violence to express itself. The violence is driven by an extremist point of view—hence, the term "violent extremism." Since the al-Qaeda attack on the US World Trade Center on September 11, 2001, security agencies around the world have focused on violence driven by extremist interpretations of Islam. But violent extremism occurs in other belief systems too: it may be motivated by racism, Nazism, and white supremacism, to name just a few. We can find violent extremism any place where adherents feel that the only way to grow their belief system is through violence. For the sake of this chapter, however, we will limit our perspective to the current concern that Public Safety Canada has identified as its top priority: al-Qaeda-inspired violent extremism.[1]

Where radicalization and the threat of violent extremism roil beneath the surface of a community, police have to sense the tremors and quell the eruptions. But they also have to mobilize and engage community capacities to mitigate social pressures from building to that explosive potential. That requires police services to recognize such threats as something more than strong imperatives for smarter, swifter, tactical manoeuvres that detect and detain those who embrace violent extremism.

Enforcement is our final option in the struggle against radicalized extremists who have chosen violence. It is the most expensive and least effective tool for protecting the public from terror. Usually, such police responses only manage to limit harms and too rarely prevent them altogether. But if we can recalibrate our sensors to detect pre-radicalized individuals who are vulnerable to the extremist message, we can redirect and support diverse community resources for more effective and far cheaper risk mitigation and prevention of violence and terror.

Framework for Risk Analysis and Program Design

As mentioned in Chapter 8, the health sector has been experimenting with and refining community-based problem-solving models for a long time. Building on these models, Williams and his colleagues designed a framework for reducing and preventing violence among youth.[2] Their model is general enough that we can adapt it to resolve any kind of community problem. It has six parts, as shown in Chapter 8 in Table 8.1:

1. Identify and analyze the problem to be resolved
2. Identify risk and protective factors
3. Design an intervention
4. Implement the intervention
5. Evaluate implementation
6. Disseminate the results

We have chosen the problem of violent extremism on which to apply this model in order to demonstrate the value of problem analysis and the importance of identifying risk and protective factors. This exercise reinforces the point that individual police officers, and the service as a whole, must develop the capabilities to research community problems and learn lessons others have learned (and published) about related or similar problems.

Identifying and Analyzing the Problem

The first step is to identify and analyze the problem—violent extremism. Police need to learn its origin, scope, impacts, and history. Often such analysis requires research among popular press and scholarly journals, plus consultation with experts and agencies, which have different specializations and therefore different perspectives on the problem. This work, therefore, needs to be done by officers who

- know how to conduct research;
- have good investigative skills;
- have a good rapport and communications capacities with specialists from other disciplines;
- can perform logical analyses; and
- have the ability to write brief, clear reports on what they learn.

For the sake of this exercise, assume that we are going to tackle the problem of violent extremism from the perspective of a police agency that serves a medium-sized municipality. There is hardly a more harmful or terrifying form of violence than that practised by individuals who are motivated by hate and malevolence. But experience has shown that tactical responses (traditional policing) are insufficient to consistently prevent it. So it is important to research what others have discovered about this problem, as a first step in designing our approach. We will start by finding, reading, and summarizing scholarly articles, policy studies, and popular press reports about what is commonly known as "countering violent extremism" or "CVE."

Violent Extremism

In January 2015, two brothers, Saïd and Chérif Kouachi, forced their way into the Paris offices of the weekly French satirical newspaper *Charlie Hebdo*, killed 12 people, and wounded 11 others. They claimed to be members of an al-Qaeda-affiliated terrorist group in Yemen, and subsequent investigations showed that, indeed, they were part of a larger cell of terrorists supported by that group.

The Kouachi brothers, associated with a terrorist organization, are different from lone attackers—that is, individuals who, while they may attribute their violent actions to broad social or political movements (like Daesh or white supremacy), become violent and act out violently without any close affiliation to such a cause or persons involved in that cause. Recent examples include Man Haron Monis, who killed a worker and held others captive in a Lindt cafe in Sydney, Australia, in 2014, and Omar Mateen, who killed 49 people and wounded 53 others in a gay nightclub in Orlando, Florida, in 2016.

What Is Daesh?

What we, in this chapter, will call Daesh is a group of militarized violent extremists who use their religion to justify their violence. Their members subscribe to the Sunni branch of Islam and believe that all other people in the world, including those who are members of non-Sunni branches of Islam, are non-believers who seek to destroy Daesh. Members use this belief to justify their violent aggression against all non-believers.

A year after the US-led invasion to remove Saddam Hussein's government in Iraq in 2003, a Jordanian, Abu Musab al-Zarqawi, rallied a reactionary force called al-Qaeda in Iraq and swore allegiance to al-Qaeda's founder, Osama bin Laden. In 2006, the group formed an organization called Islamic State in Iraq (ISI) that would accept, protect, and direct smaller dissident groups who swore to resist the invaders. Abu Bakr al-Baghdadi became leader of ISI in 2010 and increased attacks in Iraq. He also set up an affiliate, the al-Nusra Front, that joined the movement to resist President Bashar al-Assad in Syria. The merger of the Iraqi and Syrian Sunni resistance movements led to the creation of what has come to be known as ISIS, the Islamic State in Iraq and Syria. Baghdadi and his followers declared themselves a "caliphate," most easily translated as a government composed of Sunni Muslims and governed by Sunni interpretations of Islamic law, known as sharia. In the popular press, this group, led by Baghdadi, who considers himself God's deputy, is known as Daesh. Daesh expects all Muslims to move to the caliphate's captured territory and swear allegiance to it. Its ultimate goal is the establishment of a global caliphate that transcends current human-made borders. In its commitment to eradicating non-believers, Daesh claims to welcome confrontations with US-led resistance. Indeed, its online magazine, *Dabiq*, is named for the town in Syria where Daesh believes the final confrontation between Islamic and non-Islamic forces will occur, bringing about the end times.

Daesh is wealthy, relying on Islamic charities, private donors, and crude oil and byproducts that are sold and distributed outside conventional international markets. Daesh also uses ransoms from kidnappings, extortion among people living in areas controlled by it, theft, and human trafficking to finance its campaigns. It has attracted an estimated 28,000 foreign fighters, about a quarter of whom are from Western European nations or North America, and the balance of whom originate from Arab nations.

Daesh uses terror as an instrument of war that is designed to attract adherents. It does not justify its violence as self-defence, unlike al-Qaeda. Rather, Daesh sees itself as being in an all-or-nothing enterprise and prides itself on its lack of restraint in using violence. This very lack of restraint has attracted Muslim adherents from around the world. Indeed, it has attracted young non-Muslims who identify with Daesh's claim of being under duress and attack by everyone else in the world, and who seek its promise of martyrdom for those who join its cause. Daesh recruits from around the world join out of a sense of sacred mission and the desire for an idealized world of true believers.[3]

Consider the following questions:

1. Why wouldn't Daesh execute its war in compliance with the Geneva Convention or other rules of engagement that are internationally agreed upon by members of US-led forces?

2. Is Baghdadi the only religious leader in the world who claims to be God's direct representative? Explain.

3. Are you aware of any other religious groups that claim theirs is the only true religion? If so, give an example.

4. Why do you think people are attracted to join Daesh or any other group that values martyrdom and promises salvation?

Those are just a few examples of violent extremism that we can readily find in press coverage and other sources. Aside from the obvious violence reflected in these brief descriptions, what can be learned from them? It appears that violent extremism is perpetrated by two types of individuals. The first group consists of people who are radicalized by organized ideological extremists, and who are then supported and even directed by those extremists to conduct violent acts on behalf of their ideological cause. The Kouachi brothers exemplify this group of **violent extremists**—people who are willing to use, or support the use of, violence to further particular beliefs, including those of a political, social, or ideological nature.[4]

The other group is composed of individuals who may claim to belong to an ideological cause, but upon investigation are found to be acting alone. That is, no follow-up investigations uncover any affiliation with ideological movements, terrorist cells, or militants. While they may have claimed to believe in particular ideological causes, they were not contacted, directed, or materially supported by those movements. Man Haron Monis and Omar Mateen, both of whom claimed to support Daesh, represent this latter group.

Notice also that we have picked up some new language with which to understand the community problem we want to resolve. In the first group is the radicalized violent ideologue—a person who has been persuaded, or who has convinced himself or herself, to gravitate toward the radical fringe of a social or political movement that will use violence to further its cause. That suggests that we have to understand how someone becomes **radicalized**—the process by which an individual becomes motivated to provide personal or material support to an ideologically extreme social or political movement, and who may receive support and direction in conducting violent acts. The other term we picked up is the lone attacker—sometimes referred to in the press as

---

violent extremists people who are willing to use or support the use of violence to further particular beliefs, including those of a political, social, or ideological nature

radicalization the process by which an individual becomes motivated to provide personal or material support to an ideologically extreme social or political movement

the "lone wolf" or the "lone actor." The term "**lone attacker**" is probably the most accurate: the individual did attack and acted strictly on his or her own—that is, without personal, material, or other forms of support from organized, ideologically driven extremist groups. A lone attacker may be inspired or encouraged by an organized extremist group, but ultimately acts without their direct support.

Public Safety Canada, in its *2016 Public Report on the Terrorist Threat to Canada*, uses different terminology for these two categories. A "directed attack" is

> [a]n attack planned and undertaken on the instructions or with the guidance of a terrorist group. The direction can involve some or all details of the target, financing and methodology.

An "inspired attack" is defined as

> [a] self-initiated attack by a lone-actor or a small group undertaken in support of a terrorist group or extremist ideology, without the inspiring group's prior specific direction, financing or knowledge."[5]

The Causes of Radicalization

The causes and social psychology of radicalization are well researched. Not all the answers are in, but many academics, policy-makers, and practitioners agree on sufficient dimensions of the problem so that program designers should be able to identify social indicators of risk factors that allow them to mitigate violent potential. The strongest correlate to radicalization is the innate human need to belong, to be a self-actualizing and contributing member of a social group. That group may be one's family and friends, a neighbourhood, a gang, an institution, an ethno-cultural group, or an army. The basic human need for affiliation drives the pre-radicalized individual to listen to the extremist message, and the extremists use that promise to hook adherents.

The force that drives the pre-radicalized seeker into the extremist's sphere of influence is rejection—from family, friends, neighbourhood, institutions, or other social group. The individual may either be rejected by significant others or choose to reject others with whom he or she has been closely affiliated. Either situation puts the individual in the vulnerable position of needing new affiliations.

Such influences are rife in some communities. The impact of rejection can be systemic, as with poverty. Where the individual or family is prohibited from feeling valued, making positive contributions, or controlling the factors

---

lone attacker an individual who violently attacks and acts strictly on his or her own—that is, without personal, material, or other forms of support from organized, ideological extremism

that have the strongest roles in their lives, they will gravitate to social environments that promise more of those things. Another is the experience of immigration because it automatically immerses one cultural group into the culture of another—and obtaining acceptance, respect, and actualization in the new cultural context is very difficult for the immigrant population. Many young refugees and newer immigrants face huge barriers in education and employment because of poverty, stigmatization, and a lack of schooling before they arrive in Canada. Those factors lead to significant feelings of inferiority, failure, and disillusionment with the hope they once carried about coming here, profound feelings of helplessness, and ultimately a sense that they will not have any opportunity to achieve their dreams. All of these feelings can make such youth vulnerable to the recruitment messages of al-Qaeda-inspired extremist groups.[6]

What Is the al-Qaeda-Inspired Narrative?

Osama bin Laden rationalized his movement, known as al-Qaeda, and indeed the 2001 attack on the World Trade Center in New York, as retaliation against what he perceived as the West's centuries-long efforts to conquer and suppress Islam. He attracted adherents to al-Qaeda on the basis of three very simple messages, which we will call the al-Qaeda-inspired narrative:

1. Islam is the only true religion and those who do not believe in it are infidels.

2. Peoples and nations characterized as "the West" hate Islam and Muslims and seek to destroy them.

3. Therefore, Muslims have the right, responsibility, and divine mandate to fight infidels—known as violent jihad.

SOURCE: Phil Gurski, *The Threat from Within: Recognizing al-Qaeda-Inspired Radicalization and Terrorism in the West* (London, UK: Rowman & Littlefield, 2015) at 6.

Racism, whether framed as anti-immigration policy or the hurtful behaviours of social exclusion, will push the seeker to find the promise of belonging in other social groups. Or individuals can reach a stage in their lives when they question most of the values and precepts that contributed to their upbringing, and, upon close re-examination of them, reject them and the important people in their lives who promoted them.

Knowing that a profound need to belong, to be affiliated with others, drives some people to adhere to organized, radical groups suggests an area where we might begin to develop programs that can prevent radicalization. But of course we are going to have to learn a lot more about what drives these people to lose their family, friends, and community affiliations in the first place, such that they then have to seek affiliations elsewhere.

Profiles of Lone Attacker and Radicalized Extremists

Research on the backgrounds of nearly 100 lone attackers shows that they tend to be older and less educated than attackers who are attached in some fashion to a terrorist organization. Lone attackers usually have higher rates of mental illness and higher rates of criminal history. Criminal history usually means common charges like assaults, theft, sexual offences, and domestic disputes, not necessarily charges relating to terrorism or violent extremism. Interestingly, over three-quarters of lone attackers in the United States since 9/11 revealed their plans to be violent prior to acting out—via Facebook, Twitter, and other social networks. Often a triggering event preceded the lone attacker's violence.[7] For example, the Orlando killer, Omar Mateen, was, according to his father, angered upon seeing two men kissing, and he signalled his violence during his killing spree by placing a 911 call during which he claimed to be acting in support of Daesh. However, there is no evidence that Mateen had the direct support, or even endorsement, of members of that movement.

Violent extremists, like the Kouachi brothers, who are in some way actually affiliated with a terrorist organization, show a slightly different profile from that of lone attackers. According to Scott Atran:

> Most foreign volunteers and supporters [of Daesh] fall within the mid-ranges of ... psychological attributes like empathy, compassion, idealism, and wanting mostly to help rather than hurt other people. They are mostly youth in transitional stages in their lives: students, immigrants, between jobs or mates, having left or about to leave their native family and looking for a new family of friends and fellow travelers with whom they can find significance. Most have had no traditional religious education, and are often "born again" into a socially tight, ideologically narrow but world-spanning sense of religious mission. Indeed, it is when those who do practise religious ritual are expelled from the mosque for expressing radical political beliefs, that the move to violence is most likely.[8]

The Anti-Defamation League in the United States took a close look at the **demographics** of 80 US residents who were linked to terror plots and activities that were at least in part motivated by al-Qaeda-inspired ideology. The ages of these 80 people ranged from 15 to 47 years. The average age was 27 years. Among them, slightly under one-third (31 percent) were 21 years old or younger. The league discovered many more minors who have been linked to radical extremism by law enforcement agencies, but owing to their young ages, little more information was available. Most of the 80 extremists are male,

---

demographics the statistical study of populations, considering factors like gender, age, education, nationality, religion, and ethnicity

though in recent years, Daesh recruitment has targeted females with some success.[9]

One-quarter of these US residents who were affiliated with or supported by al-Qaeda-inspired radical extremists did not grow up identifying as Muslim. Through the radicalization process, they converted to Islam. One-fifth (20 percent) had prior criminal records, though past convictions were not terror related. Over two-thirds (68 percent) tried to travel abroad to join terrorist groups; 22 percent tried to provide money or materiel to support terrorist groups abroad; and 7 percent tried to recruit others into violent extremism.

That demographic information is useful but insufficient. Law enforcement agencies have neither the resources nor the mandate to put surveillance on all young males.

Analyzing the Canadian experience with violent extremism, Phil Gurski says that other demographics such as poverty, marital status, criminal background, education, and employment status cannot predict it either. He concludes:

> [T]here is no [demographic] profile or checklist of factors or drivers that can be used to predict who is at greater risk of radicalization. It would be much easier to locate and deal with this phenomenon if there were such a set. Individuals who radicalize to violence may come from any environment and any set of inputs.[10]

Tonda MacCharles adds:

> In many of the Canadian cases, the youth are from respectable, middle-class, relatively privileged families, with good levels of educational achievement, perhaps with no prior criminal record or psychological problems.[11]

Clearly, research is telling us that we should not develop programs to combat violent extremism on the basis of demographics.

At this stage in our effort to identify and analyze the community problem we want to resolve, it might be useful to decide which of these two groups concerns us most: the affiliated, radical ideologist, or the lone attacker (who may or may not claim some affinity with a radical ideology). For the sake of this exercise, let us assume that our municipality harbours a number of recent immigrant groups; that our police data and information reflect significant tensions between these groups and some of those people who have lived here all their lives; that resettlement supports for these groups are insufficient in volume and slow in coming; and that police and other acute care providers are having to direct significant levels of assistance to these neighbourhoods. For those reasons, we will continue researching the problem of radicalization, and see if we can identify risk factors that would permit us to anticipate radicalization and, perhaps, nip violent extremism in the bud.

Identifying Risk Factors

We already learned that demographics are not good predictors of radicalization. For example, many of those who became radicalized were not born Muslim; they converted along the road to radicalization. So we are going to have to look for risk factors elsewhere. Maybe we can find behaviours that correlate with radicalization.

Joosse and his colleagues summarized the research that highlights social pressures toward radicalization, violence, and terror. These social pressures consist of

- stigmatization (for example, as newcomers, refugees, blacks, or Muslims);
- existential frustration (a sense that "one's life is meaningless, directionless, boring, banal, uneventful, anodyne, soulless, aimless, passive, cowardly");[12] and
- racism, social exclusion, and loneliness experienced on a daily basis.

They point out that the alternatives offered by radicalization include:

- pre-existing friendship or kinship networks;
- Internet-mediated self-affiliation;
- excitement, meaning, and glory;[13] and
- piousness and adventure.[14]

Halafoff and Wright-Neville have depicted the road to radicalization as a wedge in which the majority of community members, at the wide end of the wedge, harbour no radical or terrorist tendencies and remain largely resistant to radical messages.[15] But as the wedge narrows, a few individuals begin to emerge who may have extremist tendencies or who may be more vulnerable than others in the community to the radical messages coming from ideologically extreme groups. On this wedge, Joosse and colleagues imposed some labels that characterize the radicalization process: resistant, sympathizer, supporter, terrorist. This continuum may also be depicted as a volcano: quiet and peaceful at the wide base where most community members live, work, and play, but extremely violent at the narrow top where a very few individuals fall prey to radical influences.

Down at the base of the volcano, where most community members live, they are resistant to radicalization and have the support of their family, friends, and neighbours in resisting it. Joosse and his colleagues discovered in a Somali Canadian community in Toronto that they had persuasive counternarratives to radicalization and violent extremism. These Somali Canadians do not want their young people drawn into that violent vortex. But as we climb the volcano, we see that some, very few, people become sympathetic to radical causes, eventually becoming supporters of violent extremists and, potentially, violent extremists themselves.

FIGURE 10.1   Four Stages in Radicalization and the Risk Factors That Predict Them

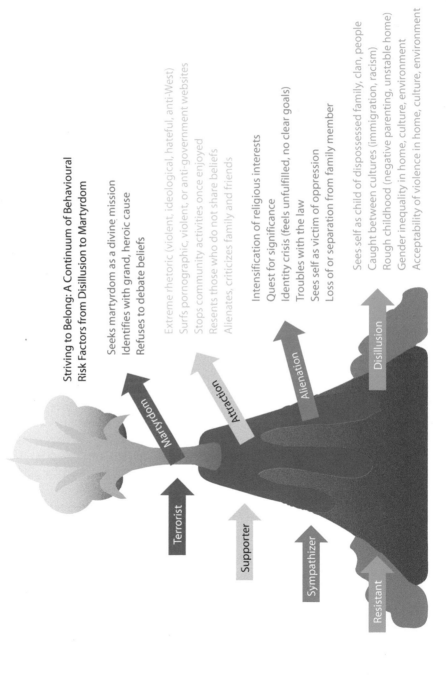

Striving to Belong: A Continuum of Behavioural
Risk Factors from Disillusion to Martyrdom

Seeks martyrdom as a divine mission
Identifies with grand, heroic cause
Refuses to debate beliefs

Extreme rhetoric (violent, ideological, hateful, anti-West)
Surfs pornographic, violent, or anti-government websites
Stops community activities once enjoyed
Resents those who do not share beliefs
Alienates, criticizes family and friends

Intensification of religious interests
Quest for significance
Identity crisis (feels unfulfilled, no clear goals)
Troubles with the law
Sees self as victim of oppression
Loss of or separation from family member

Sees self as child of dispossessed family, clan, people
Caught between cultures (immigration, racism)
Rough childhood (negative parenting, unstable home)
Gender inequality in home, culture, environment
Acceptability of violence in home, culture, environment

Martyrdom

Attraction

Alienation

Disillusion

Terrorist

Supporter

Sympathizer

Resistant

The research literature gives us a fairly clear picture of the behavioural road to radicalization and martyrdom—depicted on the right side of the volcano, above. These behavioural traits emerged out of a number of different studies. The labels, Disillusion, Alienation, Attraction, and Martyrdom, characterize a young person's progression from a sense of profound disappointment in his or her own family, friends, and himself or herself (disillusion) to a state of being separated from the family and friends with whom he or she grew up and disaffected by all that they represent (alienation). In this vulnerable condition, the person is receptive to persuasive messages about the potential of a totally different life (attraction) that promises glory and a grand heroic cause (martyrdom).

That message can come in many different forms, but we are most aware of social media's role in furthering the propaganda of the al-Qaeda-inspired narrative and other extremist causes.

The Role of the Internet

The Internet features heavily in the literature on lone-actor terrorism. It is considered by some to be a driver of the threat, by others as an accelerator, and by some commentators as a surrogate community—a social environment in which lone actors feel they belong. A substantial body of literature further concludes that given the prevalence of Internet activity as a significant feature in lone-actor cases, it also offers a vehicle through which to detect them. …

Although it has not yet been empirically proven, it appears that youth-dominated Internet sites are increasingly becoming the favoured medium through which terrorist and radical Islamist groups recruit new members and followers.

SOURCE: Raffaello Pantucci, Clare Ellis & Lorien Chaplais, "Lone Actor Terrorism: Literature Review," Countering Lone-Actor Terrorism Series No 1 (London: Royal United Services Institute for Defense and Security Studies, 2015).

Influence can also come from people who have already championed that cause—whether they are mere acquaintances or community and religious leaders and teachers. Staying on that road, with no meaningful roadblocks or redirections (counter-radicalization), the young person will eventually identify with the myth of the heroic cause. This is frequently accompanied by the appearance of profound religiosity even if the individual had not been particularly religious before. As Lorne Dawson, co-director of the Canadian Network for Research on Terrorism, Security and Society, says, "It is not a matter of Islam" but "[r]eligiosity is at the heart of this."[16]

At this point, the person is ready for self-sacrifice (martyrdom) to dull the original pain of profound meaninglessness and inability to control the world around them, and to satisfy the subsequent drive for excitement, purpose, and glory. This readiness is frequently signalled by the individual practising their adopted, radical identity in some way—for example, by making such a claim to family and friends or posting it online to see what kinds of reactions they get. Nolan summarized what an observer might see upon encountering a person on the road to martyrdom:

> increasing isolation from friends and family members; an increasing attitude of aggressive certitude particularly in relation to politics, religion, or other forms of ideology; aggressive intolerance for those whose opinions do not match one's own; reduced participation in sports and social activities; spending long periods of time online consuming extremist materials.[17]

The people who are most likely to be found on the road to radicalization and martyrdom frequently come from families, communities, and cultures in which violence is common and acceptable, and in which women are oppressed:

> Gender inequality, and the acceptance of violence towards women, is in itself "extremist" and contributes to the push factors in radicalisation. Children brought up in violent homes have a weaker sense of self and lack the support structures that might safeguard them. They are therefore more susceptible to radicalisation by charismatic organisations that offer superficial "solutions" to their identity crisis.[18]

A compounding factor is **dogmatism**—that is, inflexibility and strict adherence to a set of behavioural standards (creed, faith, religion, etc.)—which, when the young person accumulates enough life experience to question them, become great sources of disillusionment and alienation. Dogmatism can emerge in the young person's life through

- opinionated and authoritarian parenting;
- inflexible and dictatorial schooling;
- a strict, rigid, and conformist community; or
- a doctrinaire faith.

Another distinction that may be useful, especially to law, justice, safety, and security personnel and agencies, is the distinction between criminal and pre-criminal junctions on the road to radicalization and martyrdom. **Pre-criminal behaviours** are those that do not correspond to chargeable offences. That means that this junction is crossed somewhere between the "supporter" and "terrorist" stages and behaviours. Seen on our volcano image, that leaves

---

dogmatism inflexible and strict adherence to a set of behavioural standards (creed, faith, religion, etc.), frequently accompanied by imposing those standards on others

pre-criminal behaviours behaviours that do not correspond to chargeable offences

the observation that the most frequent opportunities to deflect the individual from further progress on the road to radicalization and martyrdom exist on the pre-criminal pathway. It also implies that pre-criminal actions and investments, while involving specialists in law, justice, safety, and security in some limited ways, are probably best implemented by other members of the community. We will come back to this point shortly.

On the basis of this research, we have focused our problem-solving on the issue of radicalization. We have a road map for radicalization on which we can observe the behaviours (or risk factors) of individuals on that road. We have learned that early intervention and prevention of violent extremism have only a very limited role for police and other security agencies. It remains, in the third step of our community problem-solving model, to begin to put together a program of interventions that will reduce young people's vulnerability to radicalization.

CHECK YOUR UNDERSTANDING

1. What kind of violent extremist do we see most in North America: the lone attacker or the affiliated extremist? What's the difference between them?
2. Distinguish between four levels of radicalization on the road to martyrdom (resistant, sympathizer, supporter, terrorist).

Designing Interventions to Counter Violent Extremism

Program choices to counter violent extremism range from readiness and tactical response when terrorists threaten (at the top of the volcano in Figure 10.1), all the way down the side of the volcano to advocating, investing, and supporting social influences that build strong, positive community affiliations and self-actualization to counter disillusion (at the bottom of the volcano). We have at least two significant lines of resistance to extremism in a community. One is the community's inherent reluctance to isolate and reject individuals and thereby force them into the attractive influence of extremists. The other is the community's ability and responsibility to strengthen all individuals' capacities to achieve, belong, and thrive. As Gurski has stated:

> Terrorists and radicalized violent extremists are not born; they are made. They pass through some sort of process that convinces them— or during which they convince themselves—that violence is possible, desirable, preferred, justified, or even divinely inspired, sanctioned and mandatory. It would seem unlikely that people move directly from zero to violence in one giant leap. It is more typical for an individual or

a group to travel along an idiosyncratic pathway, during which the necessity for violence is (perhaps slowly) introduced and imposed.[19]

Becoming a Violent Extremist

How does a young person become a violent extremist? The easiest answer—regrettably, one we hear voiced too often—is that the fault lies with propaganda spun via social media by al-Qaeda-inspired extremists. While the impact of social media, and this particular form of propaganda in particular, is undeniable, this answer is of little help in figuring out what can reasonably be done to protect communities from terrorism. We cannot, if we wanted to, stop social media or filter its content. We will not succeed in convincing radicals to stop spinning those messages. We cannot bar our young people from exposure to them. So that answer gives us very little to work with.

MacCharles reviewed research that shows that social media is certainly a factor in radicalizing young people, but it is not decisive in and of itself. She quotes researchers who point to "social contacts"—friends, peers, mentors, local inspirational leaders. Research has shown that the young person on the road to radicalization is rarely travelling solo. In fact, there comes a point in the radicalization process when social contacts with like-minded people are key to his or her progress down that road.

Thus, the individual is both part of a social network of like-minded people reinforcing radical ideology and influenced by violent extremist messages in social media. Both feed the vulnerable seeker with a perverted sense of purpose and direction. But what makes some young people vulnerable to inducement by those sources? Why are they attending to them in the first place? Research on this question reinforces the idea that they are on what Dawson calls a "quest for significance." Young people become vulnerable by virtue of questioning the core values and life expectations with which they were raised. At the same time, they seek to believe in something, do something, be something that carries a moral imperative and that justifies their existence. It is the classic existential crisis that most people face at least once in their lives. Dawson says:

> [T]hey are emotionally in turmoil, frustrated and the [al-Qaeda-inspired] narrative has a clean simple emotional appeal: "what's bad, what's good, what do I have to do, what will be the great reward for doing so." The fact that they're compelled to sacrifice for it doesn't turn them off, it appeals to them.[20]

Identifying the Drivers of Violent Extremism

Upon examining the risk factors leading to radicalization, Khalil and Zeuthen prescribed two conditions for programming designed to deflect young people from that road:

- programs should directly counter the specific drivers of violent extremism in the communities or other locations where they occur; and

- such programs should specifically target those individuals whom communities, or others, have identified are at greatest risk of being drawn into violent extremism.[21]

Khalil and Zeuthen use the word "drivers"—what we in this text have called "risk factors." They classify all of the risk factors in three categories of drivers:

1. *Structural drivers* are things we can see or learn about in the communities from which young radicals come, including: corruption, unemployment, discrimination, historical hostilities between subgroups (blacks and whites; Tamils and Sri Lankans; Christian and Islamic Somalis, etc.) and even Canadian or American hostilities in the original countries of Canadian immigrant populations.
2. *Individual drivers* are the kinds of behaviours identified, above, on the right side of the volcano figure: striving for meaning and purpose; adventure, belonging, strong affiliations, rejection of old friends, family, community activities; and expected afterlife rewards.
3. *Enabling drivers* are forces external to the individual that encourage them on the radical path: radical mentors (religious leaders, teachers, radicals in the social network), access to radical online "communities," and insufficient family or community support, etc.

The challenge in developing programs to counter the siren call of violent extremism is one of discerning details of these three drivers in each and every community situation where we want to have a positive influence. Denoeux and Carter stressed this point:

> Programming must reflect the distinctive features of the specific environment in which a particular [violent extremism] movement operates. … [M]any such movements present similarities in their characteristics and the dynamics that sustain them; they often are influenced by the same regional or global forces as well. Nonetheless, they also are shaped by local grievances and problems, and by idiosyncratic historical legacies and cultural attributes. Programming must reflect that situation, and avoid "off-the-shelf" or "cookie-cutter" approaches.[22]

Researching the Community

The first step in program design, therefore, is one of researching, in target communities, the effective structural, individual, or enabling drivers. That research requires someone who can develop an excellent rapport with members of the target community and who possesses a level of prior knowledge about them and their issues that allows the program designers to demonstrate genuine respect for the members of the target community. The ideal choice is an experienced community policing officer, an officer who has spent significant amounts of time relating personally and professionally with community members. Then this work can be done using community members as informants in a broad-based or focused consultation. Additionally, there are other standard research methods that can be used such as focus groups, key informant surveys, broader social surveys, direct observation, and consultation with specialists in a host of other human and social service agencies and organizations that serve the target community.

When the drivers (risk factors) that are unique to the target community are known, it does not take much to figure out the kinds of interventions and protective factors that can counter them. Khalil and Zeuthen suggest arraying them in a table such as Table 10.1.

TABLE 10.1 **Risk and Protective Factors That Become Key Components of Programs Designed to Counter Violent Extremism in One Target Community**

Types of Drivers	Risk Factors	Protective Factors
Structural drivers	Feelings of discrimination and exclusion in school	Advocacy for the individual in the school setting; collaboration with the school in designing and implementing anti-discrimination policies and programs
	Poverty and inadequate income	Education and vocational training; career guidance; financial literacy training; social development strategies; micro-credit schemes
	Community and neighbourhood tensions between groups with historical enmities	Inter-group negotiations and mediation, forums, and community events; identification and development of moderate and conciliatory group leaders; introduction of restorative justice dispute resolution methods
Individual drivers	Quest for significance	Individual mentoring; educational and customized enrichment activities; career guidance; challenging learning situations that speak to individual's aptitudes and interests
	Identity crisis	Psychosocial supports; mentoring; exposure to career opportunities; assessments of aptitudes and interests; exposure to areas of interest

Types of Drivers	Risk Factors	Protective Factors
	Anger, alienation, and isolation	Psychosocial supports; mentoring; enrollment in group activities that interest individual; support for family and community members who have rapport with individual
Enabling drivers	Radical mentors	Mentoring; development and implementation of counternarratives; support for local, moderate influencers; planned exposure to non-radical alternatives; exposure to non-violent radicals
	Online radical forums	Form online network that fosters cross-cultural communication; empower youth as activists for peace through social media; youth driven anti-extremism media campaigns
	Extreme anti-West rhetoric	Counternarratives in citizenship development: promote liberalism; suggest synergy between religious beliefs and human rights; endorse human rights; endorse rule of law; promote non-adversarial approaches to grievances; value action over inaction; promote humanitarian responses to perceived suffering

SOURCE: Adapted from James Khalil & Martine Zeuthen, "Countering Violent Extremism and Risk Reduction: A Guide to Programme Design and Evaluation" Whitehall Report 2-16 (London, UK: Royal United Services Institute for Defence and Security Studies, 2016) at 20.

Developing a Local Strategy for Countering Violent Extremism

Identifying vulnerable groups, risk factors, and protective factors is key to strategizing for CVE. However, in the CVE case, "vulnerable groups" refers not to those who would be victimized by acts of extreme violence, but those who are vulnerable to the persuasive appeals of extremist, ideological movements—like the al-Qaeda-inspired narrative.

The framework for planning community safety and well-being that was discussed in Chapter 9 will help us design four zones of CVE activity: social development, prevention, risk mitigation, and emergency response. Those zones of activity are represented by the four colours of green, blue, amber, and red, respectively, as seen in Figure 10.2.

FIGURE 10.2   **Framework for Planning Community Safety
and Well-Being**

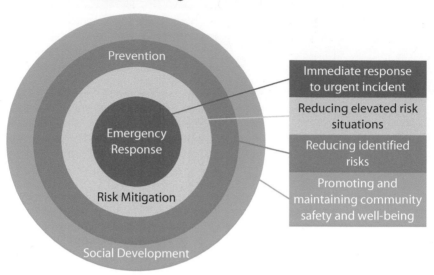

Chapter 9 showed how this framework could be applied to a community
that was faced with significant problems in the areas of addictions and mental
health. Here, we will repeat that same approach to the problem of violent
extremism. The plan for dealing with the threat of violent extremism, which
follows, is predicated on the notion that effective strategies have to be, largely,
local strategies. That is, communities and their members (individuals, groups,
organizations, businesses, agencies, etc.), much as in their struggle to prevent
crime, have to be aware of the threat of violent extremism, and address that
threat with local resources and capacities. If the vulnerable groups, risk factors, and protective factors are local, then appropriate strategies to reduce
these threats have to be local as well. That is not to say that resources from outside the community cannot, or should not, be used, but it is to assert that the
initiative and impetus to do this work must be locally derived. Any federal
initiative to deal with this threat has to, first and foremost, support local
efforts, much as Canada's National Crime Prevention Centre has learned that
its primary role is not as a preventer of crime, but as an enabler of local crime
prevention initiatives.

All of the objectives, outcomes, strategies, and measures that follow, for
dealing with violent extremism, are drawn from research on effective initiatives from around the world.[23]

We will not spend any time detailing the contents of each zone in this figure. Suffice for our purposes now to simply scan them and notice that in the
green and blue zones, and half of the amber zone, there are very few traditional policing tactics that can be usefully applied. Among other things, that

FIGURE 10.3   Community Safety and Well-Being Plan for Dealing with the Threat of Violent Extremism

	Priorities	Vulnerable Groups	Risk Factors	Protective Factors
	Identifying, preventing, and countering violent extremism	Youth, or other persons, drawn to violent extremism	• Negative parenting • Acceptability of violence • Gender inequality • Caught between cultures • Social isolation	• Positive social networks • Family supports • Positive parenting/mentoring • Early identification • Strong attachment to positive influences
Objectives	Awareness raising, community outreach, supports, coordination	Counter radicalization and prevention	De-radicalization and anticipation	Security and law enforcement interventions
Outcomes	• Early intervention • Accurate and protected information on individual • Right people to intervene • Training and orientation for interveners • Assessment of individual and their reasons for disillusionment • Collaborative determination of supports required	• Community outreach • Community consultation • Awareness raising • Trained and informed professionals	• Targeted surveillance • Warranted communications intercepts • Human sources close to terrorist cells • Targeted investigations • Counter al-Qaeda-inspired narratives	• Targeted enforcement • Interdiction of support for al-Qaeda-inspired conflicts • Prohibiting foreign travel • Peace bonds restricting movements of suspected violent extremists

(continued on next page)

	Social Development	Prevention	Risk Mitigation	Emergency Response
Strategies	• Develop select, new unit to coordinate among all authorities • Develop strategy for this unit in consultation with all authorities • Develop systems for swift and effective liaison with all authorities • Liaise with all risk mitigation initiatives • Build partnerships with human and social service providers • Plan outreach strategy to community organizations, housing associations, religious, cultural groups • Develop consultation strategy with leaders and gatekeepers in most vulnerable communities	• Design and implement fellowship and citizenship development programs • Collaborate with local associations • Develop inter-faith liaison and coordinating groups • Reinforce the value of women, youth, and children through social media • Recruit mentors and develop mentoring program	• Increased efforts with marginalized youth, including mentoring • Skill development with health care and other support staff • Strengthen collaboration to help vulnerable, radicalized people transition between and among support systems	• Targeted surveillance • Warranted communications intercepts • Human sources close to terrorist cells • Targeted investigations
Measures	• Support for community's own counternarratives • Support for community resilience and integration • Joint activities with all human and social service organizations • Frequent and two-way communications with community groups and organizations • Engage leaders of other agencies and organizations in collaborative strategies for effective personal and social development	• Tell stories of former violent extremists and survivors of violent extremism • Positive stories, films, speakers on pathways to citizenship • Programs on Canada's inclusiveness, openness, freedom of worship, and how to acquire opportunities • Education and resource packs for teachers, students, and community workers • Workshops for teachers, students, and community workers	• Social and personal supports, in exchange for abandoning adherence to violent extremism • Incentives for disengagement from any affiliation with violent extremism • Counternarratives by reformed adherents who have returned from conflict zones	• Supports for loved ones of targeted individuals • Supports for community of targeted individuals • Initiatives aimed at returnees from conflict zones • Initiatives aimed at radicalized and marginalized individuals

Community policing applied to CVE: Mobilization, engagement, collaboration, and support

Traditional policing

signals that in the first two-thirds of this plan, most of the work to protect communities from violent extremism, and vulnerable young people from the recruitment messages of violent extremists, has to be done by other agencies and organizations. In these zones then, what is the role of police? The vital roles of police in two-thirds of this plan to counter violent extremism are:

- mobilization of individuals and organizations in the community;
- engagement of other human and social service agencies;
- collaboration with the widest variety of individuals and organizations; and
- support of all those who are most directly involved in this work.

That is community policing at its best!

IN THE COMMUNITY

The Danish Aarhus Model

Around the world, there are many programs that strive to prevent young people from being drawn into the radicalization cycle of violent extremism and reintegrate radicalized people into the community. But one of those programs that has proved most successful comes from the municipality of Aarhus, Denmark. A full description of the Aarhus Model may be obtained online.[24] This Danish model contains four related components:

- prevention programs targeted on increasing public awareness about the threats of violent extremism, risk factors, and community responsibilities for dealing with them;
- early identification of individuals who are shown to be at risk of radicalization;
- mentoring that targets already radicalized individuals who have the greatest potential to act illegally or violently in support of extremism; and
- investigation and prosecution of radicalized individuals who have engaged in illegal activities in support of violent extremism.

The prevention program is implemented by community organizations with the behind-the-scenes support of police and other security agencies. The early identification initiative relies on a whole host of community organizations and individuals more than police (schools, clubs, faith groups, parents, housing officials, social service providers, and others), to recognize someone showing risk factors or vulnerability to radicalization, informing a coordinating body, and engaging in organizing social supports for that individual that compete favourably with whatever is offered by radical narratives. The mentoring program for radicalized people does not include police. Its purpose is to not only ensure that the individual can meet their basic needs, but also counter the radical narrative, and in whatever way possible, help the person reintegrate legally and functionally into the culture they rejected when responding to the clarion call of radicalism.

Obviously, Aarhus police are involved in those elements of this model that include investigation, arrests, and prosecutions (corresponding to half of the amber, and all of the red zones in our plan, above). But their role is much subtler in all of the early intervention and prevention work (corresponding to the green, blue, and half of the amber zones, above). To quote a newspaper story about the Aarhus Model: "What has made the 'Aarhus model' successful is the light touch of police involvement, and intense participation of community mentors."[25] However, the role of police in getting all of those community organizations and individuals involved, designing the Aarhus Model in the first place, recruiting mentors, and helping with public education and training on risk factors is paramount to its success. To do this kind of work, police need to have good relationships with all of these community players. Shephard concluded:

> [F]or programs like this to work, the right people must be involved. [Detective Inspector] Thorlief Link [Aarhus Police] ... is the right person. He doesn't wear a uniform often, his manner is direct, but respectful and kind, and when he listens, he really seems to listen. Link is the police officer you would want to deliver bad news."[26]

Program Implementation

Effective solutions to violent extremism will have to address the grievances of individuals on this road, the identity crises they are going through, the ideologies to which they are attracted in order to find relief, and the al-Qaeda-inspired narrative itself.[27] Police and other safety and security actors are not necessarily the most qualified people to deliver these programs. If the incentive to counter violent extremism is coming, largely, from safety and security actors, then the whole enterprise will be challenged to succeed. But if safety and security actors are capable of recognizing that their own effectiveness is limited to criminal, and some, relatively limited, pre-criminal activities, and that they need effective, collaborative partnerships with a whole host of other community actors (agencies, organizations, and individuals), then an effective strategy has a chance of working.

Research presents us with lots of lessons learned about designing and implementing programs and initiatives that can reduce radicalization and thus minimize violent extremism. We will present some of the more profound lessons learned about implementation in the balance of this chapter. In

Chapter 11, when discussing evaluation, we will come back to some of these ideas and talk about how a program countering violent extremism could be evaluated.

Separate Countering Violent Extremism from Community Building

Romaniuk based a lot of his advice about effective programming on evaluation of Britain's Prevent program. Built on a foundation of counterterrorism and anti-radicalization policies that were legislated shortly after 9/11, Prevent pumped millions of pounds into local, community-based initiatives. Many of these addressed the kinds of community issues that served as drivers for radicalization: unemployment, underemployment, social isolation, poor school performance, etc. Many developed and delivered narratives counter to that spun by al-Qaeda. Most of these initiatives were designed to strengthen community capacities to resist radicalization and support those individuals who were particularly vulnerable to radicalization—something the British call "community resilience." One of the key findings of program evaluation was the importance of disaggregating the concept and label of "countering violent extremism" from community-building programs and programs that supported targeted individuals. When applied to communities or individuals, the label "countering violent extremism" marks them with stigma, which becomes a driver of radicalization. On the other hand, effective community building, and empowerment of young community members to strive and achieve at their highest possible level, offers effective resistance to radicalization.[28]

Role of Community Groups

In keeping with the idea of disaggregating countering violent extremism from community building, most of the research on appropriate programming has repeatedly shown that programs work best when they are supported by government–community partnerships, and when the roles of government and community agencies are clearly defined and differentiated. Researchers are discovering that Muslim communities in Canada, the United States, and Britain are self-initiating programs to help their members resist the radical calling. All of these communities seek to deflect their young people from the road to radicalization and martyrdom, and often, they are frustrated with government's (including police) preoccupation with the brutality of violent extremism and blindness to the community, social, and psychological conditions that put people on that road. Too much of this community-driven work is being done without the knowledge, encouragement, assistance, or direct support of government agencies and organizations whose security officials are preoccupied with strategies for countering violent extremism. The need for these programs is great, the technical challenges are huge, they are costly, and the chances of failure are high. Government has to get behind community organizations and offer resources, support, encouragement, and collaboration.[29]

Such collaboration requires a very clear division of labour between community agencies and organizations on the one hand, and government agencies on the other. The former need to be supported by the latter in taking ownership of community-building, community cohesion, and community resilience initiatives. The latter need to acknowledge their responsibility for resourcing the initiatives, directly investing in citizenship development, and helping research and develop narratives that counter al-Qaeda-inspired appeals. Romaniuk stressed that positive narratives must include the values of a cohesive, integrated, multi-faith society and of parliamentary democracy. At the outset, these should not be negative attacks on the al-Qaeda-inspired narrative. They should be positive efforts to help disillusioned and searching young people develop a sense of belonging in Canada and support for Canada's core values. Romaniuk summarized the perfect government–community collaborative:

> In sum, governments and NGOs [non-governmental organizations] should engage broadly, and partner strategically. Nonviolent extremists should not be excluded out of hand from all efforts at engagement, and decisions about partnerships should reflect assessments of risk as well as consultation. ... Overall, on the basis of the evidence reviewed, broad-based, integrative state-civil society relationships are more likely to yield positive partnerships for [countering violent extremism].[30]

Role of Community Policing

Halafoff and Wright-Neville, reflecting on their experiences and research in the state of Victoria, Australia (Australia's most densely populated state), discovered that local communities value police in general, and specifically community policing, because community policing involves police making an effort to engage with the community and partner with them to tackle their problems.[31] They cited research that shows that community policing operates as a highly effective counterterrorism strategy in Victoria. Such sentiments were echoed by 60 foreign ministers who met in the US White House in 2015 to discuss strategies for countering violent extremism. They stressed that action is required on multiple fronts, "including development assistance and the provision of economic opportunities, educational initiatives, measures to empower youth and women, the resolution of protracted conflicts [and] community policing."[32] What are these researchers valuing about community policing?

Romaniuk listed a wide range of initiatives and activities that police, other government agencies, and a host of public organizations and the private sector need to partner on to counter radicalization, including:

- positive messaging about the values of citizenship;
- speeches, television programs, leaflets, and social media;

- community engagement and outreach;
- town hall meetings, round tables, and advisory and consultative groups;
- community cohesion and capacity-building activities like youth and women's leadership programs;
- community development, and community safety and protection programs; and
- education and training for community leaders and public employees like police officers.

The overriding purpose of such activities was articulated by Halafoff and Wright-Neville: "Community based programs that involve the police and other agencies building a reservoir of social capital ... sustained over long periods of time, and directed at audiences that transcend generational, religious, and gender divides." There is that "social capital" thing again, which takes us right back to Chapter 1. Developing and strengthening social capital is the purpose of community policing—and it is the strongest antidote to radicalization.

Reflecting on our community problem-solving model, there is a very important role for community policing in the research stage when we need to know what a target community's issues are, what their resources are, who their assets are, and what supports they need in order to help hold the community together. Quality community policing gives police officers a window on those questions that is often not open to other public agencies and organizations. When it is time to implement programming based on that research, police often have the best insights and strongest rapport with the community. On that basis, new partners can be brought into the mix, resources can be pulled together, and the community can increase its own cohesion and effectiveness in working with individuals and families who are feeling marginalized and are, therefore, more vulnerable to radicalization. As the following quotation shows, community policing is most effective in mitigating radicalization the farther away it is applied from the eruptive end of our volcano.

> Community policing initiatives operate most effectively at the large, middle, and narrow sections of the [volcano]. Police, through encouraging positive community relations, such as playing soccer with youth, attending community events, and offering assistance to newly arriving communities, foster mutual confidence, thereby lessening the risk of alienation. At the middle of the [volcano] when states and police protect and uphold the right to nonviolent expressions of dissent, grievances can be aired safely. Religious communities have historically played a significant role in critiquing states. If consultative bodies such as multi-faith and youth councils are established and individuals and communities are encouraged to air their concerns, and even more so when they genuinely feel they have been heard and are acted upon, again the risk of alienation decreases.[33]

Networks of Trust

Halafoff and Wright-Neville's last phrase in the quotation cited above, "networks of trust," takes us back to the notion of police legitimacy. No amount of community policing actions will work, will even be implementable, without a foundation of police legitimacy—that is, a quality relationship based on knowledge, respect, and rapport, between police and the target community. A more positive way to state this is that all of these community-based counter-radicalization initiatives will have a far better chance of succeeding if they are built on a foundation of trust, respect, and rapport between the community and police, as well as other agencies and organizations that are supporting them.

The "knowledge" issue also arises in this context. Halafoff and Wright-Neville talked about "greater levels of cultural, historical, and political literacy among police officers and other government officials." That observation leads directly to the idea of police and other government agencies relying on community, religious, and other cultural representatives to help officers and other government workers improve their cultural, historical, and political knowledge. If counter-radicalization programs have to be customized to each community and each vulnerable individual in that community, then it naturally follows that those who would design and implement those programs have to know a great deal about those communities and those individuals. Nothing less will suffice.

Community-Delivered, Police-Supported

Does not that heading, "Community-Delivered, Police-Supported," sound like everything we have been saying about community policing throughout this text? It is no less true for programming to counter violent extremism. If the British learned nothing more out of their Channel and Prevent programs, their most important lesson is that police are essential in support roles. (Channel is a multi-agency component of the UK's Prevent program. It is designed to identify people who are at risk of radicalization and develop for them the most appropriate supports plan.) Police and other security personnel cannot, and should not, try to direct or deliver counter-radicalization narratives, programs, initiatives, etc.[34] The other most consistent finding through evaluations of such programs is that they are most effective when delivered by members of the community who are closest to vulnerable seekers. None of that detracts from the value of police involvement, partnerships, mentoring, engaging others, researching drivers, building rapport and legitimacy in the community, etc. But police have to stop thinking that they own this problem, just because they are critical to issues of community safety and security.

CHAPTER SUMMARY

This community problem, countering violent extremism, really calls for the best that community policing can offer: building rapport and legitimacy with vulnerable communities and individuals; mobilizing community members and religious and cultural leaders to apply themselves to this problem; engaging other human and social service agencies and organizations to bring their knowledge, resources, and staff to support the community in a difficult and long-term endeavour, while, at all times, keeping a watchful presence, somewhere near the top of that volcano, on the potential for imminent violence or material support for radical, violent causes.

Nothing diminishes the importance of effective emergency response. But we can do far more to mitigate risks, prevent social alienation, and strengthen the cohesion of communities if we

- acknowledge the social influences that make individuals vulnerable to the suasion of extremists;
- increase the capacity of communities to build strong and cohesive bonds with all of their members; and
- invest in the well-being of everyone in the community.

REVIEW AND DISCUSSION QUESTIONS

1. Explain six sequential steps in a community problem-solving model.
2. List and explain two behavioural risk factors for each level of radicalization on the road to martyrdom (resistant, sympathizer, supporter, terrorist).
3. Explain why police cannot and should not deliver countering violent extremism programs.
4. Explain the role of community policing in countering violent extremism.

KEY TERMS

demographics, 287
dogmatism, 292
lone attacker, 285
pre-criminal behaviours, 292
radicalization, 284
violent extremists, 284

NOTES

1   Public Safety Canada, *2016 Public Report on the Terrorist Threat to Canada* (2016), online: <https://www.publicsafety.gc.ca/cnt/rsrcs/pblctns/2016-pblc-rpr-trrrst-thrt/index-en.aspx>.

2   K Williams, N Guerra & D Elliott, *Human Development and Violence Prevention: A Focus on Youth* (Boulder: Center for the Study and Prevention of Violence, University of Colorado, 1997) at 25.

3   "What Is 'Islamic State'?" *BBC News* (2 December 2015), online: <http://www.bbc.com/news/world-middle-east-29052144>; and Fawaz A Geres, "Islamic State: Can Its Savagery Be Explained?" *BBC News* (9 September 2014), online: <http://www.bbc.com/news>.

4   Minerva Nasser-Eddine, Bridget Garnham, Katerina Agostino & Gilbert Caluya, *Countering Violent Extremism (CVE) Literature Review* (Edinburgh, South Australia: Counter Terrorism and Security Technology Centre, Defense Science and Technology Organisation, 2011) at 9.

5   Public Safety Canada, *supra* note 1.

6   Andrea Huncar, "Advocates Say More Needs to Be Done to Prevent Youth Radicalization," *CBC News* (20 January 2015), online: <http://www.cbc.ca/news>.

7   Michael Safi, "Lone Wolf Terrorists Often Reveal Plans Before Committing Violence—Study," *The Guardian* (8 September 2015), online: <https://www.theguardian.com/international>.

8   Scott Atran, "Here's What the Social Science Says About Countering Violent Extremism," *The Huffington Post* (25 April 2015), online: <http://www.huffingtonpost.com/scott-atran/violent-extremism-social-science_b_7142604.html>.

9   Anti-Defamation League, *The ISIS Impact on the Domestic Islamic Extremist Threat: Home-Grown Islamic Extremism, 2009-2015* (New York: Anti-Defamation League, 2016).

10 Phil Gurski, *The Threat from Within: Recognizing al-Qaeda-Inspired Radicalization and Terrorism in the West* (London, UK: Rowman & Littlefield, 2015).

11 Tonda MacCharles, "'Soft Security' Measures Also Needed to Battle Home-Grown Radicalism, Experts Say," *Toronto Star* (27 February 2015), online: <https://www.thestar.com>.

12 S Cottee & K Hayward, "Terrorist (E)motives: The Existential Attractions of Terrorism" (2011) 34:12 Stud in Confl & Terrorism 963.

13 *Ibid*.

14 P Joosse, SM Bucerius & SK Thompson, "Narratives and Counternarratives: Somali-Canadians on Recruitment as Foreign Fighters to al-Shabaab" (2015) 55:4 Brit J Criminol 811.

15   Anna Halafoff & David Wright-Neville, "A Missing Peace? The Role of Religious
      Actors in Countering Terrorism" (2009) 32:11 Stud in Confl & Terrorism 921.

16   Parliament of Canada, "The Standing Senate Committee on National Secu-
      rity and Defence: Evidence" (23 February 2015), online: <http://www.parl
      .gc.ca/content/sen/committee/412/SECD/51929-e.HTM>.

17   Elanna Nolan, "Teaching CVE: A Review of the *Preventing Violent Extremism
      and Radicalisation in Australia Handbook*, and Challenges Across Policy and
      Practice" Working Paper Series No 16-06 (Waterloo, Ont: Canadian Network
      for Research on Terrorism, Security and Society, 2016).

18   Haras Rafiq & Nikita Malik, *Caliphettes: Women and the Appeal of Islamic State*
      (London, UK: Quilliam Foundation, 2015) at 6-7.

19   Gurski, *supra* note 10 at 12.

20   MacCharles, *supra* note 11.

21   James Khalil & Martine Zeuthen, "Countering Violent Extremism and Risk
      Reduction: A Guide to Programme Design and Evaluation" Whitehall Report
      2-16 (London, UK: Royal United Services Institute for Defence and Security
      Studies, 2016) at 3.

22   Guilain Denoeux & Lynn Carter, *Development Assistance and Counter-
      Extremism: A Guide to Programming* (Washington, DC: US Agency for Interna-
      tional Development, October 2009) at 1.

23   A lot of the research that informs this local plan for countering violent
      extremism may be seen in Hugh C Russell, "Making Toronto Communities
      More Resilient: Reducing the Chances of Violent Extremism" (Report for the
      Divisional Policing Support Unit, Toronto Police Service, June 2016). That
      research represents only the work and opinion of the author, not necessarily
      the choices and decisions of the Toronto Police Service.

24   Preben Bertelsen, "Danish Preventive Measures and De-radicalization Strate-
      gies: The Aarhus Model" in *Panorama: Insights Into Asian and European Affairs*
      (Singapore: Konrad-Adenauer-Stiftung, 2015) 241, online: <http://psy.au
      .dk/fileadmin/Psykologi/Forskning/Preben_Bertelsen/Avisartikler
      _radikalisering/Panorama.pdf>.

25   Michelle Shephard, "This Is How You Stop a Violent Extremist," *Toronto Star*
      (20 August 2016), online: <https://www.thestar.com>.

26   *Ibid.*

27   Jonathan Russell & Haras Rafiq, *Countering Islamist Extremist Narratives: A
      Strategic Briefing* (London, UK: Quilliam Foundation, 2016).

28   Peter Romaniuk, *Does CVE Work? Lessons Learned from the Global Effort to
      Counter Violent Extremism* (Goshen, Ind: Global Center on Cooperative
      Security, 2015), online: <http://www.globalcenter.org/wp-content/
      uploads/2015/09/Does-CVE-Work_2015.pdf>.

29   *Ibid.*

30 *Ibid* at 20.

31 Halafoff & Wright-Neville, *supra* note 15 at 926.

32 Romaniuk, *supra* note 28 at 1.

33 Halafoff and Wright-Neville, *supra* note 15 at 929.

34 Romaniuk, *supra* note 28.

CHAPTER 11

Evaluating Community Policing Initiatives

Students from the Calgary Multi-Agency School Support Team (MASST) visit the Calgary Stampeders during practice in July 2016 to learn about the importance of teamwork, dedication, and commitment. The MASST program is a partnership between the Calgary Police Service, the Calgary Board of Education, the Calgary Catholic School District, the City of Calgary's Community and Neighborhood Service department, and Alberta Health Services. The program identifies and facilitates the delivery of multi-disciplinary interventions to at-risk children between 5 and 12 years of age, addressing risk factors at child, family, and community levels.

LEARNING OUTCOMES

Upon completion of this chapter, you should be able to:

■ Explain how evaluation of a community policing initiative is different from basic research
■ Explain why it is important to include community members in all aspects of community-based research
■ Outline five or six steps to ensure objectivity in program evaluation
■ Outline the contents of a program evaluation report
■ Discuss ways to find the most qualified consultant to conduct a program evaluation
■ Outline steps toward making the police agency more data-driven and its decisions and programs more evidence-based

Introduction

We are hearing the term "evidence-based" more and more in policing and other human and social services sectors. In policing, it began to surface when intelligence-led policing became interesting to police leaders. At that time, of course, it referred to occurrence and clearance data being used to target specific patrol areas and crime or disorder problems that police should resolve. More recently, "evidence-based" has taken on much broader ramifications. For example, police leaders are asking their mid-level managers to design and implement strategies that have been shown to work—that is, for which there is solid evidence somewhere that those strategies have worked. The term is also being used to require police program personnel to evaluate their programs, to find out how well they are working and whether they are worth continuing the investments required to sustain them. That is where this chapter is going. Police managers are saying that they are going to make investment decisions, at least in part, on the basis of evidence that those programs in which they are asked to invest actually work. Therefore, it is our job to figure out how to get that evidence.

This chapter is about program evaluation—that is, how do we find out whether a program is achieving the results for which it was designed? We have always been concerned about that question, but only in recent times have we struggled with the challenge of bringing quality behavioural science into the policing arena to help us answer it. Peter Neyroud, a criminologist at the University of Cambridge in the UK, lecturer in evidence-based policing, and a scholar with 30 years of practical policing experience, commented on this eventuality:

> Policing is still a relatively new academic discipline ... . [I]t does not have an embedded presumption towards research underpinning practice. Far from "evidence-based policing," there is too much "policing-based evidence," with facts—usually crime statistics and detection rates—uncritically advanced to support initiatives. Instead of high quality research designs—randomized control trials for example—policing frequently makes do with "implementation pilots" and consultant-based studies.[1]

Neyroud is right; our policing decisions up to this point have rarely been based on qualified research about what works and what does not, and if we truly want to achieve evidence-based policing, that has to change. However, in his second assertion about "high quality research designs" in which he references randomized control trials, he is talking about sophisticated behavioural science. We need to see more of that in the research literature (that is, peer-reviewed journals on policing, criminology, social psychology, etc.), but we need to see it conducted by sophisticated behavioural scientists, not practising police officers. If qualified researchers did more of that work, we would have a sounder basis for the program decisions we are making on the front lines of

policing, but our police agencies and officers do not have the capacity, in sufficient numbers, to implement that level of science.

In this chapter, then, we are not trying to turn the readers into behavioural
scientists specializing in research designs. In the first place, we are not even
talking about basic research here. Rather, we are talking about program evaluation; and even there, we are not trying to make evaluators out of the readers
either. Instead, we are setting out to explain what program evaluation is, how
it fits in the context of police programs, what basic skills and know-how police
officers need to achieve it, and how an officer can get it done.

ON PATROL

Data Showed That There Was No Crime Wave!

A large metropolitan Canadian police service used intelligence-led policing to focus
the work of their crime prevention unit. A group of business owners brought a problem to the commander of one large patrol division. They were dissatisfied with
police response to what they perceived as an increase in crime. The business owners claimed increases in vandalism, break-and-enters and community fear over
18 months due to the opening of a shelter for homeless people in their business district. Police data, however, showed no increases. They reflected very little difference
in crime rates between this business district and similar areas.

Business owners argued that the statistics were inaccurate because the community had grown so fearful and frustrated by perceived lack of police response
that the majority of incidents were no longer being reported. The crime prevention
unit designed a survey for the targeted business community, focusing on fear of
crime, victimization, and unreported crime rates. Volunteers distributed the survey,
and businesses were encouraged to provide a prompt response. The process from
initial community contact to dissemination of the survey took three days. The survey had an approximately 20 percent return rate. The results, which were analyzed
and compared with pre-existing data, were surprising:

- The affected business community had a lower break-and-enter rate and vandalism problem than the greater surrounding business community.
- The affected businesses had a higher reporting rate than other surrounding
  communities.
- Activities surrounding the homeless shelter probably lowered the area's crime
  rate. It was posited that the 24-hour coming and goings there brought much-
  needed natural surveillance to the business area during the at-risk hours of
  darkness.

Survey results indicated that a tactical response was not warranted. Rather, problems stemmed from business owners' lack of knowledge about the monitoring and
supervision that took place at the shelter, as well as the type and nature of the shelter clients themselves. The superintendent called for a community meeting with

representation from the local police division, business owners, homeless shelter, and crime prevention unit. While the business owners seemed apprehensive at first, they were reassured that their misunderstanding of the shelter and its activities caused their false perception of a crime wave and that the shelter needed to be more transparent about their services with neighbours.

The crime prevention unit recommended that the community and patrol officers help business owners develop a better understanding of the shelter activities and its clientele. Increased opportunities for positive interaction between the shelter and the area's businesses were encouraged, including community BBQs and cleanup days.

Consider the following questions:

1. If the police superintendent had not questioned the business community complaints, what would the likely police response have been?
2. What would the consequences of a tough-on-crime response have been?
3. Would the issue have been resolved using a more aggressive tactical police response?
4. What does this example mean with respect to community involvement?

Program Evaluation Is Applied Research

Program evaluation emerged in the 1970s when people like Michael Quinn Patton (who keynoted 2016's Canadian Evaluation Society conference) began to apply what they knew about behavioural research to a question asked by program agencies and funders: "Yes, but how do we know if that program really works?"[2]

One of the first things Patton and others discovered in the 1970s was that doing behavioural research on real, live programs (and the people on whom those programs were targeted) required significantly different scientific methods than are required in the laboratory setting of university-based behavioural science where it is much easier to control **extraneous variables** (variables— factors, circumstances, conditions, etc.—that can affect results of the evaluation, but we really have no way of knowing whether or not they do) and conduct rigorous scientific studies like the randomized control trials Neyroud was talking about. In other words, program evaluation is **applied research** (the practical application of science to solve practical problems), not **basic research**

---

extraneous variables any variables (factors, conditions, circumstances, etc.) that could affect results of an evaluation

applied research the practical application of science to solve practical problems

basic research science used to improve scientific theories or predictions of natural phenomena

(science used to improve scientific theories or predictions of natural phenomena) for the sole purpose of generating new knowledge for its own sake.

The ramifications of this distinction, between applied and basic research, are huge. We have already mentioned that in the applied setting it is next to impossible to control all the extraneous variables that may impinge on the results of the evaluation; in other words, it is much harder to say that observed effects are solely the result of the program design and implementation. It is also hard to take measurements in the applied setting; or, more accurately, methods of scientific observation in the applied setting are different from those most often used in the behavioural science laboratory. In fact, it was also in the 1970s that something called "qualitative measures" emerged as important ways to gather data in the applied setting.

Program Effectiveness and Efficiency

Program evaluation is applied research that is designed to test the efficacy (effectiveness and efficiency) of a program. Whereas basic research is usually conducted by scientists who are highly trained in research design and methods, program evaluation is usually needed and mandated by program managers who probably know very little about research design and methods. As a result, they are dependent on applied research experts whom they may have to recruit from outside their own agency. That is often the case with police agencies. The unfortunate part about that is that too often the program managers, not really understanding the bases for their evaluators' methodological decisions, are stuck with reports and results whose veracity and generalizability they are unable to judge. Therefore, it is in the best interests of these police program managers to understand as much as they can about program evaluation so that they increase their chances of controlling a credible and helpful evaluation process.

Becoming Data-Driven

One of the first steps in becoming more evidence-based is becoming more aware of, and comfortable with, data—that is, data-driven. Intelligence-led policing started that movement in policing circles. We need to increase all officers' awareness and use of data in all their decisions.

Police Data

Start by bringing readily available police data into most operational decisions. At the beginning of a shift, platoon officers should look at the occurrence

---

program evaluation applied research that is designed to test the efficacy (effectiveness and efficiency) of a program

reports for the previous shift and road sergeants should help those front-line officers read a simple **contingency table** (a two-way, or two-dimensional, table that arrays frequencies of one variable in relation to another) and interpret its meanings for the work the platoon will do in their shift. For example, the platoon could look at the frequency of various types of occurrences, during the previous shift, in each of the patrol zones, as in Table 11.1.

The numbers in the cells of this contingency table are simple frequencies of each type of occurrence in each of three different patrol zones. This is the kind of data that should help road sergeants and patrol officers make some decisions about how they allocate their resources during a shift; what kinds of problems they can anticipate and should look for in each zone; and, indeed, what kinds of officer specialization they might wish to assign to each zone. For example, this table suggests that traffic officers set up in Zone 1, whereas the break-and-enter squad should probably patrol most often in Zone 3. The table seems to indicate that most of the social disorder calls come from Zone 3; that might be a good place to send some neighbourhood officers to assess the tensions and opportunities for problem-solving there.

The main points of this example are that police already collect lots of data, and the agency should work hard to convert that data to something useful for informing front-line decisions. Second, start requiring that all front-line officers become familiar with simple contingency tables like this and good at quickly interpreting their meaning for operational decisions. That is what we mean by data-driven.

Analysts in the agency can do lots of useful things with these data; contingency tables are only one example. They can and should provide everyone in the agency with daily and weekly summaries of occurrences and clearances. They should run trends—for example, how do these occurrences per zone vary with time of day, season, or from year to year? Skilled analysts can plot the

TABLE 11.1   Example of a Contingency Table That Shows the Relationship Between Types of Occurrences and Patrol Zones

Types of occurrences/Patrol zones	Zone 1	Zone 2	Zone 3
Domestic disputes	4	2	9
Neighbour disputes	2	1	7
Break-and-enters	3	1	5
Traffic violations	8	3	2

contingency table a two-way, or two-dimensional, table that arrays frequencies of one variable in relation to another

geographical location of occurences, as was discussed earlier (see the GIS map in Chapter 4). They can overlay Census Canada data so that, for example, we can see whether the high rate of social disturbances in Zone 3 of the table above correlates with a high proportion of single-parent families with adolescents, or some other demographic that the census captures. All such information can strongly reinforce an intelligence-led police service, because it is data-driven.

Municipal Data

Most police services work for a municipality, and those that work for a larger entity like the province have policing agreements with municipalities. Municipalities collect all kinds of data that can help in making strategic and operational policing decisions. But police have to access that data and figure out how to integrate it with their own data to generate meaningful recommendations about policing resource allocation. Larger municipalities also have highly qualified data analysts working for them. They are collecting and analyzing all kinds of useful data relating to economic development, demographics by neighbourhood, traffic volumes and directions, public works use and demand levels by time of day, parks and recreation use by time of day and season, health status, business and enterprise development, land use, facilities use, public consultations (including complaints), and more. Much of this data is available to police simply by asking for it. But it is best to be strategic about it. For example, looking at our contingency table (above) once again, it might be interesting to ask municipal planners to examine what their data tells us about the population living in Zone 3. What businesses are in there? What are local employment rates there? How many school children populate this neighbourhood, and where do they go to school? What are traffic flows, at what times of day, through this area? What community-based organizations operate in this neighbourhood? Which of them work with youth? What problems has the city experienced in this neighbourhood? These are just a few of the questions police should ask if they are deciding to mount some problem-solving initiatives in Zone 3.

Data from Other Human and Social Service Agencies

Every human and social service agency collects large volumes of data. They need it for their own strategic planning. They need it to justify their annual requests for operational funds. School boards, for example, collect vast amounts of information on their students and their families—where they live, how far they travel to get to school, size and numbers of children and youth at all age levels per family, participation rates in school-related activities—and that is to say nothing of school performance (academics and deportment) data that boards collect on the young people in their charge. What a useful community partner a school board might be if police chose to focus some after-school mentoring programs on youth in Zone 3 of our contingency table (above).

On the other hand, police agencies will not find it as easy to access school board data as it is to access municipal data. School boards, and most other human and social service agencies, are usually fairly reluctant to share their data with agencies outside their own professional sector. That brings us back to that old collaboration challenge again. The answer to this challenge is for police to avoid asking for open access to other agencies' data. Rather, start at the executive level in those agencies and promote the idea of "partnering" on special projects that are designed to make particularly vulnerable groups, in select neighbourhoods, safer and healthier. Then let those partnering discussions evolve to the point where both partners recognize the value of being data-driven, and figure out ways to collaborate in data sharing. One municipality in Ontario used that approach—initiated by police—in developing a "data consortium" composed of lead data analysts from a whole bunch of human and social service agencies. These analysts get together regularly to talk about how they can share data across sectors to solve particular community problems. The key point in this discussion about other agencies is that lots of data exist and much of it can be helpful. It remains for police to figure out how to access it and put it to good use in safety promotion.

Data Collection Plan

One last, very useful tool for becoming more data-driven is to charge all officers to develop and implement a data collection plan for any and all programs or initiatives that they supervise. The main point of this exercise is to get supervising officers to begin to think about data: its usefulness, how to collect it, who should collect it, how it is put together to inform management decisions, etc. So, for example, four important categories for data collection in most programs include:

- Implementation of the program: data that reflects on what it took to set up and run the program like staff time, direct costs of materials and supplies, duration of the program, etc.
- Audiences for the program: data on who participated (for example, demographics like age and gender); backgrounds, interests, characteristics of the audiences; etc.
- Outcomes of the program: any data that reflects on what the program accomplished, such as numbers of people reached, amount of press coverage, indications of behavioural changes, calls for service, etc.
- Reactions to the program: data on what people say about the program, formal evaluative comments, informal discussions about the program, comments that are heard along the way, etc.

A data collection plan would specify what data is to be collected, how, by whom, and when. Further, it would provide some guidance for data analysis by listing the kinds of questions program managers would like the data to answer. Upon conclusion of the program, program managers would tabulate, analyze, and interpret the data in order to extract from it answers to the management questions that originally informed the data collection plan itself.

Related Research

Comfort with data is the first step toward becoming evidence-based. We need all police officers, managers, and front-line personnel alike to feel comfortable with data; to have rudimentary abilities to interpret simple data tables; and to be able to develop and implement a data collection plan. Another set of important skills applies to processes for finding out what others already know about the programs, strategies, tactics, and initiatives that are being contemplated. We need officers to be able to search for relevant experiences in other services and other nations. We need officers to have the capability to do a literature study of academic research or program evaluations that have been published in peer-reviewed journals.

Literature Search

Peer-reviewed journals are scholarly journals that ensure a certain level of quality, credibility, and veracity by virtue of the fact that no article gets published in them unless it has been thoroughly vetted by scholars in the field to which the article and journal pertain. If contemporary policing is to become evidence-based, it has to incorporate the capacity to source, read, and analyze quality research that is published in peer-reviewed journals.

Most programs that a police service might consider implementing have been tried, in whole or in part, by other police services somewhere. Further, many of them have been evaluated by scholars who have published the results of those evaluations. Picking a topic at random, say, "gun amnesty," and applying that label in an online search engine (like Google Scholar), generated over 19,000 references to articles, press reports, and other documents—in less than a second. Visiting a good library can achieve the same results—with many of the generated references readily available through library services. The same could be done with any other kind of program: "neighbourhood policing" generated over 40,000 references in Google Scholar; "drug abuse resistance education (DARE)," 300,000 references; "countering violent extremism (CVE)," 25,000 references.

Learning about the availability of qualified scientific literature on such programs is relatively easy. The hard part is sorting those references out in order to glean from the best whatever is most appropriate to local program

---

peer-reviewed journals scholarly journals that ensure quality information by virtue of the fact that no article gets published in them unless it has been vetted by scholars in the field to which it pertains

decisions. One of the nice things about search engines like Google Scholar is that the order of presentation of those thousands of references is informed by the frequency with which those references have been sourced by others. So, for example, the first item in the list can be presumed to have been sourced most often, and presumably found to be most useful, by the largest number of others who searched the Internet on the same subject. Therefore, chances are best that the articles at the top of the list will be most interesting and pertinent.

But there are other clues that help sort these references out. In three or four lines of description, it is possible to learn who authored the piece, where it was published, when, and something about its content. All of that information is very helpful in deciding whether to go forward with a particular reference, source the document, and then read it, or move on to the next referenced article.

Another important skill to develop among police program designers and managers is the ability to quickly scan a scholarly article in order to discern whether it pertains to local issues and is worth reading in detail. Experience and practice are the best guides for that. As those skills develop, however, it will become obvious that, notwithstanding the thousands of references offered by the search engine, only a few of those near the top of the reference list really need to be scrutinized closely in order to inform local decisions. So, in the end, this can be a very efficient way to significantly improve the evidence base for local program decisions. But first the police agency has to value this exercise and develop these capabilities in its members.

Work by Other Police Services

It is a rare occasion when any police agency actually tries something that has not been tried by another police agency somewhere else. Often, those earlier experiences were evaluated or researched and ultimately written up in some policing or peer-reviewed journal. But at a minimum, if those earlier experiences can be found and their host agencies contacted, a visit and interview about those experiences can save a lot of lessons learned by the agency that is just beginning down the same road. Preoccupation with CVE by western police services has generated a lot of such exchanges between North America and Western Europe. In fact, this issue is currently of such high priority for Canadian police agencies that we have a national coordinating committee of police agencies set up to ensure that all learn as much as possible about each other's initiatives and experiences. With subjects that are a little less topical— for example, street sex crimes—a police service has to dig a little harder to find out what other agencies have tried and how well their efforts worked. For these purposes, police networks and associations can be very helpful.

Experiences in Other Nations

Local police agencies also have to stop thinking that policing in Canada is so unique that we can learn nothing from police agencies abroad. Furthermore, we have to open our eyes to foreign policing experiences in countries other than the United States and the United Kingdom. The Canadian Association of Chiefs of Police (CACP), International Committee, has been leading Canadian police agencies in this regard for some time. In 2011, the CACP declared that "the Canadian policing community and its leaders have a responsibility to serve Canadian citizens and stakeholders from an informed, current and global base of knowledge about all factors which have the potential to affect community safety and human security in Canada."[3] Every year, the CACP sponsors an international studies program for a group of select Canadian police leaders. Called CACP Executive Global Studies, this program focuses, each year, on one question that officers research in countries abroad where preliminary work has shown there is something for us to learn. Then, in late summer or early fall, the CACP International Committee hosts a conference to bring these lessons learned to the rest of Canadian policing. The CACP also publishes on its website the results of these global excursions. Policing is a challenge everywhere, and good police services everywhere are learning how to meet these challenges. It remains only for agencies everywhere to be willing to research and learn from each other.

Community-Based Research

One of the most significant differences between program evaluation and basic research is that program evaluation most often requires community-based research methods. **Community-based research** is the application of research methods in a real community setting, as opposed to a more highly controlled, laboratory setting. The real community setting requires that the research be done in full partnership with community members—that is, they are intrinsically involved in every stage of the research process and they share in decision-making, ownership, and implementation of the research.

Not Many Qualified Academic Researchers Can Do It

Community-based research requires highly qualified researchers who have gone to additional effort to learn about many of the things we talk about throughout this text: community building, community development, community cohesion, social capital, collaboration, etc. These are special research scholars, and they exist in special departments in universities, foundations, and other institutions. But the key point is that not all sophisticated social science researchers are necessarily qualified to do community-based research. Hence, it is not safe to presume that, just because someone has a doctoral degree in social survey research methods, he or she would be an effective

---

community-based research the application of research methods in a real community setting, as opposed to a more highly controlled, laboratory setting

consultant in doing a program evaluation study in a marginalized neighbourhood for a police agency.

Mail Surveys Won't Work in Marginalized Neighbourhoods

A metropolitan police service contracted an academic department head
who specialized in survey research methods to help evaluate a neighbourhood officer program in some select neighbourhoods. The contractor had
excellent credentials and experience in broad social survey research design.
After consulting with the police agency about what they wanted to find out
in the neighbourhood, the consultant designed a sophisticated paper-pencil
survey instrument; packaged it with a self-addressed, stamped envelope;
and distributed it to residents in the neighbourhood. The return rate was less
than 2 percent. Desperate for research results, the police asked their neighbourhood officers what could be done to increase feedback on the survey.
The result was police and uniformed auxiliary members meeting neighbourhood residents as they got off the bus in the late afternoon, and asking them
for ten minutes of their time to participate in a short interview. The return
rate was dramatically improved over the mail survey approach.

Three lessons can be picked up from this anecdote:

- Not all academically qualified survey researchers can do effective
  community-based research.
- Community-experienced police officers will most likely have a better
  idea than academically qualified survey researchers on how to get a positive response out of people living in marginalized neighbourhoods.
- But even the bus stop trick, while resolving this agency's immediate
  need for program evaluation data, was not optimal for a number of
  reasons.

The neighbourhood officers' good idea about interviews at the bus stop only
reached residents who happened to be on a bus returning to the neighbourhood around close-of-business. That probably means that most of that sample
of residents are people who have some form of 9-to-5 employment, meaning,
of course, that the sample of respondents probably excluded people who were
unemployed, underemployed, working at home, working other shifts, or
retired. Hence, this approach created bias in the results of the survey. The
response rate from the bus stop interviews was probably suppressed by virtue
of the fact that people coming home at that time of day are usually tired, anx-
ious to get into their supper and evening routines, and not as likely to tolerate
well an interruption of those routines. It is even conceivable that responses to

the survey excluded the viewpoints of primary caregivers from the neighbour-hood, as they would have been less tolerant of the interruption in the face of the need to pick up children from school or daycare. You can begin to see some of the challenges in community-based research.

Trust Is the Main Issue

The main issue that has to be dealt with in community-based program evalu-ation is trust—that is, community members' trust in the program evaluation process, its implementers, and how the results will benefit them. Without high levels of trust, research validity and reliability will be seriously jeopardized, no matter how rigorous the research design. Community members have many ways to unintentionally sabotage research, including:

- high refusal rates;
- saying what they think the researchers want to hear;
- saying they "don't know" when they do; and
- gossiping to other neighbours about the research and thereby influenc-ing their answers.

The only way to achieve the levels of trust necessary to ensure a quality pro-gram evaluation in a community is through partnering with community members throughout the program evaluation process. This has to be their evaluation; of their program; with criteria that are meaningful to them; con-ducted by **enumerators** (people who gather the data) who are known and trusted by them; for purposes of program management decisions that the community will value. The bottom line for the qualified community-based researcher is that community members must be involved from the beginning to the end of the program evaluation. A qualified community-based researcher will ensure that community members have substantial and meaningful input into questions like:

- what the program evaluation will mean to the community
- what community members know and are interested to share about the program
- who in the community should be sampled
- how to find and reach them
- how to motivate them to cooperate
- what data collection methods to use
- who should enumerate
- how to advocate for the program evaluation and data collection in the community
- how to share results with the community

---

enumerators people who gather survey data (via interviews, direct observation, etc.)

CHECK YOUR UNDERSTANDING

1. What does data-driven mean?
2. What are readily available sources of research information on the efficacy of programs that a police agency might consider implementing?
3. What is meant by community-based research, and what are the implications for program evaluation in a police agency?

Methodological Issues

As mentioned in the introduction, this chapter is not designed to make a program evaluator out of anybody. However, there are a few basic, methodological issues that, if understood by a police program manager, will greatly improve the chances of a meaningful program evaluation.

No One Is Objective

Too often, program managers look for program evaluation consulting assistance from outside their own agency on the basis of an assumption that anyone coming from outside the agency would be more objective in looking at the program than would anyone from inside the agency. Not only is that assumption erroneous, but it has too often led to police agencies trusting research consultants and their products, when both are inherently biased. Where objectivity is concerned, the first rule of thumb is that no one is objective! Objectivity is not a characteristic of people. The second rule of thumb is that objectivity rests, largely, in research methodologies chosen to do the evaluation. The only way to ensure that program evaluation results are valid and reliable is to make the best methodological decisions and know the sources of bias in the data instruments, the enumerators, the statistics used to analyze data, the research designers, and the managers who will make decisions on the basis of those program evaluation results. Knowing the potential sources of bias in the results allows the program manager to make adjustments in the interpretation of evaluation findings.

Therefore, it is important to pick program evaluation consultants who are extremely well informed about all aspects of the program, the community in which the program is being applied, the police service, and the management decisions that are pending on the evaluation results. All of those are things that many police officers are already steeped in. So it is possible that if the police agency has such a knowledgeable officer who also happens to have the community-based research skills, a more objective evaluation could come from that officer than could come from an outsider who is largely ignorant of the program, the community, and the police agency, but who may have superlative behavioural science credentials.

Populations and Sampling

In behavioural research, the concept of **population** refers to everyone to whom the evaluator expects to generalize the program evaluation findings. For example, if the police association wanted to know how all members felt about their agency's annual leave policy, they could ask all of their members to answer that question in an interview or in writing. If they got a 100 percent response rate from all members, they would have no trouble believing that the results applied to all of their members. However, if only half of their members responded to this survey, it would raise significant questions about whether the results applied equally as well to those members who chose not to reply.

Usually, especially in community-based research, it is impossible to survey the whole target population. It is too hard to get a 100 percent response rate. Therefore, program managers and evaluators have to make methodological decisions about sampling the population. A **sample** is a subset of the population that is presumed to be representative of the population on the criterion measures the evaluation is asking about. Sampling is a whole science unto itself, and we will not be going into that here. Where there are sampling challenges, it is advisable to seek assistance from qualified scientists.

On the other hand, we will provide six advisories about sampling for police program managers. First, assume that surveying the whole population is impossible. Second, realize that selecting community respondents in a way that is truly random—thereby assuring some sample representativeness that parallels the general population—is impossible. Third, decide to reach with your survey as many as you possibly can. Fourth, engage community members to advise on how best to do that: how to find them, how to motivate them to participate, what questions to ask, etc. Fifth, knowing that there are numerous sources of bias in the sample you have, round the percentages you use to analyze data to the nearest 5 percent. In other words, do not imply more precision in measurement than is probably there. Sixth, once you have figured out the variability of responses, interpret only the most extreme ones. For example, if you asked members how they liked the agency's annual leave policy on a five-step scale (like it a lot, like it some, not sure, dislike it some, dislike it a lot), report only scores for the two extreme ends of the scale—the proportions who said they liked it a lot, and those who said they disliked it a lot. Then spend the balance of your analysis on looking at the reasons people gave for positive or negative reactions and use those to explain the percentages in both of those categories.

---

population everyone to whom the evaluator expects to generalize the program evaluation findings

sample a subset of the population that is presumed to be representative of the population on the criterion measures the evaluation is asking about

Qualitative and Quantitative Research Methods

Qualitative measures do not mean that the evaluation will not use numbers or statistical tests. The distinction between qualitative and quantitative is not about mathematics. It is about what is measured and how those observations are made. Analysis of what is measured may well require sophisticated statistical work, and yield composite numerical scores, in both kinds of work.

Quantitative research usually measures who, what, where, and when—things that are fairly discrete and can be observed fairly easily with high reliability and validity. For example, "who" could be observed by noticing gender (male or female); "what" might be one choice a respondent makes for the thing they like best about the program; "where" might refer to different and distinct venues for the program; and "when" might be a simple time reference. Quantitative measures generate data that share facts and figures about program outcomes, or about knowledge gain or comprehension. For example, after a workshop on crime prevention through environmental design (CPTED), an evaluator might ask participants to select representative examples of CPTED from a list of options. Broad social surveys, analysis of existing data (like Census Canada data), and data tracking (like attendance and participation rates in the program) are examples of quantitative measurement.

Qualitative research, on the other hand, more often measures the why and how of something, like the open-ended question, "Why did you like that part of the program?" or "How do you feel about what you did there?" Both of those lines of questioning will generate a wide range of answers, probably none of which could have been accurately predicted in advance of asking the question. But that is the beauty of qualitative research; it allows the evaluator to get program participants' reactions based on their own values, and in their own words. Qualitative research provides data with more depth and description than is provided by quantitative research methods. In-depth interviews, focus groups, content analysis of documents, case studies, or content analysis of notes taken by trained observers are examples of qualitative research methods of observation.

Community-based program evaluation can benefit from both kinds of research. But where the impressions, feelings, attitudes, beliefs, and reactions of community members are valued, qualitative methods are more often chosen for the two reasons stated at the beginning of this discussion: they permit answers to originate in the values of the people from which they are sought, and in those persons' own words; and that is important in generating social cohesion and social capital.

---

quantitative research measures who, what, where, and when—things that are fairly discrete and can be observed fairly easily with high reliability and validity

qualitative research measures the why and how of something; yields more in-depth description than quantitative measures

CHECK YOUR UNDERSTANDING

1. How can a program manager ensure objectivity in his or her program evaluations?

2. How can an evaluation ensure representativeness of the population in a community-based evaluation?

3. What are the differences and similarities between quantitative and qualitative research methods?

Compendium of Measures

It is one thing to figure out what outcomes are desired from a planned program; it is quite another challenge to decide which measures can accurately tell you whether those outcomes have been achieved. This is where the program manager, program evaluator, and community partners need to spend a lot of time collaborating until they come up with both desired outcomes and measures that fit all of their needs. One of their jobs will be to research how such outcomes have been measured by others elsewhere. No doubt there is some good scientific literature on this.

In 2014, the Ontario Working Group on Collaborative, Risk-driven Community Safety and Well-being developed for the Ontario Association of Chiefs of Police a compendium of Performance Measures for Community Safety and Well-being. It corresponds nicely with the framework for community safety and well-being introduced earlier (in Chapters 4 and 10). So, for example, it provides a list of risk factors, vulnerable groups, protective factors, and performance measures in each of the framework's four categories: social development, prevention, risk mitigation, and emergency response. This is an invaluable resource for the program evaluator working in a marginalized neighbourhood where programs are designed to increase safety and well-being.[4]

In Chapter 9, we applied risk analysis to the problem of countering violent extremism using a community-based problem-solving model, the fifth step of which was program evaluation. In Table 11.2 below we bring back the program design generated in Chapter 9 to prevent violent extremism, but notice the right-most column of that table in which we insert just a few performance measures that could be used to see if this program actually worked. The colours in which the performance measures are printed correspond to the four zones of the framework for community safety and well-being planning: Social Development, Prevention, Risk Mitigation, and Emergency Response. Up to three possible performance measures for each risk factor have been identified here, though many more could be added.

TABLE 11.2   **Identifying Performance Measures to Apply to a Program Designed to Counter Violent Extremism in One Target Community**

Types of Drivers	Risk Factors	Protective Factors	Performance Measures
Structural drivers	Feelings of discrimination and exclusion in school	Advocacy for the individual in the school setting; collaboration with the school in designing and implementing anti-discrimination policies and programs	• % with six or more close friends in school • % who feel that most school people can be trusted • % reporting sense of belonging to the school community • % of youth who feel safe in school • Types, frequency of discriminatory incidents • Rates of truancy among vulnerable youth • Locations, types, frequencies of victimizing events • Numbers of meetings among school staff and partners to support vulnerable youth • Types and frequencies of agencies intervening • Number and types of calls for assistance • Referrals to human and social service agencies • Youth fears of re-victimization
	Poverty and inadequate income	Education and vocational training; career guidance; financial literacy training; social development strategies; micro-credit schemes	• Unemployment rates among employable population • % employable persons drawing employment insurance • Total employment of youth aged 15-24 per 1,000 population • Participation rates in education, vocational, career guidance, and financial literacy programs • Number of micro-credit, social entrepreneurship programs • Participation rates in those programs • Enrollment in emergency, direct, financial assistance programs • Enrollment rates in income maintenance, social assistance • Rates of mortgage foreclosures; rental evictions; loss of electricity • Participation rates in community-based organizations offering temporary shelter, income assistance, or advocacy

Types of Drivers	Risk Factors	Protective Factors	Performance Measures
	Community and neighbourhood tensions between groups with historical enmities	Inter-group negotiations and mediation, forums, and community events; identification and development of moderate and conciliatory group leaders; introduction of restorative justice dispute resolution methods	• Numbers of meetings between community groups • Participation rates and outcomes of those meetings • Number of whole-community events per year • Number and types of programs and events groups do together • Types, number of contentious issues, incidents between groups • Numbers of conflict resolution initiatives • Protocols, procedures to avert negative incidents • Locations, types, frequencies of victimizing incidents • Types, frequencies of social support agencies intervening • Community perceptions of crime, social disorder between groups • Number and types of calls for assistance • Referrals to other human and social service agencies
Individual drivers	Quest for significance	Individual mentoring; educational and customized enrichment activities; career guidance; challenging learning situations that speak to individual's aptitudes and interests	• Availability of mentoring and enrichment programs • Self-reports of satisfaction with those programs • Self-reported sense of purpose and confidence • Availability of individuals, institutions, programs offering mentoring, assistance with self-direction • Attitudes toward self, life, and future • Feelings of fit with the rest of the community • Frequency of community reports about persons in crisis • Numbers, availability, participation rates with agencies that can help • Qualities of interventions with people in crisis • Types, frequencies of calls for assistance • Referrals to community or outside human and social service agencies • Satisfaction of vulnerable groups with those services and supports

Types of Drivers	Risk Factors	Protective Factors	Performance Measures
	Identity crisis	Psychosocial supports; mentoring; exposure to career opportunities; assessments of aptitudes and interests; exposure to areas of interest	• Numbers and types of programs and supports available • Opportunities to be exposed to diverse career opportunities • Feelings of support from neighbours, friends, and families • Availability of, access to, participation in, and reactions to career, citizenship, and self-actualization programs for new Canadians • Access to career guidance, aptitude testing, and mentoring • Numbers, types, locations of at-risk individuals and situations • Types and frequencies of agencies intervening • Increased competencies of at-risk individuals • Number and types of calls for emergency assistance • Diversion rates and referrals to other agencies
	Anger, alienation, and isolation	Psychosocial supports; mentoring; enrollment in group activities that interest individual; support for family and community members who have rapport with individual	• Numbers and types of programs and supports available • % with six or more close friends • Feelings of support from neighbours, friends, and families • Availability of, access to, participation in, and reactions to career, citizenship, and self-actualization programs for new Canadians • Access to mentoring and personal guidance • Numbers, types, locations of at-risk individuals and situations • Types and frequencies of agencies intervening • Increased competencies of at-risk individuals • Number and types of calls for emergency assistance • Diversion rates and referrals to other agencies • Numbers and types of chargeable and non-chargeable offences

Types of Drivers	Risk Factors	Protective Factors	Performance Measures
Enabling drivers	Radical mentors	Mentoring; development and implementation of counternarratives; support for local, moderate influencers; planned exposure to non-radical alternatives; exposure to non-violent radicals	• Supports for new Canadians, cultural and religious tolerance and diversity • Numbers and types of community-based organizations and groups dedicated to supporting all community members • Supports from three levels of government for community-based programming to counter radicalization • Number and types of new community initiatives designed to prevent radicalization • Prevalence of counternarratives to radicalization • Community support for counternarratives • Use of non-violent radicals to send counternarratives • Numbers, types, and frequencies of acute risk situations • Types and frequencies of agencies, groups intervening • Numbers, types of calls for assistance • Referrals to other human and social service agencies
	Online radical forums	Form online network that fosters cross-cultural communication; empower youth as activists for peace through social media; youth-driven anti-extremism media campaigns	• Presence of, access to online network fostering cross-cultural communication • Youth involvement in social media for peace • Youth-driven anti-extremism campaigns • Community alerts about online radical forums • Supports for families to know whether their youth are using online radical forums • Supports for youth who are enticed by online radical forums • Numbers, frequency of reports of vulnerable people drawn to online radical forums • Numbers, disposition of interventions to reduce use of online radical forums • Recidivism and re-contact rates • Types and frequencies of calls for assistance • Referrals to other human and social service agencies

Types of Drivers	Risk Factors	Protective Factors	Performance Measures
	Extreme anti-West rhetoric	Counternarratives in citizenship development: promote liberalism; suggest synergy between religious beliefs and human rights; endorse human rights; endorse rule of law; promote non-adversarial approaches to grievances; value action over inaction; promote humanitarian responses to perceived suffering	• Presence, use of citizenship development programs for new Canadian citizens • Presence, use of restorative justice and other community-based conflict resolution processes • Numbers and activities of community-based organizations focusing on social justice, inclusiveness, and peace • Partnerships between community-based organizations and external agencies to promote conflict resolution • Availability of supports for vulnerable families and groups • Support by governments for community-based programs • Frequency and type of acute risk situations • Numbers and disposition of interventions • Calls for assistance • Referrals to other human and social service agencies

Logical Framework

Over the years, program managers have refined a simple process for designing program evaluation. The logical framework starts with what the managers have already decided the program should accomplish. Then it lays out as much detail as the manager wants to include about how those accomplishments will be measured, when, by whom, and how. Table 11.3 shows one version of a logical framework, but notice that other columns of information could be added as necessary. The logical framework should be completed by the program manager and used as the basis for discussing, planning, and contracting evaluation work by qualified professionals. During those discussions it is likely—indeed, it is to be hoped—that the logical framework will be improved and refined as the program manager gets significant and useful inputs from qualified evaluation professionals.

Data Collection Methods

There are lots of ways to make observations that can be turned into data for purposes of evaluating a program. Qualified evaluators are aware of the full

TABLE 11.3   Example of a Logical Framework for Designing a Program Evaluation

	Immediate Outcomes				
Program Objectives	Expected Outcomes	Performance Measures	Methods of Observation	Dates of Observation	Observer

	Long-Term Outcomes				
Program Objectives	Expected Outcomes	Performance Measures	Methods of Observation	Dates of Observation	Observer

range of such methods and they can be expected to advise program managers on which methods to use in order to achieve the purposes of the evaluation. The word "survey" is no longer useful as a descriptor of a particular kind of data collection method because it is too general; it can include too many different kinds of methods. So whenever a manager hears an evaluator using the word "survey," it is important to get them to be more precise about the particular data collection methods they are proposing.

Surveys come in many forms. We have already told one anecdote about a police service that contracted a **mail survey** (a survey in which the respondent indicates his or her reactions on a self-administered questionnaire and then mails that form back to the surveying organization). But surveys could also be administered by personal interviews or even online. Census Canada, for example, offers both an online and a mailed return.

These kinds of surveys are most useful for quantitative observation methods. Qualitative observation methods are quite different. **Focus groups** (in which a group of community people are asked to discuss their feelings, reactions, attitudes to whatever the program manager is interested in while an observer takes notes about the discussion), for example, are quite good at getting community members to discuss particular topics while an observer quietly listens and takes good notes about the community members' feelings and reactions. Those notes are then content analyzed in order to turn the observations into data that can be analyzed for evaluation purposes.

Personal interviews (in which an enumerator works off a prescribed list of questions and records respondents' answers in a question-and-answer format) come in many forms. For example, the enumerator could read the question verbatim off the questionnaire, or they could simply work off an outline of the important questions to ask and be more spontaneous in having a conversation with the respondent. Answers could be limited to simple tick marks on closed-ended questions with multiple choice options, or they could be discursive notes taken in a more free-flowing discussion. Because of that variability, personal interviews can be useful in both quantitative and qualitative research initiatives.

Direct observation is most often used in a qualitative research initiative. It is most useful in a community-based program evaluation. **Direct observation**

---

mail survey a survey in which the respondent indicates his or her reactions on a self-administered questionnaire and then mails that form back to the surveying organization

focus groups groups of community people who are asked to discuss their feelings, reactions, and attitudes to whatever the program manager is interested in while an observer takes notes about the discussion

personal interviews interviews in which an enumerator works off a prescribed list of questions and records respondents' answers in a question-and-answer format

direct observation type of observation whereby a trained observer attends to spontaneous actions in the community and records those observations for later analysis

involves a trained observer attending to spontaneous actions in the community and recording those observations for later analysis. Direct observation emerged out of cultural anthropology and sociology studies in which scientists sought to understand how groups of people lived and related in a community. One of the precepts of direct observation is for the observer to be as inconspicuous as possible so that they do not influence the spontaneous exchanges among the community members they are trying to understand.

All of these data collection methods, and more, are useful for various purposes at various times in the life of a program. It is important to obtain the advice of a qualified community-based researcher on which to use, when, and for what purposes.

CHECK YOUR UNDERSTANDING

1. What is a logical framework, and what are its elements?
2. What are focus groups, and how do they work?
3. What is meant by direct observation, and how does it apply to community-based research?

The Program Evaluation Report

The most important quality of the program evaluation report is its communicability to program managers who may not be experts in behavioural science or program evaluation. That is a condition that makes the difference between reports that help make program decisions, and those that sit on the proverbial "shelf." Therefore, it is important, in selecting a program evaluator, to look at their past reports for other clients and satisfy yourself that they can write in ways that allow program managers to make good decisions.

The typical program evaluation report will have the following sections:

- description of the program and its implementation
- analysis of program processes
- description of the participants and types of participation activities
- participants' reactions to the program
- observed changes, outcomes, impacts
- analysis of program strengths and weaknesses
- recommendations about the program

Hiring an Evaluator

Throughout this discussion of program evaluation, we have mentioned some of the qualities that are required of a program evaluator. Here, we will summarize them. If the program to be evaluated operates in the community—like a neighbourhood officer program, or a community crime prevention initiative—then an evaluator who has experience and understands community-based research methods will be necessary. On the other hand, if the program to be evaluated is less dynamic, and more contrived and controlled, than a community program—like a course at the police college—then an evaluator who understands training evaluation, but not necessarily community-based research methods, would suffice.

Research and evaluation skills are not sufficient for any evaluator chosen to work with a police agency. It is important that the evaluator also understand a lot about this unique agency, its mandate and role, its methods of operation, and the kinds of constraints and opportunities under which it works. It is possible to get a good evaluation out of someone who does not have that understanding if the schedule of performance in the evaluation contract gives them the expectation and time to learn those things about the agency and the program they are contracted to evaluate.

Finding and hiring program evaluators is very much like finding and hiring a contractor to work on a house. It pays to solicit representation from a number of alternative sources so that the agency can make a judicious choice among options. But to augment that process, it is important to ask all prospective candidates to submit for inspection two to three evaluation reports that they completed for past clients. Those reports will tell a lot about how well the evaluator worked to understand their client and the program they were evaluating; how well they provided evaluation results in ways that inform good program management decisions; and what kind of a communicator they are.

Additionally, ask each prospective evaluator to submit the names of three to four references. This is too often overlooked or underrated as a source of important information. But interviews with these references can disclose the strengths and weaknesses of each candidate for the job—especially if those interviews are conducted by police officers with good investigative skills.

Finally, Canada is fortunate to have one of the world's most credible professional societies for program evaluators. The Canadian Evaluation Society maintains high standards for certification as a professional evaluator and supports evaluators with state-of-the-art learning opportunities. Their website also offers a list of qualified and certified evaluators, organized by region of the country, so it is a good place to start the hunt for a qualified evaluator.[5]

Upgrading the Service's Data-Driven and Evidence-Based Capabilities

The management of all human and social service agencies (including policing) has progressed to the point where it is reasonable to expect that anyone choosing to work in those careers will come into them with at least a rudimentary knowledge of simple statistics and basic research designs. The days when it was sufficient for those skills to reside in one specialized analyst who rarely relates to what is happening on the front lines are over.

It is also reasonable for all command staff to require regular data analyses and presentations based on reliable data of all of their mid-level program managers. Therefore, it would behoove all program managers to develop data collection plans for every activity they supervise.

Police agencies are slowly upgrading the quality of their crime analysts from people who are simply good at creating spreadsheets to qualified behavioural statisticians who also understand questionnaire construction. For that matter, the state of the art is such, and the demand for evidence-based decisions is such, that program managers themselves should now be able to create, develop, and interpret spreadsheets.

In the not too distant past, a medium-sized police agency may have retained one person they designated as a "crime analyst." But slowly we are seeing the skills of those people improving and their numbers in the agency increasing. For a highly distributed police agency, like a provincial service or the RCMP, evidence-based decisions at the detachment level required submitting requests to a central office for data from a crime analyst, and those requests sat in a queue until such time as those limited analytical capabilities could serve the detachment. More recently, agencies are hiring more analysts; placing more of them out in decentralized locations where they are more accessible to frontline personnel; and also upgrading hardware and software at the detachment level so that local commanders can run some of the numbers themselves. We need to see more of that throughout the policing infrastructure in Canada. We need to push the requirement for data-driven, evidence-based decisions down the front lines of our policing agencies.

Finally, police commanders need to require that program managers base program designs, decisions, and evaluations on sound data analysis, much as intelligence-led policing did for allocation of patrol personnel. If these steps are taken, policing in Canada will become more data-driven and evidence-based.

CHAPTER SUMMARY

Policing, like all other human and social services, is becoming more data-driven and evidence-based. But that does not mean that every police officer has to enroll in graduate courses in statistics and research design. It does mean, however, that all officers must become more familiar and comfortable with data, and that police program managers must learn how to select qualified research professionals to help them fulfill their data and evidence requirements.

Program evaluation is an applied form of behavioural research. That means that, in many respects, research methodologies have to accommodate the vicissitudes of the real world, as opposed to the research laboratory in which basic research takes place. The most significant adjustment required by community policing is the addition of community-based research skills and experience.

That, in turn, adds a very significant criterion, which police agencies must add when they are selecting qualified research consultants to help with their program evaluation. It is not enough to hire an academic with basic research skills; the research consultant must also have quality experience applying those skills in a community setting.

REVIEW AND DISCUSSION QUESTIONS

1. Explain how evaluation of a community policing initiative is different from basic research.

2. Explain why it is important to include community members in all aspects of community-based research.

3. Outline three steps to ensure objectivity in program evaluation.

4. Outline the contents of a program evaluation report.

5. Discuss ways to find the most qualified consultant to conduct a program evaluation.

6. Outline steps toward making the police agency more data-driven and its decisions and programs more evidence-based.

KEY TERMS

applied research, 314
basic research, 314
community-based research, 321
contingency table, 316
direct observation, 334
enumerators, 323
extraneous variables, 314
focus groups, 334

NOTES

1   Peter Neyroud, "Foreword" in Tom Williamson, ed, *The Handbook of Knowledge-Based Policing: Current Conceptions and Future Directions* (Sussex, UK: John Wiley, 2008) at xix.

2   Michael Quinn Patton, *Qualitative Research & Evaluation Methods*, 4th ed (Thousand Oaks, Cal: Sage, 2014).

3   Canadian Association of Chiefs of Police, "Policing and Community Safety in an Increasingly Globalized World" (Agenda for the 2016 conference), online: <https://www.cacp.ca/index.html?asst_id=1121>.

4   Hugh C Russell & Norman E Taylor, "Performance Measures ... for Community Safety and Well-Being" in *New Directions in Community Safety: Consolidating Lessons Learned About Risk and Collaboration* (Toronto: Ontario Working Group on Collaborative, Risk-driven Community Safety and Well-being, Ontario Association of Chiefs of Police, April 2014), vol 3. It is publicly accessible (as of July 2016) at <http://www.oacp.on.ca/news-events/resource-documents/ontario-working-group-owg>.

5   The Canadian Evaluation Society may be sourced online at <http://evaluationcanada.ca>. The Society provides a Roster of Credentialed Evaluators, available under the Designations drop-down menu at the top of the page.

EPILOGUE

(It Is All About Relationships)

LEARNING OUTCOMES

Upon completion of this brief essay, you should be able to:

- Summarize the key learnings from the first 11 chapters of this text
- Discuss the fundamental role of police legitimacy in community policing
- Identify systemic barriers to procedural justice in police culture

Introduction

We are at the end of this text. So, in closing, I wish to summarize what we learned along the way and reflect on one of the greatest challenges to effective community policing today. This is not a full chapter like the previous 11 chapters. It is more of a summary essay.

The bottom line from all chapters is that community problems will only be sustainably solved by the people who are experiencing them—not police. Yet, police have a huge role in getting a community to solve those problems. That means that the first challenge for police is to acknowledge that for the most part, they cannot resolve the community's biggest problems that contribute most to crime, social disorder, and calls for police assistance. Their second challenge is to stop taking responsibility for solving these community problems and learn to compassionately apply the mobilization, engagement, and collaboration skills that enable community members to do what they have to do to make themselves safer and healthier.

Where police are responding most often to calls for assistance, community members have failed to develop and maintain relationships with each other that are conducive to community problem-solving. Therefore, it is up to police (and their partners) to rekindle constructive, community-building relationships. But that presents police with another significant challenge. How can they rekindle constructive, community-building relationships among community members if the fundamental relationships between community members and police are dysfunctional? This is the issue of police legitimacy that was mentioned, and reinforced, in almost every chapter in this text. It is the issue on which this summary essay will close this discussion, for it is the fulcrum on which the success of community policing rests. With insufficient levels of police legitimacy, community policing is impossible.

Summarizing Lessons About Community Policing

In Part I, we introduced the concepts of community, social capital, and social control, and we learned about the history and evolution of community policing. When safety and well-being are in jeopardy, where people fear crime or feel unsafe, and where police are responding most often, the positive characteristics of community do not exist sufficiently to prevent bad things from happening. Therefore, we have to compensate for these deficiencies by throwing police and other emergency responders at the manifestations of social disorder and crime. But by that time, people have already suffered harms and victimization, and these emergency services can do little more than put band-aids on those problems.

One of the ironies exposed by the history of community policing is that traditional policing emerged out of the state's desire to control social behaviour and maintain sovereignty over safety and security—in exchange for tithes paid by community members. As a result, it commandeered justice practices that, until then, community members had more or less adequately managed for themselves. But now, on the other end of this long, historical perspective, the state, through police and other security agencies, is learning that it has real limitations in its ability to control people's behaviours. Now, local, regional, provincial, and federal governments are realizing that they cannot guarantee safety and well-being for all. As a result, they are focusing on ways to enable communities' capabilities to take better care of themselves. That is what has to change; community policing means that we need police to rekindle social capital, social control, and the qualities of community that prevent bad things from happening in the first place. Is this a back-to-the-future moment?

In Part II, we focused on community engagement and problem-solving. The core lesson here is that police are good at traditional policing, but they have significant shortcomings when it comes to solving community problems. Police usually oversimplify the problems they perceive in a community—recognizing only the symptomatic conditions of social disorder, or crime, and failing entirely to recognize, much less ameliorate, their root causes. Police have to acknowledge that usually they cannot resolve community problems; it remains the responsibility of community members to do that. But police can and should do a lot to enable a community to do more for itself.

With that base, we began to lay out the proactive process of increasing community safety and well-being by steering police and community partners away from a preoccupation with harmful incidents and toward anticipation of community risk factors that lead to harmful incidents. If risk factors can be anticipated, then surely it is possible to identify protective factors that mitigate them.

After that, it only remains to be planful in applying this knowledge to a collaborative, community-wide process of increasing everyone's safety and well-being. This is where Part III came in, providing practical solutions and advice for mobilizing communities to make these plans. Three standard police problem-solving models are often used for this planning: CAPRA, SARA, and PARE.

But more significantly, insofar as we have already established that police can rarely solve significant community problems, we must consider the goal of community cohesion for which police should work. Community cohesion goes back to that notion of "durable relationships." It is only when people stick together that they can exert sufficient levels of collective influence to reduce risk factors and install protective factors that benefit everyone in the community. So, rather than actually solving problems in the community, police should support community problem-solving through

- effective enforcement;
- outreach, representation, and engagement;

- visible presence and encouragement;
- technical consultation and advice; and
- monitoring and evaluation of outcomes.

Police have a variety of tools to use in rekindling social cohesion in the community:

- asset-based community development
- asset inventory
- appreciative inquiry
- community circles
- management by consensus
- community justice forums

The core lesson in this is that there are a number of very useful, practical techniques for fostering community cohesion and social control. Police can introduce these techniques to communities that are striving to resolve problems that contribute to crime and social disorder. In this context, community policing is all about police helping communities identify and deal constructively with risk and protective factors. In effect, communities are becoming better at policing their own risks and liabilities.

By this point, it should have become obvious that community policing means that far more than police have to be mobilized and engaged in community problem-solving. At the same time, we acknowledge that most often it falls to police to initiate these processes. After all, problems in neighbourhoods where police respond most often would not be so severe if everyone else in the community was already effectively engaged in trying to resolve them. Police mobilizing and engaging other community partners sets up the whole idea of police and other partners learning how to collaborate more effectively. That can be a challenge for everybody, for a variety of reasons.

Collaboration among a variety of community groups, individuals, and agencies requires effective communication among them. If that communication is effective, then collaboration, most often, generates new knowledge about the problems and their solutions. It is out of that new knowledge that all community partners realize the value-added of collaboration. Effective communication across disciplines and areas of specialization challenges all agencies, organizations, and individuals in the safety and well-being enterprise. It requires levels of transparency, equity in relationship, and mutual commitment to common goals that are hard for our highly differentiated social and political structures to accommodate.

Part IV began by showing a practical application of community policing by applying a planning framework to the community problem of addictions and mental health. The planning framework can be applied to any kind of community problem. The addictions and mental health application reinforces the observation that police cannot possibly resolve such problems, but they can enable their resolution by many more community members.

We then applied this planning framework by examining the risk factors that lead to violent extremism. Here we are trying, once again, to emphasize that community policing is far more than a philosophy or a set of bold abstractions. It is not limited to hosting community picnics or playing basketball with youth. In contrast, it is a hard-core strategy for tackling some of society's most serious and potentially harmful problems. Violent extremism can be predicted well before it becomes a real crisis, based upon sound observation of the behaviours of vulnerable individuals in communities. Therefore, it can also be mitigated—but rarely by police or other security agencies. That sets up questions about which community members will make these observations, and which will most constructively intervene to ensure that violent extremism is not acted out. Last, we examined the role of police in getting this to happen long before violent extremism becomes an intelligence and tactical matter for traditional policing.

Finally, in the last chapter of the book, we focused on the challenges of research and evaluation applied to policing and community problem-solving. The first challenge is to get individual police officers, and whole police services, to value and use the tools and techniques of research and evaluation. That necessarily requires a level of skill and competence that too many individual officers and police services lack. On the other hand, all human and social service providers are beginning to recognize the value of research and evaluation. People who wish to join police services will find that if they bring research and evaluation skills into the mix, they will experience a competitive edge in recruitment for policing positions. It remains for police services to acquire these skills and apply them judiciously to the kinds of decisions and tactics that they are empowered to apply to community problems.

The Power of Relationships

As summarized earlier, "community" is defined, in part, as being composed of "durable relationships." A community's control over the behaviour of its members is a function of social capital—that is, people forming relationships with each other that enable them to work together for the common good. There, and in subsequent chapters, we learned that where social disorder and crime are most prevalent, those durable relationships are lacking. As a result, we need police and other community partners to help rekindle social capital and social control—durable relationships among the people who have the most at stake in community problems.

Effective community policing is all about building constructive, durable relationships, but not just between people living in communities that have problems. If rekindling community is going to work, it will be because members of the community that is experiencing problems have constructive and durable relationships with the agencies and organizations that are set up to help them solve their problems. These include the schools, local retailers, municipal offices, health care providers, employers, all human and social service providers—and police! In fact, relationships among all members of the safety and well-being web have to be constructive and durable if a community is going to become safe, healthy, and resilient.

Police are at the centre, or focal point, of that web because they are society's principal protagonists for safety and security. Consequently, police have to have constructive and durable relationships with everybody in the web. For example, it is the relationship between neighbourhood residents and Police Community Support Officers (civilians, recruited from the neighbourhoods in which they patrol, and uniformed and trained by police) that makes Britain's "reassurance policing" strategy so successful. The same thing can be said about Toronto, Ontario's "neighbourhood officer program." Officers who, before this program, only appeared in the neighbourhood in response to a call for service, now patrol the neighbourhood full time; get to know all of the principal players in the neighbourhood; and develop durable relationships with these neighbours, which helps them resolve their own problems. The municipality of Camden, New Jersey learned this lesson after it disbanded its police force in order to rebuild it from the ground up with a focus on community policing and subsequently saw a drop in violent crime:

> The idea is that these community-focused tactics—in which the police work with community groups, such as churches, to guide their priorities—can dismantle the us-versus-them mentality between police and residents in some places, and build a stronger police presence that's more familiar with locals and, as a result, less likely to resort to force to settle disputes.[1]

Relationships and Police Legitimacy

In this sense, relationships are the foundation of effective community policing. When applied to police, the language of relationships shifts to the phrase "police legitimacy," which is used in almost every chapter of this text. Police legitimacy is about the relationship between police and everyone else in the safety and well-being web. You will recall that it is composed of two elements: members of the safety and well-being web value what police do, and how they do it. But also integrated into this notion is the concept of "procedural justice"—that is, people's sense that police are doing the right things, and doing them well, because they

- encourage participation by everyone most directly affected by the problems being solved;

- reflect fairness and neutrality on the issues pertaining to community problems;
- demonstrate dignity and respect toward everyone involved in community problem-solving; and
- exemplify trustworthy motives.

Police Culture

The deputy chief of a large Canadian metropolitan police service reinforced ex-officer Redditt Hudson's conclusion (Chapter 3) that a small percentage of officers join the ranks to do the right thing; a similarly small percentage join to abuse their powers and authorities; and the balance behave in accordance with the "culture" of policing that predominates in their agency. This Canadian deputy chief told me that his service presumes that 20 percent of its officers are there to do the right thing and 20 percent are there to abuse their powers, leaving 60 percent subject to the whims of police culture. Police culture, in turn, is largely defined by police unions and associations, and articulated in collective agreements. For example, collective agreements and the *Police Services Act*[2] in Ontario make it very difficult for agencies to withhold pay from officers who are charged under Canada's *Criminal Code*[3] or a provincial statute. Thus, the threat of losing income no longer serves as a disincentive for officers to abuse their powers. The *New York Times* highlighted how police unions influence police culture in America:

> [M]unicipal governments have signed contracts with police unions including provisions that shield officers from punishment for brutal behavior as well as from legitimate complaints by the citizens they are supposed to serve.[4]

Another American police officer has a prescription for changing police culture in order to strengthen police legitimacy:

> This crisis in policing has to do with unnecessary use of force, racial profiling, militarization of police departments, lack of trust between communities and police departments, lack of strategies to address trauma and emotional health of police officers, unconscious and unspoken organizational agreements in police culture, and a lack of informal safety nets for people across the country. ...
>
> If we want compassionate police forces, communities must get intimately involved with their police departments. Communities need to organize and call for changes in the leadership, hiring, use of force policies, and training practices of their local police departments. And they need to do so with awareness, right speech, understanding of a police officer's job, and compassion. ...
>
> Creating the justice that leads to public safety is a shared responsibility between a community and its police department.[5]

Achieving Legitimacy

We need to increase police legitimacy in order for police to achieve five objectives:

1. reduce crime and social disorder in communities;
2. mobilize community assets in the highest-demand neighbourhoods;
3. engage diverse community partners in the long-term efforts to increase safety and well-being for all;
4. increase accountability and responsiveness of all public bodies, human and social service agencies, businesses, community-based organizations, and neighbours to the practical challenges of safety and well-being; and
5. increase active citizen and agency participation in guiding and implementing strategies, tactics, and actions of the police agency.

The year 2010 saw the advent of some tough-on-crime legislation in the United Kingdom that stressed our first objective above, "reduce crime and social disorder," as the principal measure of police effectiveness. That stimulated two criminologists, Jonathan Jackson and Ben Bradford, to research whether police legitimacy had any functional relationship to reducing crime and social disorder. Recall that in Chapter 3 we introduced evidence by the American criminologist Lawrence Sherman that "bad manners" by police provided barriers to achieving these goals. Jackson and Bradford's work confirmed Sherman's:

> If people perceive the police to be procedurally fair, and if they trust their motives … , all current evidence suggests they are not only more likely to actively cooperate by reporting crime, cooperating in investigations, providing witness evidence, even intervening in situations of low-level deviance and incivility. They are also more likely to defer to officers' instructions to obey the laws that the police in many ways still embody. In the long run, the fight against crime might be more efficiently, more cost-effectively, and certainly more ethically serviced by treating the public with fairness, dignity and respect than by instigating another "crack-down" on crime.[6]

Jackson and Bradford define police legitimacy in terms of community members' believing that police understand their needs, treat everyone fairly and with respect, provide all community members with information that is necessary to maintain their safety and well-being, and allow all community members to participate in identifying and resolving community problems. In their own words:

> If the police demonstrate to citizens of diverse communities that they are effective, fair and aligned with local interests, then this not only

makes the police more directly accountable. It also strengthens the moral connection between people and their police, thus encouraging greater civic participation and more active public engagement in domains of security, policing and the regulation of social and community life.[7]

To achieve these five objectives in policing, we not only have to remove systemic barriers to effective police culture, like racism, abuse of power, and just plain "bad manners." We also have to adopt in our police agencies policies, practices, and training and performance standards that increase rapport, respect, and dignity in the relationships between all officers and all members of the community. To quote Jackson and Bradford one last time:

> [I]t is the experience and perception of procedural fairness that fosters in people feelings of motive-based trust in—and shared group membership with—[police]. Fairness encourages the idea that citizens and the police are "on the same side," and by treating people justly and equitably, police communicate to citizens that they are valued members of the social group that the police represent ... . [U]nfair treatment communicates division, social denigration and exclusion—thus fostering an "us and them" situation.

So to close this text on a realistic summary statement: community policing is about nothing if not constructive and durable relationships. Police have a huge role to play in improving relationships in communities where the risks are greatest and where police are now most frequently called for assistance. But their effectiveness in this work depends on high levels of police legitimacy. That can only be achieved by not only recruiting good officers who choose this profession for the right reasons, but also reforming police culture so that it embodies procedural fairness.

NOTES

1   "Reforms Have Focused on Community Policing and Accountability—but That May Not Be Enough" *VOX Media*, online: <http://www.vox.com/cards/police-brutality-shootings-us/community-police-accountability>.

2   *Police Services Act*, RSO 1990, c P.15.

3   *Criminal Code*, RSC 1985, c C-46.

4   "When Police Unions Impede Justice," Editorial, *New York Times Sunday Review* (3 September 2016), online: <http://www.nytimes.com>.

5   Cheri Maples, "A Buddhist Cop's Approach to Justice," *Lion's Roar* (25 August 2016), online: <http://www.lionsroar.com>.

6   Jonathan Jackson & Ben Bradford, "What Is Trust and Confidence in the Police?" (2010) 4:3 Policing: J Policy & Practice 241.

7   *Ibid.*

GLOSSARY

accountable: accepting responsibility for one's actions

applied research: the practical application of science to solve practical problems

appreciative inquiry: an organizational development technique that advocates building on what residents already experience as positive characteristics of their neighbourhood

asset principle: the idea that even in the most broken neighbourhoods, there are people, agencies, organizations, and groups that can and will make good decisions for themselves and their neighbours, and will engage constructively in community problem-solving

asset-based community development: a community development approach that takes the stance that even the most high-demand neighbourhood has human assets that can be mobilized to strengthen the neighbourhood

backbone organization: an agency in a collaborative that agrees to undertake some of the administration, supervision, and oversight required to support the collaborative

basic research: science used to improve scientific theories or predictions of natural phenomena

collaboration: two or more social or human service organizations working together to realize mutually derived and valued goals

collective impact: working together, across sectors, to resolve large-scale social problems with shared goals, responsibilities, and accountabilities

communications nodes: connections between and among agencies and organizations that allow new information to flow among them

community: a social unit of any size that shares common values; a group of people who are connected by durable relations

community asset surveys: inventories of individuals, agencies, organizations, and businesses, including their interests and capabilities in furthering safety and well-being

community capacity-building: the identification, strengthening, and linking of the neighbourhood's tangible resources like people, organizations, businesses, housing and natural environment, and intangible resources like relationships among residents, spirit of community, pride in the neighbourhood, and willingness to work together for the common good

community circles: a technique for facilitating communication and social cohesion that ensures that all participants have equal status and equal opportunity to speak; also known as talking circles, family group conferencing, community justice circles, or restorative justice circles

community cohesion: strong and positive relationships between people who may have different backgrounds, tackling community problems together and developing a positive climate for community building

community engagement: police building ongoing, trusting, and mutually respectful relationships with neighbourhood citizens, community-based organizations, and other agencies for the purposes of resolving local neighbourhood problems that threaten safety and well-being

community intelligence: information about community dynamics that originates with community members and is used by community members to improve their own social control over issues like crime and social disorder

community justice: an approach to justice that addresses offences by focusing on the harm done to the broader community and the community's response to the offence; goals include accountability, healing, restoration of relationships, reintegration of the offender into the community, and reducing future offences

community-based organization: organization of community members that is usually dedicated to community service of some kind; frequently but not always incorporated; and most often a not-for-profit organization that raises funds to support its activities

community-based research: the application of research methods in a real community setting, as opposed to a more highly controlled, laboratory setting

COMPSTAT: a program for analysis and mapping of occurrence data (COMPuter STATistics) that is used to prioritize and mobilize police enforcement actions

consensus: a decision-making process that prioritizes the decision or outcome that all persons involved are willing to support as the best one in current circumstances

consultation: seeking, from the broader public, information, advice, input, and reactions to policing priorities, investigations, and actions

contingency table: a two-way, or two-dimensional, table that arrays frequencies of one variable in relation to another

crime prevention through environmental design (CPTED): a wide range of spatial, architectural, and physical measures applied to buildings and grounds in order to strengthen their security and the security of people who use them

criminogenic factors: community or personal characteristics that can signal the probability of crime or social disorder (like broken windows), create opportunities for them (like leaving valuables unattended), or actually cause them (like domestic violence and poor parenting)

cross-sectoral collaboration: two or more agencies from entirely different sectors, working together to achieve shared goals

demographics: the statistical study of populations, considering factors like gender, age, education, nationality, religion, and ethnicity

direct observation: type of observation whereby a trained observer attends to spontaneous actions in the community and records those observations for later analysis

dogmatism: inflexible and strict adherence to a set of behavioural standards (creed, faith, religion, etc.), frequently accompanied by imposing those standards on others

durable relations: relationships that are strong, lasting, and endure through the pressures and changes that life, family, and neighbourhood can bring

enumerators: people who gather survey data (via interviews, direct observation, etc.)

extraneous variables: any variables (factors, conditions, circumstances, etc.) that could affect results of an evaluation

focus groups: groups of community people who are asked to discuss their feelings, reactions, and attitudes to whatever the program manager is interested in while an observer takes notes about the discussion

gatekeepers: a term sociologists use to refer to community members who know the most about what is going on in a neighbourhood, and on whom others can rely for that kind of information

intelligence-led policing: the practice of using intelligence to identify the risk that offences, harms, or victimization will occur rather than as an investigative tool after offensive and harmful incidents have occurred

inventory of community assets: a bank of information about the assets in a neighbourhood, including its physical assets, community groups or associations, and human assets, that can be drawn on for resources to achieve neighbourhood improvement and problem-solving

knowledge-based policing: using information technology like social media and collaboration with partners from other sectors to obtain new knowledge about the social drivers of crime and anti-social behaviour and then intervene by managing risk

location policing: having select officers dedicated to specific neighbourhoods so that they can get to know the neighbourhood and neighbours can get to know them

lone attacker: an individual who violently attacks and acts strictly on his or her own—that is, without personal, material, or other forms of support from organized, ideological extremism

mail survey: a survey in which the respondent indicates his or her reactions on a self-administered questionnaire and then mails that form back to the surveying organization

majority rule: a decision-making process in which a decision or outcome that gains the greater share of votes (that is, a majority) is the decision that is chosen as final

mobilization moment: a brief moment in time during which police draw neighbours' attention to a community problem through their enforcement actions

peer-reviewed journals: scholarly journals that ensure quality information by virtue of the fact that no article gets published in them unless it has been vetted by scholars in the field to which it pertains

personal interviews: interviews in which an enumerator works off a prescribed list of questions and records respondents' answers in a question-and-answer format

police legitimacy: neighbours value what the police do in their neighbourhood and they value how the police do it

policing: community members' exertion of social control for the purposes of preserving order and preventing harms or victimization from crime or anti-social behaviour

population: everyone to whom the evaluator expects to generalize the program evaluation findings

pre-criminal behaviours: behaviours that do not correspond to chargeable offences

prevention: proactively implementing evidence-based situational measures, policies, or programs to reduce locally identified priority risks to community safety and well-being

problem-oriented policing: a police tactic which analyzes, and sets out to resolve, problems that underlie repeat occurrences or other patterns of offences and social disorder

procedural justice: fairness or perceived fairness in procedures

profound interventions: interventions that go deeper than incident response and enforcement

program evaluation: applied research that is designed to test the efficacy (effectiveness and efficiency) of a program

protective factors: positive characteristics or conditions that can moderate the negative effects of risk factors and foster healthier individuals, families, and communities, thereby increasing personal and/or community safety and well-being

qualitative research: measures the why and how of something; yields more in-depth description than quantitative measures

quantitative research: measures who, what, where, and when—things that are fairly discrete and can be observed fairly easily with high reliability and validity

radicalization: the process by which an individual becomes motivated to provide personal or material support to an ideologically extreme social or political movement

reassurance policing: maintaining relationships with the public that actually reduce their fears of crime and social disorder

recidivism: reoffending that occurs after the completion of treatment or sanctions for previous criminal behaviour

risk factors: negative characteristics or conditions in individuals, families, communities, or society that may increase social disorder, crime or fear of crime, or the likelihood of harms or victimization to persons or property

risk mitigation: efforts to identify individuals, families, groups, or locations at imminent risk of harms or victimization and customize interventions which reduce those risks before an emergency response is required

safety and well-being framework: a logical basis for identifying and understanding the relationships among tactics for deriving community safety and well-being

sample: a subset of the population that is presumed to be representative of the population on the criterion measures the evaluation is asking about

sector: a group of organizations with specific expertise, mandate specialization, and resource allocation

shared measures: measures (or criteria for evaluating the initiative) that all partners agree are meaningful and to which all partners have some data to contribute

silo: a metaphor for the way that many public service agencies operate with separate enabling legislation and mandates, competitive budgeting processes, and technical isolation from each other, resulting in a social service system that makes it very difficult for these agencies to collaborate

situation of acutely elevated risk: a situation that negatively affects the health or safety of an individual, family, group, or place where there is a high probability of imminent and significant harm to self or others

situation table: a regular meeting of front-line workers, from a variety of human services agencies and sectors, who work together to identify individuals, families, groups, or locations that are at an acutely elevated risk of harm, and customize multi-disciplinary interventions to mitigate those risks

situational crime prevention measures: measures that target specific types of offences—like the use of double-bolt locks to prevent break and enters

social capital: positive relationships between people that enable them to work together for the common good

social control: the ways in which people influence each other's thoughts, values, feelings, and behaviour in their neighbourhood

social determinants of health: "protective factors such as access to income, education, employment and job security, safe and healthy working conditions, early childhood development, food security, quality housing, social inclusion, cohesive social safety network, health services, which ensure equal access to all of the qualities, conditions, and benefits of life without regard to any socio-demographic differences"; in the policing sector, they are often called the "social determinants of safety"

social development: long-term, multi-disciplinary efforts and investments to improve the social determinants of health and thereby reduce the probability of harms and victimization

social disorder: a condition in which the behaviour and activities of people at a specific location lack sufficient control or order, deviating significantly from what would be considered by most to be comfortable, reasonable, or safe

social entrepreneurship: the attempt to leverage solutions to social problems with the techniques of business

target hardening: efforts taken through situational measures to strengthen the security of people, places, or things

targeted enforcement: enforcement actions that are targeted on locations where offences are most likely to occur, on persons who are most likely to offend, and at times when offences are most likely to occur

traditional policing: reactive policing based on the military model of rapid response and efficient follow-up to harmful incidents

uniform crime reporting (UCR): a standard of crime reporting that counts occurrences by type and frequency; invented by the US Federal Bureau of Investigation in 1966 in order to obtain a standard of reporting across all American law enforcement agencies, it is also used in Canada and some other countries

value-added: extra capabilities that become possible when people work together

victimization: ill-treatment like bullying, oppression, discrimination, abuse, and harassment at the hands of another person or people

violent extremists: people who are willing to use or support the use of violence to further particular beliefs, including those of a political, social, or ideological nature

wicked issues: problems that have many causes that fall into different sectors of specialization

INDEX

CREDITS

Chapter 1

Chapter-opening photo. Toronto police cruiser on lawn. Courtesy of Heather Gough.

http://www.richmond.ca/parks/about/beautification/about.htm (URL). City of Richmond.

https://www.nfb.ca/film/through_a_blue_lens (URL). National Film Board of Canada.

Figure 1.1. Ontario's Mobilization and Engagement Model of Community Policing. Ontario Assocation of Chiefs of Police, "Ontario's Mobilization & Engagement Model of Community Policing" (2010), online: <http://www.oacp.on.ca/Userfiles/Files/NewAndEvents/CrimePreventionCampaign/COMMUNITY%20POLICING%20WHEEL-2.pdf>. Courtesy of OACP.

Chapter 2

Chapter-opening photo. Halifax Police Court, City Hall, and Market Square. Nova Scotia Archives, GL Sinclair Collection, 1992-319 no. 1.

Chapter 3

Chapter-opening photo. Two Toronto police officers on horseback meeting people. Courtesy of Heather Gough.

Chapter 4

Chapter-opening photo. Smiths Falls police cruiser. Courtesy of Heather Gough.

Figure 4.1. Harms from Social Disaster. Adapted from Council of Canadian Academies, 2014, *Policing Canada in the 21st Century: New Policing for New Challenges*. Ottawa (ON): Expert Panel on the Future of Canadian Policing Models.

Figures 4.3-4.6. Adapted from Hugh C Russell & Norman E Taylor, *New Directions in Community Safety: Consolidating Lessons Learned About Risk and Collaboration: Framework for Planning … Community Safety and Well-Being* (Toronto: Ontario Working Group on Collaborative, Risk-driven Community Safety and Well-being, Ontario Association of Chiefs of Police, April 2014), online: <http://www.oacp.on.ca/Userfiles/StandingCommittees/CommunityPolicing/ResourceDocs/OWG%20Framework%20for%20Community%20Safety%20and%20Well-being_1.pdf>. Courtesy of OACP.

Chapter 5

Chapter-opening photo. Police assisting with shore cleanup. Material republished with the express permission of: Ottawa Citizen, a division of Postmedia Network Inc.

Figure 5.1. Ontario Use of Force Model. © Queen's Printer for Ontario, 2009. Reproduced with permission.

Figure 5.2. Ontario's Mobilization & Engagement Model of Community Policing. Adapted from Ontario Assocation of Chiefs of Police, "Ontario's Mobilization & Engagement Model of Community Policing" (2010), online: <http://www.oacp.on.ca/Userfiles/Files/NewAndEvents/CrimePreventionCampaign/COMMUNITY%20POLICING%20WHEEL-2.pdf>. Courtesy of OACP.

Chapter 6

Chapter-opening photo. Talking circle. Courtesy of Robert Dube.

Chapter 7

Chapter-opening photo. FOCUS Rexdale situation table participants. Courtesy of Heather Gough.

Chapter 8

Chapter-opening photo. Police and community members sitting around a table. John Nicholas/Hastings County.

Figure 8.2. The Relationship of Risks to Prevention. Adapted from Ratcliffe, Jerry H, "Intelligence-led Policing: Anticipating Risk and Influencing Action;" in press publication of the International Association of Law Enforcement Intelligence Analysts; 2016, p 2.

Chapter 9

Chapter-opening photo. Community planning training meeting. Photo courtesy of Swan Valley Communities That Care.

Figures 9.1-9.6. Adapted from Hugh C Russell & Norman E Taylor, *New Directions in Community Safety: Consolidating Lessons Learned About Risk and Collaboration: Framework for Planning … Community Safety and Well-Being* (Toronto: Ontario Working Group on Collaborative, Risk-driven Community Safety and Well-being, Ontario Association of Chiefs of Police, April 2014), online: <http://www.oacp.on.ca/Userfiles/StandingCommittees/CommunityPolicing/ResourceDocs/OWG%20Framework%20for%20Community%20Safety%20and%20Well-being_1.pdf>. Courtesy of OACP.

Chapter 10

Chapter-opening photo. Participants at discussion on the role of women and girls in countering violent extremism. Licensed under CC BY-ND 2.0: https://creativecommons.org/licenses/by-nd/2.0/legalcode.

Figure 10.2. Adapted from Hugh C Russell & Norman E Taylor, *New Directions in Community Safety: Consolidating Lessons Learned About Risk and Collaboration: Framework for Planning … Community Safety and Well-Being* (Toronto: Ontario Working Group on Collaborative, Risk-driven Community Safety and Well-being, Ontario Association of Chiefs of Police, April 2014), online: <http://www.oacp.on.ca/Userfiles/StandingCommittees/CommunityPolicing/ResourceDocs/OWG%20Framework%20for%20Community%20Safety%20and%20Well-being_1.pdf>. Courtesy of OACP.

Chapter 11

Chapter-opening photo. Children on the field with the Calgary Stampeders. Courtesy of Calgary Police Service.

Chapter 12

Chapter-opening photo. York Regional Police officer with members of the community. York Regional Police.